Nea. River to Santa Cruz.

Dec. 24   "El Zorro

Chance or destiny? Arbitrary
line drawn by the will or habits
of man is determination? Questions that
(being) only can partially answer
perhaps.

"El Zorro" the ranch owned
by our Willy Halliday, became our
destination when we left Buenos
Aires on Dec. 18, primarily
because it was the only place
where pure "criollo" horses can
be found in the southern part
of Argentina. Yet our arriving
there seemed to mean more
as ~~~~ Willy appeared to be
expecting us having prepared to
help two young North Americans
make a similar trip several
years ago ——— a trip that
fell through at the last moment

RIDING INTO THE WIND

On Horseback out of Patagonia, a Life Journey

Enjoy the ride

Elly and Nathan Foote

BOOK
NE
WORKS

Southbank
British Columbia
V0J 2P0
Canada
www.ridingintothewind.com

Copyright © 2003 by Elly and Nathan Foote
Illustrations Copyright © by Conchita Maria
All rights reserved
National Library of Canada Cataloguing in Publication Data

Foote, Elly
Riding into the wind: On Horseback out of Patagonia,
a Life Journey / Elly Foote, Nathan Foote.

ISBN 0-9732539-0-8

1. Foote, Elly—Journeys—South America. 2. Foote,
Elly—Journeys—Central America. 3. Foote, Nathan—Journeys—South
America. 4. Foote, Nathan—Journeys—Central America. 5. Packhorse
camping—South America. 6. Packhorse camping—Central America.
7. South America—Description and travel. 8. Central America—Description and
travel. I. Foote, Nathan. II. Title.

F1409.3.F66 2003   918.04'37   C2003-910196-7

Grampa Clark:
who taught me how to row a boat.

Granny Foote:
who read me the Jungle Book by a crackling fire.

The wacky Clark sisters:
who loved raw clams, raw humor, the raw truth.

And my dad:
who hoped I'd find my own soap box someday.

Nathan Clark Foote

For those who planted the seeds,
but did not get to share the harvest:

Mormor:
Your letters, tied with faded pink ribbons and smelling
of lavender brought me South America from the bottom
drawer of the rosewood chest.

Moster Elly:
the stories you told me from all the world,
the laughter we shared!

And for Mai de Broen, my mother,
who waited such a very long time for this!

Elly de Broen-Foote

RIDING INTO THE WIND

On Horseback out of Patagonia,
a Life Journey

CONTENTS

CONCHITA

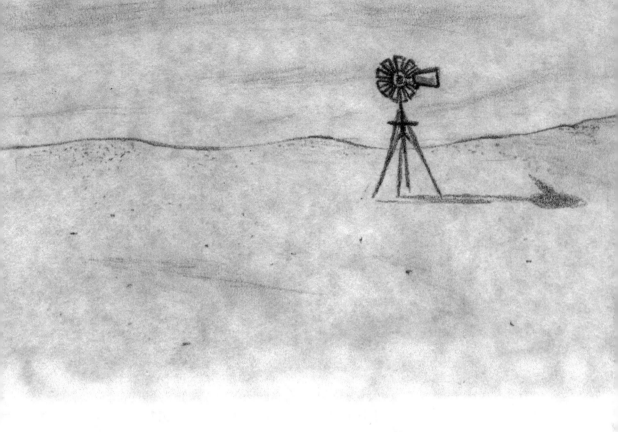

THE DAMNED LANDS

It is the summer of 1995 and I am flying alone, with all these people, keeping a white-knuckled grip on the armrest, eyes shut tight, the nails of my empty right hand digging into the palm, sweating cold, head lowered in crash preparedness position, the roar of the jet engines sending waves of white fear that might evaporate me at any moment because none of you are there to hold my hand.

I am en route from Calgary, Canada, to Stockholm, Sweden, as passenger #34D. Anyone at all with a ticket could have been the person in my seat. I am anybody, which means nobody. I hate that. I am used to being somebody unlike anybody else.

The jet shudders, jolts and bounces along on a thin cushion of air. I hold my breath, worried now about all the big people I noticed in the line up. Do they calculate passenger weight on an average? What if there are more large people than usual and what if all the large people have extra large suitcases, heavy ones, what then? Wouldn't we be over some sort of limit and what if the plane hits an air vacuum and all this mass of people and stuff fall to the ground in a million pieces? My fear is a blinding light inside my closed eyelids; my chest is about to implode. The fear is so unbearably intense I can no longer hold onto it.

What if?

Say all your fears are answered and this is it - is this how you want to spend your precious last seconds: wrapped in a bundle of pathetic angst?

No?

Okay then do something about it: how would you see yourself, going out?

The image comes swiftly:

My hands holding the reins of my horse Caicique; I am riding against the stinging wind on the Pampa de Santa Cruz, alone in a barren land.

My grip on the armrest lightens; reins are to be held lightly, with feeling. I lift my head and lean back against the seat, keeping my eyelids drawn closed. I am almost smiling: yeah, that's it! A gray sky, gravel pampa, a buckskin horse and going into the wind, not sure where the day might end, that's me!

Of all the places I've been, the godforsaken Patagonian wasteland is the one I'd have myself end on! How strange. You'd think I could have come up with a beach somewhere, or a mountain top, making love on a mountain on Corfu under the stars; that would be a moment for eternity; but no, it is a weather-beaten no-man's-land that comes to me. Brazenly, like a prodigal son, knowing it has no compare.

You keep moving, all day you keep moving and nothing around you changes. The horizon stays where it is, the grays of the land and the sky blending together. The only thing that changes is the wind, growing from the faint breeze of early morning to the iced lashing at noon and, if you were fool enough to be still out there by mid-afternoon, a merciless wind machine hurling pins at your every pore, making you want to dig a hole to escape, barter with the devil for a boulder to hide behind, willing to pay almost any price just to make the wind stop.

But, there being nothing to dig with, no boulders to hide behind, no bushes and no devil to conjure them up for you, you endure and you keep going forward and with evening the wind over the *pampa* dies down and the sky turns into a kaleidoscope of reds and pinks chasing each other on the high winds and, in a dry *arroyo*, you find a shepherd's *puesto* stacked with the flour and salt and lard needed to make *tortas fritas* and *mata negra* bushes sized for the cook stove and when the saddles are off and you sit by the flickering light of the wick burning in a tin of mutton lard, every simple sensation is a miracle.

Encapsulated here, on a routine flight, sharing the condition of – what is it, one million passengers in the air, worldwide, at any given moment? I desperately need your hand holding mine. Why is that? You have no more power here than have I. We are helpless, hapless cargo with absolutely no control over this flight. Unless you really want to believe that strapping yourself to this seat and learning how to put on the yellow plastic vest and the oxygen mask is akin to taking affirmative action.

All those little details that are designed to give me, the passenger of #34D, a sense of security and ease have the opposite effect. I am made an accomplice in a collective act of hubris, punishable by the gods. I am not sure who I believe these gods to be: some version of the wrathful residents of Valhalla, Viking gods who viciously defend their stature of being more than men and my fear of flying is the fear of being in the way when the angered gods lurch down to arbitrarily throw one of these aluminum birds out of the sky.

People weren't meant to soar to 30,000 feet on whiskey and peanuts, watching movies. People were meant to be earthbound, meant to ride a horse and be wet and dry and cold, hot and windblown. My armrest grip has tightened again; the stewardess is beginning her trip down the aisle with refreshments. Juice or pop this time.

I remain behind closed eyelids as she comes up beside me, and she moves on past, seeing how it is that passenger in # 34D who's asleep. I tell myself: good, now take control, grab your mind and put it where you want it and that place will be real and that is all that you can control: your mind.

So come on, Elly, you have been in worse situations than as a passenger on a scheduled flight from North America to Europe, how commonplace is that!

Patagonia is unique; you want to hold onto unique: go there!

Go to the very beginning, to the very first day: to the moment when, at the line fence to his *estancia*, Guillermo Halliday turns his light dun stallion, and without a backwards glance, lopes off across the plain, leaving us alone to begin our horseback journey.

The sting of the afternoon gale rips around our little troupe. Chaco plops into a heap of puppy fur, covering his nose and eyes with his chubby paws, too proud to whine; much too young to be out here walking. Guillermo tried to carry him for a while on the way, but Chaco wriggled himself free and leapt down off Indio Chico, the dun stallion.

Now he has no option, for it is with Chaco as it is with each of us: he has to make it on his own. There is no way we can carry him on any of these horses! An intense feeling of guilt reaches deep inside of me and makes a grab for my vitals. What right did we have to bring this puppy here? What were we thinking, when we asked Aranza to pick the bravest and the clowniest of the litter of yet unborn pups and send him on a plane to Buenos Aires? He had come all the way from the small village on the Basque coast of Spain where our dog Nikos, his brother, was shot by bird hunters, days before we left for Argentina. We wanted this pup to carry on for Nikos and be our loyal friend and guardian on the *pampas* of Argentina. We named him Chaco, for Cape Machichaco, our home above the stormy Bay of Biscay.

It was a lot to ask of a three month old pup.

In the far away distance now, I can make out the diminishing figure of Guillermo and his horse. All at once, I am glad he is gone and I also want him desperately to turn around and come back and ride with us for a while longer. Another day, a week, maybe more, until we can learn some of what he knows, about horses, about life on this hard land.

A sudden searing pain in my right palm jolts my attention to India, the paint mare. The wind is whipping a corner of the tarp strapped over the pack, flailing it furiously against her flank and she is pulling back, the rawhide lead burning through layers of my skin. Only one thing matters: don't let go of the mare! Turn Caicique towards her, I am telling myself, get some slack before the last little bit of rawhide eats through my palm and we're helplessly shipwrecked on this waterless ocean. Dry tears sting my eyes, as violent wind gusts snatch away any cries of pain that cross my lips. Caicique chooses to listen to my leg and hand and turns. With the wind now coming at her from a different direction, the mare leaps ahead, giving me suddenly several feet of slack. She blows a loud snort and stops abruptly, wide-eyed and shaking.

This is Pampero's cue to start bucking. He rounds his back and comes down hard and stiff on all fours. Nathan is staying with him, but has to let go of Maracas, who takes off down the fence line at a dead run.

The mare is turning her head and I can sense her getting ready to bolt once again. I won't be able to hang onto her much longer and if she runs off after Maracas, Pampero will throw another bucking spree for sure and maybe get rid of Nathan this time around.

Before any of this can happen, Nathan leaps off Pampero, grabs India's halter and is hanging onto the two of them.

But now, what?

There is nothing to tie them to. I can't go after Maracas, then the other two will bolt. Nathan can't get back on Pampero with India trying to tear away from him. I can't help because I have my hands full with Caicique.

Then, just as suddenly as he took off, Maracas wheels around and comes galloping back, rawhide lead dragging between his legs. He jolts to a stop on his front end right by Pampero, his heavy primitive face having such an expression of absolute consternation and immeasurable relief that both Nathan and I burst out laughing.

"I doubt he'll try that again! Why don't we just leave him run loose?"

And so, with Caicique up ahead, me leading India, and Nathan keeping Pampero right behind her to make sure she doesn't pull back, one slow step at a time, heading southeast, we begin our advance across the gravel plain, between tufts of hard, short and dry *coirón* grass, inter-spaced by *mata negra*. Gray land, gray sky, brown grass, black bushes, a furious, ice wind in our faces.

I get a flash image of the photos we poured over, back in Spain: *gauchos* riding sleek dark bay and gray horses over verdant grasslands, smiling garrulously under a cloudless blue sky.

Dolphins, playing in an ocean of green grass, that's how we imagined we'd be, with no house to maintain, no radio to keep us abreast of the wars and mayhem worldwide, out of time, in a place where men still measure distance by hours in the saddle. Our friend Armando, the blond gypsy, was with us at the house on Machichaco, looking over the *gaucho* pictures in La Scala magazine with us. We saw grass so abundant that in just fifty years, the handful of horses abandoned by the *conqueror* Mendoza became thousands: sorrels, duns, paints, grays and blacks. They filled the pampas to the horizon. Today there are something like seven million!

"I should be able to find one there, you think?"

Armando turns the magazine pages thoughtfully.

"I'd give anything to go with the two of you," he says and I am surprised at the emotion in his voice."

Armando is a pimp, a gigolo and a horse trader.

To me, Armando is the big brother I never had. Our relationship was uncomplicated. We were kin not by family or culture or by place. The passion for horses ran through our veins and formed a kinship above and beyond any other ties, between a kid in Sweden riding my bicycle all over the countryside, bridle over my shoulder, looking for any field with horses in it so that I might sneak a ride if one would let me catch it and bridle it and I could find a way to get on it; and a young rogue who kept a few horses in a backyard in Bilbao and, under the cover of night, would ride into the hills and stay out to graze his little herd of horses and by morning return them to the enclosure and later in the day bring them up to do trail rides for the tourists.

Like a kid sister, I tried to emulate him, and egged him on to impress me. One day I was lunging Minus, the old bay mare that we kept over winter for Jean Marc, by the pond across the road. She wasn't very good at it and it was a poor place to be doing it anyway. I was just trying to make the point with her that I could stand still in one spot and that she had to trot around me in a circle in either direction that I chose, without stopping or trying to run away.

"We used to vault," Armando tells me, "on an old grey horse, part Percheron. Did some shows for charity."

"Can you still do it?"

"Sure, why not."

"So show me," I said.

"You mean here, right now?"

"Yes, why not?"

There were a lot of very good reasons why not. The uneven ground was full of rocks and slippery wet spots. The bay mare had choppy, arrhythmical gaits and she had nothing on but the halter and a rope for a lunge line.

"All right," Armando says. "You keep her going. As even as you can."

As wide, almost, as he is tall, Armando looks like he could sooner wrestle the bay mare to the ground than catapult himself onto her back. He jogs along the rope, runs beside her for a few strides, his hands on her withers. In a bounce he is astride, sits for a couple of strides, then he's down on the other side, bouncing alongside the mare, back astride, down on the inside and then, holding onto nothing but a tuft of her mane, he catapults himself all the way back towards the inside of the circle.

"We usually have a vaulting girth," he says, walking back in to the center.

"I didn't know it could be done without one."

"Well there it is, *allí está*."

"About the horses for your journey," he says as we walk across the road towards the house. "It would be hard on a horse to take him from those green *pampas* into a desert, or the mountains."

"You're not coming then?"

His answer is to ignore my question. "And remember," he goes on, "you can take a horse from bad to better, but you can't take him from good to worse. Go to the worst place you can find and get your horses there; they'll take you anywhere."

During our last weeks at Machichaco, Armando comes by often. Sometimes alone and he spends hours talking about Life and the meaning of it all with Nathan. One Sunday he brings three of his whores, tight skirts, high heels and all and he treats them badly and then scolds them for allowing themselves to be treated so badly. Several times he comes with Constanza and her parents and lots of food for everyone. Constanza sunbathes on the grass in a black bikini that reveals a soft belly with a very large scar that is from an appendix operation. You can see the tiny holes left from each stitch and it is hard not to look and to wonder: why this girl?

Armando is there the day that Patchi, our neighbor the Basque farmer, comes to pick up our wagon. We have sold the house on Machichaco, returned the two horses to Jean Marc and will not need the wagon to drive down to Bermeo anymore.

Patchi brought his donkey, the same that carried cut grass off the field every day for the cows and the cans of milk and the vegetables to the village market. Pachi's was a well broke donkey and a nice one. Putting him between the shafts and driving home should have been a simple matter.

The donkey would have no part of the red, blue and white contraption. He shied and he danced and he balked, even brayed and kicked at the shafts and the wheels. When finally Patchi managed to get him hitched, the donkey absolutely refused to budge. He backed and he went sideways until the wheels locked and the wagon almost tipped over, but he would not take one single step forward. Pachi's stick had no effect on him. The burly Basque looked at us in helpless embarrassment. Armando caught his eye.

"Would you allow me?" Armando motioned towards the recalcitrant donkey.

"You go right ahead!" Patchi snorted." You go right ahead and drive him all you want."

What happened next was simple and amazing.

Armando walked up to the side of the wagon and took the lines Patchi handed him. Well worn hemp ropes in hand, Armando climbed aboard. He squared himself legs apart at the center of the wagon and looking straight ahead down the road, he took a steady feel of the donkey's mouth and in a quiet voice told him to move on out.

Without a moment's hesitation, the donkey did as he was bid, stepping out at a brisk clip. Down by the mimosa grove, where the road began to curve and there was a wide shoulder, Armando turned the wagon around and put the donkey into a trot back up the road.

Patchi found no words to speak.

"How did you DO that!!!!???" I exclaimed.

I know Armando enjoyed the applause in my voice, but I didn't expect an explanation from him; I knew him better than that.

It took over twenty years, but one day suddenly, driving my team in the woods of northern British Columbia, I got it:

Focus! The secret was focus!

Focus all your energies and your will power in one direction and you can accomplish anything: break a brick with your bare fist, walk on hot coals - or drive a donkey.

I wanted Armando to be out there watching me now as I drove Mischief and Sir from the landing into the woods to hook onto another log, to notice how they moved straight and in perfect rhythm and unison and watch how quiet and soft my hands were on the lines and how the team would halt and turn, in one continuous motion, heeding my voice and how they would push off their powerful hind quarters, lean into their collars and move the big pine log down the trail.

"You showed me, that day on Machichaco," I wanted to tell him. Life doesn't work that way.

It doesn't work backwards, but when Mark, my horse logging apprentice, hooks his team to a log that Mark thinks the team can probably not move and the horses feel his hesitation and stall out and seesaw and alternatively hit their collars and quit, I take the lines to show him, when he asks me to. I square my shoulders and look ahead where I want the team to move the log and take hold of the lines with an even feel of their mouths and speak to them in a quiet voice. They move ahead as one and the log comes out easily and Mark looks at me in astonishment and says:

"How did you DO that?"

Someday, unexpectedly, somewhere Mark too will understand about focus. Maybe he will tell me. Probably he won't. The important thing is that he will be able to show someone in turn, maybe even his son, and so the day Armando drove the donkey above the Bay of Biscay weaves itself forward.

We leave for Argentina. Armando stays. In staying behind, he comes with us, forever unchanged. His advice shapes our journey and takes us, quite literally, to the end of the earth.

At the office, in Buenos Aires, of the Breeders of Argentine Criollo horses, red dots on a map of the Republic show the locations of breeders of purebred horses. There are lots of red dots all over the verdant *pampas* within a few hours of the capital, fewer as you get further away. In the whole of the extreme southern region, there is but one solitary red dot.

"I can set you up with some of our breeders here close by." The secretary is very accommodating. "Many of these *señores* live in the capital and go to their *estancia* during weekends. They would be delighted to assist you."

"What about that one, way down there?"

"In the Patagonia! You won't want to go to the Patagonia. There is nothing there!"

"You've been?"

"Me? No. No way!"

"You know the breeder way down there?"

"He is known, yes."

"And he has good horses?"

The secretary shrugs. "Someone from the association has to fly down there every couple of years to inspect his colts."

"And?"

Another shrug. "He has bought a few stallions up at the *feria* in Buenos Aires."

He provides us with a name: Guillermo Halliday, Estancia El Zorro, 45 kilometers west of Puerto Santa Cruz, Provincia de Santa Cruz, three thousand kilometers to the south, deep in the *Tierra Maldita*, the Damned Lands.

"Perfect! That's the one. That's where we're going."

The secretary does not see us to the door, doesn't even manage a "good luck".

"*De nada*", he says simply, in response to our thank you. Quite clearly we are not to be reckoned with for the future annals of the Breeders of Argentine Criollo Horses; just a pair of naive fools heading for the Patagonia, never to be seen or heard of again.

Nathan captured the mood of our journey deep into the Damned Lands:

> *The train picks up speed, eating up jade carpets of alfalfa green, toot-tooting the straightest rails ever laid, and through the baggage car window, we watch whitewashed stations zip past and pastures with the fattest Angus steers you ever saw and horses rolling through waves of green. There is a beautiful* **estancia**: *box stalls under red tile, fifty yards long, a sulky at the gate, a team of Percherons, matched to a hair.*
>
> *Right into the night, hot wheels spinning and throwing off sparks, taking us closer; we hang our elbows out the open window, high on the breath of poppies off the pampa, catching glimpses of colts and calves curled up in misty pastures.*
>
> *In the morning, pulling out of another station, two boys riding bareback draw up alongside, rocking along at an easy lope, schoolbooks under one arm. They grin and wave, putting their ponies into a gallop as the train moves faster. Up close, not ten feet away, they dig in their heels and lean low over the withers and race past the water tank, to the end of the siding.*
>
> *Then the train is slipping away from them. Suddenly, they shift their weight, swing off the trestles and turn down a shaded lane, easing their mounts to a lope, to a walk and maybe dreaming -someday,* **amigo**, *we'll get on a horse and never come back!*
>
> *But we turn our backs on paradise and keep on going right to the gates of hell and five days later a trucker by name of Miguel drops us off at the windswept junction of Puerto Santa Cruz. We slouch down on gunny sacks staring at the shrinking tail-lights, like two fire flies pinned to the horizon and then night snaps her lips over them and the vastness rolls in around us from all sides and we are all alone.*

"White Indian, *Indio Blanco*, they call him down in these parts," the owner of the lodging establishment in Puerto Santa Cruz tells us. "He is as *baqueano* a white man as you'll find anywhere." He pauses momentarily. "He knows you are coming, right?"

"Actually no, he has no idea."

The innkeeper excuses himself to the adjacent kitchen. There is the sound of voices and moments later he returns with the eggs and toast we have asked for. Chaco gets a can of evaporated milk and a chunk of mutton.

"Watson, neighbor from out west, is in town for supplies," the innkeeper says. "He can give you a ride out to El Zorro."

He doesn't ask where we are from, how we arrived in Puerto Santa Cruz or why it is we want to go to El Zorro and see Guillermo Halliday.

Watson, a ruddy faced Englishman, is equally uninquisitive. He helps us load our gear into the back of the old red Ford flatbed, all ten gunny sacks that we have been dragging in and out of lorries and vans of all kinds, ever since the train left us at San Antonio del Oeste five days ago, fifteen hundred kilometers south of Buenos Aires and with fifteen hundred left to go to Puerto Santa Cruz.

"Willy should be back from Rio Gallegos today," Watson volunteers. "Said he'd be early afternoon. Of course," he continues, "if he's not home yet, you'll be lacking for nothing over at Kamasu Aike. That's our place. We've been neighbors for a long time, Willy and me, back to the time we first laid claims out here. This was the last of the homestead lands. This is what was left over after everyone else had their pieces. All the *vegas*, the *arroyos* and of course the riverbeds and sheltered lands with the better grass were long since claimed by the Menendez-Beathy. Willy and me, we were just roughnecks with a *tropilla* to our names and not much else.

The first couple of winters we survived under a tarp behind a *calafate* bush. Rule was. You had to live on the land to maintain your claim to the four leagues, twenty kilometers square.

The first well Willy dug by hand and the second winter was easier than the first. Willy hailed from the Falklands. Scotch people. Tough people. He was but a lad of fourteen when the father sent him and an older brother up north to Neuquen to find and catch a *tropilla* of wild horses and train them on the journey back so there would be using horses to sell and money to buy sheep. A pouch of salt tied onto the saddle was all the baggage the boys brought with them. It was eight months later they returned to their father with some good broke horses. The older Halliday bought sheep and sent his two boys back out on the trail again after only a few days at home, with the same little pouch of salt as their sole provision just as the first time.

They didn't return home this time, but struck out on their own. Willy was a lad of fifteen, tall and tough. Could ride anything."

A set of traveled tracks cut across the unchanging landscape. No need to build anything, move anything; it's all flat and gravel and you can drive any- where you want. There is no doubt we have found the worst kind of place on earth and that any horse surviving out here will be a tough one. Now, for the first time, so close, it occurs to me to wonder: what about us? Are we tough enough for this land?

What will Guillermo think - I like the Spanish name better - looking at the two of us and with a pup to boot and all this stuff we've brought with us? We've even got anti-snakebite remedies in the first aid kit and a folding lantern and a thermos and a set of camp dishes and way too many clothes, lots of film and even a typewriter and notebooks yet unwritten, emergency supplies in- cluding coffee and tea and sugar and flour and oatmeal and rice.

All he had with him traveling was a pouch of salt.

The descent is so sudden it feels like the earth is tipping and the gravel plain sliding away before you, revealing an oasis of green that takes your breath away as you come upon it, unexpectedly: a living emerald sparkling under rays of sunlight that are breaking through the grayness. Green alfalfa fields en- closed by a white picket fence, immaculately maintained. Three windmills spin in the wind.

The man who comes down the walkway to greet us is tall and lean, maybe fifty years of age. The wind and the cold have pulled the skin tight over his face, accentuating his aquiline features. He is dressed in black *bombachas*, a wide colorful *faja* fastened around the waist. The white shirt is ironed. Guillermo Halliday looks exactly as I have come to picture him.

"Welcome to El Zorro!" He says and his gray eyes smile.

Nathan and I start making introductions, explanations, apologies for ap- pearing on this day, on a Christmas Eve, and without letting him know.

"I can see why you have come," he says.

Like the innkeeper in Puerto Santa Cruz, like Watson, Guillermo seems to take in every detail about you instantly and read you like a billboard. Never have I felt so transparent before a stranger. It is not an uncomfortable feeling exactly, but disconcerting. We're so used to chatter and to worrying about making impressions. Appearance, I am beginning to discern, is of no consequence here. What you do is who you are and the plains will sort things out soon enough. No one asks for a personal inventory.

I toss and I turn in the guest room bed. I should sleep, I know, but how could I possibly sleep on this magical Christmas night in this faraway land!

I get up and walk across the floor and open the window wide. The warm night air flows in around me in a seductive embrace and the stars and the lingering light of dusk, or maybe it is the advent of a new dawn, reflect in the crystals over the salt lagoon that appears like a blanket of snow beneath the stars. So many stars and so close, in to me strange constellations. A herd of horses appear on the far side of the lagoon. Now and then I seem to hear the sound of a bell. It has a clear, rich sound and I think that maybe I am dreaming, making this whole thing up: this Christmas when a total stranger at the bottom of the world says to me:

"You can have any of my horses you choose. Whatever you need, it will be my honor to give them to you."

How should I sleep this night away!

Life doesn't get any better than this and I want to savor every fleeting moment. I want to run out on the starlit *pampa* and be with the horses. For as long as I can remember, all I ever dreamed of was a horse of my own. A horse I didn't have to watch being used or misused by anyone else. A horse that answered to no one but me.

People would give me money, as adults do on special occasions and they would smile: how cute! When they asked and I truthfully replied: I save every coin to buy my own horse. Little girls did not have horses of their own in Sweden in the fifties. Only the very rich could afford such a luxury. We were poor, I suppose, my mother and I. We rented furnished rooms in other peoples' homes and when we moved from one place to another, there wasn't much stuff to take along.

Peoples' condescension spurred my efforts. I would get my own horse, one penny at a time. I went house to house collecting bundles of old newspapers and brought them to the junk dealer down by the harbor and he paid me five *öres* a kilo. He paid two for the scrap iron pieces I found and loaded on my bike. I collected empty bottles in the ditches. I picked berries and mushrooms to sell and a farmer paid me five *kronor* a day to lead his horse down the furrows between rows of sunflowers, while he steadied the handles to plow the weeds under.

I was eight the summer we came to stay with my aunt and uncle in their rented beach house at Strandstuguviken, on the West Coast. They were well off and, from time to time, would bestow some kindness upon my mother and me.

"You love horses more than you love people!" My Aunt Erna said to me more than once. She meant it as a reprimand. It was the truth. People tried to control you; horses were there for you when people betrayed you, like my aunt and uncle did when they returned to the city after just one week and rented the house to someone else.

They said they were sorry.

My mother and I stayed the rest of the summer in a room off the barn that belonged to a farmer I met because he had a mare and a foal in the field next to the summer cottage. My mother got a job at the seaside hotel and I got a job too, helping the farmer look after his chickens, a thousand white Leghorns that were just starting to lay eggs. I would find eggs all over the yard. Some were small and some didn't have very good shells so you couldn't sell them. We got to eat a lot of omelets that summer and the farmer paid me five *kronor* a week to look after his chickens.

At fourteen, I had enough money saved to buy a warmblood horse. I even had a barn picked out for him, an old dray barn down by the harbor I could rent for cheap. I could earn enough now, with two paper routes, to pay for the feed and the straw and the shoes for my horse.

But the money was too late for the horse of my childhood. My world had changed, almost overnight. My idea of Freedom was so much larger now than riding a horse around familiar places. Owning a horse would moor me to the small town in Sweden that had the feel of a wool sweater that got put in the wash with the polyester by accident and went through the dryer too. It was a nice sweater so you put it on and you endure the tightness because it was such a nice sweater. Finally you can't stand it another second and you work frantically to get it off. You throw it down in a corner of your room and later you fold it neatly and put it away in the back of the closet. You keep it there because of the good memories you have of wearing it. But you never want to put it back on again.

My horse money became my travel money: a language school in Lübeck, Germany, the summer I was fifteen, off to Berlin for an International Student work camp the following summer, then England. From there southern Europe and the world.

I am not sure now if I was asleep or if I am dreaming awake. The overhead screen shows the trajectory of this plane: a red line extending into the Northwest Territories. We must have been underway for an hour, maybe two. The stewardesses have started down the aisles pushing the warming carts with food trays, all identical, all hermetically enclosed so nothing escapes: no heat, no aroma. I get my measured smile along with my tray. I wish now that I had remembered to order vegetarian. But this was not a planned trip. My mother called; she had heart murmurs. She sounded scared on the phone; she had never really considered the possibility of being ill. She asked me to come and that is why I am on this plane that is taking me back to the dark corner of the closet.

The woman in the seat next to mine is traveling with a partner: boyfriend, husband, who knows, and has no interest in acknowledging my existence. For this I am grateful. The stewardess comes back for the trays and I can close my eyes to this crowded plane that is flying back against the clock to some place I don't want to go.

I want to return instead to where the aroma of a spitted lamb roasting over the coals makes your mouth water with anticipation. In a simple act of closing my eyes and my ears, I transpose to the Christmas celebration with Guillermo and a Tehuelche half-breed who goes by the name of Tommy McCall. He is slim and tall like Guillermo. The two men, *patrón* and *peon*, boss and hired hand, are dressed with the same simple elegance: ironed white shirts, colorful bandanas and *fajas*, black *bombachas*, black boots, black flat brimmed hats. The hut is open on two sides and there are lupines growing tall along the front. The sides against the predominant winds have guanaco hides stretched across pine poles that have come all the way from the cordillera.

When the *asado* is ready, Guillermo takes his silver handled *facon* out of the silver sheath that is tucked away in the *faja* behind his back and cuts out a couple of ribs and hands them to me on the tip of a knife. I hold the food with my hands and eat squatting on my haunches on the dirt floor. The meat is so tender it melts in your mouth.

We drink wine for the occasion of the birth of a child named Jesus in a long ago time and in a place not unlike this lean-to. Without all the stuff added on afterwards about making lists and counting down shopping days and telling lies to small children about fat little men clad in red coming down chimneys and without all the tinsel, this Christmas is a celebration of being on this earth together. A Christmas about the here and now between the four of us and the ritual of sharing the bounty wrestled out of this stingy earth by the will and the labor of one man who brought water to the surface with his bare hands. The water made everything possible, even lettuce and tomatoes from the green-house. This world all its own within the white picket fence is a sanctuary, a church really, where Guillermo and those who would be his guests leave behind the cares and struggles of the plains and enjoy the fruits of their labor and their vision in peace.

We are allowing the silence to envelop the four of us. Guillermo and Tommy McCall because this is their habit. Nathan and I are trying to learn the art of being quiet, of observing rather than making endless observations. The silence is spinning the thread of a fabric to join us together.

"For years," Guillermo tells us, "I have had the dream that someone would come here for my Criollos. Give me a chance to show the world what my Patagonia *pingos* are made of. A couple of years ago now an English chap was making plans. He wanted to ride from the Patagonia to Alaska. In the end, he never showed. And now you are here."

Nathan looks over at me. Neither of us knows how to respond. How to tell him we have come here without plans? We're not out to attempt some sort of record-breaking journey on horseback. That isn't it at all.

"We built a house on the Bay of Biscay," Nathan says after a while. "Didn't know what we were doing and we didn't have much money. It was a big challenge."

"After the house was built, it became a box. A box with a view, but a box," I pick up the thread. "One day a family of gypsies came by. They camped over-night by the pond across the road."

"I grabbed some wine and we went down to visit them," Nathan goes on. "And when they broke camp the following day, we went along with them."

"Pulling the heavy caravans along the same windy roads every year and with the authorities always harassing them wasn't the free and roaming life as we had imagined it to be."

"But we couldn't go back to living in a box. A Dutch schoolteacher came by and bought the house. He'll be paying us every month for the next five years."

The plainsman hears the message, of this I am sure. Our dream may not be the same as his. We want to live on horseback and that is as far as it goes. We have no itinerary, no geographical goal. We make no pledges, no promises. Like Armando, Guillermo seems to know something about us that we don't ourselves know.

"You take my horses as far as you can," Guillermo says. "That is all I ask."

A Swiss fellow, named Aimee Tschiffely, rode two Criollos from Buenos Aires to New York back in the 1920's. The horses were Gato and Mancha, given to Tschiffely by Dr. Emilio Solanet, the one man solely responsible for saving the *Criollo* breed from being swallowed up in the mix of imported Thoroughbreds, draft horses and Arabian horses.

Tschiffely's ride was one of the Great Adventures of its day. We went to see the stuffed remains of the two horses, standing in a glass cage with all their gear on in the museum at Lujan. We spoke to Dr. Solanet on the phone, from Buenos Aires. He invited us down to visit his *estancia* and see his Criollos.

Why we didn't go there, I really can't explain. Intuition, chance, circumstance, destiny, call it what you will, pulled us inexorably towards El Zorro, allowing no deviations along the way.

HOBO'S ICON

Nothing could have prepared us for the moment when Tommy McCall brought the herd in from the plains.

The Criollos milling around below us in the corral appeared as the plain itself become animate in the hands of a creator, working with the most primitive of tools. Their shapes had come out exceedingly rough: bodies short and primitive, legs straight and stout, heads coarse and heavy on a short bull neck that lacked refinement. Their short-cropped dark manes and thick tails, chopped off evenly above the hocks, did little to enhance the image.

It was one of those moments when, touched by the magic kiss, the fairy tale frog is supposed to turn into a prince. Instead, the frog remains but what he is: a frog.

It didn't help to remember, verbatim, what I had read about the Argentine Criollo. It is a breed shaped by the forces of nature, that alows the survival of only the fittest, and it is the only one of the South American breeds to remain untarnished by the infusion of foreign blood.

Even after learning all this, I retained the image of a horse that would come floating across the surface of the earth, barely touching, his head held high, eyes and nostrils large, mane and tail flowing in the wind. Like the Black Stallion, this horse of my dream would carry me, effortlessly, across plains and mountains. Together we would greet the rising sun and he'd stay by me when the sun set.

Tommy McCall's *riata* hisses through the air and finds a target amongst the milling mass. Touched by the rope, the animal stops instantly, the herd veering away and isolating him from the rest.

"Seven year old," Guillermo says. "Goes by the name of Pampero. One of the toughest I've got. Came out of winter best of any of them."

Perched on the top rail above the mass of buckskin horses, I feel utterly at a loss for words. Nathan is sitting close and I am hoping his sidelong glance will discern my silent struggle to come to grips with the disparity between my dream and the reality of the horses before us. The truth is, these are the ugliest horses I have ever seen.

"What do you think?" Guillermo says.

"He looks tough all right, I'll try him," Nathan says, realizing that there is nothing, at this moment, that I could say.

They look like a corral full of steers! I am thinking: heavy and dumb. The herd awaits what Fate may bring with lowered heads. All except for one. This one alone looks up to meet your eye. There is inquisitiveness, defiance in his eyes. He moves around the periphery of the herd, disappears in a camouflage of buckskin shapes. Reappears again, as if to tease you.

He has a narrow, crooked spike and seems a bit taller than the rest and less stout. The withers and the hipbones are more pronounced, the neck longer, making the head appear even more heavy. He is not better looking than the rest. If anything, he is even uglier.

"That's the one." I point at him straight across from us now. "That's the one I want."

Tommy McCall seems pleased. "That's the one I was telling you about!" He says. "The one I rode twenty leagues one day and twenty back the next."

Guillermo is not so happy with my pick. "He's an odd one," he says. "I'd rather you choose another."

Nathan shakes his head. "She'd have to pick the rebel in the bunch," he says. "She always does."

Guillermo rode along with us out into the plains so that we could try out the horses: Pampero and the horse with the crooked spike, who went by the name Carpincho. Watching Guillermo, so at ease, so comfortable in the *recado* made me wish we had considered the native Argentine saddle. Built on layers of blankets and finely cured hides, soft and pliable, it is a deluxe seat designed for long distance travel. Our Prussian cavalry saddles were built for long distance marches also, but for people of a different ilk. Army surplus from the Second World War, regular issue, they were designed to be impermeable to the rain and the mud and constant use and to mold to the backs of horses in good condition or in poor. They had seemed like a good idea for a long ride. There was a bit of nostalgia here too; I used to ride remounts in Sweden in just this type of saddle.

We bought two saddles, still in their original packing boxes, at an army surplus store called *La Chiche* on Calle Irigoyen in Buenos Aires. At forty dollars each, we thought we got quite a bargain. I am not so sure about that as I watch Nathan grimace with each pile-driving stride of Pampero's. Prussian saddles were designed with absolutely no consideration for rider comfort. The hard leather would be rubbing the insides of his legs raw, the same as it was doing mine. We didn't have the tall leather boots and loose fitting jodhpurs of the cavalry; we were riding in tight jeans and western boots.

Early in the afternoon, we came upon a small herd of mares and foals near a watering trough made of corrugated metal. One mare was standing off to herself and very still, a fawn colored foal by her side. The herd withdrew at our approach, all except the one mare, who remained immobile. Her eyes were glazed with pain. You could see bone protruding in the lower cannon area of her left front leg.

"I'll have to come back with a gun," Guillermo said quietly and he turned his horse back towards home.

"But what about the foal? How will you get him back to the barn?"

"Orphans don't make it here," Guillermo said. "There is no one to take care of it."

I stared at the foal, two months old, if that, and so beautiful. Thoughts raced through my head about how we could save him, maybe pay for the supplements and the hay and how we would put it so Guillermo wouldn't be offended. Maybe we could pick it up later somehow, when it was grown a bit.

We rode away and I was too angry and upset to see that the quickened pace going back home was Guillermo's kindness, the only kindness he could offer the injured mare and her doomed foal. This happened many years before I would grow to understand such things.

 I do not sleep this night. How different is this sleepless night from the night of Christmas, the plains seeming so full of mystery than and promise. This night the plains stare at me with the empty eyes of a mortally wounded mare, with no milk to nurse her hungry foal. Before this foal, how many thousands, millions, perished so that the fittest would survive and forward the evolution of the species? I thought about the horses of the Conquerors; how many had succumbed to disease and hunger on the way over to the Americas or collapsed from exhaustion during the long marches? I felt nauseated and confused and angry and, for the first time, wished myself far away from this hard land, back to a country where a warm barn and goat milk would nurture an orphan back to strength.

 We do not speak about the mare and the foal again. When Nathan and I get up the next morning, Guillermo is sitting in the *galpon* braiding rawhide halters for us. The army surplus ones we brought down from *La Chiche* were brittle with age and too much poor quality oil; one simply disintegrated when Pampero pulled back at first sight of us and the unfamiliar gear we meant to put upon his back.

 Guillermo works the moistened rawhide strip into a tight twist and loops it to form the cheek pieces and noseband, braiding in a ring for the *cabresto* to attach under the chin. He finishes with a simple rawhide button for the strap across the poll.

 The bridle hanging on a hook above his *recado* is fashioned by his hands also, intricately detailed with thin strips cut out of horsehide, an arrowhead braided in the brow band and beautiful buttons. The hands that shaped these things of beauty are the same hands that held the gun and pulled the trigger to end the life of a foal. I try to imagine what it is to live under the laws of this hard land. What it is like to have only two acres of alfalfa, which will feed only two using horses through a winter. What it is to ride out on the plains each day to break the ice on the watering trough for the sheep and the horses and that is all you can do: bring them salt and break the ice. The rest is not up to you. If the winter is hard, you will bring many sheep hides back from the frozen plains. Some of your foals and yearlings won't make it through. If the winter is mild, you will bring in fewer hides and have more yearlings on spring grass.

Here there is no specialist to take over a task for you, no one to absolve you of it. You do each day what you can, accept the things you cannot change. The loneliness of the long evenings you braid into things of beauty.

Guillermo isn't just making a halter for us; he is weaving his dream into ours. His hands are creating a structure to our journey that had not been there before. In making for us a means to hold onto our horses, the journey is taking on a shape and form all its own.

Not a destination, but a destiny.

A destiny still there to hold onto when the plane disgorges me in Amsterdam onto a moving ramp that transports me through endless airport corridors, following numbers and signs to deposit me in the area designated for passengers to Stockholm, Sweden. Overhead TV screens show the latest Giorgio Armani fashions. The newest of the new: Panty Power. Models slither down the runway, swirling to reveal laced panties, red and blue and multicolored panties. Edit cut to the furrowed faces of the demi-gods of fashion giving erudite statements on Panty Power.

I am nauseated. I remember the first time I came to America and how I used to miss Europe. The culture, the refinement. Now I wonder what it was I thought I was missing. An intricate cultural weave taking shape on a loom, is that what I thought?

I take out my notebook and a pen and start writing a barrier against the vacuousness around me, a defense against my own fear of insignificance. Not unlike, maybe, the way Guillermo would take up a string of sinew and weave it into the exquisite star shape on a martingale. Letters, words, sometimes phrases and even paragraphs, lying dark and dormant in a slag heap by my feet, stir with signs of life. They turn red and liquid, malleable with the heat of passion. With the slightest touch then of my hammer on this anvil, molten words turn into shapes new and amazing.

Going back to this Patagonia is an inward journey to a place in time that is ours only. It is not about the geography. I know I will never travel to those places again. Returning would be like picking up a paintbrush and changing the blues and the greens and shapes of orange on a Van Gogh painting. Who'd think of doing such a thing?

Exactly!

You wouldn't even think of tampering with a sketch you did as a child because now you have better technique.

I know this now. I didn't in February of 1968.

On our way back to Cabo Machichaco from Paris, we took a detour into the valley in the Swiss Alps where we met in 1962 at Albert Schweitzer College in the village of Churwalden.

There was a strong warm wind blowing down the valley. The *foen*, the Swiss call it. Powerful gusts made driving difficult on the narrow mountain road in our VW van. But we kept on pushing against the head wind and eventually we arrived at the three-story building from our past, now boarded up and in darkness. The wind whistled along the eaves. A couple of the shutters banged against windows that we remembered lit up and with laughter percolating from the inside.

Nathan's room was on the top floor, under the eaves, where he painted on the slanted ceiling with big black letters:

SOME PEOPLE LAUGH AT ME
SOME PEOPLE FROWN
SOME SAY:
HE'LL GROW OUT OF IT
I SAY NOTHING.

Frau Ritter was furious. "You will pay for having this room painted over, Nathan!"

Nathan said, "No problem. When I leave, my poems will vanish."

My window was directly below his in the room I shared with Marlene, who was from New York and the first black person I spent time with.

Every evening Marlene would sit cross-legged on her cot and put goop in her frizzly hair and then roll it into curlers. We'd joke around about nothing in particular and everything. By morning her hair would be straight and this must have been important to her because she would never miss a night doing this thing to her hair. Marlene and I had a lot of fun. Too much fun, thought Dr. and Frau Ritter and the second term they made me share the room with Cecilia from Mexico City. Cecilia was older and more serious. She had long straight black hair. Sometimes she would go to the hairdresser in Churwalden and have them make it curly.

There were thirty-two of us. We came from different countries. Our backgrounds were different. Together we shared a world of candlelight poetry readings; raw onions and wine served to the words of Keroac and e.e. cummings. We had daytime lectures on the Philosophy of History, Existentialism, German Literature.

It was student life as it should be: learning for its own sake and with a ski lift across the road that would take you to the top of the world. You would glide along with nothing on your mind but the snow; each turn a new and complete challenge and when it was done, good or not so good, it was behind you forever and you were focused on the next one ahead.

We might have left things at that.

We don't. We go on to the small neighboring village of Malans and knock on the parish door. Dr. Wolff opens. He peers out into the darkness. For a moment, we are his ghosts from a life past. Then he offers us tea and cookies.

We try to make small talk. None of us are much good at it. Dr. Wolff is a preacher now in this small church, attending to the needs of his parishioners. Simple folk. No more college. No more students. Just the church. Just the books. His private thoughts.

We go away wishing we could have kept the college the way it was when we left in the spring of 1962: all the students still in it and Dr. Wolff sparring with Nathan over the nuances of meaning in *Das Sein Des Seiende*.

Now all our moments in that building will have an indelible ghost ring around them. We will hear the echo of laughter, not the laughter itself. Return to a place out of time and you lose it. The change remains like a cigarette burn in a leather sofa.

Time and place are inexorably bound together. Weave them forward, always forward and you keep them right there with you. Because the Patagonia and who I was then is part of my here and now, the Patagonia gives me a life raft in this ocean of people and stuff and smells and noises.

This immense passenger terminal hosts the cut-offs, the sundry pieces whirling around the weaver's floor after the rug has been taken away. Myriad of little white threads spinning in space, each inexorably separate and minute with no power to regrow a whole.

What would happen to such a cloud of specks as that in a place like the Patagonia where the winds have the power to carry an entire carpet and bury it in an *arroyo* somewhere? And I remember Armando, back when.

"If someone could tell me," he once said, "what is really real, I would give my life to know."

Armando meant it. But not enough, I thought at the time, to cast off what was his life then and go to the end of the earth to look for the Really Real. Maybe that wasn't his to do. Maybe he found his answer in the eyes of a child. Maybe he never found it. In any case, my answer would not have been his.

Leaving El Zorro is hard, so much harder than it was getting there.

We have our horses. We found them in the worst kind of place. That was all of the plan when we left Cabo Machichaco four months earlier.

Beyond this, we don't have a plan.

Children of The Sixties that we are, we believe in Happenings. We don't write a script and then try to act it out; we don't study parts or sets. We distrust lines of any kind.

No walls or boundaries to stop you in the Patagonia!

You can go off freely in any direction. Follow a fence, if you like, or cut camp, if you dare. Should you come to a fence, you lay down the smooth wire stringers and put a poncho over them so that your horses can step across. Then you prop the fence back the way it was, and as long as you do that, the owner will not mind. The fences are there to keep the sheep enclosed and separate, not the people. Your freedom is unrestrained: you set any course you wish.

In any direction you look: the stark sameness of land and sky.

"What you need to know, the plains will teach you," Guillermo says to us.

He gives us a map of the Santa Cruz Province. It is mostly empty space, like a nautical chart, with each *estancia*, each shepherd's *puesto* even, marked and named. With one person per square kilometer, there is plenty of room for such detail.

And Guillermo gives us the name of his cousin: Jimmy Halliday, at *estancia* Los Pozos, down by Rio Gallegos.

"He's a bit of a wild one," Guillermo says. "Good horseman."

Traveling as we do, with a packhorse and not knowing where to cut camp, the journey might take us a week, Guillermo figures, if we stop a day or two on the way to rest the horses.

And so it is that leaving El Zorro, we ride off in a southeasterly direction, glad to have a short-term goal, to have someone expecting us somewhere.

Just after the sun sets on the first day, we reach *estancia* Mendocino. They put out hay for our horses and meat for our dog and show us into a room at the end of a long corridor. We have pushed too far on this day and it is all I can do not to crash on the bed, clothes and all, and go to sleep. Nathan starts to wash up with warm water from the white porcelain carafe, getting ready to go for supper.

If he can do it, I can do it!

There is no mirror above the washstand, and I am glad for that because I don't want to look at my scorched face and windblown hair. The only hope of getting a brush through the tangled mess would be to wash it first, but I am not up to that. It hurts just to get water on the deep rope burn on my right palm, never mind soap or shampoo! I scoop some water and sprinkle it over my hair and pull it back into a ponytail, dig a clean sweater and a pair of jeans out of the panniers. I feel a lot better and, suddenly, extremely hungry.

We step into a dining room with a table like one you see in paintings of The Last Supper, large and made of oak and transported here, you think, by some magic. The *patrón* sits at the head of the table and he blesses the food of all whom the plains have brought together here. We eat *sancocho* stew and bread still warm, with real butter, and a salad. No one asks questions of us. Not about the day, not about the who and the why and the wherefore. We just share the meal.

A *gaucho*, red kerchief tied loosely around his neck, dark hair combed slick back from his parched face, sits directly opposite me. I catch myself studying him more than fleetingly, thinking: my camera would love the angular lines of his face. I am sure he can feel my stare but my scrutiny seems not to bother him. Probably he wouldn't mind me taking his picture.

I would mind.

His picture would become a souvenir, to show off someday, with an appropriate caption: Patagonian *Gaucho*, 1969.

And that's not it. It's not his likeness I am after. It is learning to become more like him, more quiet, tougher.

I feel certain that to him and to everyone else around this table, Nathan and I are an easy read. Nathan's cheeks are bright red and I assume my face too is flushed from the warmth of the room. The *gaucho* will have noticed how I can barely hold the knife or the spoon with my right hand and would be able to picture in detail our horses bolting and balking at being made to leave their home turf, their *querencia*. The lateness of our arrival at the *estancia* told him we had much trouble on the way, our bulging panniers how little we knew of the essentials of traveling on horseback.

Nathan rode in wearing sneakers.

Imagine that: an American cowboy without the boots, without a hat and only five foot seven and dark, looking more like a native of Chile than a gringo and speaking Spanish, very good Spanish, with a Venezuelan accent.

There is a perfectly logical explanation for the lack of boots. No one is asking and you don't just start explaining how the boots you bought at *La Chiche* got left behind and how you let *señor* Enrique know and he promised he would send them right away to Puerto Santa Cruz. No boots came. So here you are, no boots. No gloves either, because we didn't think about needing them and we are traveling in waist length leather jackets that we bought on a sidewalk in Buenos Aires.

They are not judging us; we are judging ourselves, impatient with all that we don't yet know.

"No boots!"

It is the first comment Jimmy Halliday makes to Nathan when we dismount at Los Pozos five days later. Nathan gets to tell the story then of the cavalry boots from *La Chi*che that never showed up.

"Somewhere, someone has himself a new pair," Jimmy says matter-of-factly. Before we have unsaddled our horses and stored our gear in the *galpon*, he brings out a pair of boots such as we have never seen before.

"*Botas de potro*," he says, "Made them myself. Try them on."

They're made from the hind legs of a horse, cured with the hair still on so that you can imagine the rest of the horse all too easily. He was a light bay. His hocks form a natural boot heel and you step right into his gaskins.

When the hide of an animal is cured and dyed and turned into footwear that no longer bears any resemblance to the original, you don't give it a second thought. Stepping right inside the skin of a dead horse is another matter. I am glad it isn't to me that Jimmy offers these boots.

On the *pampas*, not so long ago, when horses were roaming in abundance belonging to no one, a *gaucho* would kill one just to make himself a pair of *botas de potro* that might last him a month, this I have read somewhere. Jimmy assures us the bay died of natural causes.

"I see you have a *tobiana* mare," he says. "Good! You'll find her when your buckskins blend into the landscape. My cousin, he likes his *gateados*. For me the more color, the better I like them."

"They need shoes," he says, looking at our horses more closely. "Guillermo isn't one to shoe a horse. He's got plenty of them. One gets sore, grab another. That's how it is down here. Traveling them every day like you are doing, these gravel *pampas* will grind the hooves right off even the best-footed horse."

Our first day at Los Pozos begins with Jimmy banging on our door. It is not yet six o'clock.

"Let's get some shoes on those horses of yours. Sun is up!"

"We have been getting them used to lifting their feet," I say. "The front anyway."

"No worries. They'll know how."

A set of stocks, made of two-inch metal pipe and anchored in cement, ensures that they do. Carpincho has the softest hooves of the four. We take him first and I am surprised how readily he walks into the narrow pipe chute. A hinged pipe, front and rear, keep him in there. He struggles only briefly when Jimmy's expert hands get a rope around his left front pastern lightning fast, winch the leg up and take a couple of wraps around the pipe. A quick going over with a hoof rasp and on goes the shoe that fits, more or less, to the outline of the hoof. They take turns rasping and nailing, Jimmy, Nathan and the old *capataz*. By lunchtime, all four horses have shoes on.

Jimmy Halliday obviously loves being Jimmy Halliday: burly and ruddy, a big man to cast a long shadow across the Gallegos *campo*. But all the burly and the *gaucho* get left in the vestibule along with his boots and his hat. Inside the manor at Los Pozos, Jimmy could be mistaken for an English country squire. The lady of the house, Christine Halliday, presents a picture of proper British etiquette as she sits on a chaise lounge darning socks, her long slender legs neatly folded to the side.

I am reminded of a family in Kent, the Gordons, where my aunt sent me to spend a week in the summer I was twelve. They lived down a country lane, in a house just like this, with high ceilings and polished wood floors and the timeless decor of area rugs and laced tablecloths and curtains, even a grand piano.

How amazing are the British! At once so infinitely adaptable to climates and cultures and at the same time so unflinchingly loyal to the details of daily life according to age old patterns from a small island nation in the Old World.

"We used to ride over to the neighbors for tea," Christine tells us. "It is six or seven leagues there. We thought nothing of it. We'd play a game of canasta and then we'd gallop back home."

She laughs and tosses her head so that her blond curls dance around her head in joyful memory. Christine is trim and athletic. I love her smile; there is nothing fake here. Christine is someone who has decided to make this life in The Damned Lands a good life.

The cook has prepared a delicious broth and hot biscuits and we have salad with our meat. Jimmy takes the time to light up his pipe after coffee, but only just. Soon we are back outside at the corral, where some mares and foals are locked up.

"Time to start taming them," Jimmy says. "I like to catch the foals up once or twice at this age. Makes things easier later on."

Jimmy's rawhide lasso zings through the air and lands around the neck of a mostly white *tobiano* colt. The youngster struggles briefly, wide-eyed and trembling. Jimmy makes a couple of quick hitches around the *palenque*, the tall post set in the center of the corral, wood worn smooth from years of use. The foal tries to run away, hits the end of the rope and flips violently to the ground. You can hear him gasping for air. Soon he lies there very still in the dirt, half-choked and submissive, in the way of horses, to what may come.

Jimmy walks along the rope to the foal's head and, from behind, puts a knee on its neck and pins him down while his hands stroke and pat him all over. After a few minutes, Jimmy gets up, walks back to the *palenque* and quickly unlashes the rope to give the gasping animal some air.

The next foal is a solid dark bay. Once again, Jimmy's rope lands right on target. The foal hits the dirt with such violent force and lies there so still, it seems its neck might have been broken. Jimmy walks towards the little bay, giving some slack in the rope as he approaches.

As he bends down over the foal to check it over, it springs back to life and back to its feet and before Jimmy has time to step back, the foal rears up. Jimmy is too close and the foal strikes him in the head with a sharp front hoof. Blood streaming into his eyes, Jimmy orders the *capataz* to finish the job with the bay: choke him back down to teach him that man is his master, or he'll grow up a useless horse, good only to feed to the sheep dogs. That taken care of, he grabs the bandana off his neck, makes a knot in it and presses it against his forehead to stem the blood.

We walk with him up to the house. I am struggling to sort out my feelings. I am sorry Jimmy got hurt, glad it doesn't appear to be badly. Yet a part of me says: yeah! Right! One for the foal! What do you expect, scare the thing half to death and choke him.

I like Jimmy. I like him a lot and respect his skill. It is the whole idea of the horse as adversary, as a creature to break and use and throw away I am having trouble with. Must the foal be terrified of me for the horse to do as I ask? No wonder Carpincho doesn't like me very much. Being broke like that at the *palenque*, why should he? Someday, will he?

Or is it that the roughness of the *gaucho* is more on the surface than it would be if Jimmy were that English country squire breeding race horses and having them pampered and groomed and given tidbits, then thrown into a stee-plechase to win, or bust their lungs trying. Knowing some of the horses start-ing in the Grand National will be running their last race, is the squire kinder than the *gaucho* who teaches the colt one life lesson on the *palenque* so that he shall know his master and his own limits?

Here the colt will run free until he is two. Then he'll be castrated, thrown out again to heal his wounds on the *pampa*. He will be brought back in as a four-year-old, tied to the *palenque* to fight it out for maybe twelve hours. He'll get a saddle on his back, a *bocado* thong tied around his lower jaw and ridden out on the *pampa* until he returns broke, exhausted and subdued.

Maybe this is more honest. Maybe he has the better life compared to the pampered Thoroughbred who'll have his whole career over and done with by the time he is a long two. If he isn't fast enough, or breaks down trying to run, it's all the same. He's on the next truck to the packing plant and forgotten, all hopes now pinned on the next crop of twos coming out of the starting gates.

Maybe things aren't always what they seem.

Jimmy spends most of the evening talking on the radiophone, answering sincere concerns from some of his neighbors at twenty miles, to joshing from others. Jimmy, the *domador* of *domadores* getting himself kicked by a mere foal is big news on the Gallegos *campo* that day.

The next morning, Jimmy is up and banging on the guestroom door again before six.

"Round up time!" He calls.

"Our horses need to rest," Nathan says sleepily.

"We have horses for you. Get up! Everyone is going."

Everyone includes Christine and Edward, nine, and Jill, ten. All of us are mounted on paint horses, good solid using horses that eat up the distance in a rhythmical rocking horse canter as we head out across *campo* to bring in sheep for the shearing. My horse is an old black and white *tobiano*, much more comfortable than Carpincho, I must admit. I am enjoying the faster pace and the fact that I don't have to worry about saving my horse for tomorrow and next week and next month. This horse will work today and then not again for a week or more.

The sheep dogs do most of the work. They keep the flock tight and moving along by jumping and yapping and running across the backs of the herd if need be to keep strays in line. We ride at the rear, speaking little. The wind has come up and snatches away any word that isn't a yell and throws it far away from whom it was intended. That's okay. It is good like this, riding together and watching the Corredales and the sheep dogs.

Suddenly there is great commotion up ahead. Jimmy, Edward and the two *gauchos* are off at full gallop. My *tobiano* is running flat out too, without any cue from me. We have come upon three emus and he is an old pro at the chase. Instinctively he heads the giant birds off toward a fence. He knows he can't out run them, only outmaneuver them. The other riders are closing in on the prey from three sides and the birds get trapped into the last fence we came through. *Bolas* whine through the air, finding their target. Two of the birds go down in a tangle of rawhide and feathers.

Nathan comes storming up, all excited. "Get some good shots?"

"Are you kidding? Never had a chance to draw my camera. It was over so fast."

Now I have the time, but now I don't want the pictures. I have enough pictures in my head of hunting and huntsmen, from way back when my grandfather and his party returned from an outing with a dead buck deer on the roof rack of the station wagon.

We were out for a few days at Åsa Bruk, my grandparents, my mother and I. Also a whole bunch of people I did not know and whom I did not care to get to know. I hid up in my room under the eaves on the third floor of the big yellow mansion. I refused to come down for dinner. My mother knew to leave me alone and to run interference. What I like best about my mother is that she does not invent something to cloak the truth; she tells it how it is. And that's that.

"Elly is angry with you for killing the deer," she says. "She won't talk to anyone."

I cried until late into the night and the next morning early I snuck out to the barn and stayed with the Company horses. They were the last of the logging horses: big and brown and fuzzy. They understood.

Now, as then, what bothers me is man's taking away the wildness of a creature. One moment so beautiful and unattached. A dead heap, the next.

And for what?

Feathers?

Isn't it enough that humans fence off all the best grazing places, all the brooks and lagoons and let sheep and horses gnaw the grass down to the roots? What gives us the right to take whatever wildlife has managed to survive on the margins?

I am not looking to debate the issue. I am glad that being chatty is not a requirement here. I feel like being quiet and so I am. No one inquires if there be a reason, or tries to snap me out of a mood.

You would have thought that the slaughter of a lamb at *puesto* Media Agua, the following day, would make me cringe. Instead, I find the scene to be strangely beautiful. It is a day of high clouds moving fast and turning pink with the lateness of the hour. The color of the sky mirrors the pinks and the reds of the carcass hung from a hand-hewn beam that had once been painted a sharp blue. Remnants of the paint lie deep in the grooves of the weathered wood. I take out my camera to record the scene as the *puestero* goes about the task in the unhurried way of someone who knows the reasons for what he does.

Yesterday, this sheep was part of the flock in his care, the sole reason for this man to be living here at this lonely *puesto*, leaving wife and child back home in Temuco, Chile. Today it is the destiny of this sheep to provide for his shepherd: meat for his staple, fat to be rendered and used for cooking his *tortas* and to fuel the wick for his lamp, the fleece going to the *patrón* of the *estancia* to be turned into cash for such things as flour and sugar and *máte*.

"We will always live well in the Patagonia," Guillermo told us. "No matter what happens in the world, we will have the essentials."

I think I am beginning to grasp the meaning of what he said.

It occurs to me now to imagine this *puestero* sitting here next to me at the Amsterdam airport, watching the Desert Storm fireworks display of Global TV with me as people hustle past us with bagfuls of merchandise from the duty-free stores, their mouths full of fast food. These people here, so fractured and wanting, always wanting. I keep saying "these people". There are so many of them, with no spaces between them. Throngs, cues, everywhere you go you're in someone else's space. Space is so constricted and there is no in-between left, just one big glob. Like fish eggs.

How out of time and place would be the *puestero*; how out of place and time am I in this digital world that is not about sharing what you have, but about having more and about standing out in a crowd, any way that you can.

How ironic that the sum effect of all these desperate efforts to make an individual mark become an abstract painting with all the colors thrown in so that, in the end, you don't distinguish one single color. No single detail stands out in bold relief.

But I remember the pattern of the wool sweater worn by the *puestero* at Media Agua on that day, more than a quarter of a century ago.

There is one of him in his world and it is complete. He has his dog, he says, and his radio and the occasional visitor. His tasks keep him busy and wanting for nothing.

If I come a stranger in his land, he will show me where to put my horse for the night, he will slice some meat for my dog, show me the sheepskin-covered bunk in the spare room. He will put a kettle on to boil and will offer me *máte*. He will cook a meal and we will sit together by the stove, speaking little.

And if he come here, amongst all of these people with so much more to spare? He might be hungry and hurting or lonely. Would anyone stop to bring him what simple things he might need?

Were he to arrive at a house in these parts, chances are the owner would call the police. He might be branded homeless and a beggar. Maybe arrested for vagrancy. This for doing here exactly what we did at his home in the Patagonia: arrive unannounced, uninvited.

I am not liking where my thoughts are taking me and I am glad when my flight to Stockholm is announced ready for boarding. I get busy putting away my notebook and with finding my boarding pass and my ticket. When I am seated on the SAS plane, a window seat this time, where I want my mind to go is on the Gallegos River.

Almost three weeks into our journey and this is our first campsite. The Gallegos is not a river really, more of a stream, a mere brook. But after so many days of sameness, this small waterway fills us with a sense of wonder. The valley bottom is green and the air above teeming with large flocks of birds: geese, cranes. Far above, hawks hover. Up the banks, the *calafate* bushes grow tall and thick, offering protection from the winds.

The first thing Nathan does upon dismounting is kick off the *botas de potro* and find his sneakers in the pack. He bustles around gathering dry *calafate* branches and twigs for a fire before he heads down to the river to try out his fishing gear. This gear is an empty one pound coffee tin, a piece of wood wedged in the open end for a handle and some line wrapped around the can with a red and white spinner at the end. Nathan is convinced it will work. You hold the handle in your left hand, whirl the hooked line with your right, until you have some speed built up. Then you throw the line like a lasso, pointing the can so the rest of the line can feed out, turn it sideways to stop and, when the fish bites, you wind the line back around the can and bring in your catch.

I wish him luck. I want to stay with the horses.

We have been too busy fighting the wind and the vastness these past weeks, trying to prove ourselves tough enough. Every day has been a test of resolve and endurance, every evening a refuge in someone else's world. Riding a horse all day, every day, and then turning him into a corral for the night, or out in some large and over grazed *potrero* isn't going to make you his companion. He'll do his job and be glad when it's done so that you leave him alone. If traveling is just like that, you should better consider riding a bicycle, I am thinking.

I take out the brush and currycomb. I am planning to groom each horse in turn. Pampero isn't interested in being the object of my attention. He walks away from me and finds a choice spot of fine sand, plops down on his right side, lies flat and rubs himself vigorously: head, neck, shoulder, ribcage. Then he flips over and goes through the same routine on the left side, jumps back to his feet and shakes himself vigorously. All done and groomed, the *pampa* way.

Maracas has been waiting his turn to use the same exact spot. When he is done, the two of them wander off a short distance and start grazing, side by side. They won't stray far from Carpincho, this much we have learned. I decide to leave them be and turn my attention to Carpincho. I have him tied to a *calafate* so he can't move away from me while I give him a vigorous massage. Using a circular motion, I work from the top of his neck all the way down to the root of his tail and then back over, with straight even strokes this time, the way the Swedish cavalry taught me. Carpincho remains guarded, unresponsive. A barn horse will lean into your brush to indicate a particularly itchy spot, letting you know with soft eyes, or curving upper lip, when you have found just the spot and how much he enjoys the process.

Carpincho just stands there, enduring. As soon as I am done, he lies down and gives himself a proper *pampa* grooming in the sand.

"Okay, that's fine!" I tell him. "I need you. You don't need me."

And if I let go of you, you'll head back north, with the others in tow, back to your *querencia*. I know you still feel the pull, like a magnet. Every time I give you the reins you start to veer towards *El Zorro*. I wish you could know there are much better places up ahead of us, with grass abundant, where you won't have to half starve and freeze through the winter.

I wish I had some grain, something to make him believe it worth his while to stick around. The best I can do is stay with him where the grass is good and hold onto the *cabresto* while he grazes. Now and then he stops, lifts his head and his ears turn, ever alert to the distant sound of a guanaco down on the river, or to a flock of birds swoshing down to land on an eddy. The other three don't bother looking up, depending on him to be vigilant, as we are learning to depend on him. He is the one always going forward, the boss horse.

"I am going to call you Caicique," I announce to him. I like the sound of it with the extra i. It is Spanish for chief but distinctive, spelled that way. A name his very own"

"I know I chose the right one when I picked you," I tell him and he turns his left ear towards the sound of my voice. It is a very small movement, imperceptible almost. The faint beginnings, I hope, of a bond between us.

This river valley with no fences or sheep tracks is what we came looking for, our home without a roof or walls, under a sky so big and so clear it vacuums my thoughts right up and leaves me clean and crisp inside, aware of nothing other than the sound of my horse next to me.

Nathan returns from the river with a big smile and three fish all cleaned and strung on a *calafate* stick, ready to cook over the fire. He has brought water in the tin can with a wire handle that is our teapot. Hobo's icon Nathan calls it.

We arrange the panniers and the saddles to give protection from the south-west, in case the wind comes up and we put down our bedroll, one piece at a time. A rain poncho first to seal out ground moisture, next the sheepskins we use underneath our saddles for a mattress, a blanket spread over top and then the sheets I sewed together to make a bag. Three horse blankets, army surplus and thin and a wool poncho go on top and last a tarp, to keep the body heat in and the rain out. We stuff clean underwear, socks and sweaters into pillow-cases and presto: there is our bed.

We sit together, very close and speaking little as the outlines of the riverscape fade and the night tucks itself in around our fireside camp. Each passing moment is a juicy red grape of a cluster that you squeeze to the last drop and savor and that, over time, turns to wine. The thing about this wine from a moment savored fully is that it replenishes itself with each sip you take, growing stronger.

And it flows together with so many other rich moments of its kind, right back to the very first camp we shared, by the old castle ruin in Malans just after we met. We took our sleeping bags and spent the night together in the rain. When we came in for breakfast at the college in the morning, my hair still wet, the Ritters glared sternly and would not believe that sleeping in the rain was about listening to echoes of times past in a roofless stone structure and the wondrous discovery of each other as soul mates, not about sex. They lectured Nathan about being discreet and being careful and that's when he painted his poems on the ceiling of the third story attic room.

On the Gallegos River, Nathan writes:

I watch the cupping palm of smoke blacken the shiny surface of our tin can and in the genie vapor rising, I see a bridge above our campsite along the coast of Spain. We are telling Estanco what we are going to do next. What living on the road with him and his kin in the caravans has inspired. Estanco sits up on the edge of the wooden chair, poking at the coals with his willow cane. His dark eyes dance and I sense that the old gypsy is letting the idea take wings inside of him.

"To the pampas!" He calls out, suddenly.

His silhouette, flanked by Elly's and by mine, is thrown up large by the orange fire light against the granite arch of the bridge above and I feel very close to him. He hooks the can of boiling water off the fire

39

with his cane and sets it down in front of Eladia. The gypsy woman fills the silver tea ball and drops it in the dented old tin.

"Go!" He implores. "Go, children of mine. Go to the land of horses!"

The water in our tin can chuckles to a boil. It's bubbling voice seems to say:

"Welcome back gypsy pilgrims to your campsite behind a bush, on the outer fringe, down at the bottom of the world. Draw near and I'll warm you inside out, keep you company till you move on."

I want to laugh and shout. What an ugly little duckling of a symbol, this hobo's icon. Yet so perfect. An empty tin can: what settlers chuck out with the trash and what those who travel free always carry.

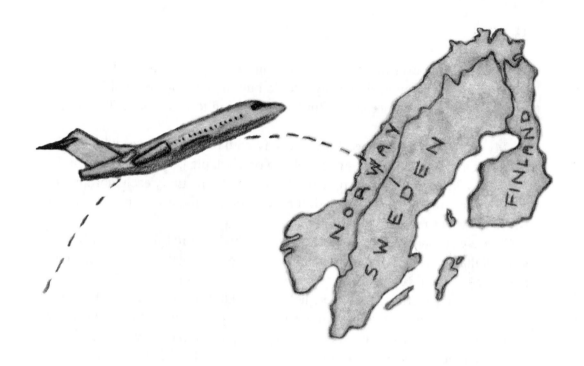

SUNLIGHT DETERGENT

The jet comes in low over the Stockholm Archipelago.
Mälarviken.
Stockholms Skärgård.
I try to get my mind around the once familiar names. My birth place, that I see from the air now, for the first time.

I should feel excitement, shouldn't I?

Should experience a tight pull around the heart that says: this is my home, this beautiful city on the water, with so many inlets, so many little islands.

But as the jet descends and decelerates in a series of rough jolts, I feel myself bracing against the motion. It isn't fear of flying now, or even of landing. It is fear of being down there, without wings. I search for memories that might override my apprehension, that might welcome me back into the folds of this city on the water.

The 1956 Equestrian Olympics, there's one!

I bought a five-day pass with money I withdrew from my Horse Fund. It was the first time ever that I took money out. I thereby broke a solemn pact with myself and it put back the day I could buy my own horse - and I was so close to having enough money! But I wasn't going to miss out on THE OL-YMPICS!

My grandmother arranged for me to stay with distant relatives who had a big flat in a stately five-story stone building on Karlaplan, which is a very nice inner city address and not far from Stockholm Stadium. Early each morning, I took the tram to the West Gate and, for five wonderful days in June, the city where I was born was my rightful home.

There were many empty seats around the Stadium; not that many people were all that interested in watching uniformed men ride patterns in the sand on their horses or fling themselves over obstacles with them.

Only the equestrian games were held in Stockholm, far away from the rest of the 1956 Summer Olympics in Melbourne. It had something to do with quarantine restrictions, or maybe Australia was just too far away. Most of the horses and the riders came from Europe and almost all of them from cavalry units.

Sweden did very well, taking individual and team gold in dressage, probably because Sweden hadn't been at war for a long time. The Crown still purchased three year old remounts from the breeders and taught conscripts how to ride at Strömsholm. For the officers, this meant having the barns and the grooms, riding halls and financial support needed to pursue excellence in dressage, cross country and stadium jumping.

There was the end-of-an-era feeling at the 1956 Olympics. People were talking about a day when there would be no more horses in the world, except maybe at the zoo. After Hiroshima and Nagasaki, what on earth would we be needing war horses for?

I felt lucky to be born in the nick of time. And sad, because the drays and the logging horses and farm teams were disappearing and with them my childhood world. Farmers did not drive teams in to the mill anymore to have barley and oats ground for their cows and there were no more horse drawn wagons hauling snow off the streets and unloading, one shovel full at a time, into the Nyköping river. Gösta still had a team and I would still ride my bike out to the farm in the summer and ski there in the winter and work with Brunte and Stjärna, the bay and the sorrel mare. But the era of the draft horse was coming to an end; I was also getting older, more focused on riding. I hoped the doom-sayers would be proven wrong and there would still be horses for me to ride. No one, back then, could have predicted the spectacular return of the horse as a partner in sport and recreation.

Security was not a problem at the Stockholm Olympics; no one worried about it. Once inside the Stadium gates, you had free access to barns and exercise rings. I spent a lot of time back there, up close to so many beautiful horses, watching riders warm their horses up for competition.

Nils Ankarcrona was one of the dressage riders. He was a cavalry officer and he was the editor of the magazine HÄSTEN, which I bought every month and read cover to cover. I felt I knew him.

Much later, I would tell him about being the kid standing ringside watching him ride at the 1956 Olympics. He said he remembered me, which was a nice thing to say, though I did not believe him.

We never did meet. When he published my articles in HÄSTEN about horses and horsemen in America and about our long ride, I felt vindicated. Nils is gone now and so is HÄSTEN and all that was a long time ago.

But, okay, then:

Let us talk about that Sunday towards the end of summer, the summer of the Olympics, when some biker friends of Marita's came up to the Oppeby Stables and went into the old cow barn where the Sunlight Detergent Company was renting storage space. The guys began playing around, opening boxes and throwing powdered soap at each other. When the cops came, they took me away to the police station, same as they did the bikers.

My crime?

Being a girl of thirteen and not stopping a gang of eighteen year olds. Nobody told me just how I would have done that. Or how it was that the Sunlight detergents in that old barn, unlocked and unattended, had become my responsibility. I was there that day. Of course, I was. I was always at the stables on Sundays and on every other day of the week, mucking stalls, feeding, watering, grooming, riding whichever remount needed miles put on him. I didn't care if they bucked, or tried to run off with me.

My punishment?

The executives of the Nyköping Riding Club were taking a strong stand against vandalism. They were demonstrating how much they cared about safeguarding the property of the Sunlight Detergent Company. They were treating everyone involved exactly the same: banishment for one year from the Oppeby

Stables. Marita didn't care. She was more interested in boys than she was in horses. She went elsewhere to hang out. I doubt that the guys who actually threw the detergents around cared; it had been a one time thing for them. They didn't ride horses and they were not members.

I cared too much: I had nowhere else to go.

All the other Sundays, all the days I had spent at the stables helping out meant nothing to the people responsible for the decision. That's what hurt the most. They sold me out to the Sunlight Company. And that was that.

It was as if they had ripped the lungs out of my chest. I stayed home from school with nowhere to go. I read furiously, big epics like *War and Peace* that immersed me in a world far away and long ago so I might block out this unendurable present. For as long as I could remember, horses were at the center of my life. Horses were my refuge: farm horses, dray horses, ponies, race horses, cavalry mounts, any and all horses, I wasn't picky. I just had to be with horses.

My mother has told me about the first time I rode a horse, so I can picture him very clearly: an old grey horse, hitched to a cart filled with refuse in the cobblestoned square in Nyköping. Stora Torget, Big Square it was called and it was the center of town.

On Saturdays, Stora Torget filled with wooden stands where farmers displayed their produce and fishermen their catch and itinerant merchants offered balloons and trashy toys. It would have been on a Saturday afternoon that the grey horse and wagon were hauling off garbage left by the vendors on the public market day, one summer afternoon in 1945. I was two years and a few months old.

I remember his large black hooves, partially covered by gray feather. He'd rest one, then the other, patiently waiting, dozing off for a few seconds now and then. Most of all, I remember his large kind eyes and that he lowered his head so I could touch his muzzle, which was so soft and smelled wonderful!

"You were so insistent," my mother told me. "You just had to get up onto his back."

Making my wish her command, my mother would have gone up to the driver, unabashed. She acted on impulse and never worried what anyone might think. She would have smiled sincerely and been so elated when the man agreed to lift me up on the back of his big horse.

The backpad of the Swedish harness is made up of a stuffed pad on either side of the withers, a curved metal bar connecting them; it is almost as if it were designed this way with the safety of young children in mind. I remember holding onto the bar with my hands and the feeling of the sweaty horse under my bare legs, soft and comforting and a little itchy.

"You didn't want to hear of getting off his back," my mother said. "Whatever this connection with horses, you were born with it."

To my mother, horses were foreign; she loved dogs, not cats, and always made friends with them. She thought horses magnificent creatures and accepted them as my chosen friends; but she kept her distance from them.

When you are thirteen, a year can be a dark narrow tunnel without end. After they slammed the door shut in my face, everything I did from then on had one aim: to get out, to get away and never ever come back.

That fateful Sunday afternoon at Oppeby, Sweden, has everything to do with me sitting astride my horse on the crest of a hill far above the town of Puerto Natales. I love the feeling of discovery, of a place with no past; of the day being crisp and clear and you know you will never pass through here again. If you miss it, there isn't a second chance. The gray and stormy waters of The Strait of Magellan hold no memory; only mystery.

For this moment, on this day, I have all I could ever want: a friend and lover to share the incredible magnetism of the new and unexplored and my horse to take me from yesterday into today.

The Chilean border post above Puerto Natales is a small quonset, painted white with red trim.

"Where are you staying in Puerto Natales?" The Chilean guard wants to know.

"Not sure, yet." I hear a very slight edge in Nathan's voice.

"May I suggest the cavalry? They will be able to attend to your horses properly."

I feel a tinge of shame; I was reacting to the uniform, not seeing the young man, far away from home, missing his own horse maybe and wanting a little piece of our journey to be remembered by.

"There is a horse trail down the *quebrada*," he goes on. "We ride it all the time. Leads you right to the cavalry barracks."

Caicique takes little stumbly steps on the steep downhill trail, struggling to find a new balance in a world that is suddenly no longer flat. I stand up in the stirrups and lean forward, the way the cavalry officers taught me long ago, to get the weight off the horse's back to help him use his hind end.

Behind us, Maracas and Pampero alternatively stall out and come crashing down on the mud and the loose boulders, all their weight concentrated on the front end, their eyes bulging and nostrils large, looking like someone threw them onto a roller coaster car.

I try not to laugh at them, but I can't help smiling: for the first time since we left El Zorro a month ago, I don't feel completely inferior to these horses that the gravel and the wind bore. Going down mountains and back up again is something we are going to learn together!

Down on the flat, at land's end, my childhood world comes to embrace me with the familiar smells of stabled horses, tied up to mangers and the sound of shod hooves on cobblestone floors; the sight of men dressed in jodhpurs and high brown boots, wearing spurs like civilians do shoelaces.

Our Criollos have no memory to connect them to cavalry stables. When, after much coaxing, they finally go inside the barn and we tie them up like all the other horses are tied, they remain rigidly standing, just looking at the feed in the manger.

We get settled in the infirmary, which doubles as a guest house and has an open fireplace. Before going to the officer's mess for dinner, we stop in to check on the horses. We find them exactly as we left them, their hay and water and grain untouched.

Caicique whinnies disconsolately at the sound of our footsteps. He looks like he thinks the roof is going to fall down on top of him, and I am thinking maybe it is, maybe somewhere back in his phylogenetic memory. Caicique can tap into the true purpose of the cavalry horse. Maybe he can feel the prick of sharp spurs and the cut of severe bits as horses are forced to engage in a battle that wasn't theirs. Maybe he can hear the cries of the horses laying wounded on the muddy fields of war.

The guard on duty appears quite concerned.

"Would there be something the matter with your horses?"

"Yes, yes, I believe so." I turn to the lieutenant who has escorted us into the stables.

"Would you mind if we just turned them out? Around the infirmary, maybe?"

"You mean loose, outside?"

"Yes."

"But there is no fence. They'll run away!"

"The grass is good. They'll stay."

Blonde young female equestrians can get away with amazing things in South America and so it was that our four horses were turned loose in the military compound. With Caicique in the lead, they took off at full gallop across the drill field and disappeared from view around the building.

"*Señora*, now what?"

"They'll be back," I bluffed. This was the very first time we let them all go with no fence around them and I wasn't half so sure as I pretended that they wouldn't just take off back the way we had come. We stood around by the barn making small talk, the lieutenant telling us about the Chilean Cavalry school up in Quillota, in central Chile, where Major Durruti had jumped the horse 'Huaso' over a wall seven feet two and a half inches high. The lieutenant was very pleased to hear that we knew of this world record jump. We chatted on about Chilean jumpers and of his own ambition to some-day make the team for international competition and finished smoking a ciga-rette together.

Still, no Criollos. We got into the lieutenant's jeep and drove around the end of the administration building, tires chewing up grass in the sharp turn. Horses AWOL!

But there they were, quietly grazing next to the infirmary. Chaco was lying on the porch, by our saddles, keeping watch.

In the morning, the officer in charge arranged to have our horses reshod to cavalry standards. A couple of officers drove us all around Puerto Natales, gave us some good maps of the region around Torres del Paine and gave us our next goal: Cuevas de Milodon.

Remains of the horse from the dawn of time, the Eohippus, a creature the size of a dwarf sheep, with four toes and slinking around in the marshlands of the Eocene Era were said to have been found in these caves, giving *hippologs* a new issue to ponder: had the prehistoric horse vanished from the Americas, walked across the land bridge into Asia, to reappear as the Tarpan horse in Mongolia?

The Caves offered no clues to such as ourselves.

Call me hopelessly egocentered, but I have trouble imagining a world be-fore me; the idea of a world long before mankind made my imagination stall out completely. Fifty-five million years would be, say, like trying to fathom the whole of Mount Everest ground up into fine sand and passing through a tiny hourglass, the kind you use for timing an egg, one grain at a time.

We camped amongst the *ñire* trees nearby, where the grass was good and there was a creek and we walked into the Milodon Grande, a cave large enough to hold a whole army and it was nice like that, in the cool of the evening with no one around.

In his diary, Nathan wrote this about the area around Mount Torres del Paine:

February 1 (1969)

Beautiful morning. I made a fire and mixed up some oatmeal with butter, sugar and powdered milk (as we had not eaten well the day before). The clothing, which Elly had washed, was hanging on the calafate bushes around the camp site, nearly dry as the sun burned off the light dew. There were indications that someone had camped in the same place many years back – a fireplace, rusty cans, and a broken spit for roasting meat (the wood still hard, but discolored with age). The horses had stayed nearby and Chaco had slept in the tent I made him out of a canvas we use to cover the pack when it rains.

The approach to Mount Paine, along the Lake Toro was the most splendid trail we have ever been on. The color of the glacial waters is rather like Lake Louise (Banff National Park) but the jagged peaks of Mt Paine are without their equal in Europe or North America. They rise several thousand meters directly out of the plain and lakes - with no gradual incline at the base like the Alps or the Rockies have.

And it was completely savage and uninhabited. Not a road, a hotel, or even a hiker with a rucksack!!! We rode several leagues without seeing so much as a hoof mark on the trail or a wisp of smoke from some shepherd's hut. The birds and animals were so tame! Swallows followed us so closely that the horses became nervous, until they got used to the whooshing sound of their small wings as they cut back and forth just behind us.

It was the rarest of treats for us to have the privilege of experiencing this area before the plague of tourism opens it up and commercializes it. As it is now, it takes a real hiker, sportsman or naturalist to pass

*over these primitive trails. But in five to ten years white collar loafers
with bellies sagging will be escorted to the lakeside in fancy cars, then
placed in yachts and given a fishing rod to hold etc. etc.*

February 2:

*Mt. Paine leaves me speechless. I won't try to describe it or our
feelings. The triple frame color slides we took at sunset and sunrise
from the south side, looking across Lake Nordenskjöld, which reflected
the mountains perfectly, will have to speak for the experience. We have
been contemplating Mt. Paine now since leaving Puerto Natales - seeing it from all angles while approaching it gradually.*

It is such a marvelous way to travel.

*We stopped at a lovely abandoned shack by Lake Pehoe. We ate
some oatmeal and drank tea. I made a fishhook out of a nail, a flat-
tened out .22 shell and some tin foil - but it was so warm and inviting
that I soon stripped and went swimming instead of fishing. The water
was so clear and cold - a color only glacial water can be. My body
was numb after just a few moments, yet the sensation of the sun bringing back the life to the tissues was splendid.*

*The trail was rather precipitous for the first time - and the shale
was slippery in places, sharp and jagged in others. Yet the horses were
doing better - more surefooted than the previous day. Even India made
it past all the steep descents without falling. Only once, out of fear, she
sat down. In a few weeks time, they shall be excellent mountaineers.*

*Hunger was getting the better of us by early evening - and we were
getting worried about Chaco who had not eaten well for three days.
We arrived at a shepherd's hut, meeting an interesting chap (who may
have been a rustler) but he had very little food. We ate a little bread
and drank tea while he told us many long tales about his exploits in the
area. He tried to convince us to stay in southern Chile, telling us that
we could get public land (8000 hectares very easily - something he had
just accomplished).*

*We moved on to the waterfall at Salto Paine where we stopped for
the night. The young couple in charge of the Paine National Park were
friendly and gave us cafe con leche with fresh bread so that we had
something in our stomachs when we went to sleep.*

51

It was a most lovely spot. We got up at sunrise to photograph - and then prepared to continue.

February 3:

A group of Japanese youths arrived at the Salto in the morning as we were saddling up. They were members of an expedition that was attempting to scale one of Paine's most dangerous peaks. On the trail, we passed a group of Czechs that also were going to climb another peak (one of the towers).

We saw much game - guanaco which we photographed with the 300 mm lens from only fifty feet, ostriches, foxes, hares and condors. I spent an hour with a herd of guanaco - edging closer and closer as they got used to me. One family were particularly curious and stayed close - posing nicely for my photographs - the father, mother, and two young ones. They looked like something between a camel and a llama. Their call is weird, an otherworldly wail, fluctuating in intensity on a high pitch. At night, it sounds like something from outer space.

The lakes we passed en route to Laguna Amarga (bitter lake) were all salty. They were full of geese and ducks. There was some marshy land to pass. Once the pack horse sank in above her knees and for one frightening moment, I thought she had broken her hind leg when she pitched forward. She lay still for a few moments, gathering her strength and then plunged out on her own. The last few days have been very tough on her - two nasty spills and then the bog.

*At **estancia** Laguna Amarga we ate our first square meal in three days, got a supply of meat and sugar and continued on another ten kilometers before camping out. I had to walk over forty minutes to get water - back up the trail we had come - so that we could have some tea before going to sleep. Getting used to the routine, we unsaddled in three minutes and set up camp in another ten. The night was unusually warm and still, which made me think that it must be the calm before the storm. And sure enough - in the wee hours of the morning the wind began to blow and scattered showers started to play on the canvas over our heads.*

February 4 :

Because of the light rain and the wind, it was hard to roll out of the sack at 7:30. But when we poked our heads out, there were patches of blue and the air was still mild. We followed the Zamora River for several hours, crossing an old bridge that was rotten and full of holes - over which the horses picked their way agilely. The only one who was scared, as usual, was Chaco, who nearly crawled across.

High on a cliff above us, on Mt.Contreras, we heard the warning siren of the guanaco. The large sentinel was running across an extremely narrow path, over which a man could never pass - head high, surveying the valley where, in the distance, very likely his herd was grazing. The guanaco always seem to have a rear guard, who warns the rest of the approach of a strange beast.

*There were signs that we were nearing a cavalry post - hoof tracks with shoes - as the **peons** hereabouts never shoe their animals for working. And sure enough, within another hour, we arrived at El Guido, a cavalry post and ranch owned by **La Compania Explotadora de la Patagonia**. We ate lunch and rested the animals for several hours before heading up the Baguales River toward the pass back to Argentina.*

A friend of my mother's named Bosse meets me at the Arlanda Airport. At ground level, following the highway around the back side, Stockholm is brown and ugly and dominated by traffic coming and going. This is what the East Coast of America looked like when I arrived in 1962, having read about urban sprawl and super highways and billboards and hating it before I even got there. Now it is plastered all over my childhood. Wasn't that what we were supposed to avoid in Sweden?

My roots are Swedish. Nothing changes that. But roots buried deep don't have anything much to do with the present of the place. Why I don't like coming here is that I am a visitor now to a strange place that once was home. We don't know each other now, my past and this present. I love my childhood and very much I love the Sweden of my childhood. Neither is there anymore and no amount of nostalgia is going to change that fact.

I don't fit in a place; I fit in between places, moving in and out, ever discovering, expanding.

It is unfair, I know, to put all that on the beautiful city by the water, but that is how it is. To see my mother now, I have to get past the dragons.

I ask Bosse to excuse me please, it's been a long flight, and I close my eyes until we are approaching Nyköping and I look out across the fields where we used to have horse races. Rows of houses stand there now, and a McDonalds.

One landmark still remaining is the Sunlight Detergent plant on the east side of town. It is oddly comforting now to see this factory still functioning, sentinel to my childhood pain and I wonder; without the Sunlight Detergent Company and the effect it had on my life, would I have gone all the way to the Patagonia to ride a horse?

SEGUNDO

The story of our journey has two voices; mine is one.

The other voice is Nathan's.

This is his story of our meeting a *gaucho* named Segundo on the *pampas* of Santa Cruz.

The pounding of hooves on the earth comes to me on a sudden gust of arctic air, moments before the herd of horses bursts out of a hidden **arroyo**, *drawing a shroud of dust behind them that billows and curls forward, a breaking wave to swallow them up from behind as their flying legs stretch and hammer on the barren plain in a race before the storm.*

I glance at Elly. She is hunkered down turtle-like against the cold wind. I edge my horse closer to hers.

"Horses, Elly!" I yell.

She hears me this time. Her windburnt face emerges from the turned up collar of her leather jacket. Her shoulders uncurl and she stands up in the stirrups, her gaze following my waving arm.

"Over there!" I holler.

She cups a hand to shield her eyes from the driving sand. A grin spreads across her cracked lips. Her whole body leans with the momentum of the stampede. I read the words the wind snatches from her mouth:

"Horses!"

Closer and closer they come. The sun, pinioned on the sharp peaks of the Cordillera to the west, beams a flash flood of orange across the plains, igniting the dwarf bushes that dot the gravel, like tufts of hair the scalping knife missed. And through the flames charge the centaurs, manes and tails ablaze.

Then the sun is gone and a purple amnesty settles over the land. As abruptly as it began hours earlier, the wind dies. The approaching herd is very near now, their path converging with ours across the endless flat.

Pampero whinnies. Then Caicique and India.

A welcoming chorus answers them and a solitary **gaucho** appears in the cloud of dust. He whistles and his **madrina** veers off a few degrees east, bringing her **tropilla** of paints and bays along behind her.

A command: "**Yegua, yegua**!" And the horses all slow to a trot, then to a walk. The gaucho gives a tug to his flat-rimmed black hat.

"**Buenas, pasajeros**. Camp is just ahead. Half a league." He points north with his chin. The horizon reveals to me nothing, but I do not doubt him.

"Good grass for your horses."

He doesn't smile, but there is merriment in his eyes.

"And maybe something for us Christians too."

We ride on in silence. In this full silence after the wind dies, every small sound is distinct and clear: a twig snapping under a hoof, the tinkle of a halter ring. The numbness slowly leaves your hands and face. Your skin starts to burn and `prickle. You feel more alive than ever before and very peaceful; the damned plain that you hated is so beautiful now in the dying light off the mountains.

"Smoke, **companero**?"

The **gaucho** has finished rolling himself a cigarette, offering the pouch of tobacco to me. I shake my head with a smile - such a one-handed feat on a moving horse isn't one of the skills I have mastered in our first month on the trail.

"Later, **gracias**," I say.

He tilts his hat forward, shielding the match struck with a thumb-nail. An orange light flickers, revealing a raw-boned serenity in his swarthy face. He settles back in his wide fleece-covered saddle, rock-ing smoothly back and forth, his gnarled hands crossed in front of him.

Whenever he speaks, coughs or just shifts his weight ever so slightly, the ears of his paint move, attentive. Up ahead in the lead, the **madrina** pays him the same heed. I watch intently. I want to pick up the cues, unravel this secret of his that brought the herd of fourteen half-wild mustangs galloping toward you as one. There is nothing to see. No whip, no ropes. But you can feel it, this bond between the man and his horses and his dogs, like a spell of some kind.

Up front, the bell mare suddenly disappears from view, then three of the others, four more, five and soon we too are funneled off the plains, along a gentle slope of sand and down into a small island of green. It is so unexpected that, for a second, you think that this cannot be. The dry cold is lifted off our shoulders by a warm updraft that smells of sod. I catch the welcoming scent of burning **calafate** and roasting lamb.

Sheepdogs bark all around as we ride into the grove of poplars towards a crackling bonfire. Chaco moves in between Maracas and Pampero for protection from the howling pack.

A command bellows from the fireside and the yapping ceases. The **gaucho** continues tending to his roasting lamb, pulling the steel cross out of the ground, turning it and then driving it back in at a sharp angle to the fire. With a hooked stick, he rakes hot coals in under the spread-eagle lamb. Straightening up now to face us, boots planted wide apart, he jams his large fist against his hips and gives us a gold-flecked grin.

"Touch earth, **compadres**," he says, wrinkles making merry with his scorched face. "And make the backs of those poor beasts grate-ful."

"Segundo!" Our travelling companion leaps from his saddle to *embrace the older man.*

"Tonio! Back from Chile so soon!"

*"Yes, **amigo**, I have returned."*

"Every horse of yours has sweat marks," Segundo shakes his head of bushy red hair, fringed with white.

*"I saw my wife. **Mis hijos**."*

*Segundo makes the sign of the cross on his hairy chest, his expression suddenly stern. "You only stayed long enough to put another **inocente** in her oven."*

"Ah, boss. My good woman can do without me, bless her. But you cannot."

"You are right. Absolutely right." His face is still serious yet his gray eyes dance. "Without Antonio Salazar, how do I find eight thousand sheep in these foothills! How can I shear and dip them all!"

*Segundo turns to me. "Tonio will stake out his **madrina** on the west side. You will find good grass on the east side, just beyond the poplars over there. Leave your panniers and rigging right here near the fire if you wish."*

I glance up to find him watching me across my horse's withers as I tug at a jammed buckle and his eyes are still playful, but also intense. It is the way that Guillermo sized us up without one question when we appeared on his doorstep. I feel awkward, transparent.

*He moves over to the far side of the little dun, making a soothing, whistling sound. Deftly undoing the straps that hold the bedroll atop the panniers, he works without looking. Then his mouth puckers and his eyes smile and we each lift off one side of the panniers at exactly the same time and put them down on the grass, side by side. He loosens the rawhide **latigo** for the back cinch, leaving the front one for me and when I lift off the packsaddle, he takes the fleece pad with one hand, runs the other down Maracas' back, from the withers all the way to the tail. He turns and puts the fleece near enough to the fire to dry off the horse sweat and then busies himself with the roast once more.*

We lead our horses to the east side of the water hole, just beyond the trees and take the saddles off. The three geldings we let go; they'll stay with the mare. I find a rock and pound in the stake that anchors her fifty-foot rope. This done, we stand for a moment, arms around

*each other's waists, watching the horses roll in the grass, lunge back
to their feet and shake themselves. Then we return to the fire and sit
down on the sheepskins laid out for us. Elly holds her hands out toward the flames, rubbing her palms together, watching Tonio pack*
hierba máte *into a silver gourd. The blackened teapot gurgles to a boil
and whistles. Segundo hooks it off the coals with his stick and sets it
next to Tonio, who fills the gourd with boiling water, puts a silver straw
into the brew and passes it to Elly.*

*"***Señora***, this* **amargo** *will warm you."*

*Elly cups both hands around the gourd for a moment, absorbing
the heat, then takes a long sip. Her face looks serene; she is at home
here, she has learned to enjoy even the bitter taste of this* **hierba máte**.
*I watch her windburnt features, the fire highlighting that long-ago scar
on her left cheek, the very blondness of her long hair, gathered into a
ponytail against the ravages of the wind. How tough she looks! And
how much like a kid: that grin of hers as she returns the gourd to Tonio!*

*Next, it's my turn to sip from the silver straw. The bitter warmth of
the* **máte** *spreads a sensation of intense wellbeing, takes the edge off
the hunger. I return the gourd to Tonio, who refills it with boiling water
for Segundo. After Tonio's turn, the* **máte** *passes between us all for a
second round. No words are spoken; none are needed. You share the
relief after the many hours in the wind and the vastness of the plains,
the anticipation of digging into the roast. That is enough.*

Segundo pulls his sleek, silver-handled **facon** *out of the ornate scab-
bard he wears on his back, tucked under the wide cummerbund. With
swift strokes, he cuts several ribs off the spitted lamb, gives them to
Elly. I pour some boiling water on the blade of my old knife - the same
one I used for trimming India's hooves yesterday - and cut some for
myself.*

*We gnaw eagerly on crisp tender meat, tossing the bones into the
shadows where the dogs wait. Tonio fetches a wineskin from his* **recado**,
*passes it around. We eat until we can eat no more. We drink until the
wineskin is empty.*

*The soft yellow twilight is fading ever so slowly into deepening
shadows. The far off peaks of the Andes are still fringed with a golden
halo, though my watch tells me it is almost eleven. Only the brighter*

stars prick the pale sky. To the west is a constellation I now recognise.
"Las Bolas Perdidas." *I ask Tonio. He nods.*

"Yes, that's the one."

Even with a name, it has no past for me. There is only this present that I am building. Watching the horseman next to me roll himself a cigarette gives me the same feeling as rowing around the end of Beale's Wharf with the smell of low tide and lobster bait and tarred wood. My bare feet are small in huge boots that are rolled down, like the herring fishermen's when they skull out to their boats standing up. Grandpa Clark is facing me on the stern seat of the dinghy, his hands next to mine on the heavy oars, pulling with me evenly, feathering on the back-stroke so that the flat tips just kiss the surface. My short arms stretch out toward him and my face comes close to his before we dig the oars back into the green water. Those gnarled working hands push toward my chest, hands unlike any others I've known, and I'm glad they're his hands and that they are teaching mine.

Elly's laughter reverberates into the night. She has spilled most of the tobacco in her lap, trying to roll herself a cigarette. She makes a paper ball and throws it into the fire.

"Looks like I'll have to give up smoking!" She says.

"That tobacco of mine," Tonio says. "Gets all shaky at a woman's touch."

Segundo nudges me with his elbow. He holds a tightly rolled cigarette in his outstretched hand. The edge of the paper is left unlicked.

"For your **señora**, *" he says.*

I nod, acknowledging his care not to offend.

"Well, look at that! A runaway star!"

There is excitement in Tonio's voice. Our eyes follow his pointing finger to a speck of light that is sliding rapidly across the heavens.

"That's no star!" Says Segundo.

"What then, boss?"

"Sa'.....te'.......li.....te. One of those contraptions they throw up there to show up on God's Creation." Wonder and scorn mix in his voice.

"Without shame!" Tonio exclaims. "Sailed right through **Las Tres Marias**.*"*

Tonio keeps blowing smoke rings at the sky as we lie on our backs watching its trajectory east. A weary smile comes over Segundo's face. He cracks his knuckles and sits up.

"They're all done dividing things up down here. So now they're unrolling the wire up there." His large hands weave in the air, a sort of cat's cradle. Tonio is digging in the red-hot coals with a long stick. I sit up erect, on edge suddenly. I listen for the gentle gurgling of the teapot, the sound of the horse bell; wanting to hang onto the way it was just moments before.

But it's too late; I am no longer far away behind a bush at the bottom of the world. I am right back underneath the shadow of a giant mushroom cloud; a member of TOCSIN, handing out pamphlets outside the movie theater in Boston after they showed On The Beach, knowing it is futile. We're a whole generation doomed to live our lives in the face of certain annihilation.

"And what if?" Tonio whispers with a mocking scowl. "What if they hurl down one of those atomic bombs next time around?"

*Segundo's eyes flash. "Let them! Go ahead. Blow a billion **dólares** on four saddlebums behind bush! Be like trying to catch a fly with **bolas**!" He whirls imaginary **bolas** over his head.*

"Like throwing balls at a horsefly, boss!" Tonio blurts through another burst of laughter.

"Let's face it, guys," Elly giggles. "We're not worth a billion dollars."

We roll in the grass and laugh until our stomachs ache. The wineskin passes around until it is empty once more. We smoke a last cigarette. Then Tonio goes off to check on his horses. Segundo lays out his bedroll by the fire. I scoop up our bedroll and follow Elly toward the sound of India's bell amongst the poplar trees.

In the early light of day, a whistle, the jingle of spurs cause the horses to drift out of the misty poplar grove in twos and trees and the low rumbling of hooves gathers in the earth all around you. Without a cue, your horse too moves forwards, ears erect, anticipating.

I spot Segundo's bell mare breaking away into the lead at a fast trot, pulling the others behind her: twenty, thirty of them. The whole mass is picking up momentum, pulling you along, up and forward, as powerful haunches pound and churn up the steep slope toward the cleft in the canyon wall. Segundo's dapple grey is loping in place on the right flank of the trotting herd, held in check by a single finger on the rein, like a stone in a slingshot waiting to be released. On the other flank, Tonio's paint gelding is doing the same dance: jigging sideways, head poised, listening. Amazing! Under me Pampero's stout legs are prancing.

"What's gotten into you?" I give him a pat on the neck.

Segundo's yodeling yell cracks the din:

"YEGUA! YEGUA!"

The stampeding herd hurtles upwards, a flying wedge against the blank sky. The rim of the basin splits in two and we're over the top suddenly, horses exploding out across the flat, bucking and zigzagging in all directions. I'm fighting back the reflex to tighten up - just let him go! Hang on, roll with it! That's it; let's run with the force of this smoking typhoon! For the hell of it, the joy of it. For whatever is up ahead in those mountains.

"Yes, Pampero, smell the snow water and wild grasses on the breeze!"

*I'm talking out loud, giving him all the rein he needs and with an eager reach of his neck, he lengthens stride, eats up the open **pampa** with these freewheeling mustangs. The homing instinct is loosening its grip on him at last! This is the way I wanted it to be. This is the image I've carried with me for so long. All the way from Cabo Machichaco, even further back than that. From way back: Elly and I galloping across school playgrounds on different continents, our manes and tails flying. We were tireless, untamable and no one could catch us!*

The herd is slowing to a trot, coming back together. The mare's copper bell clangs back and forth, on and on, coaxing minutes into hours of constant rump-bobbing motion. I pass one hand lightly over Pampero's roached mane, my eyes resting on Segundo up ahead as he rocks along with sinewy ease, a cigarette forgotten between his lips, his gaze resting quietly on the spires of ice and rock rising up ahead of us. His expression has not changed for a long time. I intuit that his direction never varies, that his journey is one, while in my head thoughts bounce around like grasshoppers.

A shrill whistle cuts the air. The bell mare immediately swings a few degrees to the west. In the distance ahead, flashes of silver: tin roofs under the noon sun.

Too soon, too soon, you're thinking, because now you want to go on and on, until thoughts become instincts; want to share more fires with Segundo, more good lies. But when the herd veers towards the holding pens of La Tercera, moored to a stand of poplars that lean in the direction of the predominant wind, we don't follow. Segundo reins in alongside us, slowing the grey to a walk. He points his riding crop towards a white sawtooth that rises straight out of the plains, etched in chalk against the blue sky. "Mount FitzRoy," he says, "You will find a **puesto** *this side of the river crossing."*

He brushes up the corners of his mustache with the back of one hand, picks up the reins. "May Lady Luck guide you to your destination."

"She already has," Elly says.

He smiles broadly, gives a salute with his **rebenque** *to the brim of his hat then gallops after the herd led by the black mare.*

No smoke curls from the crooked stovepipe of the little grey **puesto** *in the meadow above the fording place of Rio de las Vueltas. No dogs yap from under the stoop. But there is kindling by the chopping block, water in the bucket by the steps. A quartered lamb hangs in a tree.*

The reins go slack in my hands. Pampero takes this as a cue to drop his head and begin to graze. Elly rides on with the packhorse, dismounts and ties up to the hitching rail.

I remain another moment, with no desire to move. Not even the short distance to the day's end. There is something here that I don't want to let slip away. This little box of a shack so far away from anywhere throws me back to the long forgotten Secret Fort that Clipper and Mike and I built when we were ten. We'd crawl inside and sit in the semi-darkness. Very excited and very serious, with the real world far away. We'd take a pledge to never tell anyone. Except for those few Braves who passed the test. We'd cross our wooden swords:

Death Before Surrender!

Our voices would shake just a little, for we knew they would come. We would have to fight to keep our fort.

*This **puesto** is the home to whoever works for **estancia** La Tercera. It is also the rightful home to **pasajeros** such as ourselves in need of temporary shelter and food on the way.*

*Real men fought, real men died, so that we would share this right with all who travel the Patagonian plains on horseback. We had seen the big earth mound behind the shearing shed at **estancia** La Anita, where the men lay buried.*

The present-day foreman at La Anita told us the story.

"The company brought in workers for the shearing," he said, "and for the dipping. And when the season's work was done, they kicked them out. It was hard times. There were men roaming hungry all over the plains of Santa Cruz.

*"They gathered at La Anita, one of the many big **estancias** owned by Menendez-Beathy and the Patagonia Sheep Company.*

"You cannot turn a man out, like a horse, to fend for himself on the frozen plains with no food and no water when you're done working him, they said. A man must have the right to food and shelter, they said.

"The Patagonia Sheep Company complained to the government up in Buenos Aries. A Bolshevik Revolution is brewing down in the Patagonia, they warned.

"The year was 1921. The Government in Buenos Aires dispatched a Colonel Varela with a company of men and orders to solve the Bolshevik problem. They gave him a free hand to act as he saw fit."

Tears clouded the eyes of the old foreman when he told us:

"The Colonel had the men go into the big shearing shed. For a meeting, he told them. He had them all shot dead in there. There were about a thousand men gathered."

They did not surrender. They just died. Trapped and slaughtered, like so many sheep. They were men like Segundo and Tonio.

The sound of a thousand bullets would reverberate across the plains and give rise to a new Law for this land; no longer each man just for himself. The Law of The Land in the Patagonia dictates that each estancia must provide food and shelter to whoever so asks for it: for himself, his **tropilla** of no more than twelve horses and up to six dogs. Any **pasajero** has the right to remain for twenty-four hours. After that he must work for room and board.

Están en su casa. I ponder the literalness of the Spanish invitation to be and to do as in your own house as I tilt my chair back against the wall, inhaling the aroma of the roast lamb we have cooking in the wood stove, the scent of the lemon tea still in the air.

Elly is writing in her diary, sitting by a table covered with a flowered oilcloth that is worn threadbare at the corners. Pages from English newspapers and magazines - some more than twenty years old - cover the wall above. A calendar with the tenth of November circled in pencil is hung from a nail.   Perhaps the shepherd's last visit to the **estancia** to pick up supplies?

These are the necessities of living pared down to a minimum: an enameled dishpan on a rough-hewn shelf under the window on the north wall, a row of chipped enamel cups hanging from nails and jars of flour, rice, sugar, tea and salt in the cupboard made of an old wooden crate nailed to the wall.

A transistor radio sits on a barrel in the corner and next to me a rawhide lariat, half-finished, hangs from a wooden peg driven into the wall. The tools belonging to the **puestero** lie on an upturned box. I pick them up, one at a time, roll each in my palm, holding it long enough to warm it, to feel the grip of the man who sits in this same chair whittling wooden handles for his awls and knives by the wavering light off a strip of rag stuck into a tin can of mutton fat. I feel the patience of those work-warped fingers that pick up the thongs, pause to moisten the rawhide with saliva, to sharpen a tool, then pull one strand over another with deliberate slowness, twisting, tucking, tightening; marking the passing of the lonely hours, weaving one long evening into the next.

Before turning in, I flick on the radio. There is some static, then nothing. I turn it off again without making an effort to find a station; there is no need for me to hear the latest news. Right now, it is more important that I listen for the mare's bell to know that the horses re-

*main nearby the **puesto**; that I hear the teapot gurgling on the stove, to know that the fire is going.*

The bunks in the tiny cubicle off the main room are padded with uncured sheepskins. You can feel the hard edges where the drying hide curled inwards from the sun. But as I nestle down in the middle, fitting my body into the dip made by those who have slept here before me, I am soon comfortable. I close my windburnt eyes and drift off to sleep.

In my sleep, we ride across an endless plain. All along the way people are waiting for us. Their skins are of every color, their dress of every imaginable design, yet they speak a common language. They all wave at us. Some want to go with us. Others ask us to stay with them, or pray for our safe return.

But to where? This world here? To the worlds we left behind?

It doesn't seem to matter.

Then the shepherd passes the leather thongs of his lariat into my hands. I begin to braid where he left off. The thongs are the colors of the people's faces and as I weave them together: the yellow, the red, the black and the white they become one - the living golden brown of the hybrid man.

This image is so vivid when I wake up in the morning that I am surprised to find the half finished lariat hanging from its peg exactly as it had the night before. I pull my boots on and step outside. The horses lie in a semicircle above the riverbank, noses touching the ground.

I whistle. They lift their heads. Once, very clearly, the bell tolls.

I realize I woke up because India's bell had been silent for some time and I knew I had to check to make sure they hadn't strayed. Maybe they are going to stick with us now. I feel very happy that I came outside when I did: the light is just sweeping into the glade and it catches the frost-tipped grass in such a way that a wave of tiny rainbows rolls past. It lasts only seconds. Then the river metamorphoses from a gray avenue of shadows into molten gold at the alchemist touch of the rising sun. In the eddy by the bank, a flash of silver, as a single trout breaks the surface. The dactylic code of an invisible woodpecker in the iron oaks punctuates the stillness.

*By the time we finish the morning chores, put the **puesto** back to how it was when we arrived and get down to the fording place, the sun* *has taken the cool edge off the mountain air. Up close, the river is clear blue ice. Only when a leaf races past do you see that the current is moving very fast. The horses drop their heads to sniff the surface, but they've watered themselves during the night and aren't thirsty. I urge Pampero forward, just one step. The water boils up around his fetlocks and you can feel the spinal quiver of the strong current right through the horse. He snorts and paws the water, splashing cold drops on my face. I scratch the side of his stout neck.*

"Something new, eh boy?"

Elly glances over at me. "It is big," she says.

"Must be melting in the glaciers, like Segundo said."

I try to ignore the note of apprehension in her voice, but I am feeling it too. Crossing the Gallegos River with the water lapping the bottom of our stirrups was a piece of cake compared to this. Two sandbars divide the Rio de las Vueltas into three arms. Altogether sixty yards wide. Or more. The first arm is the widest and looks to be the deepest.

"Well," Elly says with forced cheerfulness. "People ride across it all the time."

"Tonio said we'd get a good Christian dunking," I say.

"Not funny!" Elly says without cheerfulness.

There doesn't seem to be anything more to say. From downstream comes a rumbling so low that you can hardly make it out at first. Where the riverbed narrows into a canyon there is white mist rising.

Rapids!

"Better tie Chaco to the pack horse," I say.

"Good idea," she says.

Her eyes are riveted on the white water downstream. She is listening intently. Looks very serious now. But says nothing further. I dismount to get a piece of rope from the pack and tie one end to the D-ring in Chaco's collar, the other to the bedroll strap atop the panniers.

The horses push and bounce forward in slow motion through the icy flow. Halfway across the first arm, when the river bottom gives way, their powerful legs churn as they start to swim, instinctively angling upstream, keeping their chests against the current. You can feel, too, the down-dragging swirl of the undertow and realize suddenly that alone, without a horse to hang onto, you could not stay afloat in this maelstrom.

We sink or we swim together.

This thought makes me feel very close to Pampero.

And vulnerable.

And scared.

Caicique is a stronger swimmer than the others. He and Elly are far ahead, almost to the first sandbar when she looks back. She starts to wave frantically.

"He's gone under! Cut the rope Nate!"

I turn. No Chaco! The rope I tied him with disappears in the water underneath India's belly. He must be caught inbetween her legs. I grab my knife from its sheath, lean out as far as I can towards the pack horse and manage to grab hold of the rope. I start sawing at it with all my strength. The knife is too dull and I don't seem to be making any headway at all into the hard nylon cord. I keep on working furiously, not thinking, feeling him tugging on the rope under water. Then it snaps. He is free!

My eyes rake across the glassy face of the river. Twenty yards downstream, a yellow ball bobs to the surface. His black nose is pointing upwards and he's paddling very hard. But he is no match for this current. He grows smaller and smaller while everything inside me is clawing out to reach him. This whirling undertow pulls my guts down, turning me inside out as the yellow speck disappears into the shroud of mist. Above the rumble of the rapids there is a shrill puppy howl that swells to thunder inside my head. This was Nikos all over again, on that futile drive to Bilbao, careening along the narrow roads as she held Nikos' head in her lap, feeling the convulsions of a life not wanting to let go, even with half of his head blown off. Right on top of the hill before Bilbao, Nikos' heart stopped. Then we just sat by the side of the road, Elly and I, cradling our dead dog, not knowing how or where we would go from there.

What have I done!

I cut him loose! I gave him to the river!

"Chaco! Chaco!" The anguish in her voice sears right through me like a hot flame and throws me from this nightmare into the other:

Elly crying uncontrollably after Nikos was shot and Aranza hugging her, consoling her, promising to send us a pup from the new litter. "The strongest. The biggest little joker! Maybe even with the same soul as your Nikos, you'll see. By the time you get to Buenos Aires, he'll be three months old."

Pampero lunges out of the water and onto the sandbar. It is hard to look at Elly because everything is coming apart inside of me. What will I tell her now? That I should have carried Chaco in my lap! I should have pulled him up. Should have jumped into the river to untangle his rope!

Nikos died twice and this time there is no Aranza.

Caicique plows chest deep into the waters of the second arm and moves steadily across, the other horses following. Without a pause, he continues across the small third river arm, trotting out of the shallows, Elly hanging on, a mere passenger. His attention is downstream, his ears pricked to a high-pitched howl that grows miraculously louder and closer from out of the dwarf trees where the river turns.

Around the bend, a yellow mongrel bounces into view yapping like crazy, coming straight for us. Up close, he darts off into some wild zigzags and dashes around us in a circle. He jumps up to kiss the horses on the muzzle and they lower their heads for him. Pampero nudges Chaco right off his feet, but the pup comes back for more. We get down on our knees in the sand and he's all over us, but when Elly tries to hug him tight, he wiggles free. Then he dashes off around the horses again, carving out more space for his feelings.

Maracas picks up the mood and starts chasing Chaco around us. When he skids to a sudden halt and whirls around in the opposite direction, the pup pounces on us, then takes off again after the horse. They head down the riverbank, spin around and come racing back again, the horse bucking sideways as he runs, the dog bounding and pouncing and twisting and yapping.

When they tire of the game, we build a fire to dry our clothes. We put some water on for tea. We don't talk about the river and what happened; we just sit there feeling the warmth of the fire and listening to the water in the tin can boil on the coals, bubbling so cheerfully, reassuringly.

When our clothes are dry, we ride on up the bank of the River of Many Turns. The root-snarled path takes us through shrub oaks, skirting the logjammed eddies of the river, then a bottleneck canyon spills us into a basin. Meadows of waving grass capped with orange and red, roll away up the valley. The hush folds around us - truly, this is a sanctuary that makes you think of staying around for awhile, you fantasize of homesteading even and the last thing in the world that you expect to see is a billboard, orange letters on white, grinning at you like a Cheshire Cat.

MILITARY ZONE
RESTRICTED

DEATH MESA

We will always wonder what it might have been like, riding up the valley past the military and on to Laguna del Desierto, over the pass at McLean's to Lago San Martin, the way the *gauchos* at la Tercera told us to go.

No one noticed us arriving at the military encampment of La Florida. We rode right up between the rows of tents and sixty pair of eyes looked up from tin plates in great surprise when we appeared in the doorway of the large mess tent. We could have just as easily continued on by and, chances are, they would not even have noticed our hooftracks in the dust.

Strange that no one had thought to tell us about this impressive military presence in the remote Andean valley, replete with one small aircraft, tanks, personnel carriers and a corral full of mules. We had envisioned spending this evening by a campfire, listening to the parrots in the *ñire* trees and maybe to the wail of guanacos. Instead we wound up on straight-back kitchen chairs in the field office of Destacamento La Florida, listening to the irregular clicks on an old Underwood as the corporal typed up a lengthy report, using only two fingers:

    Our full names,
    nationalities,
    names of fathers, maiden names of mothers,
    passport entries,
    detailed itinerary,
    ages and brands of horses,
    serial numbers of all camera equipment,
    typewriter and reasons for carrying such,
    description of diaries,
    contents of first aid kit,
    and so on and so on...

The whole of the report was relayed via radio to army headquarters in Rio Gallegos that same evening after 2200 hours.

When we pressed the corporal for an explanation, a justification for their keeping us overnight at La Florida, not detained exactly but not free to leave either, he allowed that there had been "an incident".

In a drunken brawl over a woman, one man shot another man and because the one was Argentine and the other Chilean this bar-room brawl became a pretext for fanning smoldering border issues into a wildfire. The exact location of the border between the two sister republics had never been legally agreed upon. One side considered the highest peaks to be the legitimate reference points and the line drawn between them to be the true border. The other nation claimed the flow of the rivers as the determining factor. If the river flowed westward, its origin was considered to be Chilean territory; if it flowed east its point of origin was Argentine.

The trail we wanted to take - the only trail north through this region - passed from Argentine into Chilean territory for a few kilometers and back into Argentina again, following the lay of the land. There were a few *estancias* up in there. That's all.

The response to our request for free passage from the High Command in Rio Gallegos was prompt and brief:

"Send them back where they came from!"

The corporal returned our passports with the added explanation that Laguna del Desierto was not an authorized border crossing.

And that was that.

Going back east instead of heading on north felt like we were in retreat. When it feels like that you tend to lose track of the fact that, whichever direction you go, there are all the other options that you didn't explore. You tend to focus on the one that got away. Silly really, since that one became the direction only because you made up a plan for yourself, shaped by a mixture of chance and circumstance. Now this plan of yours has been foiled by another mixture of chance and circumstance.

Could've, would've, should've can torment you much if you let them. And let them we did, when the Argentine High Command in Rio Gallegos sent us out of the beautiful mountains and back onto the barren *mesetas* and the plains.

We could not know then that in retreating, we were also advancing towards some of the most amazing places of our entire journey up the Americas. Looking back, we would think about how Columbus was searching for a better way east by going west. In looking for India, he found a whole new world.

The alternate trail to Lago San Martin goes over the Cangrejos Pass and it is a warm sunny morning almost a week later when we start to climb towards it. We meet a *gaucho* on his way down to *estancia* La Margarita. He tells us he brought a *tropilla* of horses across the Cangrejos the day before and just to follow his tracks.

This works fine until the wind off the *cordillera* turns cold and wet in the afternoon and brings in snow. It is the kind of snow you'll have in late November in Sweden, or in Canada, the kind of snow that envelopes you in a white hush so that you might lose your way going home from the mailbox up a familiar road.

We are in unfamiliar territory, following horse tracks and the occasional bits of manure and when the snow covers these, we have nothing at all to guide us through the maze of shallow gullies and treacherous volcanic bogs of a little used Andean pass. Without Caicique, the rest of us would have huddled to a stop and turned tails to the wind in the hopes that the snow would let up so that we might figure out where we should be going.

Caicique just keeps on walking right into the face of the storm with me aboard and the rest of our troupe trudging along behind. Every now and then, he drops his head to sniff the ground, occasionally letting out another one of those chest-rattling coughs he started having a couple of days ago. They are getting worse. He is going on raw willpower; it's the same kind of power you see in the eye of a show jumping champion when he attacks a difficult course, one fence at a time. The difference is that Caicique is doing this without the help of a rider. I am just sitting there, cold and miserable and lost. With a rider like that, the best show jumper in the world would have stopped out after the third or fourth fence. Caicique keeps on going, pulling us all along.

Eventually we reach a plateau of some sort. The mist is too thick to determine if we've reached the top of the pass. Caicique seems no longer sure and he stops. The horses bunch together, tails to the wind. We dismount to stretch our legs and to try and figure out where to go next. The black sand is steaming as patches of snow are evaporating. The mist is very heavy, making our world seem very small, yet at the same time boundless

"It feels like being becalmed at sea," Nathan says. "I remember sitting in the fog like this for hours in Silverwing. There'd be nothing to focus on."

"Right."

With the horses remaining completely still in the center, we explore the microcosm of a ten-yard circle around them. Next to Pampero's left hind, I discover a dark green stone. It is flat with irregular square edges - petrified wood! I keep it and pick up a flat yellowish stone lying in front of India and as I turn it in my hand, I see that it is loaded with tiny seashells. Seashells on a mountain top - this is an amazing!

We continue moving slowly around the periphery, like the hands of an invisible clock, picking up objects at random that measure time in a way that the mind can't entirely grasp. One minute of this clock would equal a million years, maybe ten million. We are talking about a prehistoric forest of enormous trees dropped to the bottom of the ocean, then thrown back to six thousand feet above sea level by volcanic cataclysms, the proportions of which totally boggle the mind.

A shudder goes through every cell of your body, like when you touch a light switch with wet hands and the current zaps right through you and in that split second, everything is clear: your whole life, the life of mankind flash by in an instant, shorter than a butterfly's. All time co-exists in this one moment and matter, in its changing form, flows by you, creating an illusion of temporality, of flux and duration.

We sit down on a couple of boulders and listen to the wind and look

at a slab of sandstone we found in which there were perfect impressions of plants and small insects.

Then, all at once, the mist parts, revealing far below us Lake San Martin as a giant starfish wedging turquoise arms in between green-shouldered hills.

The image fades to black and white in the trailing mist.

Blooms again into full jeweled extravagance.

Back and forth, from gray to living color, the veil of creation is being lifted before our eyes and slowly the world below us expands: ice-capped peaks to the northwest, two black mesetas dead ahead and out to the east, the plains sprawling to merge with the gray sky. Shafts of sunlight streak through gaps in the clouds, bathing the hills and the lake with moving spotlights, dozens of them race across the landscape in shifting formations. One touches a tin roof in the tundra basin straight down below us.

The descent from the Cangrejos is very steep.

Our horses have learned a lot about how to negotiate downhill trails since that first one into Puerto Natales a month ago. They are rocking back on their haunches in the black sand, taking us safely down between jagged limestone spires into the tundra basin. The tin we saw reflected from atop the pass turns out to be the A-framed roof of a small lean-to, the simplest of shelters, the kind that a child might build for a fort.

The grass is good so we decide to stop and make camp. There are dry chunks of sage and *calafate* scattered about and even an old wood camp stove that Nathan picks up and brings into the A-frame. Soon we have a fire going, our sheepskins laid out to sit on and the saddles for backrests. Water is boiling in the tin can. We drink tea and watch the horses roll in the grass and I think how wonderful it is to live like this, needing so little to make a home.

I fashion a blanket out of our tarp for Caicique, to keep the rain off his back. His cough is definitely getting worse.

It rains on and off all night, but in the morning the skies clear. We are in no hurry to leave. I am happy to stay around the camp, to mend some gear, read a bit maybe and just watch the horses graze. It is a good place for Caicique to get some rest. Nathan takes the binoculars and the camera and heads back up the trail toward the tallest of the limestone spires we passed on the way down.

He wants to try and scale it.

Nathan actually likes heights. He remembers a fig tree in the backyard of the house where they lived in Stockton, California, the way I remember the grey dray horse at Stora Torget. The fig tree was the beginning of his climbing career that would include such conquests as the roof of the three-story parsonage in St. Paul, at age seven, where he'd play Indians with the few friends who dared put on a loincloth and war paint and join him. Later, at age ten, he crossed the bridge across the Mississippi –by walking the four-inch iron girders beneath it! His favorite part of building our house in Spain was stringing the second story rafters; he'd walk across the grid and tell me what a great panoramic view of the Bay of Biscay we had from up there. Walking the rafters is how he caught the eye of the gypsies, who stopped to make camp for the night by the pond across the road from us.

"Hey, Hercules, want to join our circus!" Taunted the youth we would come to know as Jobo.

"I have to finish the roof on our house," Nathan answered.

"How so? You want to live in a box?"

"A house needs a roof," Nathan said.

"So you want to put a lid on the box!"

When the Ivanovich family broke camp the next morning, we went with them along the Basque coast of Spain, because they had spoken more truth than we. I am remembering now, warm in the sun like this, where we stayed over for a day and Malika did my nails bright red and I did hers and afterwards we lay in the sun on our backs, watching the clouds go by.

High above the limestone spire, a condor hovers, motionless against a blue sky. Then there are two of them, then three. Then I don't see them anymore and I wonder how Nathan is doing and I try not to worry about him.

For an indeterminable time I sit on the edge of a precipice at the foot of the orange and pink monoliths that shoot straight up two or three hundred feet. Sculptured by gales and ocean waves of immeasurable force to a diameter of only twenty feet at the base, they taper upwards to a spiked fist, a wordless challenge.

The urge to climb is irresistible.

I get up and start doing some stretches to warm up before I begin. The ascent is surprisingly easy, because the wind and the rain have carved shelves into the soft stone and all I have to do is follow the upward spiral.

I am half-way up to the top when I become aware of a moving shadow and the humming of enormous wings. I tilt my head back to look: there are two of them, a male and a female condor and their bodies are enormous! I remember reading that between several of them, they can knock a man off his horse and kill him on the ground and that they can lift a sheep or a young guanaco into the air.

I am feeling very exposed and vulnerable as my fingertips slide over fossil shell Braille, in search of another crevice. I find a shallow groove in the ledge above and knock off my boots, so that my bare feet can grasp the message my fingers decipher.

I look up once again and this time I catch a glimpse of the red in the eye of the condor. My balance quavers. Still, I keep on watching him, spellbound, as he keeps circling, coming closer to me each time. Suddenly I can feel myself losing hold and press in tight against the rock, closing my eyes and telling myself to breathe in - breathe out - breathe in – breathe out.

The cunning buzzard was hypnotizing me! Almost got me!

The air from giant wings buffets against my shoulders as he comes back again; he's playing for keeps! If he can make me lose my fragile hold, I'll fall to my death and become carrion to nourish his young in the nest atop one of the spires.

Back off, you bloody fool! I command myself.

You want to reclaim the supreme confidence you had at age ten standing on a four-inch girder, two hundred feet above the Mississippi? Look guys, no hands!

Back off! That can never be!

Without looking again at the condor, slowly, stiffly my hands and feet find their way back down to the ledge and I take several long deep breaths until the dizziness is gone and I dare lift my eyes again and glance at him as he is rising straight on the up-draft, without once cocking his head to look down.

He no longer cares where I go.

At the base of the spire I lie for a very long time on my back and above me - a thousand feet above me - pinned to the sky like an iron cross vaporized, the condor hovers.

*When I get back to camp, mud up to my knees and wet hair tied up
with my handkerchief, Indian style, I feel like a ten-year-old kid home
from some Saturday afternoon adventure.*

*Elly has the fire going and a pot of curried rice ready to eat. She
has met a shepherd who lives in a tent about a league down the valley
and he has invited us to stop by. We saddle up in the late afternoon and
go down to have supper with him.*

*His camp is something to see, carved right out of a grove of **calafate**
bushes and bordered by a low wall of stones brought up from the riverbed with a roof made of wire and old gunny sacks. Around the fire, he
has large rocks covered with sheepskins to sit on.*

He makes a tasty stew and fresh tortas for supper.

There was frost on the ground in the morning. Caicique was getting worse.
He had developed a deep, rattling cough and yellow mucus was streaming
from his nostrils. We had to find somewhere to stop where we could take care
of him.

We continued down toward Lago San Martin to *estancia* La Angelita. The
grass was good, but there was no shelter from the weather, which was turning
bitterly cold. The rain whipped like ice. We went on to nearby La Federica,
where there was a barn for Caicique, but nothing to feed him in it.

We dragged on for two days until we found La Laurita where they had both
a barn and plenty of feed. The old Asturian horseman checked Caicique over
and treated his lungs with eucalyptus smoke to clear out the phlegm. He showed
us into the master bedroom and we slept like kings, knowing our horses were
being well taken care of, something that did not happen all that often in the
Patagonia. After a few days, Caicique seemed to be much better and we moved
on towards the next pass, across Meseta del Carbon.

According to our map, which was printed in 1945 and based on source
material that included a Chilean military survey of 1907, Route # 40 across
Meseta del Carbon to Tucu-Tucu was under construction.

A quarter of a century later, no road existed.

Maybe construction had been scrapped because funds were diverted to more
essential projects than a road connecting isolated ranches in this sparsely popu-
lated region. If construction had been planned, we reasoned, a feasible route

would have been marked.

This assumption placed us far up the Fossil River. We had climbed for hours across rocks and boulders and the further up the river valley we came, the more impenetrable appeared the dark wall of the Meseta del Carbon far above us. All evidence pointed to the impossibility of a road ever being built up this steep valley crisscrossed by deep gullies and increasingly large patches of volcanic bog. We found orange stakes left by what we assumed were road surveyors and we found some rusty tin cans. That was all.

Still, we continued on.

The *meseta* loomed dark and menacing, impenetrable like a fairy tale fortress, shrouded in mist and black clouds, the kind inhabited by evil witches in a reign of darkness. We didn't have a fairy godmother with a magic wand to help us transcend the obstacles thrown in our path by the forces of evil; we were just two people stubbornly, blindly, taking four horses and a half-grown pup on an exhausting ascent into a cul de sac.

We work our way slowly up the rocky slopes, from one orange stake to the next. Caicique's hacking cough chops the silence behind me, but I don't look back. All I can think about now is reaching the next orange stake. There aren't any and, without warning, I'm at the edge of an abrupt chasm, staring down at a streambed of boulders spilled out by the overhanging glacier above. There's got to be a way down and back up - if the surveyors did it, I can do it!

"Guess that takes care of our shortcut through the mountains." The tone of defeat in her voice makes me angry. I try to keep the lid on it.

"We're almost there. I think I see the way across." I point to a narrow shelf angling down.

"Good grief, Nate. Give it up! You're driving us all into the ground. A horse could easily break a leg in that mess of boulders down there!"

I avoid looking at her. "You stay here until I get across with these two. Then bring the other two."

"What's gotten into you? This isn't worth the risk. Let's go back."

Her last words snatch at my shoulder as I urge Pampero down the steep shelf, leading India with the pack. Everything inside of me is hardening, all doubt gone.

I don't see. I don't hear but the one thought: to go further, to last longer - to win. Everyone gives up; everyone quits when they're almost there.

Elly comes on Maracas and way behind her, Caicique begins to follow again. When he reaches the bottom, he stops, looks towards us and lets go with a frantic whinny. He is not used to being left behind like this. The other three horses answer in chorus: they don't like it any better than he. He's the boss horse, belonging up front. There is another shrill whinny and then Caicique comes charging straight across the boulder-jam at a full run, dodging some, hurtling others, iron shoes striking sparks.

Elly lets out a scream as she watches him misjudge a large boulder, toppling sideways as his front legs catch on the rock. She is off Maracas and hurtling back down the bank as her horse goes down, kicking out violently. Then, abruptly, she stops short: the big buckskin has lunged back to his feet. He limps a few steps, favoring the right front, then whinnies once again and plows on across the stream and comes charging up to where the rest of us are.

Elly is pale under her tan; she doesn't say one word while she checks over the ugly gash on his right foreleg, runs her hand over his other legs before she cleans the wound and dresses it. Only then does she speak, holding back her anger.

"Now are you ready to call it quits?"

I hesitate, stalling for time. Hoping she'll cool. "Look, we'll take it real easy. The gap in the **meseta** *wall is just ahead."*

"There is no gap in that goddamned wall!"

"Pull yourself together! Just this one more hurdle."

Elly drops further and further behind as I force Pampero on up the muddy incline. The Fossil River is now no more than a dirty trickle coming out from the base of the gray ice mass that plugs the gap between the stone peak and the **meseta** *wall.*

All of a sudden the lead rope burns through my hand. Behind me, India is wallowing in a patch of volcanic quicksand. Her struggle just sucks her deeper into the black ooze. The canvas panniers stay on the crust, like an oversized and useless life jacket.

This time there is no scream. Elly just gets over there quickly, grabs onto the mare's halter rope, all the while talking softly to her. She doesn't glance over once while I struggle with getting a rope secured to the cinch ring, another tied into her tail; she just keeps on speaking to the mare even as she ties the lead to the ring in the back of her saddle with a slipknot and gets back up on Maracas. I get the rope from her cinch tied to the back of Pampero's saddle and hold onto the one to her tail. Wordlessly, we work side by side, our horses pulling together like a trained team, tightening the ropes and gradually inching forward, without jerking.

Back on solid ground, India remains on her side, shaking and panting, while Elly brings out the first aid kit once more and cleans and disinfects her leg wounds from the sharp volcanic cinders. Then she gives a few gentle tugs on the lead and when the mare finally heaves herself up and stands there trembling, Elly turns to me.

"We're lucky!" She says.

"Let's rest awhile. Then we'll put the pack on Caicique for the last stretch."

"Last stretch!" She erupts, her face dark red. "Are you out of your mind? There is a wall around us a hundred feet high!"

"We took the wrong turn. We can't quit now!" My voice sounds alien, yet familiar in a scary way.

"We've almost gotten two horses killed. Two of our friends! Just who the hell do you think you are?"

"Go on. Cop out on me! I'll do it alone!"

"I've never seen you like this! You're like a bloody soldier with no brain!"

"The map says this is the way."

"The map! Screw the map!"

"The U.S. Air Force flies by these maps!"

"Look at you, so afraid of giving up, you're trembling all over!"

She spins and heads back down, leading Maracas and Pampero. The mare follows slowly, then Pampero falls in behind them. And Chaco.

I remain, frozen with a rage that has no outlet. I swirl around and face the wall and pick up a rock and hurl it upwards. As I do, something high above snags my eye: a condor pinned to the gray-white sky, motionless. Before my staring eyes, he slips his mooring and rises on the updraft until he is nothing more than a tiny puncture in the under-belly of a cloud.

When I read about the Klondike Gold Rush, years later, and the account made a passing reference to the thousands of pack animals that perished along the trail to White Pass, I felt a wave of anger and shame. Shame for all those men who put gold and fortune above the most elementary decency and I wondered how these horses died; did they just lie down after days without feed and call it quits? Did someone put a mercy bullet in their brain to end their suffering?

If a kind and gentle man like Nathan could become so obsessed with a goal, I would not even begin to imagine the obsession of harder, of lesser men, who believed all they had to do was conquer the pass and that beyond lay a land of treasures untold that were theirs for the taking.

On the way back down to the grasslands, we discovered the skeletal remains of five horses - how many more lay hidden deep in the volcanic ooze?

I lay awake for a long time looking at our four horses, standing motionless by our camp. They grazed for maybe an hour after we stopped and then they just stood still in the same place. They had been pushed to their limit. But they would have continued on up the pass, beyond exhaustion, cut by cinders. They would have extricated themselves from one more bog and then one more, until spent. They would have stopped struggling somewhere and just let the bog swallow them up.

Through the ages, this is what horses have done for humans. Human history, I thought, is built on mountains of dead horses and I remembered the story I wrote in grade four about what I would do if I had a million Swedish *kronor*.

With a million, the child would buy a farm with big fields that were forever green. She would buy all the old and the crippled horses and retire them there; because the child had seen, on a tour put on by the school of the local slaughter house, how the two big work horses had to stand there awaiting their turn, their manes and tails shaved off already, smelling the blood and hearing the moans from the steers being killed in the next room.

And one of the children asked why the horses had no tails and the guide told the children they made mattresses out of the horse hair and that's why they took it off in advance; so it wouldn't get soiled by the blood.

This was how the team was rewarded for a lifetime of doing all the field-work in the summer and pulling the logs in the winter and giving sleigh rides on Christmas.

A spinning quill of dust glides along the horizon in a parallel direction, moving at a much faster clip than we and etching a straight line across the vastness that underlines the obvious: all roads in the Patagonia come out of the maze of inner mountain canyons to the supply centers along the Atlantic seaboard.

*Black Mesa looms massive next to us: a two hundred-foot wall that escorts us in the opposite direction we both wish to go. And Black Mesa is just a small part of Death Mesa, which is part of the even larger **Meseta** of the Wind. The particles of black sand that we ride on were once blocks in the **meseta** wall. The walls keep tumbling down but always, right behind, is another wall.*

There is a lesson here, but I'm too distracted and pissed off to be instructed.

There was another way!

I spotted it right on the map. But Elly was too mad to listen. Too mad about what a toll my blind attack on the Carbon Mesa had taken on the horses. She told me to tear up and burn the map. I was far too perturbed - more than humiliated - by my irrational behavior to present my arguments sensibly.

I should have said: let's rest the horses for a week, or whatever it takes to bring them back to condition, then plan our route with the help of the shepherd at Bajo Comisión. He said he might even go with us, over to McLean's, if we'd wait awhile.

Instead I locked horns with her; and now she's on strike. So, for that matter, am I. That's why we are marching east into the desert instead of northwest into the mountains. All because we can't agree on a better way; so one will cancels out the other and we both go where neither wants to go.

When we're stubborn in the same direction, nothing can stop us. When we're stubborn in opposite directions, anything can stop us.

Around us, the land is changing. Gullies are now deep slashes, *difficult to get across or around. Clumps of **calafate** bushes appear like islands, some rise ten or twelve feet above us – that's how much soil has been blown away. Stretching from island to island, the line fence is more like a tangled power line - we can ride right under it. But Elly has trouble keeping Maracas moving. He balks and shies and keeps trying to turn back. Pampero is behaving much in the same way and India, the packhorse today, has to be dragged along. At the elevated line fence, Caicique quits following us and circles back, his head high and nose into the wind.*

Estancia Kach Aike can't be much further and I know Elly is eager to end the day so I tell her to go on ahead with the packhorse and I'll get Caicique and catch up.

But Caicique keeps circling away from Pampero and me. He holds his ground until we're up close, then he blows air out of his nostrils like a stallion scenting danger and gallops off a short distance, drawing us further back the way we came.

Silence greets me as I cross the bridge over a dry *arroyo* and ride on towards the corrals and the shearing shed. I can smell smoke on the wind, but no dogs come running to greet me. Strange, there are always dogs. Every *estancia*, every *puesto* has dogs because, without them, you could not work the sheep.

By the corral, Maracas stops and veers to the side, so suddenly he almost throws me off. He will not take one step further. Maracas is not a very brave horse, not like Caicique, so I get off and walk ahead of him to show him that there is nothing to worry about. But, there is! In a dried pool of blood in the middle of the corral lies the severed head of a steel grey horse. He has a running star right in the center of his forehead. A sign of good fortune amongst the Bedu, I have read somewhere. What a strange thing to be remembering just then!

I lead Maracas and India on past the corrals and get back in the saddle; I don't want to be on foot in this place! Further up the driveway, I pass a shed housing an antique car. It is covered in layers of dust, but otherwise it looks to be in mint condition. Maybe it's a Buick, maybe from the forties. I couldn't tell you, I don't pay attention to cars. As I approach the fence around the two-story main house, I spot a woman, shrunken with age, walking towards a small cottage just outside the fence. There is a wisp of smoke rising from the chimney. I call out *buenas tardes* repeatedly. She keeps on walking. Finally, on the threshold, she turns around.

"Excuse me, *señora*, could you tell us whom we might speak to about a place to stay for the night?"

She stares at me with strange blue eyes.   Her chin is covered by white facial hairs, I notice - a beard almost.   I simplify my request.   "We need *alojamiento* for the night, my husband and I."

She lifts a thin arm and points off to the right. "Go to the worker's quarters," she says. "You will find everything you need there."

I thank her and she disappears inside the small hut. I continue on where she indicated and find a building, about twenty feet by sixty. The end door is wide open. Inside, it looks as if a twister swept through the place, taking out all the furniture, except one broken chair, left lying on its side. Ripped mattresses, old magazines, pieces of clothing, beans, rice, broken liquor bottles and mouse droppings litter the floor.

I turn around, suddenly feeling so tired and hungry and at a loss. I had conjured up a cozy kitchen, painted bright yellow and red and blue, where a cook would offer you tea and, if you were lucky in your timing, freshly baked *tortas*, deep fried in mutton lard. Warm and rolled in a little bit of sugar, *tortas* are the best donuts you ever had. Cold, you take them with you and eat with your meat on the trail and they are good for a week or more.

We had come to take for granted the *estancias*, scattered across the plains, offering reprieve from the long stretches of cold and hunger. But there isn't going to be any *tortas* for us at *estancia* Kach Aike.

Worse than that, there is no grass.

I decide to look in the barn, a short distance from the ravaged worker's quarters. To my surprise, I find some loose hay in there: tall stems of timothy, brome and alfalfa. Judging from the state of the place now, this hay must be very old. It is surprisingly green. I grab a handful and offer it to Maracas and India and they eat it.

A chorus of whinnies announce the arrival of Pampero and Caicique. They had spooked at the horse head, just like Maracas did. Nathan wants to move on. He says the place gives him the creeps. I don't. It is late in the day; we do have hay to give the horses and that is all that really matters to me. Nathan takes our tin can and cooking pot and heads off in search of water and any food the old woman might be able to give us

He returns with a purplish chunk of meat in one hand, a rectangular loaf of bread, hard as a brick, under his arm. The water he has brought in the pot is brown.

"She said it won't kill us," he says.

"And what's *that*?"

"Beef heart," Nathan says.

"Beef... there is no cattle around here."

"That's what she says *he* told her."

Chaco won't touch the heart. He waits for us to make a fire in the cook stove in the kitchen at the back of the worker's quarters and cook up a pot of food. Straight oatmeal tonight, that's all there is left of our emergency supplies. Nathan and I eat just enough of the sticky goo to line our stomachs so that we will be able to go to sleep without hunger pains. Chaco devours the rest of it. Amazing guy! He must dislike oatmeal as much as Nathan and I do, but he will eat that rather than the heart of a horse!

There is a locked door off the kitchen. This seems strange. Curiosity takes us around to the back of the building where we find an empty oil drum to stand on so we can look through the high window. Everything inside the small room is neat and tidy. The single bed is made, the papers on the desk in the far corner are arranged to one side, a pair of glasses lies in the center of the writing pad. A jacket is hung up on the locked door, a pair of shoes parked below it. The very ordinariness of the bachelor pad amidst the chaos and decay that hangs over the rest of the place gives it an eerie quality.

"Must be where he lives, whoever **he** is," Nathan says.

We collect our pot and few utensils and head back to the hay barn for an early night. We want to be up at dawn and put this awful place behind us as soon as possible. A pale moon is coming up behind the broken windmills. The wind has stopped and it is very quiet. Much too quiet.

The horses have left the mound of hay we put out for them next to the barn and are nowhere to be seen. We have gotten used to them staying with us now, wherever we stop for the night. Caicique would know that this old hay is the only feed for miles around. Why would he leave?

A horrible churning panic grabs hold of us. We run through the dry *calafate* bushes, which tower above us, frantically looking for tracks, for piles of manure in the dark. Had someone scared the horses off while we were cooking up the oatmeal, leaving us on foot in the company of a deranged old lady and some guy who kills horses?

Eventually we have to give up the search and find our way back to the hay barn. Nathan barricades the door with the broken pitchfork. We crawl into the bedroll with our clothes on. Chaco snuggles up between us.

Her heavy breathing tells me that Elly is sound asleep. So is Chaco, his head cradled in the hollow of her back. I count their even breaths, trying to lure sleep.

But there are so many other sounds in the night: the crippled arm of the wind mill creaking back and forth, the shrill screech of an owl, followed by the faint whir of its dive, then a thud, a flurry of wings and just one squeak from the victim. The pale moonlight slices through cracks in the wall, casting bars across the loft, like in a prison.

There was subdued panic in the night like this on the chronic ward at the Massachusetts State Mental hospital, with everyone breathing from the darkness all around me and the sound of keys in metal doors throughout the night. The crazed eyes of the old woman has stirred up memories of Ethel D, who has forgotten that it is spring outside these barred windows and that there are wildflowers all along the highway into Boston and that the ocean is not far away with its salt spray and gentle rollers sweeping endless miles of beach so clean it makes you want to run very fast with the wet sand between your toes and the seagulls overhead race with the clouds and with you and the curling waves.

Only Professor Cantor knows.

To the other patients and the wardens I am just another chronic admission, vulnerable, without hope. Of the ten Harvard students admitted for the experiment, only two of us last the month.

When my time is up, I want to yank them all out of those metal chairs and take them with me out of this cage, away from this hopeless stench, to run with me until the sea spray washes away the masks of dread.

Her face is still on the other side of the glass partition and she tries to smile even though she knows she will see me no more.

"There is no place for me out there," says Ethel D. "You live for me."

Another sound in the night, familiar and comforting, brings relief. It's the sound of the horses munching hay outside! I resist the urge to get up and look out and maybe even tie up Caicique, just to make sure. Instead, I curl up around Elly and Chaco; if the horses came back on their own, they'll be there when I wake up and that will be soon enough.

In the morning, with the sun up and no wind, I set out to find the old woman to ask her how we might help her. I walk through the shriveled garden and take a moment to look through a window in the large mansion. All the furniture is covered with white drapes, paintings are turned against the wall, as if someone left on an extended holiday but planning, someday, to be back.

She does not answer the door. There is no smoke from the chimney.

Driven by an inexplicable curiosity, I return to the corrals. The head of the grey horse is still there. I open the door to the shearing shed and, hanging from an iron hook, is the rest of the steel grey, skinned and gutted. His hide is lying in a crumpled pile on the concrete floor, entrails on top. I push back the nausea from the sweet-sour odor and take a quick look around; there are bales of wool, stacks of dried sheepskins covered by thick dust. The sheep droppings scattered across the cement floor are bleached white. Years old! The plug-ins for the electric shears have been torn right out of the walls, so have the light fixtures. There are no tools, no strapping press for making the big bales of wool. No generator.

I hurry back outside, without looking this time at the carcass of the horse and run back past the hut. Elly has the horses saddled up and ready to go. We ride straight east over large dunes that appear to be rolling in the direction we're going, the wind snatching a wisp of sand off each crest, shoving us along at a steady clip.

Thinking we are doing the right thing, we bring the plight of the poor old woman at Kach Aike to the attention of the owners of *estancia* La Bernarda. *Señor* Leyenda stands up abruptly from the table in the bright yellow kitchen of his house and the look on his face makes me wish I could throw out a hook and reel my words back in.

"You think we should help her?" He says.

He invites us to come with him, in the way of a demand and I am apprehensive almost, as we drive with him out into the plains in the Land Rover. He drives fast, straight west, and he says nothing on the way. At the line fence between La Bernarda and Kach Aike, he stops and we all get out of the vehicle. The fence is not stopping the dunes from drifting in from Kach Aike. *Señor* Leyenda bends down and digs around in the sand with his large hands. When he finds what he was looking for, he straightens up and turns to us. He is holding a stem of grass between his fingers. It is dried up and shriveled.

"The *medano* grass was our last hope," he says. "We planted acres of it to hold the soil. Then came the summer winds."

I can feel the sand coming in on the afternoon gale, tiny particles that burn your face and your eyes. I think of Guillermo's mare with the broken leg. I have come to understand that *survival of the fittest* means there is no place for the weak in this land. There is no margin for error.

"Kach Aike was one of the best *estancias* around," says Leyenda, "not so many years ago. Before *she* took over.

She came down to housekeep for the old bachelor of Kach Aike," Leyenda tells us as we drive back home in the Rover.

"She was a floozie he met up in Buenos Aires. Married him practically on his deathbed.

She knew nothing about this land. Or about sheep.

The old foreman left. She hired another. Then another. The one over there now is number five. Each one took off with what they could: sheep, machinery, furniture. Now, as you saw, there is nothing left.

The last foreman is working the lawyers to take over the land for back wages owed.

Maybe, when the land is his, he will look after it. Maybe then things will turn around."

Señor Leyenda sounds so very tired.

"The hay we found in the barn would have been very old, then?" I ask, looking for a neutral thing to say, a way to backtrack from our comments earlier about the poor old woman, half-starved and living in mortal fear.

"Eight years, maybe nine," he says and then we are silent the rest of the way. Back at *estancia* headquarters, *señor* Leyenda stops the Rover and gets out to check on the dipping of recently shorn sheep. Each animal is put through a narrow trough, filled with a poisonous mixture that kills lice and mites. An old *gaucho* uses a forked wooden stick to push each sheep below the surface. He is a colorful looking character. I decide to go and get my cameras. I want to step back, be a photographer and just record what I see. I don't want to wrestle with an answer to the question:

What would I do, if the old widow were my neighbor and this my land?
There are no easy answers.
What *could* I do?

That night we snuggle down in child-sized beds with colorful patch-work quilts; twin beds for a brother and a sister, away now in a board-ing school. The hard wind blowing outside is muffled; the hand em-broidered curtains hold the darkness at bay.

The following night, we are lodged in the simple *puesto* that belongs to La Bernarda, up the *quebrada* at the rim of the Meseta de La Muerte. This is their summer range. The sheep have not yet grazed close to the *puesto* and the grass is good.

The night after that, we are straggling across a sterile moonscape. We have been walking all day, due north, advancing so slowly. There is no trail to follow. No one travels north across the Meseta de la Muerte. No one has any reason to. We pick our way over cinders that are sharp and irregular. The horses stumble often and we have to get off and check their hooves for chunks of lava that get wedged in there. We don't feel right riding them. I don't know if our walking makes it that much easier on them, but it puts us down there on their level, makes us feel less guilty.

We come to a hollow and find shelter in a cave that smells strongly of sheep. The ground is covered with droppings and chunks of wool. Nathan uses the *machete* to sweep a place clean to put the tarp down and we lean the saddles up against the wall of the cave. We put a rope on Caicique but find nothing to tie onto, so Nathan just hangs on to the other end and we sit like that, huddled. Caicique doesn't try to move. He doesn't even lie down, like the other three. He just stands there with his head hanging low.

In the gray of dawn, we continue on. We walk next to the horses, picking our way carefully through the chunks of lava. My feet hurt. They are swollen from too much walking in boots, not meant for walking. The thin leather soles don't protect from the cinders and they pinch in the back of the heels.

Everyone else's feet hurt too.
In different ways, we all hurt.

The rim of the mesa comes up quite suddenly. Below us lies a crater, a turquoise lake at its center, encircled by waves of soft pastel colors. As we gaze down into the basin, an incredible burst of pink, gray and white birds erupt into the air.

Flamingos by the thousands!

The explosion of wings fills the whole of the salt lagoon, a crescendo of drums, the voice of an ancient volcano as tier after tier, they lift out of the basin, whirling straight up, a typhoon of living color.

The top of the spout curves slightly northwards, pulling the whole twister right off the ground, reshaping itself into a flying wedge heading north, from fall into spring into perpetual summer, as far as Mexico and beyond, heeding the primordial command and somewhere deep within me stirs a lost instinct to follow. The screeching grows fainter until the hush is total and we are alone on the edge of the chasm.

Caicique finds the trail off the *meseta*. It is narrow and steep like a goat path, but the horses don't hesitate. When we get down to the bottom, we join in with a wagon trail and we follow tracks made by metal-rimmed wheels and a yoke of oxen.

We haven't had a meal since yesterday morning and when you're hungry like this, your senses start playing tricks on you. The wind up the canyon is bringing me the aroma of pancakes. I am trying to entertain myself, wondering what you'd call a mirage that played on your sense of smell, not your sight: an olfactory mirage, an *olfage*, maybe?

But when Caicique starts trotting, tired and sore as he is and Chaco dashes off ahead of him, I realize that the smell of pancakes is for real. Our noses lead us to a small dwelling built right into the rocks, with a slate roof and a stovepipe coming out the side and where Horacio Español is making pancakes in an iron skillet.

Horacio brings out a whole sack of oats and empties it into a wheelbarrow that he pushes down the slope into the pole corral. The horses crowd around him. He stands back and watches them eat, with a big grin on his face. These oats have come all the way from the coast. He makes the journey for supplies in a hired truck, twice a year, he says. The last stretch up the mesa is by oxcart and takes most of a day to complete.

And he just takes and dumps out a whole bag of this precious feed for the horses of a couple of strangers! I will remember Horacio Espanol as the most generous man I ever met.

He brings us inside his mountain home and feeds us a stack of pancakes. We drink goat milk and listen to Horacio talk and when we're done eating and drinking, he says for us to do the talking. For us to take him away from this place that he has been dealt by Fate and by his father, who left Andalucia to seek his fortune in this New World.

We take Horacio back with us to our Spain, to the Basque Country, where the hills are green and where we arrived one day in February 1965, when the sun was shining and it was so beautiful, driving up along the coast from Bermeo.

At the highest point along the road between the village of Bermeo and the village of Baquio, right where the road turns sharply and you can see far in all directions lies the Atalaya. It is a round tower made of granite rock, built by the Bermeo fishermen. A man named Jesus sits on watch there with binoculars. He keeps radio contact with the fishing boats in the stormy Bay of Biscay and alerts them of schools of fish jumping and of storms moving in.

On the other side of a hill from the Atalaya there is an old quarry. They used rock from here for the breakwater in Bermeo. We see a perfect spot for building a house in the lee of the triangular rock that remains. You have protection from the north and from the east. You can look across green fields, all the way to the coast of France. We decide, on the spur of the moment, that this promontory and no place else is where we will build a house and make it the center of our world.

No matter we had so little money and so little experience in building.

We had plenty of stubbornness and enthusiasm.

No matter the owners didn't want to sell.

There were twenty-seven of them, heirs to a large holding that stretched over much of the mountain behind the Atalaya. Representing them was a cultured and pleasant man, a lawyer, who we went to see in Bilbao.

"Sell us just enough for a home site. Your investment will pay off tenfold!" We told him. "A hundredfold, when people see your property with new eyes."

Señor Fernando de Ruiz listened to us and, for one hundred and forty dollars, we acquired legal title to the old quarry.

A group of fishermen, idle in port and looking to pass the day, walked the four kilometers up from Bermeo, carrying shovels and picks. We leveled the land and mixed cement, we moved rocks and built the foundation. From the village of Bermeo we salvaged tiles and bricks and roofing from old mansions that were being torn down to make room for apartment blocks. We found an old oak beam they had taken out of the church and used it to hold up our second story. When the walls to our house were halfway up, a newspaper reporter from Bilbao came by. He made a front-page story about a university-educated couple building a house with their own hands. The result of that was that the building inspector could not ignore the fact that a house was going up, for which there had been no permit issued.

We went to plead our case with the inspector. Winter is coming, we tell him and we need to have a roof over our heads for when the storms come in off the Bay of Biscay.

"Could you perhaps give us a permit to continue building without a permit? Until we can get a proper permit?"

This he did.

Then the gypsies came by.

And we take Horacio Español along with us in the gypsy caravans:

With a wicker jug of wine and a beatup guitar, we run behind the wagon, grab his gnarled hand that reaches down to lift us aboard the green and yellow caravan - yes, that's how it all begins - our roofless house disappearing from view behind us as the road uncurls along the cliffs over the Biscay where fishing boats buck out to sea like runaway horses hurtling moving walls and we're toasting old Estanco and singing a song we brought back from the roads of Greece:

"Ain't got no money,

Ain't got a dime,

We're gonna leave this cruel world behind."

*We pass green hills and meadows with stone walls all around them. Along the roadside, gypsy women in long colorful skirts pick **caracoles** from mossy crevices.*

And we're going up, up this long straight hill, every one of us piling out of the wagon to help push, because the old grey mare and the lame donkey can't do it all alone and then, coming over the crest with the lush valley pouring out before us, we all scamper and leap back in as the wagon picks up speed and Estanco shoves the eucalyptus pole into my hands and grins:

"Hercules! You're the brakes!"

I lean way out to the side with the pole braced in under the wagon, pulling it hard against the metalrimmed wheel which is spinning so fast now you can smell the wood burning and the smoke is like incense rising up with the steam off the asphalt after the rain with the hot sun dead ahead.

The wind is whipping your hair and Jose won't stop hitting the guitar with the flamenco beat and you're leaning so far out over the pavement you're almost horizontal and the road keeps whirling right under you and it is the longest hill in the world.

It ends, around a curve, in a hollow and beneath a canopy of firelight under the overhanging trees, Malika and Elly whirl around and around, tambourines clamoring in the air and Lalito rolling somersaults through your legs and Estanco grins, his chin balanced on his folded hands resting on the head of his willow cane and the new moon slides through the branches overhead.

And no clock measures this night.

THE FRY PAN

The black face of Meseta de la Muerte sinks slowly into the shimmering heat waves, ever so slowly, from a proud fortress to a penciled mustache, to a faint ripple above the desert floor behind us.

I squint so hard tears blur the sinking island of black rock in the distance, bringing it closer, writhing, twitching: a grin over a mouth you cannot see. A grin so enormous, so undefined that it's beyond existence and at the same time all around you and wrapping you in more tightly to a random spot in the middle of this white-hot sea of the Pampa del Asador

*And way up on top of the **meseta** I conjure up Horacio and he's black ebony too. Little lines run all over his face and he's cracking up with one monstrous laugh after another, ranting and giggling, cracking into pieces that fall off his face and reshape into a mammoth ship of ebony that is breaking apart in a soundless, windless storm; a storm inside out like vacuum: a black hole sucking it all back into itself.*

Grinning ever larger as the face disintegrates further, he is shaking his fist at the sky; a captain without crew going down with his fortress, the tattered flag of defiance on its stern suddenly starched flat with no breeze and you see the purple snake spinning, its own tail in its mouth, a hoop snake whirling right off the pennant he wore around his neck and across the horizon, then all the way around you, growing smaller and faint as the black ship goes down in one final broadside of cannons, loud as ten thousand flamingos, an explosion of wings heeding the call of return, pushing and pulling you ever closer to the edge where below is just one tiny wisp of smoke and his last rebel's laugh:

"The worst is never behind you," he says, "only the best."

One huge belly laugh, a belch of indignant joy, and then the horizon is naked. And you are more alone and desperate than before because none of it makes any sense. I take my shirt off and wrap it around my head; the sun is poaching my brain.

Elly and Caicique are thirty yards ahead of me on a sort of bulldozed runway, a piece of the devious Route 40 that got off the map and onto this desert, slicing due north, luring us on ahead. But so slowly, so painfully slow.

And like a somnambulist merged with the afternoon shadow of my horse, Chaco keeps on flicking his paws so fast, in such unwavering cadence. Those big puppy paws...

*You know how raw his pads are after the **mesetas**; you can feel what the burning gravel is doing to them now. Chaco has a heart big enough to match paws he has not yet grown into and he is giving it all he's got.*

Even with my eyes turned away and looking at the unchanging horizon, I see those paws clicking away. His unquestioning loyalty is a pain that sears right through your crotch and into your guts and you think: it would hurt less if they were my bare feet down there on the hot plate, with the sweat cutting white trails down your black legs and your black feet are glistening; you're so worn out you could drop but Backy Morgan and Stu and Clipper and Tony aren't going to quit now, so you keep on driving yourself. No one is saying out loud how much it hurts. You just keep thinking of the cool lawn and the sprinkler and the Kool-aid with ice cubes that is waiting close by. Everyone is keeping

score out loud:
>*"Thirty-eight. Thirty-nine. I've got forty!"*
>*"How many you got?"*
>*"First one hundred wins!"*

It was a game we played on the street in front of the parsonage on Goodrich Avenue, with the smell of lilacs everywhere and the quiet of Sunday with no cars going by and you have to keep moving because the tar is so hot it is all soft and bubbly and if you are really fast, running in pace, you can pop the little black bubbles with your big toes without breaking stride. We are nine years old, going on ten.

Caicique is plodding ahead out of blind stubbornness and Elly, who never ducks the elements and won't wear a hat in a downpour or on the worst scorcher of days; she now has a green towel draped over her head.

Abruptly, Caicique changes direction and heads straight for the base of a red butte to the west, maybe two miles away, maybe four; the shimmering heat waves make it impossible to gauge the distance. Elly comes out from under her green towel. Her bare back, blackened by the sun, straightens up.

*She won't believe me. She does believe him. He doesn't fabricate a green **pampa** just to cheer her up, covered by a carpet of luxurious cool grass spreading as far as you could dream on a soft summer's evening under the fragrant umbrella of a large mimosa tree; cool water anywhere you needed it, with gentle banks sloping down to rest on while you drink with lips barely touching.*

*Caicique knows. And we follow. This cranky gelding with the lopsided blaze is never wrong and it irks me. If he could deliver pancakes on the **meseta**; what will it be on this Pampa del Asador, this Fry Pan Basin?*

Impossibly, a lagoon appears: a sheet of shimmering blue directly below us. We've been fooled before, coming off the crest of hills, but the thirst is so unbearable that you believe, because desire has turned to pain and out in front of you is Chaco, passing Caicique at a dead run and then you're sure this water will not vanish.

Chaco drops onto his belly at water's edge, poised to dive in headfirst. But his cracked nose jerks back up. His sunk-in body recoils with a wrenching inner howl so muffled it reverberates in your own gut.

The horses drop their heads and tear into the marsh grass at the edge of the pond. Chaco just lies there, motionless, his golden eyes staring past you at nothing.

Then you catch the stench of brackish stagnant water. Undrinkable. Unusable even for cooling face and limbs. Chaco knows from other lagoons what salt feels like in open cuts, what it does to cracked paws and how much harder it is the next day to keep up in the shadow of a horse.

I dampen my kerchief with the last few drops from the canteen we carry just for him, kneel down next to him and dab his nose and lips gently. He licks the cloth. Gives his tail a feeble thump and puts his head down on his forepaws, eyes closed.

"What are we going to feed him?" Her voice is vacant, far away. She has slumped down onto her knees next to Caicique, her arms dangling at her sides. "We can't even cook."

Her words and his eyes are digging into me like hot claws, twisting my insides; I've got to give them something.

*"We've still got a pouch of rice and some garlic." I pump hard to get some life into the words. "Just the thing for a **Patagonian dry-fry**. Guaranteed to fill up the hole, once the fried rice swells inside your stomach."*

Her expression doesn't change. She doesn't smile. Doesn't scowl. Just stares at me, pushing me away. The-here-and-nowness is gone. No tough tomboy left. Just shutting down.

I kneel down in front of her and put a cigarette between her lips and light it. "Come on, puff! Take a puff. Chaco needs you to make him some moccasins or something, okay. I'll cook."

She inhales slowly, nods. Let's the smoke out through her nostrils. I go over and get the sewing kit out of the panniers and put it in her lap. She hasn't moved and she doesn't now, but she is watching the horses graze along the banks of the lagoon. I want to kiss her, just touch her. But I don't. We've crowded each other for weeks now and she needs space.

Before going to sleep next to our small fire made from twigs, I say to her back: "We have to stick together. We can make it if we stick together."

A few coals give off a last glow as a breeze comes up and I can see India, Maracas and Pampero lying down together near the lagoon. Caicique stands watch, nose into the wind. I drift off to sleep, startling awake at intervals. Each time, Caicique is there and one time, very late, or maybe very early in the morning, when I open my eyes I see thousands of stars dancing around him, like fireflies. His silhouette is very large and black and fills half the sky.

Too much nothingness, too much sun! Rest, I tell myself, or you won't be able to crawl out of the sack and rekindle the fire over yesterday's ashes and invent a reason for dragging on that she'll listen to.

"Only to there, El. Then we've got it made. We're almost there."

She doesn't buy it today any more than yesterday and I can't look at her right alongside my horse, knowing she's crying and not wanting to see the tears searing her blistered cheeks. Can't think of anything to say, because she has never broken down before. I want to take it all inside me, so she won't have to feel it, like I did at Albert Schweitzer College when she had a headache and I drew it out of her forehead and into mine, where I could isolate the pain and kill it so we were free to ski with torches into the night, with hot sweet wine below at the end of each run and the beginning of another.

That was then.

This is now, with everything upside down. This helplessness is like acid, eating away at us, turning us into strangers, manacled together, trapped in motion on the Asador; the needle of the compass burning deeper and deeper into your brain.

North. Always to the north now. No more turns, right or left.

She's sobbing now. I don't want to look over. She slams a fist down on the pommel of her saddle.

"Goddamn these plains, I hate them!"

"Get hold of yourself, loves. Right now we don't have a choice."

"You're driving us into the ground. Push, push, push - that's all you ever do!"

"Blaming me isn't going to get us out of here any faster."

"Who put us up on Carbon. Huh?"

"This isn't Carbon, damnit. We've got to keep going."

"Look at Chaco! Look at the horses! Half dead - don't you care anymore?"

I'm fighting to keep a lid on. "Look, El," I say, "our only hope lies straight ahead."

"You've been saying that for weeks. How far? How long?"

"Just a few more days...to Casa de Piedras. Perito Moreno, maybe." My voice sounds empty, unconvincing. Phrases die without completing themselves.

"Perito Moreno! That's two hundred miles!"

Her jaw clenches. She shakes her head, crunches the towel into a ball and throws it at me as hard as she can. "This is bullshit! You are full of shit!"

"Oh yeah! Look at yourself! Every time it gets a little rough, you throw a cat-fit. Well, screw you! I'm not taking this crap any longer."

"So go bash your head into a wall. Just leave me out of it!"

She turns Caicique, heading to the east of north. I turn Pampero west of north, the distance between us growing. Further and further apart we ride: Caicique and Maracas going one way, Pampero and India the other. Out of shouting distance, almost a mile between us, our lines become almost parallel, the horses unwilling to separate any further. I have to keep a steady pressure against Pampero's side with my right leg to prevent him from drifting back towards the other two.

Behind me, the mare whinnies. Maracas answers from across the gap. Followers both, now confused, their plaintive duet drifts over the emptiness. Then, at the edge of my vision, I discover Chaco, alone in dead center, his paw still flicking with smooth mechanical speed. So tiny, so brave and vulnerable.

It stabs me like an icepick: he's got no shade to walk in out there all alone!

The moccasins she made him, they're gone. Stubborn, heroic little bastard! Won't wear boots! Won't let himself be carried! Won't go on strike or lie down! And now: won't choose between us.

I want to shout: "Chaco, let me help you!"

But I can't, anymore than she can.

Because he is already split in half and it would only make him swerve and if he came this way, then he would have to go back the *other and you know he is doing the only thing he can do and it's your fault and you must give him back his shade.*

My leg relaxes against Pampero's side, letting him drift to the east. Caicique is starting to move over this way too. Without a cue from me, Pampero begins to jog. No longer just converging, we're running towards one another.

Chaco slides into Pampero's shadow, his tail wagging, but he does not try to jump up and kiss his buddy as ordinarily he would. I reach out my right hand toward Elly. She doesn't seem to notice, but I keep holding my hand there, until hers rises slowly, wearily, and the tips of our fingers touch, just lightly brushing together.

His name is Rafael.

He owns an *estancia* at the base of a butte, a few kilometers off Route 40. We have never seen the man before, yet he receives us as if knowing all about us. This is not an unusual thing in the Patagonia, but with Rafael the feeling is intrusive, not respectful and accepting.

Turns out that about a year ago a young German chap arrived at this ranch on horses he had bought at Cerro Guido. He had planned to ride them to Santiago de Chile. This was as far as he got.

This man Rafael bought the two horses and his gear too and the chap hitched a ride north with a truck. He'll buy our horses too, says Rafael, because winter was bad this year. Horses were eating fence posts and each other's tails, that's how bad it was and he lost a *tropilla* of twenty. He could use a few extra head. And he wants to help us out of our situation. We could be on our way tomorrow, with no more horses to worry about.

This man Rafael has a loft full of alfalfa hay, brought in from the coast. But this Rafael is no Horacio and will not spare us one bale of it for our horses. Not at any price. They'll be okay overnight in the *potrero*. That's what he says. One bale wasn't going to make any difference anyway, he says. What our horses needed was a couple of months of rest. They'd recuperate enough on their own to make it through winter.

Caicique tours the bare paddock and comes back to the gate and parks himself there, waiting. He knows there is feed, I know he does. He can smell the alfalfa up in the loft, just as I can smell the ribs that Rafael is preparing for us in his kitchen.

I don't want to eat this man's food if he won't feed my horse.

We saddle up and move on and leave Rafael to wonder what on earth we were thanking him for, seeing as we did not sit down at his table.

What I was thanking him for, very sincerely so, was snapping me out of the mood I was in and making me mad enough to ride on.

On the last day of March, ending our third month on horseback, we awoke to frost on the ground. We remember this campsite with special clarity because, amongst the frost tipped *coirón*, close to our bedroll, we found a small fetus. It was perfectly formed, no larger than a lamb. It lay enclosed in its sack, full of protective liquid still, a little buckskin colt. It had a small star on his forehead. A star for good luck, just like on the severed head of the black horse at Kach Aike.

We looked at each other. Each of us knew better than to force conversation, so we just stood there together, alone in grief, staring at our little family. Now and then, Caicique coughed. Maracas coughed a couple of times too and there was yellow mucus in his left nostril. India stood apart from the others. Only Pampero was grazing. Even he was so gaunt looking now.

When you move, move; when you stop, stop.

Guillermo told us that. It was simple advice. But we had done the opposite. We pushed to get to better pastures. We pushed to get ahead of winter. We dragged on for twenty-seven out of the thirty-one days of this month. There were places where we could not have stayed; there were others where we should have stayed but we didn't.

Chaco didn't want to get up this morning. We had to pull the bedroll right out from under him. Even after we did that, he lay down again on the ground and curled up in a ball. Once we started moving, he got up and followed way behind Maracas.

This sorry looking troupe arrived at *estancia* Pago Chico around noon that day. We didn't know what to expect, you seldom do. The place looked neat and tidy, a whitewashed barn and sheds and the second crop of alfalfa coming up in the irrigated fields. The house was low and made of adobe, Spanish style and freshly whitewashed. Pots of flowers adorned the garden and there were birds chirping in the poplars and the crab apple trees. A chime sounds as I

Guillermo Halliday, The White Indian

The house on Machichaco.   A permit to build without a permit

On the road with the gypsies in northern Spain

Guillermo created Estancia El Zorro in a wasteland no one else wanted

Criollos at Estancia El Zorro

Nathan wears botas de potro on the Gallegos River

Elly with Caicique and Maracas, Gallegos River

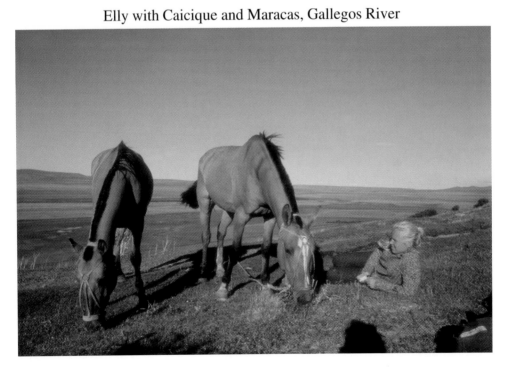

Ultima Esperanza, Chile

Ultima Esperanza, Lago Toro

Shepherd's puesto

Campsite in the cordillera

The rains never stopped in southern Chile

Pampero crossing river in southern Chile

Along the coast of Chile

Living off the sea

Springtime along the coast of Chile

Nathan and Pampero taking a siesta

Morning shadow on a bulldozed track through the desert

Ghost town in the Atacama

Gustavo's compass helps us find our way in the desert

The horses give shade for Chaco

At Pan de Azucar, fresh water out of the Pacific

Chaco and Pampero share a pot of water

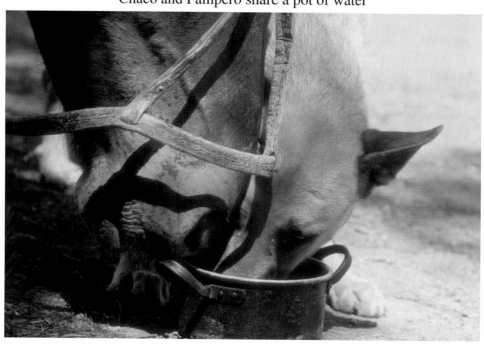

Pampero drinks from a bottle too!

Rene's ancient truck goes off road to bring us water and feed

The fig tree Don Lucho planted

The fig tree gives us shade and fruit

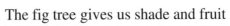

The old hermit cooks us a meal at Blanco Encalada

Approaching Rio Loa, Atacama desert

Railroad cart brings feed to Camp Siberia

Lunch break in the Atacama, the driest desert on earth

At Cerro Moreno air force base

Nathan and Chaco on sick beds

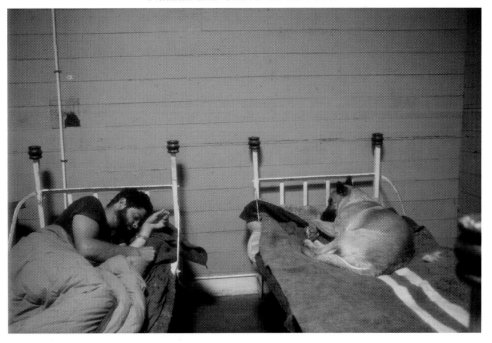

On the way down from Paso Condor at over 5,000 meters

Purchasing llama meat from an Aymara family of the altiplano

The twins by campsite in a cave

Nathan in sheepherders' wind break

The Enchanted Valley, Peruvian altiplano

Encounter

Encounter: burros loaded with ichu grass

Weaver outside his home of ichu grass

Encounter: llama pack train

On top of the world, Northern Peru

Moments after Pampero fought his way out of a rock slide

Pampero walks a trail not made for horses

Impromptu speech to villagers in northern Peru

The grass is greener in the church yard

Crossing Chinchipe River at la Balsa

Andin watches raft with our saddles on the Chinchipe River

Climbing the old Inca Road

Rains have turned the trail
into a trough

Nathan and India follow in the
steps of many

Section of the Zumba-Yangana
trail, Ecuador

Arturo Dragon sniffs out a hidden abscess

India goes up and onto the Monica

On the beach somewhere

Nathan on Pirata with migrant workers, southern Mexico

Chaco hides from the downpour

Horses and Chaco share
concentrate feed

Nathan with the twins

Swimming in Lago Atitlan, Guatemala

Riding into a sunset

Voyage's end

open the small wrought iron gate. I knock on the door.

A woman opens. Her smile illuminates her face and with it the whole doorway where she stands. The smile comes from deep inside her eyes,

"My husband will be so disappointed to miss you!" She says. "He won't be back for a couple of days!"

I can feel my lips tremble as I struggle to shape my mouth into something that might be mistaken for a smile and that might force my tears back. I don't want her to see me stand there crying, not knowing how I will find the strength to get back up on my tired horse and ride away from this beautiful place.

"Would you wait for him?" She asks us now.

It takes us a few moments to realize that she is not turning us away, not at all. She is pleading with us to accept her hospitality and to wait for her husband's return.

"We have lots of room, now that my children are gone. Please stay!"

I don't know what might have become of us, had we not found our way to Pago Chico on this day. Our journey might have ended. But beyond exhaustion, we finally found the end of the rainbow.

We ride borrowed horses from Pago Chico to get help and medicines for our troupe back at the *estancia*. The trail is good, the horses are fresh. We put them into a lope and they move out, side by side and egg each other on faster and faster. I look over at Nathan and he looks at me and a smile comes over my face and over his and we let go of everything but the exhilaration of the moment. In that split second, we rediscover the heart of our journey.

The staff sergeant at the cavalry regiment in Perito Moreno is a very good friend of Gustavo Truttman's. He loads several sacks of oats into his jeep, grabs his medicine kit and drives right over to meet us at Pago Chico. He checks our horses over carefully. He knows the country we have come through.

"Tough horses you have," he says.

Chaco is lying on a blanket in the barn. He hasn't touched the milk Audrey brought for him. His nose is dry and cracked and there is puss in both of his eyes. The staff sergeant's face is grave when he turns to us.

"Looks like distemper," he says.

"But we vaccinated him against it!" Nathan says.

"Sometimes they get it anyway," says the sergeant.

He gives Chaco a shot of penicillin and Audrey invites us to move the pup into the kitchen. Chaco won't get up, so Nathan carries him in his arms, like a sick child, and beds him down on a blanket next to the stove.

"We must hope for the best," says the sergeant.

But his face is not so very hopeful.

We take turns, sponging the puss out of his eyes, dabbing water on his hot and dry nose and his worn and cracked pads. We keep a bowl of milk on the ready, should he want some. In the vigil of this one night, we try to make up for all the many days that we had pushed too hard. Helplessly, we watch his big puppy paws flicking back and forth, so smoothly and so mechanically as he runs in a fever, hour after hour.

We watch with unbearable pain, each of us remembering the immeasurable joy of the moment when the yellow pup came bounding across the galley floor of the Spanish freighter docked in Buenos Aires and into our waiting arms:

I bend down to pet Chaco and that's all the prompting he needs: he leaps up, slobbers kisses on Elly and is off spinning like a drag racer, folds of yellow fur wiggling and bouncing, sliding across the polished floor, bumping into the walls, his large paws slipping out from under him at every turn. Undaunted, he hops right back and charges straight for us. Skids to a halt and cocks his head, and litfs his left forepaw.

"He knows you already!"

Aranza's uncle is astonished. "How can that be?" He is the captain of the ship and he brought the pup from Bilbao, Spain as a favor to his niece.

"He has the soul of his older brother, Nikos," Nathan says. "Shot by a bird hunter. Right by our house on Machichaco. Two days before we left for Argentina."

Aranza's uncle asks no more questions. We take Chaco away with us in a taxi, right past customs and immigration, to a small pension where the owner was okay with us bringing a pup. A few days later we are on a train going south to the Patagonia.

Then for three long months we marched him into the eye of the storm and he would hide his pain and exhaustion and keep on going, a little pup making the trek designed for a full grown dog.

But what have we done?

Sending this wonderful pup, so full of enthusiasm, to march into windstorms on gravel prairies, cutting him loose into the icy waters at Rio de Las

Vueltas, dragging him over the shales and the cinders of volcanic *mesetas*, across the whole Pampa del Asador.

In the morning, just before dawn, Nathan carries Chaco outside so he can relieve himself and when he comes back in, he drinks from the bowl of milk by the stove and when he sleeps, he just sleeps. Only once in a while, one of his paws would twitch, but he has stopped running.

The road from Perito Moreno lifts us gently, without urgency, amongst the soft bellyfolds of golden brown hills; when you're in a dip it's cool and all you see is a narrow slice of blue off the lake below, then you reach another sweeping curve and the panorama floods in around you. You hover, a sleeping yo-yo spinning on its magic thread, inhaling the first cooling scent of the mountains ahead on the hot breath of noon. Overhead, small clouds do not drift nor change their shapes.

There is a hum in the air. At first you don't really hear it; you aren't paying attention. But it keeps nibbling away at the edge of awareness and now you notice that the horses all have their ears turned backwards, catching the sound that keeps on tapping you softly on the shoulder, asking for recognition.

The drone of the motor fades as the road loops into another bellyfold and you begin to doubt the whole thing because of how you don't like to let go of Gustavo and the sound of the old green Chevy truck that woke you each morning at Pago Chico as Gustavo brought a bale of alfalfa to the barn for the horses.

A little higher and closer and louder, the sound returns and you can imagine the old Chevy now and see Gustavo so clearly, the way you want to remember him from the photograph that is sitting on the mantlepiece made of a huge slab of driftwood, fished from some river with the silver sheen of old wood licked clean by fast water. Gustavo Truttman is pictured astride a bay mare, alone atop a mountain pass high above the tree line, wearing the black wool poncho of a Swiss farmer and he is taking a reading from a hand compass.

In his eyes, you see the whole horizon and you know how hard it is for him to stay when we boot the stable doors open on their hinges and the horses catapult into the open, eyes large, heads high. They spin on their haunches, half a turn left, quarter turn right, letting out short squeals that might have been whinnies in a more mellow mood and on a soundless cue, they stampede straight into the sunlit purple of the alfalfa fields in blossom, kicking and bucking sideways, farting at the heavens. And in front of them runs Chaco, yapping like crazy.

It is so good to see Gustavo again, in a happy-sad kind of way. Happy because he is a kindred spirit, the first person we've met on the way who truly loves horses and life on the open road. Sad because now we have to say goodbye all over again and it wasn't easy the first time.

The horses nicker at the sound of his voice, the same voice that greeted them each morning, bringing them feed and speaking to them in Swiss German. They are not disappointed. Gustavo has brought a bright green bale of alfalfa in the back of the Chevy.

"They certainly have picked up," he says with pleasure. "Even the mare looks good."

"Thanks to you!"

"I love horses," he says simply and he strokes India on the side of her neck and brings his hand up to just in front of the withers and rubs his fingers on both sides.

He brings out a bag from the front seat of the pickup and pulls out a black poncho. It has a tailored collar and buttons down the front and is cut the same way you cut a bell skirt, out of a circle, so the cape falls softly over the shoulders. I recognize the poncho from the picture in Gustavo's study and know what it means for him to be giving me this and I don't know what to say.

"Thank you, Gustavo," I say.

He smiles back at my smile. "It kept me dry on the trail," he says.

To Nathan he gives a compass in a leather pouch. It is the one from the picture and I feel my throat tighten and I don't look at Nathan because I know there will be tears in his eyes and I am not sure I would be able to handle that.

"I am so happy to have found someone to give this compass to," Gustavo says.

Then he turns quickly around and picks up the chunk of meat he brought along for Chaco and then we sit there together by the side of the road, the three of us, watching the horses munch their hay. Right in the middle of the hay lies Chaco, thumping his tail as he works his teeth into the leg of lamb, and the horses eat carefully around him.

LEAVING PATAGONIA

It is time to leave the Patagonia and move on to all that followes.

It is hard to leave.

I have been comfortable in this place so far away, so stark and unforgiving. A place that defines me, the worst and the best of me; a place devoid of clutter. A place that does not ask questions of you and only demands that you endure.

Patagonia is addictive.

Patagonia is the place where I needed to lose myself that long night in July in my mother's room; the room where I lived during four teenage years and where I still reside a teenager.

The beer coasters I collected in Germany the summer I was sixteen and worked at an international student camp in West Berlin remain pinned to the left side of the window, in rows of four, on wallpaper that has remained unchanged for forty years.

Forty years!

I cry without tears and without a sound.

Beer mats! Anything at all that reminds her of the teenager who used to live here; who left forever.

And I didn't even like beer!

In the early hours of the new day, I take them all down and throw them in the wastebasket.

Forty years have left empty circles on the wall. The effect is worse.

I take one of the straw mats off the table and pin it over the area. In the morning, I vow, I will buy yellow paint and cover all of it.

But, in the morning, I understand that I am not in charge of this mausoleum to an only daughter who left.

It is not mine to do, I know, unless now that I have come back I can, somehow, make her want to move on.

Yes, it is time to venture beyond the vastness where you can see so clearly, where splotches of primary colors across an unbleached canvas etch minute details in your memory. There is so much still untold. But you make choices.

Chance, perhaps, and the mood and the space you find yourself in when writing has much to do with what goes on the page for all to see and what remains private memory.

The mood of that night removing the beer coasters off the wall in my mother's apartment puts us riding in the rain towards the Corcovado River.

At first, coming down into this thickening forest, we throw our heads back and drink raindrops; the rain soaks us to the skin and the chill feels good, because you remember all those days on the plains and the mesetas and the Pampa del Asador when it did not rain. The horses stop at every large puddle along the trail and put their heads down to wet their lips and slurp in a playful mouthful or two even when they aren't thirsty anymore and you let them because it makes you happy.

But this rain does not cease.

You become numb with a chill lodged deep in your gut, like a cramp from holding on too long and then you can't let go. The heavy mist has closed in around you and all you can hear is the rain drumming on the canopy of leaves overhead and you are trapped within a wall of trees and inside yourself, without sky, without horizon.

Chaco is slogging along in the muck next to your horse, no longer dashing for each puddle as if it were both the first and the last, no longer even shaking the wetness off his coat; a portrait of abject misery now.

Ahead of me rides Elly, a solitary horseman of the Seventh Seal, right out of the Ingmar Bergman movie, the hooded black cape so heavy with water it does not even flutter. Lost is your vision of the black cape flagging around her like the wings of Pegasus as we rode high above the tree line where the wind blows in gusts from many directions and where in her eyes you could see the whole horizon.

How soon you forget the dance in the rain.

How quickly your vision shrinks to this rutted trail we're following, pushing ahead into darkness towards the village of Corcovado on the other side of the river, holding onto the one thought: you'll get a hot meal there, find a bed, maybe there's a small hotel, anywhere under a roof that does not leak will do and will be better than where you got up this morning, stiff and sleepless from huddling all night on a mud floor, listening to the rain leak through the roof of the small hut of a shepherdess and into twenty-seven cups, bowls and tin cans, your eyes blinded like hers from the smoke off the hearth in the middle of the hut, with no chimney in the roof above for the smoke to escape.

Caicique stops.

Before us, the lights of Corcovado scatter across the moving surface of the river: a painting hung in darkness of a town washing away in the rain.

An uprooted tree whirls past on the turbulent waters of a river that is much faster and much bigger than we had anticipated so we turn away from the promise of shelter and warmth on the other side and ride back up the rutted trail to a house perched, like a fort, high up on the bank with a slab fence around it.

Pedro Samhuesa is some time in responding to our pounding on the gate in the tall slab fence. He holds up a homemade lantern to illuminate the darkness and our rain soaked apparitions. His face, in the flickering light, is a mass of wrinkles gathered around a toothless grin.

He beckons us to come on in, leaving our introductions, our expla-

nations and apologies trailing behind as we follow him, sloshing through the mud across the yard. He's been wet and cold like this; we're his son and his daughter in misery.

*"**Están en su casa**," he says, "You are in your house."*

And in this our house, we huddle on short legged stools near the open mouth of the large adobe oven that fills half the small room, hugging old wool blankets tightly around our naked bodies as the old woman shuffles from the oven to the wash-tub, where she wrings out our socks and hangs them next to our other clothes that are still dripping and starting to steam, on a line strung from corner to corner above our heads, all the while muttering, cooing, chuckling to herself and to us and to others no longer here.

And she hugs us like a son and a daughter and kisses us on the forehead and kneels down in front of my stool and rubs Elly's feet with her long and bony fingers and then she slides on a pair of old slippers with small patches of fur that may have been white rabbit.

"You have feet just like mine," she says and she smiles with more gaps than teeth.

*She serves us potato soup and heavy dark bread that is moist inside and has a very hard crust. And then we drink **hierba máte**, the four of us, the silver straw passing from mouth to mouth.*

Candle in front of her, she leads us into a narrow bedroom, Samhuesa shuffling behind. She hands us night clothes and we all change in the wavering yellow light, then we crawl into the beds, which are plank shelves covered with raw wool hides. When she blows out the candle it is very quiet, except for the rain on the tin roof and their breathing.

Sometime in the night, she lights the candle again and gets out of bed and lifts her flannel nightgown and squats over the bucket between the beds and I try and hear the rain and the wind; grateful that the smell of wax is so strong after she has blown the candle out.

I know my grandmother kept her teeth in a glass jar by her bed and I knew that in the aftermath of her fabulous parties she re-used the grounds for her own coffee and ate the crusts cut off the sandwiches she had served to her guests. But I cannot begin to imagine being so close as this to my grandmother.

All night long it rains.

The following day, the rain turns to snow and we remain by the hearth and listen to Samhuesa talk, one yarn spinning into the next as he cuts the rough cloth of what had been his life, for us to take along with us on our journey beyond this river and this valley and on into a land and a time where there is too much plenty; a land and a time where they need to know a man like Pedro Samhuesa.

Pedro Samhuesa does not ask why, children of privilege that we are, we would choose to live exposed like this. He does not look for a reason for our journey. He asks nothing at all of us but that we listen to the stories of his life.

This is one story of Pedro Samhuesa's that I recorded in my notebook:

"I laugh," he says and his big steely eyes have a warm glow, "I laugh at my poverty in those days."

His hands grip his knees underneath the patched *bombachas* and he laughs again. I look at those hands, finely shaped hands that don't seem to belong to his big-framed body.

The old man notices my gaze. "And only once," he says, "did I sell myself to work for the Argentines. It was in those years when you were having a war in Europe. We had a lot of need here. It was very bad.

'Go to the *estancia*,' my woman said. 'All I've got left here are two hens,' she said. 'And then what?'

Well, I went. They knew me there, knew I was good with the oxen, so they gave me work. For one month, for two, I worked. Then, when I left, I asked the *mayordomo* if I could have some meat to take with me.

'Well, yes,' said the *mayordomo*. 'You can have some, Samhuesa, if there is any in the locker room.'

We went and we looked and there was a sheep's head hanging there. That was all there was. I took the head and I left.

She was mad when I came home, after two months, with a sheep's head.

'And you worked for two months!' She said.

I said nothing. Nothing at all. But she cooked up a soup with the head and I ate and I felt better. I took my ax and I went off up into the forest.

Never, I said to myself, will I sell myself again as a *peon*. I had learned what my share of it was: a head of sheep.

Until dark, I worked up there, chopping down straight old trees with my ax.

We did not speak to each other in the evening, my woman and I. But the next morning I went back up into the forest with my ax and when I had cut what I needed, I went to borrow a yoke of oxen, for in those days I did not even have my own. Then I set to work, carving basins.

They laughed at me, I know. 'What are you going to do with those chunks of wood?' They asked.

I went on carving, one basin in the morning I could finish and another before dark. And when I had as many as my packhorse could take, I saddled up.

I'm going to Trevellin, I said. I'll be a few days away. And I left. On the way, I met certain Josè Vargas. He was going to the Welsh colony with a cow to trade for flour. That's where I am heading, I said. 'Let's make company.'

We made camp together that night and the next day, early, we got to the colony.

'And you think the Welsh are going to buy your chunks of wood!' Said Josè and he too laughed.

Well, I said, let's see who gets the best trade.

And we left, each his own way. I took my packhorse and went to the house of *señora* de Owen. A girl opened the door

'Good day, Samhuesa,' she said. 'What brings your here?'

She recognized me. I know the Owen family.

I would like to see your mother, I said. I am bringing her the basin she asked me for.

'She's in the corrals,' said the girl. 'Just a moment.'

And off she went running, the little Welsh girl. Soon they came back, the two of them, mother and daughter. And I took out the basin from under the *poncho* and showed it to her. She took it. Handled it. Turned it.

'Nice work you do, Samhuesa,' she said. 'Better than those factory made.' She said. 'Only I have no money to pay you. But could you use ten kilos of butter, Samhuesa?'

Well, I said, Yes, I could take butter. How much did you say you sell a kilo of butter for, *señora*? I asked her.

'Fifty *centavos*, Samhuesa,' she answered.

That was not the price she got for her butter and I knew it, so I said to her:

The other time, didn't you say it was forty *centavos, señora*? But, never mind, you give me bread for the journey.

She went off and returned with a big can of butter and a loaf of bread, one of those two kilo loaves that the Welsh used to make out of oatmeal. And I loaded my packhorse, said good-bye and moved up the road to the Jones family. They too had no money.

'But would you take a sack of flour, Samhuesa?' Asked *señora* Jones and I accepted the deal and packed my horse and went on with the rest of the basins. In the next house, I got a good-sized bag of sugar and another of *hierba **máte***. In the next, a sack of peas and in another one a sack of flour. My packhorse was loaded with as much as he could take and so was my saddle horse. There was nothing else for me to do but go walking, but this I did on light feet. I went back to camp where Jose Vargas was waiting with two sacks of flour, but no cow. He looked at me walking, leading my two horses.

'I see it went well with you, Samhuesa,' he said but he did not smile. It seemed something was on his mind that night by the camp-fire, for he did not talk much. The next morning we turned back home, I was on foot and he was in the saddle. He disappeared at a trot, while I kept slowly walking and when I came to the river, my woman was there to see me.

She smiled this time. And all summer, I worked in the woods with firewood and we ate *tortas fritas* and pea soup."

When the rains let up, around noon on the second day, we saddled up and crossed the Corcovado River with the brown waters swirling above our stirrups. At the *boliche* we bought hay and grain, and meat for Chaco, and sat in our rented room and wrote down the yarns Pedro Samhuesa spun for us.

And the next day we traveled the trail that Samhuesa had gone so many years before to the Welsh Colony of Trevellin. We knocked on the door to the home of one family Howard to ask for pasture for our horses. We were received with surprise, then delight and, as so often happens to travelers such as ourselves, we were made the guests of honor at their table. Our stock in trade is as old as history itself: the excitement and the tales from faraway places that the traveler brings to those who stay put. It's the lure of the gypsy - made palatable because we are the children of privilege. Because we do this by choice, not out of necessity.

And from Nathan's diary:

May 7, Ranger Cabin on Lago Verde:
We had to hurry to catch the ferry which transits Lake Futalaufken and follows the Arayanes River up to Lago Verde, a trip of two hours. The park administrator phoned ahead to tell the captain to wait for us. We saddled up in record time and trotted the four kilometers along a lovely forest road by the lake to the dock.

The horses behaved well, even though the ferryboat was so small that it rolled when they shifted their weight. Pampero was the nervous one as usual and tucked his nose up under my arm, as he had done when we crossed Santa Cruz River and the Leon.

Chaco lay next to the pilothouse licking a nasty wound on his thigh where a mongrel boxer had bitten him. Poor Chaco is now the age when the adults pick on him, as though to initiate the raw adolescent into the ways of the world: too old to be rendered the immunity due an innocent, yet too young to fight for himself.

And into the wilds once more!

Virgin forests lined the lake, green for the first few hundred feet up the steep slope of the mountain and then red from the frost line on up. The area was similar to the lake region near Mount Paine - a beautiful cross between Swiss Alps and Norwegian fjords. The water was so clear that we could see the bottom perfectly at a depth of thirty feet or more.

After an hour, the ferry turned up a narrow sound between steep cliffs and entered the river. The colors were superb for photographing the snow, the foliage, the water, the horses and the boat itself. By the time we arrived at the park hostel in Lago Verde, we had shot a roll of Ektachrome. It was an exhilarating voyage and quite a change of scene and pace.

The captain refused to charge us for the trip and the park guard invited us to use the upstairs of his log house headquarters. I never cease to be astounded by the way most people treat us. And why? We are nobody in particular, neither celebrities, nor politicians, nor millionaires - just two joyful young hoboes. Yet many like to have us around for awhile, so perhaps we are symbols of some sort, perchance of the freedom they are denied.

May 8,9,10 Lago Verde:

What a choice spot for quiet sitting! The forestry guard was away most of the day, leaving us to ourselves. We sat by the fireplace, strolled by the lake, photographed flowers and birds, trimmed our horses tails and manes, tried in vain to teach Chaco to heel, hiked up the mountain behind the cabin. We even went for a spin in the outboard skiff to Lake Menendez. With the guard, we took turns preparing meals, cleaning up, and chopping firewood.

I thought a great deal of settling down in an area similar to this, of building another house (log cabin), of installing a small turbine, raising horses and dogs, and writing a long novel covering the twenty-five years between Hiroshima and Vietnam, a magnum opus on the scale of **The Odyssey: A Modern Sequel** *(Kazantzakis).*

I felt tranquil, unhurried - free of compulsion to achieve - as it seemed that my life was flowing naturally in this direction, all the experiences of past and present joining into the mainstream like tributaries into a growing river. It seems that with scope comes patience, the neutrality to encompass life's extremes and contradictions.

But the Patagonia never leaves you.

It isn't a place, you understand. It is not a destination. You cannot conquer it. You can't go there and take a tour for the experience.

You want to do that, go to your closest IMAX Theater and let them treat you to the current thrills and spills of vicarious living. It will be better than what any tour operator could offer you.

Patagonia is about being out there without protection or guidance.

You alone in a landscape so vast that you go day after day and it does not change and in that unchanging vastness you marvel how man found the spirit to live, facing the overwhelming evidence of his own smallness.

Everything is drawn with such sparse strokes:

Plain.

Sky.

Wind.

Day after day after day you ride, yearning for the moment you reach the horizon where the plains end.

And then, someday, when you are crowded in and suffocating, you close your eyes you look into the never-ending horizon of the Patagonia and let the wind whip your face and the cold penetrate you and you let yourself imagine how it is to see a *gaucho* come towards you on the horizon and how it is to have the wind bring you the faint aroma of *calafate* burning and of ribs cooking and how it is to arrive at a shack tucked in a hollow and to know that you are welcome because you are human and there are so very few in this unforgiving land.

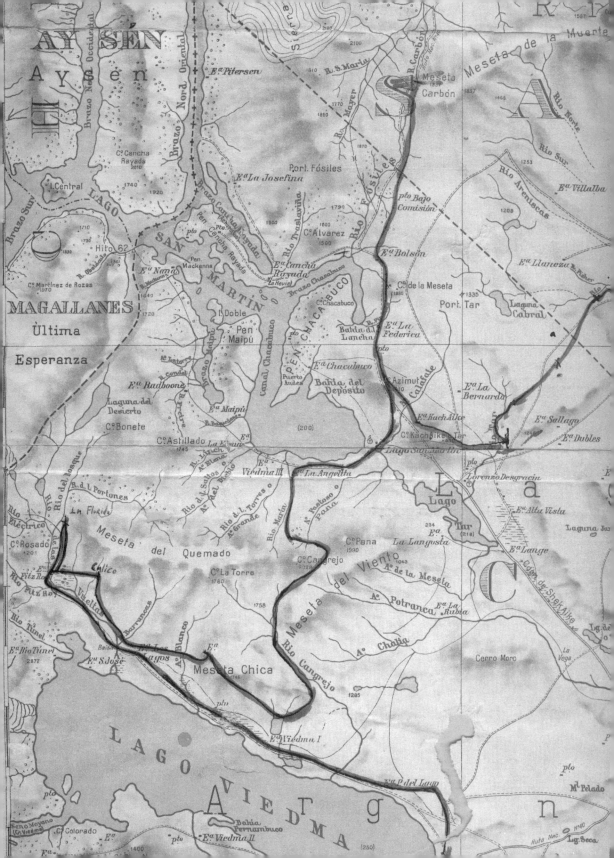

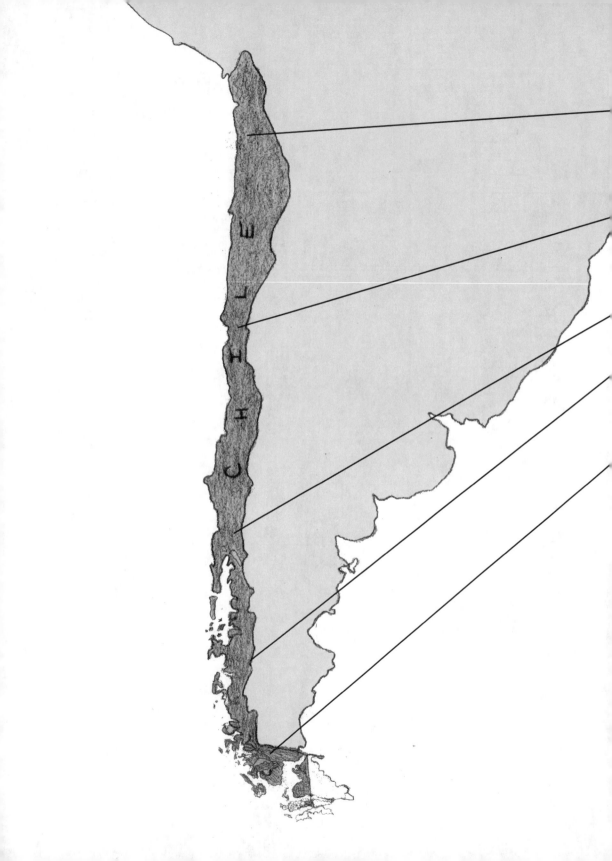

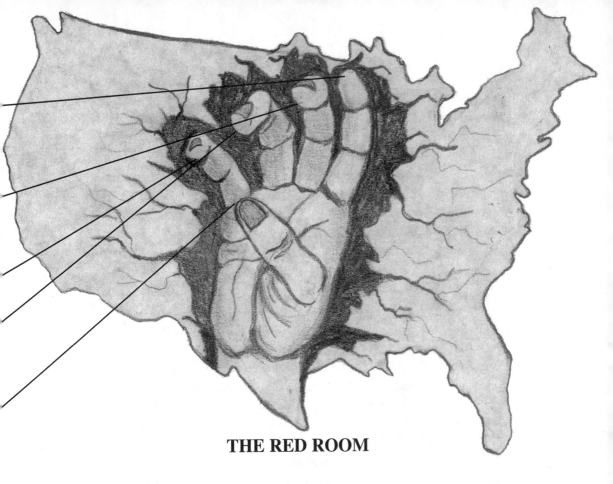

THE RED ROOM

It is a clear and cold day when we cross the Puyehue Pass from Argentina into Chile, through snow that is dry and crusty where it has drifted across the road during last night's storm. The horses' iron shoes make a rhythmical creaking sound as they pick up the pace and the mood from Chaco who is really going wild up here! He bounds ahead of us through the fluffy powder, scoops up mouthfuls of snow and burrows into drifts like a hopped-up canine steam shovel, spinning around and plopping down on his belly with a devilish look in his eyes.

At the top, the panorama splits in half: above us an island necklace of sky piercing thorns; below us billowing clouds of vapor roll in over a dense rain forest. The metamorphosis is so sudden that you have the sensation of dropping through a trapdoor from one reality to another as you let the mountain road take you down the Pacific side of the Cordillera.

The shallow gully deepens into a steep walled canyon and the snow *becomes sticky, packing up in the horses' hooves. They kick out random snowballs that grow bigger as they roll away, exposing slashes of black sand. Some of the snowballs make it all the way to the ditch and bob away on the churning brown riverlet until they get sucked into a culvert and shoot out over the chasm next to us and into the river below that is louder now; you hear underwater boulders turning and you breathe the river on the mist that rises all the way up the cliffs.*

Soon there are streamlets everywhere on the road, etching webs in the black sand and the running water washes away our tracks as soon as we pass.

The horses slow to a choppy, tense walk with every nerve on high alert, their nostrils open wide to take in the scents that come to them on the mist off the trees with hanging vines, some in flower - this alien smell of life and death in a rut that is new to them.

The mist lifts off the top of the ridge, revealing a gap in the wall of giant trees, where a piece of the mountainside has fallen away and slid down into the river, leaving a door open to a magical place where you glimpse the tip of a snow-capped volcano catching fire in the red sunburst at the end of the day.

Then the door closes and the grays of the sky darken to charcoal and a liquid stampede overtakes you and circles back. I surrounds you and throws needles at your face and your bare hands and your wool poncho captures the biting rain and brings it inside your jacket and saturates your sweater and then your underwear is wet too. Little riverlets begin to form, one running down the center of your back, another from the collar bone straight down to the umbilicus. The next thing you know is that your toes are soaked from the water flowing down the stirrup leathers and filling your boots.

The only thing clear to you as you force your horse forward, your eyes cast toward the muddy ooze below, is why nomads live in desert climates. You can cover yourself from the sun and protect yourself against the cold, but there is no escaping the rain, except by being under a roof, inside a house and after a few days of being rain-whipped like this, all we can think about is to reach Ruperto Vargas' house near Villarica.

Ruperto storms out in the rain to greet us, his forty-year old face an open boyish grin under a red and white stocking cap that makes you think of Dr. Seuss' Cat-In-The-Hat. The buckles of his galoshes click wildly as he goose-steps through the haphazard line-up of totem poles that surround the yellow house at end of a long and narrow valley.

"Something told me you would turn up today! Darn nice to see you!"

He gives us each a big bear hug.

"So, how was it?"

"In a word?" Nathan says.

"No, wait!" He takes us both by an arm and walks us past red and yellow-beaked Mapuche totems, several Easter Island *moai* made of wood, flats of pine seedlings and into the big house where we will have plenty of time over the coming weeks to give Ruperto the long version of our life on the trail.

Every morning, the maid would tiptoe into our room. She would pull the curtains and put the breakfast tray on the night table and we would scrunch the pillows behind our backs and drink hot, sweet tea and look out at a gray morning where the rain drizzled, or came down in sheets, or hammered down furiously. And we would so relish being warm and dry and cozy and sharing the world of a kindred spirit.

In this same bed have slept such illustrious guests as Nobel Laureate Pablo Neruda, a communist, and Jorge Allessandri, the ultra-conservative political candidate of the day. Ruperto embraced both extremes. In Ruperto, we began to know Chile as it was when politics played like a national sport.

So who *is* this Ruperto?

We met Ruperto on our way through Santiago de Chile, before Buenos Aires, before the Patagonia and the beginning of our ride. It was a Sunday afternoon and we went to the National Museum, for something to do. Most of the rooms in the three-story building were filled with portraits of generals and dukes and the pomp and paraphernalia of colonial history. It wasn't terribly interesting to us. The archeological section, relegated to the basement, was a fascinating jumble of skulls, pottery fragments, textiles and stone artifacts. Some lay spread out on metal shelves, some with tags, some without. There was a lot more in boxes and just in piles on the floor.

"Lack of funds," the curator said apologetically. "What money there is goes to the upstairs."

Nathan answered the curator's request to sign a petition for funding with

129

an eloquent plea on behalf of pre-Columbian history in Chile, signed in the name of Harvard University.

What all this has to do with Ruperto is that, as one favor in return for another, the curator agreed to stash some of our excess baggage in the basement of the National Museum, until we would return to Santiago on horseback in a year or so. We marked the box: the Foote Collection. The curator thought it was a good joke. And because it was such a good joke, the curator called up his great friend Ruperto Vargas to come meet us. That was seven months before we appeared at El Coihue. Events appear randomly but then, when you look at them together, a pattern emerges. Isolated pieces, you begin to discern, form part of an overall design. With the horses as our ambassadors, doors open to privileged experience in this journey of synchronicity.

Ruperto embodies the opposing elements of the flamboyant love affair with freedom that was Chile at the time. He becomes the central figure in the patch-work quilt that is our experience of the Chile we came to know.

It is hard to know where to start. Maybe I'll just start with archeology, which was the thing that brought us together after all. We went in to Villarica with Ruperto to supervise his dig - actually municipal works excavating for a new sewage line. The job was done with picks and shovels and paid for by the city of Villarica. Ruperto urged the workers to handle their tools slowly and carefully in the rain soaked ditches. He paid them a bonus for buckets of pottery fragments they salvaged. Ruperto and Nathan jumped into the ditch and rummaged in the mud like a couple of ten-year-olds. They found broken tiles and burned wood from the old town that was razed by the Araucanian Indians and pieces of tile ceramics, an old coin, a knife and a bullet. Ruperto seemed pleased with the head shaking and mirth of passers-by, who obviously knew him.

"They think I'm crazy!" He said with apparent relish.

He waved his trowel at a woman who stopped to peer down at us from street level. She was immaculately and incongruously dressed in a tailored suit, each strand of her hair neatly in place underneath the protective cover of a large white umbrella.

"Ruperto! How is your mother? Remember me to Doña Eladia, por favor," she said.

"Yes. Yes, of course."

He held out a muddy mess of porcelain pieces for her perusal. "May I offer you some fragmented culture, Doña Marí-Inez?" He said. "My mother is fine, thank you."

"I am glad to hear that," the woman said and she turned around, ignoring his offering. "I must excuse myself, Ruperto," she said.

"Elegant lady," I remarked.

"She is from one of *The Families*," he said. I tried to read his expression. I saw a boy who enjoyed being bad, knowing he can't be punished because he has mastered the art of subtle insolence.

The Vargas family arrived in South America with the first *conquistadores* and Ruperto's great-great-great grandfather was the owner of three entire provinces in the south. Up until 1928, a whole city block in Santiago, right opposite the National Library, belonged to the family. The Vargas were politicians, doctors and lawyers.

Ruperto was a lawyer. A non-practicing member of the profession, he told us proudly, since the day he put a fighting cock up on the witness stand. The judge was not amused. Ruperto left Santiago and took up residence on the Easter Islands, where clothes and titles were not important. He learned to harpoon fish and drink hard liquor and he met Patricio Pate-Pate. Eventually the Vargas family got over their anger. Ruperto returned to Chile to live on his own terms at El Coihue. Patricio came with him. Ruperto set out to plant trees, where his forefathers had cut down, pillaged and burned.

The day we met Patricio was the day that 600 million of the earth's people watched man take the first step on the surface of the moon. There was no television at El Coihue so we could not have joined them had we wanted to. There was no radio either, because Ruperto had forgotten to buy new batteries for the transistor. Maria Angelica accused him on forgetting on purpose and maybe he had.

Patricio lived in a forest glen and carved the *moai* of his native island out of ancient tree trunks at El Coihue. The day was warm and sunny, one of the very few this winter.

The soft dappled light splayed through the leaves of the branches overhead, rippled over Patricio's sweat-polished shoulders as he coaxed the brutal countenance of some sea deity with his chisels, every tender, sure stroke an echo of his people's soul. Watching him, you forget time and place, as he does, and you feel the energy flowing from his hands into the wood, from the wood back to his hands: the beaked nose, the cruel laughing mouth, the hard piercing eyes of the unforgiving Adversary (yet with such loving strokes of worship he brings him forth!) against which man has pitted his will and wile since time immemorial.

When at length he had put on the finishing touches, his whole body relaxed and a look of peace came over his face. He placed the statue in front of him and smiled, then he jumped up lithely and stretched.

"Do you like to eat trout?" He asked.

"Sure."

"I cook them well, but they are not real fish." He smiled.

"Oh?"

"They drink only fresh water. And a man is not a man either if he drinks nothing stronger than water, no?"

Nathan got the hint and that is the how, for twenty dollars, we acquired a mini Easter Island *moai*. We wrapped him up and sent him off by mail and, miraculously, he arrived in the United States and now he sits in the livingroom of our log house in northern British Columbia, a reminder of all that we don't understand about life on this earth and the neverending struggle to pull the masks from the Enigma.

One morning, a few days later, Ruperto stormed into our bedroom before the maid brought the breakfast tray. He was already fully dressed.

"Get your clothes on!" He said, "I want you to meet someone."

During the night, communists had taken over the *fundo* belonging to Doña Marí-Inez and her husband. They left for Santiago. Behind them, the agitators for land reform burned the old mansion to the ground. That's all Ruperto would say. Maybe that's all he knew.

I found myself wondering, of all things, about the fate of the white umbrella. Was it one of the things Doña Marí-Inez picked up in her haste? Or did it get left behind and burned?

On this day, Ruperto took us high up the mountain, past last year's pine plantation and past the house where the Mapuche Pablo and his three sons worked carving bowls and spoons and plates. This day we did not stop in for a visit. We rode single file through second growth forest and all the way to where a few virgin coihues had been spared from the lumbermen's slash fires. Ruperto stopped underneath an enormous coihue and gestured for us to dismount. It was dark under there and quiet, like in a cathedral, and a bit damp. Nothing grew in the shadow of the old giant. Its silver gray trunk was scarred; stubs of amputated limbs jutting out like the broken booms and gaffs of a storm-battered brig. Huge roots spread in all directions, an arboreal octopus with a death grip on the living earth.

"This tree," says Ruperto, "was here long before Columbus discovered America."

The way he says it makes you feel that he is speaking of a revered ancestor. We did not understand then about the feeling for land and for trees. We were nomads, not ready for commitments to anywhere in particular. We were at home in the world, which is vastly different from feeling yourself the guardian of a certain portion of the earth.

"Looks to be a thousand years old!" Nathan says.

Ruperto nods. "This tree has stood through the turmoil of the centuries, to triumph as the sovereign of the forest. It now holds the soil and the sky," he says with solemnity. "And legal title to El Coihue," he adds.

"You're joking?"

"I am not joking. When those *coyotes* of the Agrarian Reform come to take over El Coihue, they'll have something to howl about!" He says with vehemence. "This land already belongs to the true sons of Chile. To the *coihues* and *araucarias* and the pines."

"How?"

"I'm a lawyer, remember. From a long line of distinguished members of the profession. This deed is my single most important contribution."

He let loose one of his peculiar shouts that sounds like a bull moose on the make and that he used to call his men to work, to announce his arrival at the house, to herd cattle, and to express the inexpressible from the core concealed inside of this outward buffoon; of this man who grew up and then changed his mind and returned to the chaotic audacity of youth, to remain a living protest, a childlike outrage, in the face of corruption and hypocrisy.

Ruperto was quiet on the ride back down through the forest, where light flowed through the foliage the way I had once seen a candle flicker through an aquarium. We were feeling very close to Ruperto and at the same time we knew that it was time for us to move on.

Our horses gather around us eagerly, knowing in the way horses know things, that the time has come to leave the confines of this one pasture where they have been getting their ration of oats regularly every day and where they have spent much time standing under a clump of large trees, watching the rain fall. It is time now to go find new pastures over the next hill.

Beyond this valley somewhere, we'll come upon a stretch of beach and sit late into the night under a starry sky and watch the moon rise over the ocean and maybe then we can imagine the moon back to the way it was before an American flag got planted on the lunar surface.

Because I want to believe that the world is huge and flat; I don't want to know it is just one infinitesimal speck whirling around in space, with pictures from away out there to prove it.

Because I need to feel the world roll out beneath the hooves of my horse; I don't want technology to yank the rug right out from under us and leave us suspended on electric waves, gnats caught in a spider's web.

And there on the beach, or on the top of a mountain or on a plain somewhere, we'll feel closer to Ruperto than we do with the walls closing in on us in his and Maria Angelica's house.

Nathan's Diary, July 22:

I tossed a rope around Maracas neck and jumped on to bring him over to the house to saddle up - and WOW what a powder keg of energy! He galloped, cut, bucked, snorted, reared, and spun around. I was surprised to find myself still on board, holding his mane with one hand and pressing my knees tightly against his sides. By the time we had reached the house, I felt like a veteran rodeo-star with floating kidneys and a Marlboro hangover.

Elly had made a new pair of saddlebags out of tough green canvas, this time with different pockets and pouches for our humble possessions: tent, tools, medicines, clothing. We had to get new shoes on Pampero before putting the pack on and things kept turning up (a book, leather strap, medicine, etc) for which we had to find space. Finally at 10:30, we were off. Ruperto walked aways up the road with us, then stood and watched as we crossed the river and began to ascend the mountain which separated us from Lake Calico.

Mud, mud and more mud! After the heavy rains of the preceding week, the cart path we followed up over the mountain was a river of muck. The horses slid, sunk in, strained forward so that by the time we reached the top, they were breathing hard and sweating. The effort, after three weeks of rest was double. They had put on weight, but also lost some of their condition.

The rain forest was so thick that I could see only a few yards from the road. They were mostly young trees, perhaps twenty or thirty years old, which had grown up after the lumbering and burning. Here and there I caught a glimpse of the national flower shining like a red lantern in the green shadows - the coihue, a vine that lives symbiotically with the trees. Many trees were budding in the spring air, and some bushes were already sprouting.

It felt wonderful to be back in the saddle, alone and wandering slowly through the countryside. I felt a peace I had not achieved while resting at the Vargas ranch - a sense of liberation, as when a ship leaves port and enters the open ocean. It was a departure from the restless activity and accumulated possessions and anxieties of the urbane and security minded, a renewed affirmation of the simple mobile life, of belonging nowhere and everywhere, of possessing nothing yet being in possession of all.

Chaco was ecstatic, back in the lead again, heading up a new trail with all new smells and sights and sounds to explore. The long rest had done him good. He had grown into himself, big and strong.

The journey over the next few weeks became about trying to time departures for when the deluge let up, about finding cover during the worst of the storms, about learning to endure the winter rains of southern Chile. During the month of July, half a meter of rain fell in the Lakes District. That is enough to overflow your bathtub. In a season, three meters of rain falls and that would go all the way up to the ceiling of your bathroom.

Like a winter-numbed earthworm, the rutted road into the coal mining town of Curanilahue slithers down a moss-banked gulch, elbows back listlessly and spills us out of the dense woods into a smog-filled hollow. Uneven tiers of makeshift shanties cling to the muddy hillsides. The drumming of the rain on the corduroy sea of rusty tin roofs throws me back to a tropical downpour in our Venezuelan barrio *with Chelito careening stark naked down the street, red mud squishing between his toes and splashing his face, yelling **aguacero**, **aguacero** with happy abandon.*

*The **barrio** was Technicolor dynamite, boiling with clatter and red-chatreuse-green-every-shade-of-blue-purple-day-glo-rainbow-yellow-pink. This is a silent black and white flick.*

Here nothing moves. No one shouts.

*We leave the road for a shortcut down a steep pathway between gray shacks as a train clanks into the station below and through the ground fog laid down by the steam locomotive, coal blackened workers shuffle silently up the crooked streets. Not even looking at our rain soaked gestalts, they disappear behind doors and we continue on through the empty streets of the town, breathing sulfurous air, and finding our way to the green and white barracks of the **carabineros**.*

When I walk in to see if we're okay to keep our horses here overnight, Caicique marches through the gate, up the concrete pathway and right up to the porch behind me. The staff sergeant is a big fellow who is amused by this and he smiles wide. His is the first smile we have seen in a very long time, going from one coal soaked mining ghetto to the next. He is very glad to be of assistance, he tells us, and suggests we go up the hill to the parish where, he assures us, the Jesuits will be glad to provide shelter for road weary travelers such as ourselves.

It rained continuously through the night and the next day, so we stayed put in this clamshell town buried in fog and coal dust. On the second evening, we went out looking for something to do and were drawn to the *plaza* by a loudspeaker that spit static from the second story of the town hall:

"Tonight Doctor Rafael Carmona will lecture on the history of the labor movement in Chile. All members of the working class are welcome."

Small clusters of miners are gathered in the dim light of a bare lightbulb at the edge of the *plaza*. They begin to disperse now; boots tromp wearily off into the mist. Only one miner knocks the coal dust off his helmet and heads for the open portal. We follow in tow, up a narrow wooden staircase that siphons us into a long, dark hallway.

At the end of the hallway, we fall right through the looking glass and find ourselves standing in a brightly lit room. All the walls are painted scarlet red.

A Sherman tank lurches right at us from a life-size photograph and we stand face to face with a young student being crushed under iron tread. Large black letters proclaim: YANKEE IMPERIALISTS TOPPLE DEMOCRACY. The miner ambles on past and finds a seat towards the front of the room. We remain standing face to face with the dying student and right in line with the bayonet held by a GI in the other giant picture next to it, not knowing, at this moment what is up and what is down.

Have we walked into a cell of the MIR? But right in the town hall? How can this be? Red cells are usually secret and out of sight, aren't they? You don't actually expect a *red cell* literally to be red! MIR, the Leftist Revolutionary Movement, is made up of people who meet surreptitiously in hidden places, who pass information in secret codes and who believe kidnapping and setting off bombs in public places are legitimate steps on the road to independence; they don't hold meetings, like this. This much, we thought, we knew.

The scene playing out in front of the red room is even more amazing. Against a backdrop of posters depicting the life and death of Ché Guevara (Ché in jungle fatigues, Ché doctoring a wounded comrade; Ché grinning from a speaker's platform in Havana; Ché dead on a slab of concrete with a Green Beret standing guard at his side), two uniformed, but unarmed Carabineros are debating the legality of holding tonight's meeting with an intense young man.

"Our apologies to you, doctor," says the corporal, "but the governor has ordered this meeting closed."

"My friend, under the constitution of Chile, he cannot legally prohibit any peaceful gathering." The words of the young doctor carry the gentle assurance of a medical expert diagnosing a common ill.

"Doctor, please understand. We have no personal choice in the matter. Our duty is to defend the Constitution."

"The core of which is the right of citizens to assemble."

This said, he hands over a pink slip to the corporal. "Here is our permit to meet. Issued this afternoon by the office of the mayor. And now, if you would like to join us, I shall begin tonight's lecture."

Doctor Carmona does not wait for their answer. He opens his black satchel and takes out two books and lays them on the table in front of him. He looks up and smiles at no one in particular. The tips of all ten fingers touch the tabletop.

"An idea whose time has come is stronger than mace or gun."

His eloquence sends chills down my spine as he speaks of more children dying every year in Chile from preventable causes, than rebels during the entire Cuban war of liberation. The smoke from the coal miners' cigarettes fills the air and his hands weave cat's cradles in front of the posters of Ché Guevara. The uniformed *carabineros* sit quietly listening, caps in hand.

So many years later now, I am grappling to comprehend how reasonable men such as these *carabineros* could have followed orders from General Pinochet to draw weapons and summarily fire them into such men as sat next to them then: coal-dusty miners, tired from the long night underground, humble, working-class people.

And how this defiantly scarlet room, this almost whimsical symbol of a Chile intoxicated by the freedom of political expression could mutate into torture chambers, where the blood of innocent victims splattered the walls with red.

If this could have happened in Chile, it can happen anywhere. Anytime.

And as I sit here in my log house, grappling with what it all means to me, now so far away, I go downstairs for a break from writing this book, this chapter. It is after one in the morning. I flip through the channels of the satellite. And there it is: a documentary of the return of a film maker to his native Chile, twenty-three years after he filmed the days of the coup. His story is about memory and memories.

A female student who is being filmed as she watches the documentary from the coup speaks through her tears. "I am so proud," she says, "so proud of my people for daring to dream."

Yes, that is what Chile is to us!

Not was.

It is.

I feel hopeful, looking at the face of this student and the others with her. They connect back with the Chile we knew. They will pick up their long tradition of freedom and they will weave it forward from there. In their faces, I recognize the faces of the students in the sixties when we believed we could save the world and set out to do this, everyone in a different way.

They have wonderful faces, these students of the nineties in Chile, mirrors of dreams and aspirations. And the pain they feel for what happened back then will propel them forward to make a better world.

When the doctor opens the floor to questions, one of the miners stands up and turns around and looks directly at us and he says:

"It would appear we have visitors here tonight. Would the *señores* care to identify themselves and explain their presence to us!"

His tone is not friendly.

"Our Union has had more than enough meddling from the CIA!" Says the miner, awaiting a response from us.

We hesitate. How can we tell him about riding horseback across the land? How can we tell him we came here because there was nothing else going on in town? I wish we had something of substance to offer this man, even if it be from the wrong side of the political spectrum.

"I can assure you," says the young doctor, who does not know us, "that this young couple is sympathetic to our struggle."

His eyes are very intense and they connect with Nathan's and Nathan begins to tell the small group of miners about our life in the *barrio*. He tells them how we were recruited by *Acción en Venezuela* from the Harvard campus, to work in community development in the *barrios* in Venezuela. And how angry we were when we learned that *Acción* was a front for the CIA and our real job was to gather information about the state of political unrest in the *barrios*. Nathan tells the miners that we can identify with their suspicion of us now. They are right to be watchful of the CIA.

The miner sits back down. Maybe he believes Nathan, maybe he does not. Either way, will it make any difference for him? This man grovels for subsistence in the bowels of the earth. He goes down into the most dangerous mine in Chile, where accidents happen daily and the coal extracted is so low grade that there is no possible way that his life can become any brighter, no matter who holds up what political beacon.

The message of this red room, allowed to exist right here in the open, seems suddenly clear: protest all you want, working men. But know this: we can close the mine any day. Then where will you be? Of the thousands of miners, only a handful are here. If the few cause disruptions, who will the hungry mob turn upon?

I watch the young doctor speak with passionate intensity about the coal miners of Chile being pioneers in unionism, the facts and the figures and the very eloquence of his speech sending my mind wandering back again to Puerto Cabello. We were part of a dynamic and idealistic group of students who came

139

to Venezuela to help the people of the *barrio* help themselves. Some of the group went back home when we realized we were to be tentacles of the CIA, to help determine if and when American intervention might be called upon to prevent a Cuban style revolution in Venezuela.

Nathan and I stopped sending in monthly reports then and just lived in our *rancho* in Barrio Universitario and did what we could. Nathan worked with Benito on a stone retaining wall for a road in front of his shack and they named it Calle El Milagro. I talked about birth control with Dorka, who was eighteen and had four kids. And we found a family in the American enclave in Valencia where Victor could live and study, a foreign exchange student in his own country. And we had goats and chickens in our backyard. When *Acción* wanted to send in a film crew to stage a documentary of a-day-in-the-life-of-a-volunteer-couple, living and working shoulder to shoulder with the people in the *barrio*, we said sure come stay with us and follow us around if you want.

They wanted to stage the whole thing in a day, maybe two.

We wanted it all to be real.

We would not compromise on reality so no film crew came. I bought a Pentax camera and Dorka and Antonio and Cruz and Angelica and José and so many others let me follow them around and I was more comfortable like that, documenting lives as they were, not trying to change them according to some ideology or concept of social structure.

Dr. Carmona, who thought that by our presence in the red room he knew what we were about, invited Nathan to his house the following evening. He invited me too, but I didn't go. It wasn't my kind of thing.

This guy is all energy, wired on an evangelical adrenaline rush like I've seen before, in other places, and he's talking as he ushers me into his pad at the rear of the clinic with a metal cot crammed in-between a medicine cabinet and the antique Fridgidaire. "Want something to eat? Or drink? Maybe a beer?" He opens the beat-up fridge and there's nothing in it except beer and a row of vaccine bottles, syringes, and a tray of blood samples in test tubes. He closes it and grabs the bottle of red wine off a shelf, waving me toward the small table with cigarette burns around the edges and two metal chairs with the paint chipping off. I sit at the table, sipping Merlot and the smell of rubbing alcohol and disinfectants makes me feel like a kid on the edge of my chair, waiting for a nurse ten feet tall to show up with a large needle and I toss down the glass of red and he refills it without missing a beat. "You and I, not much difference. Both on a mission." And, without a pause: "I felt it at once." I watch his delicate surgeon's hands that deliver babies and are not made for carrying guns or planting bombs under cars, as he dangles dream catchers in front of me. He is doing all the talking and he never takes his eyes off me, very sure of himself because it works so well on miners and students and Indians. Once he has snagged you with his eyes, he never lets go as he circles around you and you know he feels your resistance slipping as he paints with the brutal colors of women bleeding to death in childbirth and moon-faced babies that would have lived if El Ministerio had given more money to the clinics. Suddenly he's talking with his face very close to mine, now about the killing of the Kennedys and Martin Luther King and the students at Kent State and the disillusionment I must feel and he's got it all figured out about an expatriate on horseback. He is playing me and slowly I start to play him back because he doesn't know anything about me building a school one brick at time in the barrio with Benito and Antonio and too much rum in the tropical sun because I don't believe in violence and I convinced the hawks on the draft board why I wouldn't go to Vietnam. But he keeps on casting and reeling, never letting go, not hearing what I'm saying about Gandhi because it doesn't mesh with his agenda. His intensity is contagious. His face is a déjà vu of Mac MacKensie's, this place a double exposure of Mac's attic off Brattle Street. 1959/1969, from then to now, there to here, and it's all one place, one time. Wall-to-wall cigarette smoke and a pyra-mid of Budweiser cans rises off the pool table and we're brain-storm-ing blueprints for TOCSIN and SDS, another all-nighter because the next day we're heading out, campus to campus, all across the nation and a roller coaster of a ride with two hundred thousand showing up at the D.C. rally. The highest of highs! And then, free fall into the abyss. Everything we believe in being gunned down. And we distrust our own dream more than the CIA and our charisma and the eagerness of peo-ple to follow because they won't think for themselves. They'll march to any drummer and even drink Kool-Aid with cyanide in it if you say it the way they want to hear it and make them feel more important than they really are. And when Mac sees this, he erases his identity and evaporates into Africa to do something "insignificant, but worthwhile," and no one sees him again. Maybe that's why I'm here now at this table drinking too much red, not wanting to convince Carmona, but wanting him to convince me that embalming a revolution in a novel isn't good enough. I tell him that I will think about it, knowing I can never stop thinking about it. I leave him standing in his open doorway watching me disappear like Mac into the night.

When Nathan returned, he opened and closed the door quietly. But the ideas he brought in with him invaded the room like a swarm of locusts, bouncing off the walls of the parish guestroom with the picture of Christ above the headboard and the Madonna on the wall by the wash stand window and I woke up.

"What time is it?"

"I thought you were asleep," Nathan says and sounds glad that I was not.

"So what time is it?"

"Late."

"How late?"

"Almost three."

"He must have covered a lot of history!"

"Yes. And... he offered me.... offered us, a job as liaisons. We'd be stationed in Montevideo and link the revolutionary movements in South America and North America."

The locusts were attacking the world as I knew it! I sat up in bed, wide awake now.

"Boy, he sure got you going!"

"They need people like us."

"I'll bet! I don't want to get shot."

"We wouldn't be in the front line."

"And you'd quit the ride just like that to go play revolutionary? What about the horses?"

"Rafael has a friend where we can leave them."

"That's nice."

We talked about the pull between wanting to be part of something and be free of everything. We talked about identifying with South America. We talked about Luis, who brought the urchins down from the *barrios* of Caracas to paint butterflies and flowers all over the Plaza Bolivar. They stalled the traffic and, for one brief moment, we believed with Luis that art might really conquer the world. We talked about Benito and helping him make his life better, one rock at time for Calle El Milagro and we talked about why Swedes are so lost and so unhappy in the Welfare State and about Nathan being the heir of a great Unitarian tradition: four generations of ministers. He was the one picked for his time.

"Isn't this the same choice you already made, not to preach to people, not to pretend to lead them, not to save them?"

When the pale light of the new dawn seeped in through the parish window, we curled up together, very close, in the narrow bed which was meant for one. Our own version of commitment came not from inside an ideological framework, not through following the rules of any established movement; our chosen task was to stretch the limits of personal freedom. It wasn't for us to lead others, just blaze a new trail. A selfish choice?

Some may think so.

Who is to say?

As we rode away, out of the hollow filled with coal smog where a train just disgorged another shift of miners, I felt very sad. Then a boy, maybe nine, came running down a trail from between the shacks and he ran right up next to us and he smiled with a big open face and he asked to pet our horses and we stopped so he could pet them all in turn and his hands were fine and sensitive and he stroked each horse with feeling and he said:

"Someday, I will have a horse just like your paint mare."

And I believed that he would someday ride out of this town and not live underground in the mines and I felt much better.

A few days later, we would awaken to the morning bell at *fundo* Quilpolemo and look through lace curtains as the day began, the same as it had for two hundred years: an oxcart laboriously advancing across the cobblestones, bringing water in oak barrels, women and children emerging from the communal bakery with loaves of bread and two old men slowly sweeping the courtyard with brooms made of alder bows.

The maid brought us breakfast on a tray: poached eggs in silver porringers, tea and hot milk in silver pots and monogrammed linen napkins, folded to resemble a swan. We leaned back against hand-embroidered pillows and I slowed my breathing way down to hold onto this moment in which *War and Peace* had become transposed to Chile and Nathan and I swept into the epic. I wanted to savor this illusion of tranquility and permanence and forget what we had learned the night before from *señora* Irma Caceres de Almeyda, our beautiful hostess.

"Change is inevitable," said *señora* Irma and she smiled politely across the coffee table and ran the tips of her long fingers around the collar of her cashmere turtleneck. "It is our role now to guide the people into our New Society."

"You see no contradiction in being a landowner and a Marxist?" Nathan asked in his direct way.

"When the coalition of the left comes to power after next year's election, we shall turn over the *fundo* to the *peons*."

"You are not afraid the extremists will just take over your land in the meantime?" She smiled. She told us of her husband, Clodomiro, who was teaching at the University in Santiago, paving the way for the Marxist coalition that would win the next election. She answered with a question.

"Have you heard of the Camelot Plan?" She did not pause to find out if we had. "I had a visit from an American sociologist last year. He was also very interested in the history of Quilpolemo and our plans for the future. Do you know why?"

"He turned out to be CIA?"

Her deep brown eyes revealed no surprise that we should have known, or guessed. "The CIA ran an extensive survey in Chile to find if there was support for a coup amongst landowners and business people."

"And is there?"

"Violence is alien to our tradition," said the wife of the man who wrote the blueprint for a Marxist government in Chile. She took another cigarette out of a monogrammed gold case and inserted it into the holder. "Your Camelot Plan is bound to fail."

They had it all figured out, *señora* Irma and her husband Clodomiro.

Salvador Allende did indeed become president-elect in Chile. Clodomiro became his foreign minister.

They lasted but a season.

*We stopped atop the ridge for one last look at the old **fundo**. The giant **coihues** on the northern edge of Quilpolemo were being cut down, chopped into pieces and taken away on trucks. We remained there for ten minutes, maybe twenty, and listened to the steady tapping of four axes in cadence. Then the tree fallers scurried off to a safe distance while, for one interminable moment, the silver-bodied regent remained perfectly balanced under a spacious crown of spring leaves. A gust of wind came up the valley and with a bullwhip crack, the kingpin came thundering down. In the quiet of the aftermath, a sparrow hawk screeched and we rode on down the other side of the mountain.*

As I look now with the hindsight of the events that followed on September 11, 1973, when General Pinochet took power and Salvador Allende took his own life, I see a people who believed themselves sovereign in their faraway land, cradled between the mountains and the sea. An image comes to me of a young girl, her long hair blowing in the spring breeze, standing by a road to hitch a ride, confident in that she knows who she is and that this knowledge will protect her from the Highwayman.

It doesn't.

Chile's proud tradition as the oldest democracy in South America did not protect her from the Behemoth from the north, either.

Henry Kissinger, then US Secretary of State, said in 1970:

"I don't see why we need to stand by and watch a country go communist due to the irresponsibility of its own people."

The Chileans have an expression when someone pretends not to understand, *hacerce la sueca*, turn into a Swede. After a year of riding the length of the country, I wrote an essay that I called 'A Swede Turning Chilean'.

It was a declaration of love for this singular nation that embodied all the contradictory flamboyance of the sixties, a country where everything was possible, where Ruperto Vargas could be both an *enfant terrible* and a man of influence.

Chile became our spiritual homeland.

Salvador Allende became the first democratically elected Marxist president in the world, while we were riding through the *sierra* of Peru. One thousand days later, his reign and his life ended when the military bombed La

145

Moneda, the presidential palace. The dreams of Chile, like the sixties' dreams elsewhere, were turned into a nightmare of political oppression.

We fear what fate may have come to the fervent young doctor who spoke to a handful of miners in the red room in Curanilahue. Individuals were summarily executed by Pinochet for much less than openly proclaiming the revolutionary overthrow of the government.

Of Clodomiro and *señora* Irma we know, because in the winter of 1973, a man walked through the snow and knocked on the door to our log cabin in Northern British Columbia. He had to bend way down to fit through the doorway because the little homestead cabin had sunk into the ground over the years. I still don't know how he found us here.

He was an aid, he told us, at the military hospital on Dawson Island in Magallanes, where Clodomiro Almeyda and so many other leaders from the Allende government were taken as prisoners after the coup. He told us of a sick and broken man.

Ruperto would be okay. I don't know this for sure, but I want to believe that, for many years, Ruperto would ride up to the high ridge where the giant *coihue* stood and he would call out his vibrating baritone yodel across the valley; an ode to the sovereign individual. And that the artisans of El Coihue would continue carving their gods and their bowls and, eventually, things would become all right again in this and the other valleys of Chile.

We followed a cart road that lifted us toward a patch of blue and, cresting the bluff, waltzed down out of the forest into rolling drunk farm land where poppies bobbed and hill-bottom puddles were as big as ponds and fence posts had to sink or swim, where putty-legged calves bucked and skated the mud and where birds sang overtime, where fresh wash sucked up sunshine on lines and kitchen doors were left open.

We trotted through a village with TV antennas sprouting through old roofing tiles, the horses pulling at their bits, smelling the new grass along the sidewalk and as we passed a Catholic Mission, the school children lined up on the low stone wall and a young nun in white led them in song:

*"Caminando, the travellers are going on, **se van caminando, caminando**..."*

At the end of the day, we came to a beach.

Spider crabs and sand pipers retreated from advancing hooves on the smooth black sand as we rode towards a driftwood shack that clung to the dunes where wildflowers grew thickly, a short distance above the hedge of debris tossed up by winter storms. A torn veil net waved from a dwarf pine, a broken oar stood by the open door and up under the eaves above the crooked window someone had etched with charcoal in childlike scrawl:

NUESTRO CHILECITO: our little Chile.

A dip-billed pelican rose off the rusty roof made of hammered-out tin cans and flapped lazily northwards above the endless curve of white breakers.

We lined the saddles up on the silver trunk of a fallen tree and let the horses loose to graze the spring-green troughs between the dunes. Elly picked dandelion greens and penca stalks for a salad and I collected mussels and crabs from the tidal pools for a clambake.

And late into the soft spring night, as the flames danced in front of the lopsided shack and the swells reclaimed the territory lost to the ebb, I tossed mussel shells into the heap of so many seasons before me.

Now and then, a gust shaved the top of the dunes and the scrub pines leaned against their bare-knuckled grip on the shifting sand.

In the morning, all tracks would be gone.

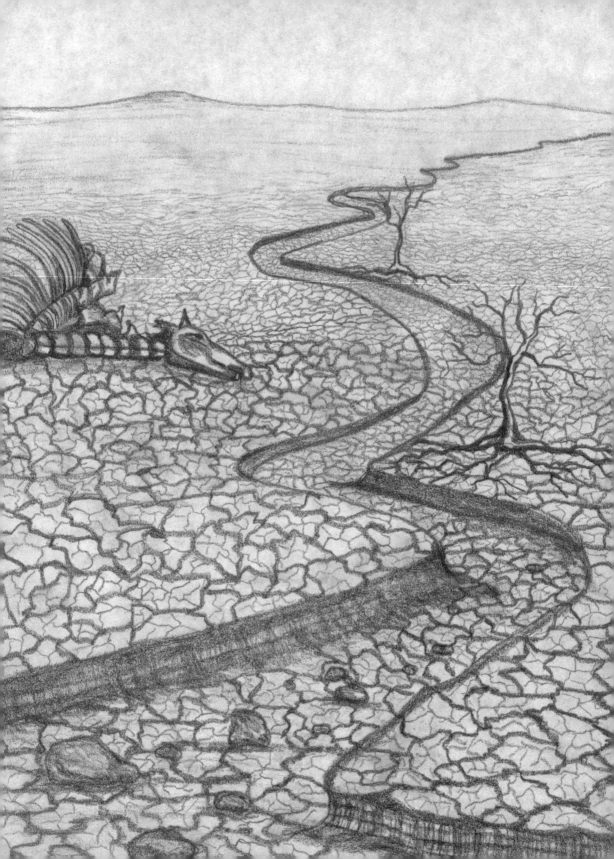

THE WHITE COLT

Between the south of Chile, where it rains up to three meters in a year and the north where it does not rain, not ever, there is a transition zone, the Norte Chico.

This arid land is dependent on the winds to come in from the south, bringing rain. For the past three years the winds had, instead, come out of the Norte Grande and brought the desert down with them. We rode into ranching country that had not seen rain for three seasons.

The drought in the Norte Chico has for me a shape, a voice. It drags itself along, one painful step after one painfully slow step in the bone-dry *arroyo* between withered bushes, its belly swollen the way a white balloon looks filled with water. But you knew there is no water in there, no feed either. Just hunger gas. Seeing us, the white colt lifts its head and lets out a hoarse wail, allowing itself a feeble moment of futile hope.

Now I understood about Guillermo making haste to return home so he could fetch his gun and return with two bullets: one for his mare with the broken leg and the other one for her suckling colt with no milk to drink.

And I understood that it was the same with the colt as with the pups the stray bitch whelped in the backyard of our *barrio* shanty. They were yelping more than usual one day. I went to look. I found a wriggling, twitching mess of white maggots and pups. One pup was half eaten up from behind, screaming in his blind helplessness. I was the only one there. I could not just stand by in horror. I grabbed a rock out of the stone wall and began to smash the mass of puppies and maggots until, at last, the only sound left was of my own crying. The surviving maggots continued their feast, now on inert flesh. I went to the back of the *rancho* and got a basin of water and washed my hands for a long time.

Our neighbors, hearing of me stoning the pups to death, shook their heads and pitied me.

"Killing a dog is bad luck," they said.

"The worms were eating them alive!" I said.

"*Así és*; that's nature's way. Not for us to change."

On our ride up the Americas, we carried no gun that we might use now to bring a swift end to the colt's slow journey towards certain death. How could we stand by and watch such unspeakable suffering?

"Let's feed him some oats," Nathan says.

"No!"

"We can spare some," Nathan says.

"So that, what? He can suffer a little longer?"

"I thought you were the one who wanted to take care of all the unwanted horses in the world?" Nathan says.

"There is no hope for this one. Please do something! Can't you please do something!" I was crying. "You have killed sheep before. You can use the knife."

"I can't kill a horse," says Nathan.

And at that point, he could not. He didn't know then that later on he would, when it was the only thing left to do. In this, he had much more courage than I.

The white colt stayed by the withered bushes with the two other emaciated horses, the glimmer of hope now extinguished in his eyes and we rode away on our well-fed horses, knowing that up ahead, towards evening, we would arrive at a *carabinero* stable and that we were assured hay and grain and water there.

The scorching silence of the empty pastures of the Norte Chico was terrifying. For the first time, that night, we became apprehensive of what might lie up ahead. The desert had come to meet us and caught us unprepared.

We had not planned to come this way by horse. If you had told us, when we chugged south along the Pacific coast on the Utlande at 5 knots an hour, we would be going north on horseback, we would have said no way! Not here! We saw nothing but sterile desert, all the way down from northern Peru, for days and days! We would have painted a picture for you of the verdant *pampas* and told you: that's where we will be heading!

So why?

If we were to cross the Andes from central Chile back into Argentina and the green *pampas* to continue north, we would end up in Bolivia. Because of events in Venezuela in 1965, that was a place we did not want to be.

One such event took place in the village of Aroa. We had spent a couple of days riding mules in the hinterlands, visiting subsistence farmers in the area, part of background studies for a book Nathan was writing on urban migration. We had just sat down to dinner when three armed men came and told us to come with them. They marched us through the dark streets before cocked guns and drawn machetes.

The guardsmen believed they had captured Chè Guevara himself, because Nathan's beard rendered a one-point resemblance to the revolutionary. In me they saw Tanya, his companion in arms, because of my blonde hair. They threw us in the local jail. Around midnight a large black car appeared. We were told to get in. No explanations were given.

Nathan was put in the front seat, a guard with a semi-automatic by his side. They sat me down in the back seat, flanked by two guards, their guns on the ready toward Nathan's back. No one spoke. When they stopped the car on a dark and lonely stretch of road, I tasted fear. I forced myself to swallow it deep down so the guards would not catch the scent of it and I tried to think of something to say. Should I ask them for a cigarette? Make a comment on what a clear and beautiful night it was? Tell them about the *barrio*, about working for Acción and about the book we were preparing with collaboration from their own Instituto del Caribe de Antropologia? I decided I would ask for a cigarette, even though I didn't much like the sound of it; too much like a prisoner's last request.

The guard to my left answered. "Sorry, *señora*. I don't smoke," he said.

The driver got out of the car to urinate and then we continued on to the provincial capital of San Felipe. They kept us in the jail there for the next two days while our courtesy visas and references were checked out. Then the governor called and bawled us out for being such fools as to ride through the hills and putting the whole state on red alert.

"You could have gotten yourselves shot!" He said, "There is guerilla activity in the mountains. Infiltration from Cuba. People are nervous."

This happened to us in a country where we worked in community development for two years and where we knew people in high places. It happened after we had duly introduced ourselves to the authorities in Aroa, stating the purpose of our muleback excursion into the hinterland. What might happen to us in Bolivia if we rode through the backcountry? Bolivia had no tradition of the *pasajero* on horseback that opened doors and made our journey self-explanatory in the Patagonia. Bolivia didn't have the freedom of expression of the Chile we had come to know.

Bolivia was where Chè Guevara, a doctor and an educated man fought a battle in the hills on behalf of the people. Bolivia is where Chè was shot to death, just two years before. Would the authorities believe that we were just saddle tramps passing through? We thought the risk of a misunderstanding too great to chance riding through Bolivia.

After the idyllic landscape of south and central Chile, the challenge of crossing a desert appealed to us. The desert, we thought, would be a bit like the Patagonia, but hot instead of cold and without the wind. The desert would teach us what we needed to know as we went along, as the Patagonia had taught us, the way Guillermo said that it would.

With the noon sun and the dust chasing us, we arrive at a little rest stop next to the dirt road in a *quebrada* called Pejerreyes where a man named Francisco Duran has brought a bale of alfalfa for us from Ovalle in his vintage yellow bus that earns him a living, taking people to market on Wednesdays and Saturdays. Today is Thursday.

Francisco Duran hails from Antofagasta. In the cool of the evening, he comes over to tell us of the sandstorms over the salt flats between Antofagasta and San Pedro de Atacama. Storms rage for days sometimes, he says, driving a man around in circles. Even a man like him, Francisco Duran, who knew his way and who made a living taking freight on a mule train back then.

Francisco Duran has some well-considered advice for us.

"Get a covered wagon," he says. "A wagon is the only way for you to cross the desert. There is your shade, your water and your feed. And a place for your dog."

After Francisco Duran bids us good night, Nathan and I stay up late into the night talking about driving up the Pan-American as he suggested, hitching up two of the horses, tying the other two behind the wagon and switching teams every few hours.

He's right about the dog. We've been getting an earlier start, leaving in the pre-dawn darkness at five or six. But the distances are getting longer. There are fewer places to stop. There is no shade.

A wagon would solve some problems. And create an enormous new one. We'd be tied to a strip of asphalt, moving along at four miles an hour, with trucks whistling by. Travelling in a wagon, we would find no trail along the rocks and patches of sand, close to water's edge, where the night's mist off the ocean gets trapped and produces a carpet of pink flowers. There would be nothing like that along the Pan-American. No wet cool sands where Pampero would roll over and over; no waves for Chaco to romp in.

A wagon would mean the loss of our freedom. The whole terminology involved with the hitching and driving of a wagon spells constraints. The collar, the neck yoke, the traces and holdbacks and the shafts, the tongue and the very lines for driving all connote restrictions.

And what about the hills? Further north there would be deeper *quebradas* than the one at Pejerreyes. We knew what effort it was for the gypsies' mule and old mare to pull uphill, even worse coming down with all the weight of the wagon pushing.

We're not good with itineraries that have to be followed and thinking too very much far in advance. We'll have to adjust to the desert, in our own way.

We're going to have to find feed, like we had in Ovalle and find someone, like we had Francisco Duran and find a place, such as this *quebrada* and avoid riding in the daytime. If we couldn't give Chaco a wagon, we'd have to give him the cool of the night instead.

In 1969, the *carabineros* still used horses, even up in the few towns and villages of the Norte Grande. In the South, we had learned we could count on the

full-hearted support of the *carabineros* most anywhere we stopped in. Now
we also had a letter, directing each and every commander of a post to give us
full collaboration. The letter was signed by the general of the *carabineros* in
Santiago. How we had come by this letter was because Ruperto Vargas introduced us to the General. The way things work in Chile is that when a member
of a family such as Ruperto's asks a favor of somebody, it is a done deal because such a family is related to everybody who is somebody in Chile.

On our way to the *reten* in Los Choros, we come upon an old woman in
black, resting in the lee of a big boulder. A scraggly donkey loaded with her
belongings stands patiently by her. Four emaciated goats huddle close to share
the shrinking shadow on the left side of the rock.

"The devil is playing tricks with us poor mortals," she says and crosses
herself repeatedly, not looking directly at us. "I roam the plains from east to
west and from north to south and this is all that is left of my good herd. And
now you come with these fat horses. I say the Devil is at large upon this land."

I feel blasphemous astride my shiny fat horse and with the carelessness of
the morning hours still over my face. I want to have something to say to her,
tell her about the pink flowers along the coast, not far from here, and about the
little shack down on the dunes with Nuestro Chilecito painted in childlike letters. I want to tell her that this beach, this shack is reachable, one step at a
time, if she would just head on slowly in one direction: south. But I don't say
any of those things. I just ask her the direction to Los Choros and she nods,
unfolds a bony arm: north.

The water boils in the tin can on her fire and she asks us to share her *máte*.
We squat on the sand and drink out of the same cup and the same straw. Then
we leave her by her rock and ride on northwards, feeling her dark eyes in our
backs.

At Los Choros, I have a nightmare: we're at the center of an enormous
disc, following a white line. As we move, the disc moves. The horses are
mere skeletons under parched hides, they're straining in their traces, stumbling on before the raised whip of a woman in a black cloak.

I wake up in a cold sweat, feeling trapped and scared and wanting to turn
around and go back south, before it is too late. Why do I see the futility in her
circles, but not in our own trek headlong into the longest and the driest desert

on earth?

What if?

There are so many of those. A horse could go lame. Chaco could get hurt, or one of us. We have no backup of any kind. No one expects us or would know to come looking for us if something went wrong out here.

I don't often think that way. If I did, I'd be busy building a nest somewhere and wearing pathways of familiarity to a neighborhood store and a job with a dental plan and a retirement package.

Thinking of a life run on parallel tracks puts me at peace with how things are in this here and this now. I get up and look out the window of the *carabinero reten* where we are spending the night. The horses are sleeping in the corral outside. The air outside is cool and crisp. I realize I am happy that there is nothing at all familiar about the path I'll take in the morning, because sameness is one thing that truly terrifies me. I snuggle up with Nathan and have no more nightmares.

We ride further into the desert, one step at a time. One day about three weeks later, we are travelling in the noonday heat when an oasis appears in the hazy distance. We've been trudging across lifeless dunes all morning. The air is so still you can hear the silence ring. The morning shadows have shrunk to thin lines directly below us. Chaco has already drank all the water in his canteen and we're down to the last lemon. The piece in my mouth feels like cotton rubbing against cotton. Ahead, the mirage hovers above the desert floor: an island of green, a mini jungle suspended between the scorching sand and the cloudless sky. You read about this sort of thing: mirages that taunt and then dissipate into heat waves, ever receding, luring the heat-crazed traveler further out into the wasteland with false promises of shade and cool water.

This island sinks slowly at our approach, until it is firmly anchored to the ground and we smell citrus blossoms in the air. But even as we ride up an avenue of eucalyptus saplings, along water reservoirs the size of hockey rinks, we have trouble believing that La Castilla isn't just going to evaporate into thin air.

The manager welcomes us in the name of Don Caesar Sumar and opens up the modest cinder block dwelling that is Don Caesar's house and also the guest-house.

By his deeds we come to know this singular man who pours millions into the desert so that lemon and orange trees may blossom, alfalfa fields bloom and tomatoes and cucumbers ripen. Life seems much too good to be true as later we tube about on the tepid waters in the reservoir and look at our four horses, knee deep in what is possibly the most expensive alfalfa field in all of South America. And we imagine Don Caesar surveying us all, godlike, from his private jet overhead.

Don Caesar looked down over the lifeless desert plain, so the story goes, imagining a subterranean lake, a kind of desert Atlantis. He decided he would bring this water to the surface. He would create a desert emerald, a landmark in this barrenness to feast his eyes upon during his frequent business trips between Santiago and Lima. Oasis La Castilla was born: a vision powered by five Worthington pumps and, ultimately, by the profitability of Don Ceasar Sumar's textile factories in Santiago and in Lima.

He tried to give La Castilla to the government, the manager tells us. They won't have it. Costs too much. He can't bear the thought of letting La Castilla revert to desert, so they keep pumping water from seventy feet below the desert floor, trying to find something more profitable than tomatoes to grow.

After three days of plenty, we leave La Castilla and ride on north in the early morning light. The desert closes a veil over the shimmering oasis behind us and, just like that, it is gone. We're alone again with the sand and the heat and with no capricious creation to look forward to, making you wonder: was this really real? Did this happen or was it just a dream and we're awake now with the mirage evaporating on the hot sand?

And does it really matter if it had been real or imaginary? It's all the same in this moment. Either way, now the oasis exists only as an ephemeral illusion, as memory.

On November 21, we cross the line, just north of Copiapo.
Officially now, this is THE ATACAMA DESERT.
It is the driest, the most sterile desert on earth.
Everybody, including the Carabineros who receive us after the grueling march to Huasco, tell us the same thing:
"You cannot cross the Atacama Desert on horseback!"
When Diego del Almagro, the Conquistador, tried to reach Santiago de Chile from Peru, via the Atacama, Indian slaves were forced to carry exhausted horses on stretchers. Indians were plentiful and horses were literally worth

their weight in gold. Thousands of Indians buckled under in the effort. The horses died too. I saw etchings of this desert march in a book in the amazing equestrian library belonging to Colonel Lepe, in Mexico City, two years later.

At this point, entering the desert, we had little idea of what lay ahead. After what we witnessed across the Norte Chico, we felt relief that now there would be no white colt with a muted scream for help appearing behind a dry bush. We would not chance upon an old shepherdess taking her skinny goats across the burned plainscape, in search of some scrap of vegetation that they might have missed on a previous day. There would be no more truckloads of emaciated goats and sheep and horses heading south. No more skeletons in the dry *arroyos* and no more people sitting in doorways and looking with empty eyes across barren lands, remembering what had been.

And no more would we have to feel blasphemous, riding into town on shiny, fat horses. We would not be meeting families who did without to buy another bale of alfalfa to feed an emaciated horse for another while, clinging to the hope that the rains would come and the land would turn green once more.

The reign of the desert was now absolute.

The two bales of alfalfa we sent on from Copiapo are waiting for us in the shade of the *posada* at Barquitos, which is a cinder block building right on the beach, bright pink and in the form of a ship. The owner welcomes us with open arms and insists we be his guests for dinner.

Everything worked perfectly on this our first day in the desert!

Not quite.

When we open the bale of alfalfa, sold to us by the *capataz* at a farm outside Copiapó, put on the ore train and then dropped off for us at Barquitos by the Carabineros' Paddy Wagon, we find a steaming, slimy mess.

The second bale is just the same as the first.

There isn't much use in cursing the *capataz* for selling us rotten feed. We have four hungry horses. What to do?

While we debate what we should do: let the horses starve or risk a fatal colic, our four equines approach the compost pile and, without so much as a fastidious wrinkle on their noses, they begin to munch on it.

I think now of all the horses we have fed all these years since, and how careful we are to discard anything that may be spoiled. How we introduce any new feed gradually, always water before feed, always give hay before grain, to minimize risk to the fragile equine digestive system, which has to push feed through a hundred feet of intestines. Excessive gas will kill, because there is no way out. You can punch a hole in the side of a cow to let the gases out and the cow will live. You do that to a horse and he will die of peritonitis.

We should have removed every last scrap of the putrid feed, watered the horses and groomed them extra carefully and tied Caicique up for the night. And hoped that they would forgive us for letting them stand there on empty stomachs while we ate too much and drank too much with the owner of Barquitos.

Instead, we leave them free to choose whether to eat or not to eat.

The next morning we wake up with a hangover and stomach cramps, from too much greasy food in our system. Next to the stern of the pink cinder block ship, the four horses are dozing peacefully. There isn't a scrap left of the putrid hay.

We feel foolish and very, very lucky as we move on to the town of Chanaral where there is a *carabinero* post and we will get proper feed for the horses. But in this town, which grew up around the Kennecott Mine, the captain of the *carabinero* tells us:

"We are not here to promote your North American Mission!"

"Didn't you receive a call from Copiapó? Didn't you tell them you had feed?"

The captain gets angry.

When we show him our letter of recommendation from headquarters in Santiago that has been a magic wand at every post, the captain gets angrier.

"Why don't you go see the manager at the mine about **your** problem?" He says.

I manage to keep my mouth shut and get back outside. I have absolutely no idea what we will do now. In all our many months in Chile, nothing like this ever happened. The *carabinero* and the Cavalry always went out of their way to help us in every possible way. The horses would receive the best of care and we were often invited to the homes of the *carabinero* for dinner, or to stay the night. No one had ever labeled us 'North American' before!

I am getting angry now and I feel like getting off my horse and going back in there and telling him: Hey, I am Swedish! And I certainly don't agree with US policy in Chile, but that is beside the point. You told Copiapó you had feed and would assist us. Now you are breaking your word. How is a mining company supposed to be able to help us feed our horses?

Before I have a chance to storm back in, the young constable on guard outside the reten turns to us.

"The company imports meat from Argentina, *señora,*" he says. "On the hoof."

I feel like kissing the man. Of course! Where there is cattle, there will be feed!

There are about forty head in the slaughterhouse corrals belonging to the mining company, big, black and white with long horns. The whole herd of them approach the horses, one timid ox pushing another timid ox ahead of him.

But our Argentine ponies aren't having any of this national brotherhood stuff; they head straight for the grub line. The steers follow, until flashing yellow teeth and iron shod hooves stop them short and turn them around in confusion. The steers stay in their corner with their big sad eyes watching the horses gobble up their feed.

The old man in charge shrugs: what's the difference? But we make a rope partition so that the good-hearted critters can finish their last supper in peace. Then we go for a dinner of rump roast in the mansion on the hill - what inconsistent monsters we are!

Our host, the mine manager, who is English and very proper, shows us a book written by a couple of former visitors, who drove a Citröen from Buenos Aires to New York in 1962. I take it with me to read at the guesthouse.

The two Englishmen don't make inspiring bedfellows, in spite of their overactive imaginations and production of drama. In their book, the small-time prospectors and hard working miners of this desert become lawless riff-raff and bandits ready to rob you blind the minute you have a flat tire. The book gives me a different perspective on the attitude we got from the *carabinero* sergeant.

I wonder what the two Citröen Brits would have made of the fishermen Nathan met in a harborside bar. Parched by the sun and withered by too much booze, they were a rough looking bunch we entrusted with the precious hay the mine gave us for the next leg. At five dollars each, the two bales were probably worth more than what they might catch in a day of fishing!

The fishermen agreed to bring two bales and two barrels of fresh water for us in their boat, in exchange for the two empty barrels, which were worth two dollars each. They would meet us about thirty kilometers up the coast, at a spot that went by the name of Pan de Azucar. They would be there, the day after tomorrow, at sundown.

We reach a cove by a large cone shaped rock around five in the afternoon. Pan de Azucar? Has to be. We unsaddle, gather some driftwood for a fire and sit down to wait.

The sun grows oblong on an empty horizon. The horses are getting restless. Pampero leads Maracas in a protest march along the beach in front of us. When I find a hunk of hard bread in the pack and start chewing on it, Caicique stomps over to give me his most indignant glare.

"Okay, okay, we'll all starve together. It didn't taste very good anyway."

"Worse than a bunch of kids!" Nathan says with an uptight edge to his voice. He walks out to the end of the point for a second time. What if the fishermen don't show? We're fifty kilometers from Chañaral, more than that from Las Bombas, which is inland. If we don't get supplies, we'd better saddle up and get going right away. The horses have plenty of reserves to use if they have to, after their three-day binge at the slaughterhouse corrals in Chañaral. But Chaco would never make it through the day without water.

Just before dark a skiff putt-putts around the point and into the cove. They can't pull in close because of the heavy ocean swell that would smash the boat against the shoreline rocks, so Nathan strips and wades out into the icy water. How bizarre it is that the waters off the desert are as cold as those of the North Atlantic! I, the landlubber, get behind the camera and snap away. The horses line up at water's edge and don't seem the least bit surprised when Nathan comes wading ashore with an eighty pound bale hoisted over his shoulders. Pampero forgets that he is mortally afraid of waves and runs right into the ocean to grab a couple of mouthfuls, nearly knocking both bale and Nathan into the salt water.

The fishermen roll the two barrels of fresh water into the ocean and the waves bring them in closer. I put a saddle back on India and ride her into the water and Nathan ties one end around the barrel and the other to the back of her saddle and she pulls it out of the sea. We siphon the water into our big cooking pot and the horses drink, one after the other until the whole forty-gallon drum is empty. Then we use the pot to cook rice for Chaco and ourselves.

When all this is done and the animals are snoozing contentedly, we throw some more driftwood on the embers. The water clucks gently against the rocks and out on the bay we can see the lights from the fishing boat. I feel a little ashamed for having doubted, even for a moment, that they would come through for us. I am learning that in this desert, where we are all so alone and vulnerable, there is a sense of community and of trust between strangers.

I feel oddly secure in this soft silent nothingness, this demanding place where you must always keep on the move, struggling onwards: to the next watering place, the next bale of hay.

I like that.

The next bale is supposed to be at a mine called Las Bombas. And so it is, when we arrived in the early afternoon. The Kennecott Mine gave it to us, put it on the ore train and here it is, under a big Pimento tree. A perfect place for us to sleep a few hours, before we take off for the long march inland to a trucker's stop called Charito, where we arranged for another one of the Kennecott bales to be dropped off.

A miner named Pedro, who lives with his son in a cubicle just big enough to hold two sagging spring beds, will hear of no such thing.

"The sap dripping all night will turn you *loco*," he says.

To save us from such a fate, he doubles up with his son in one bed. He insists that Nathan and I share the other. After a few hours of such comfort, our poor backs are killing us. The stuffiness of the tin cubicle makes you gasp for air. We sneak out and lie down for an hour under the tree. Then, before we go *loco* and the fearsome sun rises, we saddle up and start on the long trek inland.

It is a hard march.

Chaco can hardly breathe and his paws are burning, when we finally reach the makeshift shack that is Charito, where a family lives to attend to such passersby as would stop there. We dunk Chaco in a water barrel and he conks out on the cement porch. He won't even look at the goodies that the cook has saved for him.

Two boys, about eight and nine have been preparing for our arrival, ever since the trucker from Chañaral dropped off a bale of hay the day before. They even built a room for us to sleep in, out of some pieces of tin. We tell them we'll try it out later on. Bet you could bake bread in there! They have a box of food saved for 'the donkeys' - fish heads and guts, mainly.

They are so sweet and so excited about the whole thing and it is hard to think of a way to tell them our horses can't eat fish. How do you explain about herbivorous animals to kids who have never seen a blade of glass, never mind a donkey, let alone four horses?

A northbound trucker stops in the *posada* for a glass of beer.

"Look," he says to us, "there is no way you can make it from here to Antofagasta with those horses. And the dog! Some vehicles don't even make it! There is nothing between here and there! Two hundred and thirty kilometers of nothing!"

He is going up empty anyway and he won't charge to take us.

We'd be in Antofagasta by nightfall.

We're not about to hitch a ride with anyone. We've made it this far; we'll make it to Antofagasta too. But we decide not to take the inland route. We're gambling on there being some way to follow the coastline towards Antofagasta, and head down a steep quebrada to the coastal town of Taltal. We phoned the Carabinero post from Copiapó ten days earlier to inquire if they would be able to assist us with feed in Taltal. They told us that they would.

But the feed truck hasn't arrived with a shipment that was due several weeks earlier. The Carabinero horses are down to half rations. There is none to spare. The Carabineros are very attentive and apologetic; they love horses, but there is little they can do to help us out.

This time there is no big mining company to save the day for us. We begin to regret not having taken that trucker up on his offer to give us a lift. What are we trying to prove anyway?

We can't stay in Taltal without feed.

We can't look for a way up the coast, if we have no feed.

And we can't go back the way we came, because there is no feed back there either.

There must be *something* we can do!

"You might go see the butcher," says the sergeant to us. "His name is Hugo Rojas."

What a perfect name for someone of his profession, I mutter as we walk towards his shop: Hugo The Red. I conjure up a big hulk of a man smashing in a steer's skull with a single blow from the sledge.

But Hugo Rojas is a man of slight build and, as we stand there watching him guide the knife through an intricate maze of tissue, sinew, muscle and bone with an expert hand, I find myself captivated by his skill.

The butcher as artist?

One more prejudice down the drain.

Now and then, Hugo Rojas tosses a piece of meat in Chaco's direction. He smiles shyly in ours.

We need six bales to get from Taltal to Antofagasta.

Hugo Rojas must know he can ask five times the going rate for a bale. We would have no choice but to pay. Instead, he just gives us the six bales we need on the condition that we accept a seventh and with it his invitation to stay the day in Taltal as his guest.

"I have never done anything daring or extraordinary," he says. "Now I can say I helped two persons who did."

He has prepared a chicken for us to take along when we leave for Paposo. Meat for Chaco, some cheese, cigarettes even.

"Don't forget this little corner of Chile," he says. Smiles shyly.

No Hugo, we haven't.

The *carabineros* arrange to have the six bales sent up the coast for us to Paposo, a forlorn little village at the end of nowhere, clinging to a narrow sand strip where the desert plateau ends and the ocean begins. No one has bothered painting boards or blocks and every yard is strewn with junk, rusty wagon parts, trucks and cars.

Here we are with our six bales and absolutely no idea how to proceed.

No one is fishing up the coast, we are told.

No one goes up the road inland, towards Antofagasta from here.

No one knows anything about anything.

The only advice everyone can give us is: "Go see Don Lucho."

From the outside, his house blends with the rest of this godforsaken place: unpainted and dreary. Don Lucho receives us in his inner sanctum, which is a stately blend of oak and white lace. He is a heavyset man with a commanding aura. He makes me think of an Arab sheik. He listens to our story without any of the common interjections.

"Come back in an hour and we'll see what we can do," he says and escorts us to the door.

An ancient red truck is parked outside the house when we return. Don Lucho introduces us to the driver, his nephew Renee. Renee is going up the coast on a guanaco hunt, Don Lucho tells us. He will be able to take along our bales and the drums of water he will provide to Punta Plata, to La Higuera and Blanca Encalada. These aren't places, just reference points up the coast that Don Lucho knows well because, for many years, he was in charge of maintaining the telegraph line up that way. He travelled up the coast by mule.

From Blanco Encalada, says Don Lucho, we will have to march straight on through to La Negra Linda, a *posada* on the Pan-American above Antofagasta. He will arrange to have a bale dropped for us there.

It does not occur to us to ask any details or to doubt that, with Don Lucho, what is said is also done. A man who sends a nephew out hunting in a sterile desert to downplay, perhaps, the tremendous favor he is doing a pair of strangers who washed up on the shores of his world, such a man does not need to explain himself.

When we see the green hills north of Paposo, I am ready to believe that the guanacos are for real; that the story Don Lucho told of a Russian prince who came to live out his days in Paposo is true, that there is gold up in those hills and that someone used to keep a milk cow and goats. Looking into the deep green gorges under the heavy morning *camanchaca*, I am ready to believe anything. It is the first natural green we have seen in over a month.

The right conditions for trapping the mist off the ocean prevails for only a few kilometers, then the coastal range is less abrupt again and there is no more sign of life.

If Renee brought a gun, we didn't see it. We camped together in the lee of a large rock the first night out: Renee and his wife, two small boys and elderly father-in-law who had all come along for the outing.

"What if something goes wrong, way out here?" Nathan says, feeling guilty that such an old truck had been sent out to take care of us.

Renee points to a Saint Christopher hanging over the dashboard. Crosses himself.

"He is watching over us," he says. "Not to worry."

How could we not worry as we watch the ancient truck chug along the narrow tire tracks, far beyond road's end, slalom into a ravine, sinking in to the hubs, and then careen across the dunes and wheeze and shake as it climbs up a corrugated hill, bouncing and rocking from side to side, steam puffing from the radiator! Renee carries no spare tire. His tool kit consists of one crescent wrench. Some faith that man has!

La Higuera is a real fig tree that has grown from the sapling Don Lucho planted by a water hole at the edge of the ocean many years ago. It is now a single tree oasis, at the center of a fan of animal tracks coming in from all sides.

The figs are dark purple and sweet. We help Renee and his family pick some. Then they leave to drop off the last bale for us up ahead at Blanca Encalada before they return to Paposo. We spend the day under the canopy that reaches all the way down to the edge of the Pacific. We make a fire and cook the crabs Nathan catches in the tidal pools. Chaco spends most of the day submerged in the cold water up to his chin. We would like to spend another day, but that is not possible. We have to move on to the next bale.

From La Higuera it is an easy ride to Blanco Encalada, which used to be an important port back in the days when Bolivia had access to the Pacific, before the War of 1879. Now an old caretaker lives by himself in a cave right by the sea. We don't ask of what he might be caretaking. He shares his fire and some fish with us and does not ask who we are or what we are doing out here either. We just sit together at the edge of the sea, so far away from anywhere. In the early afternoon, with the sun still high over the ocean, we saddle up and begin the twenty-hour trek to La Negrita, back up on the desert plateau.

Throughout the night, we walk for ten minutes, trot for twenty, walk for ten. This is the formula I remember from cavalry marches I read about. You keep focused on small and doable segments that way. The whole night is chopped up into 20-10-20-10-20-10-20-10. Every two hours we dismount. Air the horses' backs. Turn the blankets. Change saddles. Remount and begin another 20-10-20-10-20-10-20-10.

Just before noon, under the merciless desert sun, we reach the couple of tin roofed shacks that is La Negrita. The last of Hugo Rojas' bales is there waiting for us, just as Don Lucho promised that it would be.

They have a room for us, just off the small restaurant. We feed the horses, but we are too tired to get something for ourselves and just crash. We manage to fall asleep on the swaybacked beds, in spite of the flies and the heat and the noise from the jukebox and the trucks outside.

And then someone comes knocking on our door:

"*Señores*, your horses are on the highway!"

Standing peacefully right in the middle of the Pan-American are our four Criollo ponies. Trucks are lined up in both directions, patiently waiting to get by. There is no use trying to sleep now. We eat and wait for the sun to dip low on the horizon and then we saddle up and ride through another night.

At the cavalry unit in Antofagasta they give us a hero's welcome.

They tell us to stay as long as we want. They have plenty of feed. And since they also have plenty of grooms to look after our horses, we decide to take a few days and make a trip inland by bus to see the largest open pit mine in the world at Chucicamata and visit Padre le Paige and his mummies at San Pedro de Atacama.

Intriguing places both, but we did not enjoy being tourists. We felt orphaned, cut off from the sense of place we had come to take for granted in our daily life together as we met each new and unexpected challenge. Just looking at places and things, detached from our little movable gypsy world, wasn't all that interesting.

We continue on. Too late, we realize we shouldn't have. A case of Asian Flu colors Nathan's perceptions:

Antofagasta levitated in the sky behind us, a hop-splotch of shimmering yellow-orange rectangles on a rusty cloud of smelter smog. It hung there most of the morning, moored to the red sulfur hills at the edge of the sea, bleaching out slowly under the white heat lamp sun until it evaporated: abracadabra, moved to another gallery of the mind.

An aqueduct, partially buried in the salt crusted sand, divides the plain into equally empty halves. I listen for the life-force pulsing through the metal artery, flowing from Andean ice fields down waterless gorges, over bare hunch-backed hills, for hundreds of miles through motionless dunes, trapped without capillaries.

But all I hear is the throbbing of my own blood as urban microbes dance in a fever pitch and heat waves roll through my brain. I cling to my horse, watching our shadows dangle over the sterile epidermis of the desert floor. Then a metal arm drops to block our path:

ALTO

PROHIBIDA LA ENTRADA

A squadron of low flying jets scream in over a runway, one after the other, tossing billows of white and from inside a glass sentinel booth two soldiers stare in disbelief. Lips stumble with a message: phantom horses at the gates!

A Landrover comes careening straight towards us. Soldiers roll out of the back in a chain of blue. They all line up.

"How good of you to bring an escort, lieutenant!" Elly says and she beams a smile at the row of men in blue.

*"Your mission, **señores**?"*

"Captain Medina invited us to spend the night."

"This is Cerro Moreno Air Force Base!"

"Then we are in the right place." My ponytailed realist is very matter of fact.

She hands him the magic paper wand and up goes the metal arm and none too soon because the invisible strings holding this marionette up on his horse become rubber bands, bouncing me this way and that. I sink to the ground on the front steps of Main Headquarters and gaze out through Pampero's fuzzy legs at the flock of Phantoms arranged in groups of three along the airstrip.

Questions descend like artificial rain:

Why this?

How that?

When?

What?

Where?

Who?

Hands trained to hold the stick steady at the speed of sound are now fumbling with rawhide straps, hemp ropes, buckles and canvas panniers. A squad is sent to deposit our gear at the infirmary, (I hope they bring back a stretcher for me).

*"I'd like to water the horses, lieutenant." The **señora commandanta** has taken charge of the situation. "And where is the feed we sent out from Antofagasta?" Two more details are formed and head off in different directions. A fire brigade returns first, water sloshing from bright red buckets onto spit polished shoes. The horses dispatch one bucket after another; back and forth run the men in blue.*

*"**Señora**, how many buckets will they drink?"*

"We could take the horses to the water."

*"No outside faucets, **señora**."*

The bale of hay arrives on a red toy wagon, pulled by two air force men and comes under immediate attack by the hungry equine guerrilla. Maracas butts his way through and grabs a mouthful. The wagon retreats. The lieutenant looks to Elly:

*"**Señora**, where shall we put it?"*

"Over there, by the patch of green grass." No hesitation there.

*"But, **señora**. That's the sewage disposal plant."*

"That's okay. It's fenced in. It'll keep them off your runway."

With the boys in blue pulling, the horses follow the toy wagon across a checkerboard of concrete. The ominous birds pull themselves up behind lengthening shadows and, far out over the Pacific, the vapor trails of three bombers stretch across the apricot sky like a three-wire barbed fence.

Off Limits. No dreaming beyond this point.

A bugle wails: the day is done, gone the sun.

Overhead a powerful searchlight threshes the stars and in the officers' club, the bartender asks

"What will you have?"

"Gin and tonic," Elly says.

Penicillin, my body suggests, with the revolving stool wobbling under me. Three images stare back at us from the long mirror through a menagerie of liquor bottles: two sunburned faces under dusty sombreros and a handsome unlined face.

From the next room comes the clack of billiard balls and the jukebox hums and our host salutes the Johnny Walker, Gordon, the Domec and White Horse.

"We keep those bottles there in the memory of José Aguirre. He was killed in a crash last year."

Tilt your glass now and remember the whole grease-lighting-split-second-chain-of-reactions ending suddenly in a cartwheeling flame of wreckage. Yes, it could happen to any of us. Routine can be fatal. Shall we drink a toast to the inspiring fictions we live by? And die by?

"Argentina bought a dozen French Mirages last month and we can't

*afford to be left behind. Security, **entiende usted?** "*

"More Phantoms?"

*(He doesn't hear what she means) "**Seguro que sí, señora**."*

Phantoms here and Mirages there to make a desert safe for democracy. What are Peru and Bolivia getting for Christmas? It's a real bargain, neighbors, surplus planes and tanks for cheap copper, tin and oil. The dice are loaded, so divert their attention. A billion starving people watching vapor trails in the sunset, but never fear (for just ten dollars a month you too can become a foster parent to some orphan like little Pedro Murillo staring out from the back pages of TIME).

A room with rocking walls and an air conditioner for lungs. Cool, cool sheets.

Elly sits on the bed and I dictate:

Riding under your copper sun, leased by Anaconda,
Dear Chile:
the electro-dynamo Big Daddy of the north could not do without you; he is eternally grateful and shows it with CARE and AID and all this dime-store weaponry (for which you pay Wall Street prices) and every time we throw a switch, fire a bullet, plug in a cable, start a generator, trigger an air-to-ground missile, open a refrigerator, turn up the heat, phone the neighbor, fill up a car radiator, charge the batteries, make a Nevada countdown
believe us, Dear Chile,
a silent prayer goes out of our hearts to you and your hungry people
("Roll over Nate, this is penicillin and will only take a minute."
"Gracias, doctor")
we are forever in your debt and even though it is you who are forever in the red, your faith will be rewarded: we shall show you the way into the future, reselling you all the copper coils, ammunitions, Bell telephone wires, light bulbs that you can't afford at very special interest rates,
which your great grandchildren can pay off to our great grandchildren,

for we trust you, dear Chile,
and know that you appreciate the hand that feeds you (while the
other bleeds you),
thank you for sharing your copper sun with us, it helps make the
Lights of Liberty glow brighter, and when it's all gone,
well, we'll think of something....

"You still awake?"
"I don't know. What did you think of that?"
"Go to sleep, Nate. We have to ride tomorrow."
Because the hay will be gone and the next bale is fifty kilometers
away in Mejillones. You don't just stop because some medic thinks you're
an idiot to go out there and fry your brains with a fever of 103.
All or none, all for one.

It was a day of hours.........just hours.........on an equine seesaw with
Elly bobbing up and down up ahead and me trailing, Kafka-esque im-
ages pouring out behind like goose feathers from a torn mattress:
metal birds with radioactive eyes
billiard balls in cages
a computer half buried in the sand
a walkie-talkie in an ice cube, rising up an escalator into the white
sky.
Hold onto Elly, she is real (always so real!)
She'll get you out of this nightmare.
The ground sagged, then swelled up toward me.
On and on.... until the green and white walls of the reten at Mejillones
rose before us and the nauseating motion ceased.
I was hardly aware of being helped from the saddle, olive green
shoulders steadying me, leading me off into a big barrack with rows of
cots, olive green blankets.
Her face was swimming above me (all or none, all for one).
"The horses," I mumbled, "the horses..."
A cool hand on my burning forehead: "Everything is all right, Nate.
They have a barn full of good hay."
When I came to, I discovered another patient in the cot next to

mine, paws in the air and breathing heavily. I reached out to touch his hot nose. He rolled over toward me and opened his swollen eyes.

"Poor Bumper. You look miserable."

"No worse than you." Elly said and came in the doorway with a pitcher of water and filled my glass and Chaco's dish. He shoved his nose in, slurped and sank back against the pillows with a groan.

"Elly, what's the matter with him?"

"He picked up your Asian flu."

"It looks like distemper again."

"Actually, I think he is jealous of all the attention you were getting. He'll be all right when you are."

THE ATACAMA

On this Christmas Eve, we left the little town of Mejillones and rode alone out into the desert and I wanted to begin a new chapter thus:

The Evening Star glowed purple and orange in the last aura of the setting sun and we followed along the edge of the ocean where breakers crashed and came hissing up the sand, foaming around the horses' legs, swept back again and then we trotted across a mirror of wet lava.

*The full moon rose out of the jagged mountain range to the east and we left the beach and followed an old mining trail through the dunes where the shadows played in the unearthly white light and, unfolding behind us, through winds and forests, rains and mountains, across plains, rivers, flowering meadows, snowfields, past campfires and shepherd's huts, a fragile thread connecting all the worlds back to where it all began, one year ago in a sod lean-to where Guillermo and Tommy tossed the **taba** while the spread-eagled lamb roasted over the*

173

coals.

Guillermo told us the plains would teach us what we needed to know and they have. One day at a time, we have evolved toward this night when being home for Christmas means being right here, right now, riding our horses under a blanket of stars.

It is easy to feel close, this night, to three wise men following a star on a magical journey to a newborn babe, two thousand years ago.

Moving into darkness, we have faith that we will find our way.

There is peace on earth this Christmas night.

New Year's Eve is a masquerade marathon. In the town of Tocopilla they mob us, mother us, maneuver us, devour us ("Gringos on horseback have come to town!").

Starch-stitched lives are ripping at the seams; the citizens of Tocopilla are zapping their coils, bombing right out of the small town quagmire with gin-wine-beer-whisky-brandy-pisco-cuba libres-fruit punch detonators. It is a veritable test of endurance: you must be here, we'll take you there, they'll want to meet you, let's drink to that. A Bloody Mary won't do. Here, try some champagne.

Lions Club, Fishermen's Ball, Dance at Anaconda, the Alcalde's party, and just the chosen few at the Lara's house. Elly is whirling through serpentine dances in boots and buckskin jacket ("Can I dance with the señora?" "Why of course, if you wait in line"). A Cueca, señores, let's see you swirl it out! Banquet tables overflow with motley gestalt: olives, caviar, roast pig, duck, beef, avocado salad, Spanish rice, empanadas, blue cheese, Miracle Whip, fruitcakes. Fill your plate; it's now more than ever.

The hour is approaching. Ladies careen towards the powder room for a facial touch-up. The village dentist sits with his chin on the table. A Cleopatra of waning charm and artificial pearls leans on my arm.

Fire crackers and sweaty abrazos at the stroke of twelve, New Year's resolutions cranking up from acid indigestion, hypertension, apoplexy.

Twe-e-e-e-eetooooooot screech the plastic horns; confetti and streamers spume out over our heads. On to the Union Club for another supper; the night is still young and tomorrow the desert again.

Pampero groans under the extra weight of brandy, turkey, sweet bread, cookies, candy, a heart for Chaco, canned olives, jam, fruit, and tied on top of the bedroll in a box is a chocolate cake (a chocolate cake!!!) with PROSPERO AÑO NUEVO in curly butter fudge letters. A troupe of kids swarm along behind us as we head out of town.

"Hey, Ringo. Where are your pistols? Ringo!"

I spin the mare around, drawing my Colt 45's and fire at our pursuers. They fan out and hit the ditches, throwing a volley of lead after us.

"Arrrrrgh."

A bullet tears into my shoulder and I topple backwards over the rump of my startled horse. Up and running, the posse charges forward. Firing from the hip, I drop three of them in the dust, leap back on the mare and dig in my heels.

They fall further and further behind, yelling:

"Did you see that!"

"Ringo flipped right out of the saddle!" Laughing, still not believing.

"They're getting away!"

Real Hollywood bandits right here in Tocopilla, riding off into the setting sun.

It is their memory (their parents have others) and we are glad to give it to them, but now we are off their screen, alone again riding railroad trestles toward the upper plateau of the Atacama.

Midnight.

The twin irons slither on up the gorge, coiling back upon themselves, taking us higher, just ahead of the rising banks of mist that pursue us from the ocean, until in the wee hours of the morning, the peaks of the coastal range have become an archipelago of floating islands far below.

From the crest - strange mountain with only one slope! We step out onto the Atacama salt flats and the air is suddenly dry ice. The clouds advance no further. The wind ceases. In the eerie silence of another realm, we are the only survivors on a cinder planet.

Phantasmal ruins of a lost civilization, surrounded by giant cupcakes appear all around us and bulldozed tracks crisscross the flats, making it look like a military campaign has taken place here, leaving nothing it its wake.

Vertical shafts of light rake the wall of darkness ahead, then two fireballs burst out of a hollow and roll toward us with a crescendoing rumble and a truck hurtles past. Air brakes hiss, a red wake of lights flash - has he even seen us? The truck accelerates again and continues on north.

The Pan-American is not far away then. All we need to do now is find the ghost town named Prosperidad, where an old caretaker will have the bale that the carabineros in Tocopilla arranged to have dropped off for us.

It was a good plan, except for the fact that we have arrived here in the middle of the night. We take out the map again. It shows a cluster of abandoned nitrate towns right off the Pan-American: Empresa, Esperanza, Iberia, Ricaventura and Prosperidad. One of these ghost towns is Prosperidad. Which one? While we stand indecisive, Caicique takes charge and starts walking down a paved side road. We trust his sixth sense and follow along.

Imagine this:
Hoofbeats resounding on empty streets,
clippety-clop,
past hollow-eyed houses,
clippety-clop,
tin roofs rattling in the wind,
clippety-clop,
Cats and front-end loaders hunkered by a water tower,
clippety-clop,
right into a small square with a sagging grandstand and dead trees.
And imagine this:
Footsteps (mine) echo on the boardwalk. A rocking chair creaks on a porch. Look through an open door. Neat stacks of papers on the desks. Two drawers in the filing cabinet open.

Continue on up to the street corner, a giant crane juts out over a line of loaded railroad cars, casting a tall shadow against the wall of a power plant. Push the heavy door inward. Let eyes adjust to the darkness and make out the shapes of transformers, generators, switchboards, a web of black cables crawling up the walls, all coated with a phosphorescent dust. The dust has filtered through every crack, hole, rupture and broken pane of glass. The same white powder covers tables, sidewalks, machines, and withered hedges.

Creeping paranoia.

Everything still in place. But the populace is gone without a trace. Without an explanation. I close the door behind me and retrace my steps, resisting the urge to run back to Elly and the horses.

The horses are rustling twigs and dry leaves in the gutter. She stands up. "I am hitching back to María Elena to see about the bale," she says. There is no use telling her to wait until daylight so we can see where we are. Her horses are hungry and she is going to do something about it. Right now!

She walks back to the highway.

Imagine this:

It is 3:30 am. Hovering by the side of the road at the fringe of the hellish spook towns is a white-haired female wrapped in a black poncho that is flapping like the wings of some prehistoric bird. She is waving at you.

Would you stop?

*No trucks came by, so we'll never know if one would have stopped. Elly returns after about an hour, cold and distraught. We drink some brandy and share the Happy New Year's cake with Chaco and when morning comes, we climb up one of the nitrate **mesas** which is hollow inside like a crater and scan the rubble towns emerging from darkness. So many of them! Sprawling out across the nitrate flats, the ghostly suburbs of a lost world.*

At the center of the nearest one, not far away at all, a small crown of green emerges above the tin roofs - a live tree! That means someone is watering it.

We put the saddles and the pack back on and ride in the direction of the one tree and find a bright green alfalfa bale and an emaciated old caretaker, who seems more bothered by our visit than pleased. We ask him for water. He points to a rusty barrel with some water in the very bottom of it. We give him the bottle of brandy and he disappears inside his dwelling and does not come back out. We spread the alfalfa in the plaza and take our bedding and put it under the sagging roof of the bandstand, in what would have been the center of a bustling town, where couples would walk in the shade of the big trees and talk, listen maybe to music playing from the grandstand. It is very hot already with no breeze and I toss and turn.

"What has come to naught is in my care."

(He looks around, laughs, then wheezes)

"Not a human being for hundreds of miles, not a buzzard in the sterile sky. Yet the sun peels the paint, the nitrate gnaws at the iron plates, the wind strips roofs from empty rooms. I watch the pilfering. I take note of the daily losses."

(Pauses and looks at his thin hand)

"Even the witnesses are whittled down. There isn't much of me left."

(He jumps up, moving mechanically like a marionette and dances around a withered tree).

"Puppets we are, building dams against time. Magnates with giant tombstones, mutilated soldiers with honorable mentions in history books - IN SMALL PRINT, mind you IN SMALL PRINT!"

(He stoops down and inspects the trunk of a dead tree, then shakes his head)

"Termites. They are invading the vaults, the archives, the libraries, the government files! The world is made of papier-mâché. It rots and crumbles away!"

(He clutches his head and reels backwards)

"Illusions! Into the factories, the mines, the offices, onto the battlefields, there's a cause to be won!"

*"**Pero hombre, era una rica aventura**! Man, it was a rich adventure."*

(Sinking down, he lets his chin fall against one propped up knee)

"Ah, my genius lay in knowing when to run, when to lie low. Folly has devoured them all."

(He wraps his arms around himself and shivers.)

"Brrr. It is so cold. My reward: I am the sole heir. The heroes and the loyal slaves are buried in the sand. Only I am condemned to live IN

THIS GODLESS SILENCE WHERE THE TERMITES GNAW!"
  (He collapses and crosses himself.)
  "Have mercy upon my soul!"

In the heat of the afternoon, waking from a fitful sleep under a silent bandstand in the center of a ghost town, the origin of the old man's monologue is unclear. Did I dream it? Imagine it? Hear it, maybe?

The horses have cleaned up every scrap of hay and are nosing the empty water drum that is sitting in the middle of the street. It is time to move on. There is no sign of the old man. Poor old geezer, when he wakes and finds no one, he'll wonder who hit him over the head with a bottle of cheer.

Heading due east from Prosperidad, we will get to Rio Loa. We know this, because we have a map and the map shows the western branch of the river not far from Prosperidad. Rio Loa runs through the desert in the shape of a giant U. We have been looking at it on our tattered map for weeks now. But remembering other maps, showing a Route 40 across Meseta del Carbon, when there is no road and never will be one built, we are cautious. We won't believe anything until we see it.

The horses just seem to know. After six weeks of water barrels, rancid water holes and desalinated Pacific, they trot eagerly eastwards across the sand, up one slope and then another and break into a gallop - our placid, bone-heavy Criollo ponies! We stand in the stirrups and stretch our eyeballs, yearning for that gurgling, sweet crystalline river. But doubting still a little bit.

Quite suddenly the plain parts in front of us, revealing a shimmering emerald in the navel of the earth: Acres and acres of alfalfa. Chaco plunges into the rolling waves of green with all the joy of a canine dolphin. We dismount and take their bridles off and then we just stand there, waist deep in sweet-smelling alfalfa. The horses stuff in enormous mouthfuls and slowly eat their way down the slope. At the bottom, they discover the mighty Amazon of the Atacama: a bold trickle in a deep ditch, all of three feet wide. They kneel on the bank, rumps in the air, and slurp in the magic liquid while Chaco floats downstream with the current, only his nose and the tip of his tail showing.

So the Loa isn't a mighty torrent - who cares anyway? What other river could claim such a feat: crossing a desert without tributaries or rains to help it along. No forest to shade it, no mountains to push and guide it.

We stay right there all afternoon, in and out of the river and when night falls, we feast on Tocopilla party favors. We spread our bedroll on the riverbank. No one disturbs us. Life is perfect, except for the bugs particular to this paradise, which are swarms of large and vicious mosquitoes and legions of bats that arrive on the scene at dusk.

The next day we move on up the river to where the valley widens. In the town of Quillagua we meet an old mule driver who used to make charcoal for the nitrate companies out of giant trees he found buried in the sand, just a few feet under the surface. Imagine that! This was a jungle once. And these very old trees, perfectly preserved, were used by the nitrate mills to produce gunpowder and explosives. That I don't like to imagine.

We find it hard to motivate ourselves to leave Quillagua. We stay a day. We stay another. We stay a third and then we ride straight north out into the nitrate fields where, every day, the wind rages. It is this noonday night that Francisco Duran warned us about at our camp in *quebrada* Pejerreyes, so many weeks ago; desert storms that will send a man moving in circles.

> *The horses plow on, heads lowered, into a darkening wind tunnel, the whiplash hail of burning sand stinging our faces and hands. Under us, the desert turntable twists, obliterating all sense of direction and time, making it entirely possible that, on the other side of this unfathomable daytime night, we would ride back into yesterday and an oasis named Quillagua and meet an old mule driver who would tell us stories in the cool of his citrus grove where the alfalfa grows waist high.*
>
> *At dusk the wind dies abruptly and leaves you with a deafening silence that drinks you to the dregs. Then night comes quickly and phosphorescent buckshot makes a sieve of the purple dome overhead.*
>
> *The sandblasted railroad tracks unravel twin silver threads and mile markers nailed to telegraph poles lure us deeper into the heart of darkness:*
>
> *616*
>
>   *617*
>
>   *618*
>
>   *619*

an abstract progression of numbers, leading somewhere,
above:
dancing particles of ice-fire
and the potter's wheel spins in the void,
unseen hands centering shadow into a transparent vase
where a weightless crystal glows
620

621

622

623

Three a.m.
The twin silver threads split into four. Black letters against a white
rectangle spell:
SOLEDAD
(SOLITUDE)
The small station is vacant.
But a bale of hay sits on the platform and on the siding a tanker car
is parked, a bucket hanging over the faucet at the end.
Offerings in the night: ***Gracias a Dios*** *for our anonymous allies!*
The horses drink three buckets each and while they eat, we catch
some sleep. In less than three hours' time, we are underway again
following the railroad. It is cold enough to see your breath against the
predawn gray, then the globe of liquid radium catapults into the sky
with such scorching intensity; you can hear the nitrate cracking all
around you.
Chaco hangs in the shadow of the horses to keep out of the blowtorch
glare. When we stop to give him water from his canteen, he shifts from
paw to paw on the hot crust. By ten there is no more shade.
Our timing is off.
Should have stayed the day at Soledad. Or should have pushed
right on through to the camp at kilometer 654.
Now we are caught without shade.
Spouts of dust are gathering in the east and begin to twist across
the flat, coming at us like a locust army.
Suddenly it is terrifyingly still. You're aware of an ultrasonic ping
inside the bell jar cranium and of mounting pressure.

Then a tidal wave of sand rears up and the fissioning molecular madness blasts right over us, a mighty screaming comber of bats out of hell. The horses skitter sideways and they bunch up close together.

With the sand grinding into eyes-nose-mouth-ears, plugging every pore, we cling to the trestles, crawling along. After the first black rage is past, the storm gradually winds down to a droning backdraft. Next come searing heat swells and every now and then we catch a glimpse of a Jack-o'-lantern sun creeping toward zenith behind a peppered veil.

Then through the shifting haze, four men appear along the tracks ahead of us, armed with shovels and looking at us from inside yellow pug-nosed masks. Desert frogmen?

Why not! After the nights on the nitrate flats and in the ghost towns, little will surprise us out here.

"Welcome to Siberia!" Speaks a muffled voice.

It is time for the two o'clock northbound to come by so the railroaders shoulder their tools and lead the way down the tracks to Campamento 654 where they remove their masks. They are a tough looking bunch.

A bale is waiting by the side of the tin shack and there is enough water in the tanker car to hose the horses down. A couple of the railroaders help Nathan with this. The horses lean into the spray and turn their heads to try and drink from it and the men begin to miss the horses on purpose and spray each other and laugh like a bunch of kids. The water makes a hollow, hissing sound when it hits the hot tin of the shack behind.

The cook invites us to share a plate of beans with the gang. Inside the tin shack, with the coal stove going, it is hotter even than out in the noonday sun. And the hottest place of all, the hottest maybe in all of the Atacama Desert, is the end of this rough plank table, right next to the stove, where the cook slouches, wiping off sweat onto his apron and watching to see if you need more coffee to wash down the gooey bean mash, spiked with enough pimiento to curl your tongue.

Gathered around the table, hooking down mugs of steaming black coffee, the camp crew tell tall stories, aimed to shock you, the way the gypsies would play up to an audience around a roadside camp fire. We became part of the caste of a real life gypsy performance before some stranger, with music and song and dance and the clapping of hands and Eladia reading palms and tea leaves. Entering the railroaders' world on horseback like this places us some-where between the ins and the outs of this gang doing hard time.

"This is, you might say, the end of the line. Jose here got liquored up and slugged a foreman. He'll be here awhile."

Jose looks from the speaker, named Juan, to us:

"We don't really mind. No boss around."

"Just the desert. So, what do you think of our Sahara?"

"Your Sahara?" Nathan deadpans. "I hear that over in Sahara they're asking what people think of their Atacama!"

They laugh at that and their tales grow taller. Chicho and Miguel took an engine for a joyride down in Tocopilla. That's how they earned their ticket to Camp Siberia, a.k.a. Sahara.

"Every day. Every *jodido* day the desert buries the tracks and we shovel it off!"

And Juan tells of the mummified mule they found and propped up near the tracks, all decorated up with a scarecrow on its back, for the train passengers to look at and wonder.

We tell them stories from the trail and try to ignore the infernal heat and the flies.

I think of sitting behind a bush with Segundo and Tonio and laugh-ing together over the idea that anyone would want to waste a bomb trying to hit four saddle tramps at the bottom of the world. It is the same around this table in a shack in the desert: a grease-collar, rough-out, don't-take-no-shit-fraternity of fist-wheeling parolees, but well meaning (no doubt about that) and no-holds-barred-tell-it-like-it-is-honest.

*Elly laughs at the archetypes I create of these men, who speak with a common voice out of **barrio** shacks and gypsy caravans, from plains and mountains, men like Jose who sees that your flashlight is broken and fixes it with parts cut out of a tin can while you sleep with your head on greasy pillows in bunks belonging to Migtuel and Juan.*

This is where it's at.

I am close here to my Grampa Clark, who cupped his hands over mine on the oars so I might feel the rhythm of the strokes and learn to row the skiff by myself.

But free from my Grandfather Foote's hand behind my neck, push-
ing my face into scalding hot soup, so that I shall never ever bend
forward to smell my food again, but eat what is before me and do as
I'm told.

I never forgave my grandfather, the Reverend Foote.

But I am thankful now for him humiliating me this way, so I would
go my own way and find the men of the plains and of this desert.

In the cool of the evening, we saddle up and continue our journey
through the Martian world of the salt flats, hanging onto the railroad
and in the quiet under the toehold moon, you can feel them coming:
dry-bone timpani rattling in the bowels of the earth, gathering forces
under the expanse of giant cornflakes (because that's exactly what the
salt flats look like). You could make a sci-fi movie and you wouldn't
need to build a set; it's all here.

CRAAAAABRAOOOOOOM!

Claps of seismic thunder reverberate as the cool air of the night air
collides with the buried heat from the day and the earth contracts and
splits and you imagine that the railroad ties are strung over a chasm
where the jackals of the underworld are twisting and writhing in chains
of matter, rising up and smashing through:

"Release us. All is stellar dust and gas!"

Fissures are radiating out, the scaly crust peeling back on both
sides of the trestles and you know that if you strayed out onto the egg-
shell surface, it would disintegrate and swallow you up, horses and all,
into an intergalactic ooze.

It is that weird!

A total perceptual shakedown.

And you hold onto the tracks with the fear of God, beginning to
think that if the subterranean bombardment goes on much longer, you're
going to be zonked right out of your brain cage.

BAAROOOOOOOOOM!

Two nights and two days that we've been marching, almost without
sleep. It keeps getting colder and the putty globe keeps shrinking, then
little by little, the stars melt into a pre-dawn whiteout. A group of
windmills rear up before us.

And you think: Oh no! We've living fiction again, thrown into the never-never land of Don Quixote and here are the windmills I am supposed to do battle with, but I am too tired to draw my lance. I feel more like Pancho anyway on Pampero. These windmills are not dragons; they belong to Pumping Station Number 3 which is part of La Victoria, the only nitrate mine still open for business in the Atacama Desert of Chile, once a symbol of glory, for which thousands gave their lives during the Nitrate War of 1879.

With the ground still pitching beneath us, we drop our gear under a tamarugo tree and lie down on a bed of dry leaves and pull a blanket over our heads to ward off the swarms of flies that have appeared out of nowhere. The horses drift off to graze the tufts of grass that grow around the pump house.

We sink into a deep sleep, that lasts all of an hour before two vehicles come hauling dust up the gravel road, honking and swerving around the pumping station and jerking to a stop in front of us.

"Here they are!" Someone says. "Look, they are having a siesta!"

"Tell them I'm out," Elly groans from under the blanket.

I shove the cotton back from my dry gums and try to flash a grin to the welcoming committee from La Victoria: office-white friendly orbs fibrillating with curiosity and beaming out a ten-mile smile.

*There was no way they were going to let us sleep away our fifteen minutes of fame under a tamarugo tree. And so it came to pass that two trail weary desert prophets stood in the back of a GM chariot as it cruised into La Victoria, up the wide Avenida one way and down the other, through the marketplace and into a funnel of soot stained workers' dwellings, honking and bouncing, high on pure exhaustion, all the mamas waving, thrilled to have a little piece of some action, and careening along past elevators, giant rock crushers spewing out dust, under a labyrinth of pipes, cables, conveyor belts with workers staring at us from the loading platforms, dumbstruck: "What have we here?" and finally pulling in for a flashbulb reception at the **comandancia**.*

Much later, we drop into a double bed in the mine superintendent's mansion with Gerry Mulligan's saxophone rasping from an old Victorola in the musty downstairs living room (if such a shell of colonial elegance would still classify as a room for living), staring up at a fan, big as a propeller, gyrating slowly and noisily in the center of a cracked ceiling.

We're yearning to be back under the tamarugo tree at Pump Number 3, even with all the flies, for this inhabited ghost town is more uncanny than Ricaventura. It is doomed and everyone knows it. Walls remain unpainted, streets without repair, but the rock crushers pound on wearily through the night. A rattletrap bus bounces down the Avenida with the next shift aboard.

The show goes on, for where would they all go?

The superintendent has been dreaming for twenty years, he said, of a little cottage in Kent and upstairs I imagine our Max Factor hostess removing her spider lashes and tucking them into a drawer in her dressing table, holding on, keeping up the blues.

After the barroming salt flats, what a reality warp: OUT HERE!

The record ends and the blunt needle scratches on:

saaa-aaa-rrrr-ooom, saaaa-aaa-rrrr-ooooom

a whirling cocoon spins across the surreal cornflakes wrapped in faded crepe paper streamers, like gauze over a bandaged face

frogmen with pug-nosed filters rise up through the fissure in the crust and dance along after it drunkenly

saaaa-aaa-rrrr-ooooom,

the cocoon hangs on a thread and spins and spins,

the needle stops scratching

and then all you hear is the ceiling fan.

I wish I had taken a picture of Juan Morales, lying there on his back in the sun in the cemetery outside Huara, arms crossed over his chest, his tan face looking so peaceful, his bushy mustache neatly twisted at the ends and his polished boots shining. So you could have seen, with your own eyes, how absolutely amazing he looks in his Sunday best. If it wasn't for the casket and the tablet telling you he is one Juan Morales 1837 - 1881, you could have mistaken him for one of the oldtimers of Huara sleeping off a hangover. There was nothing to suggest he was eighty years dead. Looking at the mummies of San Pedro de Atacama that, or should I say whom Padre le Paige dug up, some of them three or four or even ten thousand years old, that was one thing. I took pictures of those and marveled at the detail. You could see the wrinkles around the eyes even! But this Juan Morales is too close in time. It is like meeting up with your own great grandfather out there. You are not prepared for how Time eats away at the adobe crypts in the cemetery so the apartment houses for the dead crumble into banks of sand, leaving the mummified occupants exposed for all to see.

The dance hall in Huara has a poster out front, announcing the arrival of authentic Parisian can-can dancers. Wow, you think, that's amazing! Then you look closer and see that the event was to take place forty years ago! And the poster still looks almost new! In contrast to the faded signs for the hardware store and grocery, pharmacy and liquor stores, all closed and boarded up, as if someday the owners are planning to return.

Oldtimers, whole rows of them, lean forwards on benches along the boardwalk and watch us ride into town. We stop for a moment to ask the way to the *carabinero reten*. They hold onto us with their eyes, their memories tumbling out for us to hear.

"When the English built the railroad, towns popped up like mushrooms."

"Mr. Humberstone wore his tweeds and necktie even on the hottest days."

"Some days the sky was black with the smoke from all the *salitreras*."

Wrinkled leather faces shine younger, one picking up where the other pauses for breath, they vie with each other for our attention.

"After the war in Europe, the Germans came up with synthetic nitrate."

"No one believed it when they started closing down the nitrate mines."

"Almost overnight, everyone was gone."

We continue on down the main street, leaving clusters of old men still talking.

"No one believed it."

"No one saw it coming."

We ride past the railroad station where an old man is watering some flowers and a few trees from a tin can and across the tracks to the *reten*, which is also a prison and where we put our gear in one of the open cells facing the courtyard.

An old man is cooking his supper in a tin can hung over a small fire outside. He invites us to share his fire, should we wish to. We fill our *pava* with water from a tap inside and put it on the coals next to his and bring out some rice and a can of tuna and an onion. He doesn't speak to us but remains close

187

by, smoking hand rolled cigarettes that smell of pipe tobacco.

We think the old man might be a custodian. We are surprised when the Corporal in charge tells us that he is a prisoner, brought in not long ago on a murder charge. He caught his wife with another man and pulled her entrails out with his hands and killed her. A rightful punishment for an adulterous wife, by the laws of the people in his remote mountain village.

"We haven't told him that he will never see his village again," says the Corporal, sounding regretful almost. "He doesn't understand. We have told him he must wait for a judge to come to town. Patiently, he waits."

Just like the oldtimers wait on their benches all along the main street of Huara, passing the time until Death comes their way and the desert embalms their last moment for eternity, as it did Juan Morales and the other casualties from the Six Year War fought over these nitrate fields: Peruvians, Bolivians and Chileans, and all who came here afterwards, in search of a better life. You are not prepared for a murderer held prisoner by the desert, with no need for walls or chains.

The desert is so much bigger than we. It can swallow us up, just like that. We spend a long time brushing our horses this afternoon and cleaning our tack, we even polish our stirrups with steel wool, waiting for the cool of the evening. We leave with the sun still high, eager to get out of this town where history coagulates the present.

I am thinking of a pantomime about freedom as we ride along. The usual premises would be reversed for comic effect (i.e. greater consciousness brings less freedom in terms of possibilities).

CAGES

*There are five cages across the stage, interconnected by passages of wire mesh and progressively larger, left to right. **Actor**, in blue overalls and a metal safety helmet, sits curled up in the smallest cage. As the curtain goes up, a film is projected onto a large screen, showing **Worker** riding a train through an industrial labyrinth, staring straight ahead at dark red smoke. Loud sound of metal wheels clicking. The train stops and **Worker** descends, walks across an elevated steel bridge and down a ramp toward a maze of smokestacks and pipes. There is* *loud cacophony of industrial noise.* **Worker** *enters a long hallway, walks along assembly line, punches time clock and takes his position on the line. The film changes to black and white and fades out.*

Cage 1
Actor *coming awake: rubs his eyes, stretches and looks around, gripping the bars of the small cage, then crawls through the passage into the next larger one. He does a cramped dance in the limited space. Removes helmet and overalls, revealing a baggy suit. Puts on a wide necktie and accountant's green visor. Walks into the next cage. Marches lethargically around, stooped over because of the low ceiling. Stops and sits down on a stool in front of the adding machine. Film shows closeup of his tense face, then walking through urban canyons of a large metropolis, camera receding until* **Actor** *is a mere speck. Closeup again: he enters a chaotic stock exchange hall and makes his way through the crowd. Loud clicking of ticker tape machines. He punches time clock and enters a small booth. Sits down on a stool in front of adding machine. Film becomes black and white and fades.* **Actor** *is dozing on the stool in the cage.*

Cage 2
Actor *wakes slowly, rises stiffly and performs a dance simulating slow-motion calisthenics. He yawns, rubs his eyes and grips the bars of the cage, dances into the next passageway. Removes visor and suit. Hangs them on a hook and emerges in grey slacks. Dons tweed jacket, lights a pipe, moves into third cage. He does a hopscotch dance. Sits down in a leather chair by a bookcase with large volumes. Films now shows* **Professor** *in an old Volkswagen stuck in a thruway traffic jam, walking through an apartment house jungle, up a cement ramp to a large library. He shows ID card at a desk, walks down an endless tunnel of loaded bookshelves. Comes to an alcove and sits down at a messy desk. He blows the dust off a large volume that is falling apart and leafs through the yellowed pages. Film turns black and white and fades out.*

Cage 3
Actor *comes awake slowly and staggers into a drunken, but graceful*

dance around the cage. He passes by the bookcase several times, turns in fright each time and retreats. Finally, he escapes into the next passageway and erupts into an elated dance of great agility. He steps behind a divider and emerges in a trim business suit and dapper hat. Walks briskly into the fourth cage, nodding and smiling and flowing into a casual, self-important dance around a desk with six telephones on it. Sits down and props his clasped hands underneath his chin.

*Film clip of **Executive** inside a jumbo jet, drink in one hand, a folder in his lap, then stepping out of a limo, nodding, smiling, alone in an elevator, walking past a boy holding open double mahogany doors into an enormous office. He sits down behind a large, modern desk and begins to juggle phones and papers. Film becomes a negative, then fades. There is soft music in the background and an incoherent jumble of voices over several telephone wires.*

Cage 4

***Actor** starts awake, lifts his head from the desk. Shakes it. Looks irritated. Begins a frenzied dance around the cage, bumping into the bars, knocking over a potted tree and the chair. Sweeps the phones off the desk. Pulls off his necktie and jacket. Suddenly clutches his chest and sags to his knees. With great effort drags himself into the passage. Puts on a gay sport shirt, a yachting cap, dark glasses and finds a fishing rod. He goes into the fifth cage. Sits down in a deck chair and casts out over the top of the cage.*

*Film clips of the leisure king hunting big game, waterskiing, skydiving, car racing, mountain climbing, submarine fishing, playing roulette, swimming at a nudist colony, jumping on horseback, playing tennis, drinking at an elegant club, and bringing a glider in for a landing. The film speeds up and the images begin to repeat themselves, they split and whirl, becoming a negative kaleidoscope. **Actor** asleep in deck chair turns fitfully from side to side. He starts and awakens abruptly. Leaps out of the cage and circles around it making paranoid gestures to shield off blows. Runs to stage center in front of row of cages and stops, paralyzed, one foot off the ground, one hand pointing off stage. The cages are moved off into the wings. The screen projects an endless*

*desert. **Actor** begins an explorative dance, moving warily about the
stage. Stops. Stares off into space. The dance becomes more expan-
sive and audacious: he spins and jumps, he does backward somersaults and cartwheels. Elation gradually turns to confusion, then to
fear. He moves slower and slower. Retreats to the rear left of the stage.
The screen goes black. **Actor** stands on his head, motionless, the spot-
light on him shrinking slowly until the entire stage is dark.*

CURTAIN

*All this inspired by riding across the Pampa Tamarugal at dusk
(and written in the Lluta Valley in the house belonging to Enrique Araya,
author of The Moon Was My Country), watching my own shadow
lengthen and the wind wipe away the hoof tracks behind us. Ahead of
us a dim unchanging horizon that recedes as we approach.*

We follow the old telegraph line across the Pampa de Tana, an orphaned
copper wire that leads you back into yesterday. The network is still intact, still
standing are the dusty offices with the telegraph receivers that have keys of
ivory, polished by someone's fingers and boxes full of yellowed telegram re-
ceipts. A mosaic of details link you to thousands of anonymous lives that
shaped the course of events for a brief time.

I wish I had kept the telegram about the *piano mules*, so you could have
seen that one too. But we left it where we found it. The telegram was dated
November 17, 1934 and it said:

-sending-pianomules-immediately-

Signed, Edward.

A husband's message to his wife, isolated up in a nitrate boomtown, yearning for home, for culture? No, that didn't make sense. An agent down at the
coast maybe, confirming that the piano was on its way?

Piano mules, an old man in Camarones told me later, were two mules the
same size and with the same gaits, teamed up to carry each end of an awkward
and delicate load, like a piano. Imagine a piano walking slowly across the
dunes to bring Mozart to some boomtown like Huara or Victoria or Prosperidad!

After Tana, the salt flats are behind us. Now we don't need to cling to railroad trestles, bulldozed tracks or telegraph lines to get us safely across the giant floes of salt locked in a waterless ocean that is completely unpassable outside of an established line. The desert floor is sand now and we can go anywhere we want.

The sky is so close it might just land softly on you for a moment and you could reach up then and touch a star with the very tip of your finger. You look at yourself, at your little troupe moving across the sands into the night and you are astounded to be alive. Amazed to be making this journey through the desert unplanned, uncharted, playing it by ear and improvising as we go along, confident that wherever we will end up, it will be okay. And even if it isn't okay, we'll get through it and move on and then it will be okay. And if not then, the next day after.

You see things differently in the desert. You can put what's inside your mind out there and have a look at it. Nathan says this is how he feels out alone in a boat on the ocean. He is a Pisces and at home on the water. I am not. I am a Taurus and the desert is my kind of ocean, with the dunes rolling in under my horse in shadowy waves. The slightest hollow might be a gaping chasm, because you have no perception of depth, but that is okay because you're on a horse and he knows and he carries you through.

And I am okay even when suddenly the desert plateau tips over and up becomes down and far below us we see a star, shining brightly all by itself. The horses step off the very edge of the world then and pitch their weight into a vertical zigzag and the whole mountain begins to fall away and pull the desert into a whirlpool in the sky below.

The star of the upside-down sky turns out to be a bare lightbulb shining against a corrugated tin wall, at the bottom of a very deep canyon. A squat, sleepy-eyed woman in a torn slip and plastic sandals speaks to us from her doorway.

"I didn't hear you coming down the pavement," she says. She yawns.

"We came down the side of the mountain," I say.

"*Niños*!!! No one do that. You get buried alive." She crosses herself. "The Quebrada of Chiza is a kilometer deep!"

She tugs her shawl around her rounded shoulders and motions for us to follow her into the kitchen where, at two o'clock in the morning, she prepares fried eggs and black beans for us while guinea pigs of all colors and sizes scurry around her feet on the dirt floor.

A little later, a trucker pulls in and she mothers and feeds him also.

She is still tuut-tuut-ing and shaking her head when we get up to go and sleep.

"You very loco, *niños*. God must have protected you!"

"Thank you for everything, *señora*," I say. But there is no way to properly thank her for filling up an empty space like this, for sharing her simple fare and her heart with you, making you feel that your are her *niños* and that because you are, her God will be looking out for you too so that no harm will come to you.

In the morning, when we can see our tracks coming down through the loose sand in almost vertical descent, we feel very lucky not to have been buried alive. If we had known what the side of the mountain looked like, we would not have dared. And that was true of the whole of the ride across the Big North. Had we known more about it beforehand, we would have joined in with the chorus who sang:

It cannot be done!

We spend the day in the shade of the tamarugo trees and drink lukewarm Pepsi Colas, waiting for the cool of the evening. When the sun begins to drop towards the Cordillera in the west, we begin our climb up the other side of the canyon, up the Quebrada Seca, along a narrow bed of sand through the rocks. Near the top, many of the boulders have hieroglyphs from long ago and dates and names of more recent travellers.

We stop and carve our own symbol on a stone. We don't do this sort of thing very often, but it seems appropriate to leave a record here. We have earned our place along the other travellers through time. If you go by that way, you will find our simple sign: NE 1970 next to the mementos left by Carlos Rodriguez in 1820 and Juan Bellini in 1836.

On January 25th we ride into the northern city of Arica, right up the middle of the main avenue. Our reflections wobble along walls of glass and multiply into a whole cavalry unit of victorious campaigners taking the city by storm. Palm trees wave in the wind, rollers crash against the breakwater in salute. No one else is around.

We're intoxicated with our own sense of triumph.

We made it!!!

And just look at our horses: sleek and shiny, in better condition than they have ever been! And Chaco! If Aranza could see him now, how amazed and how proud she would be of the clownish little yellow pup she sent off to the New World and who grew into this Basque Conqueror, equal to none!

We're so used to the people of the great solitudes helping us out anytime day or night that, without hesitation, we knock on the large oak doors at the entrance to the Tarapacá Regiment, at four o'clock in the morning.

"We have arrived!"

The guard has no idea why two gringos and four horses and a yellow dog are standing at the gates. We insist that we are expected and managed to convince him to call a superior officer. The guard does not relay his exact words. Suffice it to say that our night of triumph ends in a shantytown at the fringe of the city. We set up camp under a railroad bridge. Chaco curls up on the panniers and promptly goes to sleep. He has learned to take every opportunity to rest, for he never knows when he'll be going on, or for how long.

We make a small fire out of some paper and a few twigs and sit there for a while, huddled in our ponchos and then we crawl under the tarp and go to sleep. The horses stand guard by a slimy trickle of polluted water amongst a scatter of tin cans, orange peels, threadbare tires, cardboard boxes and plastic bottles, waiting for their bale to show up somehow, from somewhere.

This time, there is no bale. This is the first time, in all the many weeks across the deserts of the Big North, that we fail to feed our horses.

Weight of Pack, 18 marzo 1970

61 kgs

Pack saddle: (12 kg
Big brown poncho   2 3/4 kg
Grey blanket   1 1/4 kg

Total basic saddle: 16 kg

Basic pack:
Medicine kits   2 3/4 kg
diaries   1 kg
Fishing X shoe kits   3/4 kg
mending kits   1/2 kg
Thermos   1 kg
Waking up kit   3/4 kg
Horses shoeing kit   1 1/2 kg
2 horseshoes X nails   1 kg
(horses brushes)   1/2 kg
eating utensils kit   1/2 kg
Nathans shoes   1 kg
my sandals   1/2 kg

Misc clothing (my thin pants, blue shirt, N pants
bathing suits , grey wollen t shirt, 2 pairs socks,
2 long johns)   2 kg
my heavy pants   3/4 kg
2 pairs corderoid pants   1 kg

3 nylon shirts   3/4 kg
2 wollen sweaters   1 kg
underwear X T/ shirts   3/4 kg
Tripod for camera   3/4 kg
1 roll blue film.

Total   22 kg

Top of pack:
Tent (material only)   3 1/2 kg
2 Jackets   2 kg
Sleeping bag X tarpollen 5 kg
Space blankets   1 kg
Tent poles   1 kg
Type writer   4 kg
Horse shoeing kit + shoe 2 1/2
Hwe' bushes   1/2 kg

Total top of pack :   19 1/2 kgs

Sack contains N: shoe + tube   3 1/2 kg.
+ 2 cups

(15 1/2) , 12 1/2
- 3 hrs.

THE HIGHEST HIGH

Dogs bark. Dishes clatter. Children argue. Women yell. Car horns blare and a train thunders across the bridge above our heads. The Arica shantytown is awake and ready to tackle another day.

We emerge from under our railroad bridge and ride back into the center of town. We have a letter to deliver, in an envelope crumpled and stained from being in our pack, through the rain and snow of the south and the salt and dust of the north.

The letter is addressed to a *señor* Lautaro Ortega.

The address is Hotel del Paso, Arica.

The person who wrote this letter is Enrique Araya, author of a book called *The Moon Was My Country* and Consul General of Chile in Bariloche, Argentina. We had dinner at his house one stormy night, eight months earlier, and Don Enrique told us to use his little place in the Lluta Valley of Arica. He gave us this letter to deliver by Pony Express. And now here we are, handing the weathered envelope to a bellboy, at what looks to be the best hotel in town.

Moments later, *señor* Lautaro Ortega comes out of his office, brimming with enthusiasm and hospitality.

"A letter Pony Express across the Atacama! That is really something!"

We are to stay at the hotel as his personal guest. He insists. And he means all of us. He sits Nathan and me down to an exquisite lunch, attended to by not just one waiter, but two! Our table has a full view of the ocean and the hotel garden, where presently Pampero is checking out one of the flowerbeds. The other three are, so far, sticking with eating the grass.

Señor Ortega really, actually means for our Criollos to stay there. Obviously he has little idea what four horses would turn a bright green lawn and garden into. We suggest the Tarapacá Regiment as a more suitable place for our voracious foursome. *Señor* Ortega immediately springs into action. He makes a phone call and this time when we ride up, the oak doors swing open wide. No one makes mention of our earlier appearance at four o'clock this morning. Eager hands take the horses over to the stables to be given the attention they so well deserve.

With the horses in such good hands, we immerse ourselves in the luxuries of the Hotel del Paso and our status as its great and honored guests. When we return to the Tarapacá Regiment the following morning to check on the horses, we are in for a shock. Our horses are not in the stables, nor in the yard. This is very strange! We begin a systematic search of the buildings around the inner courtyard.

We find Pampero first, in a section of the stables used for storing feed. He is parked in an alley, between two enormous piles of whole oats stored in open tie stalls on either side. Caicique, India and Maracas are standing by a stack of alfalfa bales. None of the horses are presently eating. One of Caicique's ears turns at our approach. Maracas lifts his head slightly. Pampero remains immobile, large and Buddha-like.

A lot of things go through your mind in a moment like that.

Who could have been stupid enough to turn horses loose in a mountain of grain?

Don't they know horses colic and die! That they develop azoturia from the protein shock. How could they do this!

And then you realize that whoever it was didn't mean harm. You begin to calm down inside because you see that this is amazing! Someone wanted our horses to have the biggest banquet any horse ever had and you don't want to yell at anyone for being too good to your horses. Most people don't care nearly enough. Remember Rafael, way back down in the Patagonia? Rafael would not sell you a bale at any price. You meet too many people like that. You are just very, very grateful now that the Criollos have the amazing constitution that they do.

You look at Pampero and think of the old classic: a donkey starving between two piles of hay because he cannot choose which one to eat. Instead of yelling, you start laughing then, because whoever thought that one up didn't know anything about donkeys. Or Argentine Criollos. Humans worry about free choice; donkeys and Criollos don't. They'd munch on one pile and then the other, back and forth, until both piles were gone. No dilemma.

Looking at Pampero now, I remember when I was six, maybe seven and my grandfather made a tub of vanilla ice cream, just for me. I remember the feel of the wooden handle and the sound of ice and salt crunching and how turning it got heavier as cream and sugar and vanilla churned into icecream. My grandfather sat me down at the kitchen table at Slottsgatan # 7 and he told me:

"Eat all the icecream you want."

Until that moment, I had always thought that this was a whole lot more than it turned out to be. I would never have said so, but the truth was that the second bowl did not taste nearly as good as the first. The third was quite a chore to finish. I sat at the table for long time before I would admit there wouldn't be a fourth bowl. I had reached my ice cream limit.

Just as Pampero clearly reached his oat limit. He follows Nathan out into the courtyard without halter or rope. I put baling twine around Caicique and lead him like that and the other two follow and we walk them around for a while and then we jump on bareback and ride them around and around the courtyard for an hour. Their walk is the same as always: short and choppy and very slow. Then we find their *cabrestos* and tie them up in stalls and tell the officer in charge not to feed and especially not to water them.

Back at Hotel El Paso, people are waiting for us.

You have done this amazing thing. People always want to know why?

What made you do it?

They expect you to tell them you are making a record, or breaking someone else's record, or you are doing it to raise awareness about something, or funds for something.

People want crisp answers and it is easier to give those. You say things like: we wanted to ride the length of Chile. The desert was there, so we crossed it.

Close enough to the truth.

When you live on the trail, which is vastly different from making an expedition, what you have accomplished comes as a surprise to you when you look back after weeks and months of travel. You realize then how extraordinary it is.

With an expedition, it would be the reverse. I have never made one, but I think that's how it would be. The goal would totally overshadow the journey and I'd be afraid of missing the whole thing on the way to The One Moment.

This is not a discussion you want to get into with newspaper reporters and people who just want to say they met someone travelling from a here to a there. All they need is a label to properly categorize and file you. Another thing people want to hear are the numbers. How far? How long? How much?

Here are some of the numbers.

From El Zorro to Arica, we rode a total of 6823 kilometers. Very little of this distance was over roads. We estimate distance through counting the hours in the saddle. The Criollos walk an agonizingly slow four kilometers an hour. Slower yet across volcanic *mesetas* and boggy trails, somewhat faster in the desert, where we trimmed the pack to a bare minimum and did intervals at a trot.

We spent three months in the desert and covered a distance of 1764 kilometers. In November we came 611 kilometers in 17 days, in December 588 kilometers in 15 marches and in January 565 kilometers in 16, for a total of 48. Most of the time, we travelled during the night. In the desert, we rested almost as many days as we moved.

We covered almost as much territory during our first three months in the Patagonia: 1741 kilometers. But we moved a total of 73 days, 23 days in January and February and 27 days in March, resting only 17 days in the three months.

Arriving at Pago Chico, the horses were exhausted and sick.

Arriving in Arica, they were fit and healthy.

The difference was the feed.

The horse culture of the Patagonia is based on horses being plentiful and cheap. If one isn't serviceable, you grab a different one. *Gauchos* travel with a *tropilla* of eight to sixteen horses, using each horse just a day or two in a month. The code of hospitality assures you a roof, a meal and pasture for up to a dozen horses at the *estancias*. The *potrero* where you turn out is usually over grazed from too much use by too many. The *estancias* are not set up to provide the kind of care you need to travel the same horse day after week, after month, after year.

"Buckskin sooner dead than tired" is a saying anyone familiar with *gaucho* lore can quote you. I am not quite sure I know what it really means. These same people will also tell of Criollo horses that just keep going and going, on whatever they can scavenge at night.

What I know to be true is that with good feed and care, an ordinary horse can perform well, without it you will ruin the best of horses in short order. Every night when you can't find good feed for your horse, he will use up more of his reserves. He will start going down and, eventually, he will not be able to go any further.

In all of February, in the Patagonia, we were able to grain our horses but once.

In the month of December, in the desert, we grained them 24 days. They consumed 342 kilos altogether, or about 3 1/2 kilos per day per horse. We were able to feed them high quality alfalfa hay each and every day. They consumed a total of 1530 kilos during the month, or about 12 1/2 kilos per horse per day.

Most of this feed came from the Carabineros. Cavalry and mounted police horses are issued a standard daily ration of six kilos of alfalfa hay and four kilos of whole oats. In 1970 most of the Carabinero horses were of little practical use anymore in the desert communities. They were worked only lightly and some hardly at all. There was usually feed to spare for our four horses at the *retens*.

Without the Carabineros, our ride through the desert would not have been possible. They fed our horses, often us as well. They gave us places to stay, they gave us respect and they made us feel that what were doing was a great and wonderful thing.

When the novelty of living in a luxury hotel has worn off, we ride up the Lluta Valley to Parcel # 23: twenty hectares of desert that belong to Enrique Araya and where Olga and Bernardo live in a small block house, painted white and shaded by two *algarrobo* trees, the only two trees on the parcel. It would be hard to imagine Don Enrique Araya out here, our elegant dinner host who had his picture taken with Prime Minister Nehru of India and with his intimate friend, Nobel Laureate Pablo Neruda. To this simple desert plot this worldly man says he will someday retire. Maybe he will and maybe it will be perfect.

For us, at this moment, it is the perfect place.

Physically we are fit, mentally we are exhausted. No more room for input. We have to stop the flow and sit down and try and figure out what it all means. We need to have an address where people can write us letters, take the same bus down to the same store and watch the sun rise and set over the same piece of horizon. Because if you don't stop like that, you will lose the edge and everything will start to blur, because you are just moving through geography.

We stay in the white block house for two months.

We write about the agrarian reform in Chile, about MIR, about the history of the Chilean Creole horse, about the Carabineros. Nathan writes several short plays. I write articles in English and Swedish and Spanish. We eat Olga's *empanadas*, we play bareback jostling games with dry corn stalk lances. We go to the beach on Sundays and we help Bernardo with the alfalfa. We irrigate, spray the emerging shoots and make bundles every evening to send to the racetrack. Bernardo gets nine crops a year, spraying each one. The poison that kills the fat green worms also gets into the ground and into the racehorses and onto your hands and you breathe the stuff and it is the same they used to fumigate our *barrio* shack in Venezuela. We swept the bugs off the floor afterwards, two gallons of roaches, black spiders as big as your hand, moths, flies, fleas, and mosquitoes. Then we washed the floor and moved in and lived there for a year and a half. We didn't worry what the poison that killed so many bugs might be doing to us! And we don't know to worry enough about the DDT now. It is off the list in Chile, as in the US, but it is legal in Peru. When Bernardo goes to Tacna, just across the border, to pick up some, we come along to see Colonel Flores at the Tacna Cavalry regiment. We want to talk about riding through the Peruvian *sierra*. Colonel Flores is brief and to the point:

"Horses don't make it in the *sierra*!" He says. "They'll keep going until they drop with *soroche*. Then you'll be on foot."

Colonel Flores has plenty of historical data to back up his opinion. The great Liberators Simon Bolìvar and San Martìn lost thousands of men and horses to pneumonia and mountain sickness.

"In Santiago they told us we couldn't possibly cross the Atacama on horse-back," Nathan says. "I wish you could come and see our horses now!"

Colonel Flores knows his *sierra* and he is a man not accustomed to being contradicted.

"Many passes up there are over five thousand meters. And you say your horses are from the *pampas*! What do they know of mountains!"

"They'll learn," I say.

He shakes his head. "Get mules," he says. "You want to go into the *sierra*, get yourselves some mules."

Seven months later, if someone had come to us and asked about crossing the length of Peru on horseback, we would have told him what Colonel Flores tried to tell us then: stay along the coast. Because after seven months, we had found out what Colonel Flores knew: the *sierra* of Peru will zap you physi-cally and mentally. With every pass you conquer, you will find another pass to climb. It will be higher than the one before, or just seem that way, because every day you are growing weaker than you were the day before. You under-stand then why mountain regions do not cradle horse cultures. In the moun-tains you can hope only to endure, not to flourish.

We do not know any of this when we ride up the Lluta Valley. With us come Olga on a burro and Bernardo riding a borrowed horse. We have a picnic together in the shade of a big tree and then Olga and Bernardo turn back home to Parcel # 23 and we continue on.

And that is how it should be. What is the point of travelling, if you have a known destination and a road already mapped out and if you know what you are going to encounter and all you have left to do is walk or ride or bike or drive along the pre-arranged line.

Our aversion to pre-planning is personal and extreme. We don't want to repeat the mistake we made when we built our house in Spain. We had a blue print for a house, which we brought with us from Sweden. We sat in my mother's apartment in November, dreaming of being somewhere else, and drew up these plans. Then we superimposed this pre-designed structure on the site we discovered on Machichaco. The house was wrong for the site. If someday I get a lot of money, win the lottery or something, one of the things I would do is go back to Machichaco and remove the house we put there and build the one that belongs: low and made of rock from the site, blending in with the old quarry.

But you don't get to do things over again.

Anyway, I don't play the lottery.

What we learned from our house on Machichaco is: don't bring blueprints with you. Go see what you see, do what you do. Don't spend too much time studying the topography, fauna, flora, ethnic and cultural structure of a region before you get there. Allow yourself to be surprised.

Colonel Flores did give us one concrete piece of advice:

"Advance by stages," he said, "Go to 2000 meters, then to 3000 meters and stay a while at each. Get yourselves and your horses used to the altitude."

That is exactly what Don Filiberto Ochoa tells us in the village of Putre, which lies at 3524 meters and where we arrive six days after leaving Parcel # 23. Don Filiberto is eighty-two years old and proud to have you know this and to marvel at his youthfulness. He is a village elder and in charge of the vacant agricultural experimental station where, he says, we are to stay until our blood thins. This will take at least until after the Semana Santa celebration, which is a very big thing in the village of Putre.

Today is only Wednesday. Don Filiberto has places to go with us before the Easter Procession begins. He bursts into our room at the experimental station before six on Thursday morning with what is left of an old cavalry saddle slung over one shoulder. He is planning to ride India on an outing with us.

We get to watch from the rear and try not to worry about our octogenarian as the mare trips and stumbles her way down a precarious trail carved right into the sandstone, barely wide enough for a horse. Don Filiberto does not explain to us where we are going or why but a few times, on a switchback, he looks back and smiles and you see into the eyes of a boy. We stop for a drink of water at a grotto to the Virgin Cristo Rey, which is right by a stream with clear running water. Don Filiberto takes out a crumpled paper and sits down on a rock and looks out across the valley and writes down some thought that he has. We ride on along fields of alfalfa and ripening corn in this mountain Atlantis wedged between sterile slopes, Don Filiberto always up ahead.

This old man knows to seize a moment when it comes to him in the shape of a beautiful paint mare, all the way from the southern *pampas*. And he lets himself be carried into the past, back to the places where he used to grow corn and where he raised eleven daughters and had a weaving factory. Our journey is now also his, in that way special to strangers, unburdened by a common past and with no future together.

Don Filiberto picks some ears of corn in a field and takes us to the Cave of Ancestors. We make a fire in the shade, where many others have before us. The corn tastes smoky and sweet, roasted in the husk, with goat cheese that Don Filiberto brought along in his pocket.

He is the son of a Baptist missionary and an Aymara woman, he tells us now. He speaks Latin, he says, better than most priests. Then he sends us to explore the cave and the orange and red prehistoric wall paintings of men and llamas. He stays by the horses to write down more thoughts on his piece of paper. Back in Putre, he reads to us from the rumpled piece of paper, fragments from a poem about our epic journey.

"They travelled soon to be forgotten trails, tracing rivers back to hidden sources."

We don't get to see his finished poem. Maybe it remains unfinished. The Easter Procession is now upon us. Don Filiberto is a moving spirit behind the pageant, we the outside observers. We do not speak to each other again.

Aymara Indians float into Putre out of mist-clogged gorges, hidden mountain valleys, from the tundra between crags, the most lovely, harsh, inhospitable upper reaches. They float down the deep-rutted trails between cacti, walled terraces of oregano, alfalfa and maize and disperse into the adobe colonnades of shadows, chewing green wads of coca with vacant wonder in their large brown eyes.

All flow together into the plaza for the Christ burial procession on Good Friday, packing in tight around the tall oak doors of the church: clusters of Aymara women in Charlie Chaplin hats and town elders in long ponchos squatting on the cobblestones, hooking down aguardiente from proffered bottles. The cool mountain air is spiced with eucalyptus incense, sugarcane liquor, manure, mud and mold; the hum of voices mounts steadily. From within the adobe womb of the church, the baritone chanting increases in volume and intensity until everyone outside is rocking back and forth.

The large oak doors open suddenly and through the gaping mouth of the high-domed conch, an enormous glow worm begins to emerge, inching forward in rhythmic cadence, rocking from side to side under a sea of flickering candles, crawling towards a Bethlehem to be reborn. And just in front of the glassed-in coffin, reading aloud in a hybrid tongue from a leatherbound tome is Filiberto The Baptist, leading the pagans and the Catholics!

All eyes are on the icon incubator swaying on the shoulders of black robed pallbearers, voices joining the river of the mourners' chants that swell out into the night, as the procession humps forward inch by inch, monotonously swinging to the pulse of the mantric song:

Una limosna para enterrar a Cristo
Alms for the burial of Christ,
Alms for the burial of Christ,

The death march goes on through the night in hypnotic low key, throbbing through the adobe catacombs, a Gregorian rhythm echoing on a pagan drum, the primal beat: a-tooooom, a-tooooom, the heart-beat from the statue inside:

a-tooooom, a-tooooom until all I perceive through weary eyes is an aura of flames drifting by, a glass time capsule undulating through space and I can almost share in the collective illusion of a wooden heart of the Son of Man beating and bleeding in our midst. I stumble up the aisle to witness the Christ being lifted from the cocoon, arms spread out like the wings of a moth, and placed above the altar, symbol of the perpetual rebirth of death into life.

For the Indians and the townsfolk, this séance is only a prelude to the celebrations that will go on non-stop for days. Without the coca to erase the ordinary limits of fatigue and hunger, all we want to do now is go home and sleep.

Far above the village of Putre lies a region so separate, so untouched, you feel you have entered the magical world inside of a glass ball. We come upon a shepherdess and her children, spinning red wool with a top and giggling as they herd a flock of llamas and alpacas across a carpet of green, laced by silver riverlets. Beyond the tundra marshland, twin volcanoes pierce a clear blue sky with brilliant white.

I take photograph after photograph of this world beyond the grasp of language, a world I want to take with me and keep always and return to when I am feeling crowded and swamped by the inane details of daily life. The way you would hold a glass ball in your hand when you were a child, turn it over gently and then watch the snow fall silently inside.

But when the gods shake this world, it isn't gently.

The blue sky disappears and snow comes on a breath of liquid ice from the glacial peaks. It hits you full in the face with whiplash ferocity. We keep riding into the storm. We're heading for the carabinero post at Chuncuyo an hour away, maybe two.

But the angry god of the volcano opens his bomb hatch to drop a couple megatons of ice balls over us. They ricochet off boulders and bounce on the moss. And they hurt! A moment later, a horizontal shaft of lightning splits into a dozen branches and a ball of light rolls across the tundra not very far away from us, and explodes.

Now we believe the stories of tight bunches of llamas incinerated at a stroke. Now we believe that the shepherds run from their flocks in the instant storms of the Bolivian winter. We don't want to keep going exposed like this on iron shod horses that might draw the lightning to us. We decide to stop and pitch our tent. It goes up like a red balloon and we manage to hang onto it and peg it down and lash a ground sheet over our saddles and panniers. Then we crawl inside and huddle together under soggy horse blankets as the peat bogs tremble underneath us. Our little nylon igloo blinks on and off as the blitzkrieg rages. Chaco buries his head under the blankets and trembles at every clap of thunder. I just keep my eyes closed, most of the time.

As suddenly as it came, the storm moves on and becomes but a distant rumble of retreating artillery. All is quiet again. Too quiet. We're afraid to look outside. Maybe the horses stood too close together, their tails to the storm, and the electricity between them brought all of them down in one stroke. Or maybe they took off and ran until the thin air stopped them dead in their tracks. Maybe they dropped with *soroche*; maybe Colonel Flores became right after all.

They are grazing on the frozen marshland not far away. Their slick summer coats are wet from the storm, but they seem totally at home here as they shove hail the size of golf balls out of the way with their lips. It is as if the storm never happened to them.

If we saddle up right away, we should arrive at Chuncuyo well before dark, where we'll have a hot meal and a bed. But now that the storm is over, we find no reason to leave this random spot that makes us feel at home in a way that we haven't since we travelled the solitudes of the Patagonia. This grass isn't much more than filler for the horses, but they obviously enjoy eating it. Maybe the taste reminds them of home. We have a ration of oats we brought along from Putre to give them. They'll be okay until we get to Chuncuyo in the morning.

We can wait to eat until tomorrow. For now, we just want to watch the storm clouds retreat around the volcanoes and enjoy this freedom we feel on the rooftop of the world where the grass is green and the water blue and we can allow ourselves to realize just how hard the desert marches really were.

This is a fine place to sleep a first night in the new red tent that Nathan's parents sent from Maine to Arica and that has now weathered a storm so well on the Pampa de Chubire at 4600 meters. We crawl into our bedroll with Chaco curled up in a tight ball at our feet, asleep long before we are. During the night, as we sleep, he uncurls himself and inches his way between us. When we wake up, we're the ones in a tight ball on either side of Chaco who is sound asleep with his head on the pillow, his front paws drawn up under his chin against my back and his hind legs braced against Nathan.

The tent is white with ice crystals. We kick Chaco out of bed and peek outside. The horses are munching on the short prickly grass above the creek that is now encased in ice, clearly unfazed by the cold. Chaco pussyfoots around the frozen earth just long enough to relieve himself and then comes charging back into the tent. We snuggle together and wait for the sun to gain an edge over the morning frost.

We arrive at Chuncuyo in time for lunch. The carabineros had been expecting us the night before with supper and a bed prepared for us in the telegraph operator's room. They worried that we got lost or took a wrong turn and seem disappointed now that we are planning to continue right after lunch.

We quickly change our minds about leaving when storm clouds come racing in with hail and lightning. We stay by the fire in the cozy little room instead and take the opportunity to pick up the threads of our writing projects. Nathan is working on a scenario he calls Pies, one of so many inspired by the desert. I am still working on the article about the Chilean Horse. There is a passage I found in El Huaso by Tomas Lago. It is from the War of 1879. Says one Captain Ramirez Rosales:

"Almost all the mounts were purebred Chilenos. There were squadrons that kept their horses saddled day and night for three or four weeks at a stretch and in spite of this and of having their backs full of worm infested sores, not a single soldier was unable to fulfill his mission because of his mount failing him."

I am trying to decide if I am including this with my article or not. The author means to illustrate the hardiness and valor of the breed. I see only man's brutality and stupidity. I decide to leave the passage out and talk instead about the Araucanian Indians who rode their horses bareback, with only a leather thong for control.

"They conditioned their horses, the same as they did themselves, training them in all kinds of exercises such as long jumps and jumps over obstacles, races, turns. If the horses were not very good in all these activities, they killed them and ate them."

At least they made it swift. Araucanians did not just let the worms eat their mounts out from underneath them! The Araucanians were never defeated by the Spaniards.

I am going to use some pictures I took in the Lluta Valley of Chileno horses belonging to Lautaro Rojas. He rides occasionally on some Sunday afternoon and employs two men full time to care for them. The horses have no purpose other than the ostentation of Lautaro Rojas. In his meticulous care of them, does he make a small right for so many wrongs done to horses in the history in the Americas? Probably not.

We drift across the Pampa de Chubire in slow motion, moving fifteen kilometers in a day, maybe less and wind our way around the inlets and streams of Lago Cotacotani at the foot of the two white volcanoes. Sometimes we follow trails, sometimes we just follow our eyes to hidden ponds speckled with birds, flamingos, ducks, loons and black and white geese, herds of llamas and alpacas, shepherd's huts and solitary churches. Every hamlet has a small chapel, made of rock and mud and with a cross in a cage in front of the door.

Painted on the walls and the ceilings inside are the demons of the European spirit of the seventeen hundreds. Devils and lizards and beasts, just like you see them in the paintings of Hieronymous Bosch and Breughel in the Christian churches of central Europe. But why here, in this pristine place so far away? As if these simple shepherd people, who learned to live at the foot of volca-noes and endure the electrical blitzkrieg each and every day, need the evil spirits, the purgatory and hell of Europe. The priests are long gone now. The plains are depopulating. In the town of Visviri, which is at the very top corner of Chile, there is a brand new school where we stay the night. It is built to hold a hundred students. There are ten in residence. And when they learn to read and write and to want and wish for more, are they going to stay in these forlorn villages tending to flocks of llamas that provide them with meat for sustenance and wool for warmth, in a cycle that goes back to the beginning of history?

Are they?

Or will they find their way down the mountain, to the coast, to the streets of Arica and, once there, will they ever climb the mountain again?

On April 7 we ride across an arid pampa, between two volcanic mountain ranges that are layered in red, yellow and black. At some point, we cross a frontier and enter the Republic of Peru. We stop at an isolated hut to ask directions to the post of the *guardia republicana* and the Aymara family invites us to share their barbecued lamb. They are all turned on from coca leaves, mixed with *ceniza*, formed into balls and kept in the side of their mouths.

We continue up a valley and find the *guardia republicana* post at Laguna Blanca. The *guardias* are busy painting the place, which has the look of a youth hostel more than a military outpost. No one is wearing a uniform. No one is interested in seeing our documents. Their job here is to ride mules in the mountains and they are not interested in hearing the details of our riding horses. What they want to know about is the war in Vietnam and free love and the racial problems in the US. We are glad to oblige. They honor us with a great meal of steak and french fries, while they eat spaghetti. We talk late into the evening and don't worry about tomorrow.

On April 8, our first full day in Peru, we ride to the top of the world!
We conquer the Condor Pass, at 5168 meters!
Our horses did it! No trouble at all!
I wish there had been someone to witness, especially of course Colonel Flores from Tacna, how Caicique walked up the steep switchbacks, slow and steady. He would stop often and stand still and breathe in and breathe out, slow and steady and deep. When he was ready, he would start moving on his own and go another while. Stop again and go, with everyone following behind and with me just sitting on his back, trusting him. The same as I trusted him all the way from the Lluta Valley, along the cliff-hangers above Socorama. You

could look straight down into the village and throw a pebble, Nathan said, and it would land right in the plaza of the matchbox village far below. I didn't look, I couldn't look. I can't even look down from ten feet up, never mind thousands! All I could do was trust Caicique to carry me up which, if you stop and think about it, made no sense at all. What did my big plains-bred gelding know of climbing mountains?

The *apacheta* at the top of the Condor Pass is a very large pile of stones. Some of the rocks look to have been picked up from the site, others must have been carried all the way up by travellers over the centuries. Inca runners, slaves, warriors, miners, traders all placed a rock on the *apacheta* as a symbol of the burden you leave behind on top of the pass.

I want to put a big stone right on the very top of the pile! I spot one and get off my horse and walk over to get it. I don't even get to pick the rock up before I am out of breath and my legs fold up under me. My chest is suddenly tight. I remember to focus on my breathing: in and out, in and out. I feel better after a few minutes and look up to meet Caicique's mocking gaze that seems to say that I haven't conquered a mountain, he has.

The sun sets a thousand meters below us and, for one fleeting moment, the last rays bequeath a crown of fire upon the gray heads of extinct volcanoes. Then the shadows climb the mountain and we begin our descent into a valley that slowly fills with night.

*We find a cave just above the trail and stop for the night. The horses eat their rations of grain and go off to graze on the hard **paja brava** along the creekbed below.*

We make a roaring fire at one side of the entrance, so the smoke will be drawn out of the cave and lay out our bedroll on the opposite side. We climb in right after supper, intending to write for an hour or so. But I find it impossible to use the written word in this setting. The smell of the smoke, the firelight flickering over the wall, the cold wind humming past the mouth of the den bring images, feelings, impulses churning up from the phylogenetic reserve, from the collective unconscious. I picture women stooped over a fire, preparing meat, men painting the walls at the rear of the cave and I sense fur pelts against my own skin, a stone implement in my hand. I feel warm and secure.

*Yes, IN A CAVE on the inhospitable, solitary **altiplano** in the south*

of Peru!
   Caveman Foote, Esq.

Forty-eight hours later our world is blown apart.

You need to blame someone, so you blame yourself.

You always blame yourself.

I shouldn't have been so triumphant, so gloating.

If only I had kept my head down and been more humble, the gods might not have noticed us coming up the side of the mountain and we could have continued unnoticed down into the valley on the other side. If we hadn't made so much noise about it, there would have been no reason to punish our *hubris*.

We hadn't done anything else wrong. From the cave, we went on down the valley, all the way to the post at Challapalca, where the *guardia republicana* let us have some alfalfa and oats. We turned the horses loose at night, like we always did, knowing they'd be around in the morning looking for their breakfast.

And they are nearby waiting, when we get up to feed at daybreak. But there is something very wrong with Caicique. He has rancid smelling green slime around his mouth and nose. His eyes are wild and his belly is swollen. His heartbeat is very rapid. He staggers and his hindquarters seem to be paralyzed.

The *guardias* shake their heads when they see Caicique. They know what is wrong with our horse. Caicique has eaten a poisonous plant they call *garbanzo*.

The *guardias* also know the outcome: death.

"What a shame," says the lieutenant. "Such a good big horse."

"There must be something we can give him for it. Something we can do!"

"Not for *garbanzo*," says the lieutenant. "We lost a couple of mules ourselves not long ago," he adds by way of commiseration.

It makes no sense. Why would Caicique eat poison? He is the smart one, the one who brought us here safely from sea level. He didn't do that just to die at a border outpost in the middle of a desolate plain 4600 meters above sea level.

Nathan gives him an intravenous injection of Dexhitril from our pack, to eliminate toxins from his liver and kidneys. They tell us *muña* tea might help and show us which plant that is. We make tea from the light green leaves and give Caicique drenches with a Pepsi bottle into his nostril. Nathan grinds up carbon pills and mixes them with powdered milk and oil and makes him swallow a gallon of the mixture, a little bit at a time. We give him a series of enemas, concocted from *muña*, soap and salt, via a piece of plastic hose. The hose also helps eliminate gases.

We walk him. We massage him. We talk to him.

But all day long he keeps getting worse.

The stars are frozen in black ice and the mercury continues to drop as he lies quivering under an army blanket in the corner of the corral, his head in Elly's lap. Her face is pressed against his neck, speaking muffled sounds.

Each time spasms of pain gouge at him from within, he grates his teeth and his powerful legs strike out and each time he retracts them to his swollen belly slowly, with such agony, that a tear runs down the side of his face onto her knee.

I throw more wood on the embers, prod the fire back to life. The horse looks up at me, crooked spike tilted and then his head sinks back into her lap and I watch the light dance against the round stones of the corral and drive the shadows back into the crevices. The heat snatches away the frost vapor from her breath, from his and mine. I squat by the pot of boiling muña tea, blue jeans burning against my shins, and mix in more carbon tablets, vegetable oil and salt. When it is cool enough, I watch her feed it to him slowly, pushing the neck of the bottle into the side of his mouth, cooing nonsense, crying again, smiling bravely at the same time.

He is listening to her. But his body is so cold! With my ear against his side I can hardly make out a beat anymore. Gently, I massage his belly, trying to ease the toxic gases, but I am powerless against the pain that wrenches his hindquarters and shoves him forward in the mud. He lunges, head twisted sideways up into the gaping hole of darkness. He finds his footing, staggering one way, then another, dragging the old blanket that slid off his back to his rump, a torn and bloodied matador's cape that will not fall. Elly steadies him, straightens the blanket and leads him around the fire, circling slowly several times before he stumbles and falls.

He lies absolutely still, his gaze fixed on the dancing flames, un-blinking, while she talks on and on. A tear has formed in the corner of his eye, but it too seems frozen. I want to run forward and check for a pulse, to listen for his heartbeat, but I can't move.

Is he gone?

He is staring straight into my eyes now, reading my fear, my loss of faith. How weird he looks. How ashamed I feel. In his raging eyes is the indomitable spirit that Elly loves more than any quality in man or animal. He might die this night, but he will not be defeated.

Dawn comes and finds him prostrate by the dying embers of the fire, Elly and I huddled together under a blanket right by Caicique. We are powerless prisoners of this unendurable moment, wanting it to end, fearing what will come next. We cannot bear to look back and we dare not look ahead.

The other three horses are over by the corral gate, looking out over the plains, listening with their backs turned towards their fallen leader. When the warming rays of the sun reach us, Caicique stirs and then, with one enormous effort, he gets his front legs under him and rises to his knees and then heaves himself up. He braces himself, he staggers, but remains upright and walks very slowly over to where the other horses stand.

Elly opens the corral gate for him, crying like a child, and we watch him walk out alone to the head of the bluff above the river, still weak-ened by the siege of the past thirty-six hours, but steady now, sure of his feet. He lifts his head to the breeze.

Clouds of dust, red-brown in the dying light, converge from all sides of the basin as shepherds bring their flocks in. Dogs barking and the acrid incense of dung fires come to you on the dry breeze. The outlines of thatched huts and cactus corrals emerge from the haze: walls the same gray-brown colors as the hills beyond, grass roofs parched yel-low like the plain.

Over to our left, an old man finishes the last furrow in a narrow plot of red soil, maybe fifty yards wide by a hundred long. He unhooks the long-stemmed wooden plow, hefts it up and comes slowly toward us behind his yoke. We wait for him to join the trail.

"Excuse me, señor," I say. "Would you have some grain you would sell us?"

He unshoulders the piece of hardwood shaped like a broken wishbone that is his plow and straightens his stooped back with effort. Up close, we see that his face and hair are tinged with dust but that he is not older than we are. His yoke are two skinny cows with dried udders.

"For you? Or for the horses?"

"For the horses."

"They may feed grain to animals where you're coming from, señor," he says.

"Here there is no longer enough for bread."

He points to the plot he has just worked. "My brothers and I have only one fifth of the land my father had. He had one quarter of what his father had. My children, señor, will get one furrow each for their corn and potatoes. My children's children will starve".

"What about the agrarian reform?" I ask.

He gives a weary laugh. "They promise us new land." He motions to the steep-walled basin.

"There is no land for them to give us."

He strides away without another word. I watch the wishbone plow sway back and forth on his shoulders and his cows amble wearily toward the adobe corral topped with broken glass and I cannot begin to imagine what it would be like to labor without hope. If he knew how much protein is fed to pets and slaughter steers in our faraway lands, would he be dragging along behind that plow?

*We set up camp by a small creek within earshot of cocks crowing and children playing. The horses drift off to a marshy area that is shaved slick as a putting green by sheep and llamas. Elly goes off to fetch water in the **pava** and I gather llama droppings and make a pile inside a circle of stones. I have some paper and dry grass to start and then try to fan the smoldering llama chips into a flame with my hat.*

A child comes out of the adobe hut and walks towards us. She wears a blue school uniform and her black hair is braided neatly. She smiles at me.

"Bring your pot into the kitchen where the fire burns brightly," she says.

We duck in through the low door after her and squat on the mud floor beneath a ceiling of orange smoke. From the far end, the father bows slightly. It is the man with the wishbone plow. We are here at his invitation. The young mother fills two gourds with barley gruel and passes them around the circle of children for us and then she places our pot on their mud oven to cook. I watch a small child crawl toward the earthenware pot from which everyone is helping themselves. Her ragged dress is not long enough to cover her muddied buttocks. She sits next to the pot and begins stuffing in one small sweet potato after another: four, five, six. I try to avert my stare: eleven, twelve, thirteen. Impossible! Sixteen, seventeen, eighteen, nineteen potatoes!

And still she is hungry.

Pampa de Chulire — 12,000
Condor Pass — 16,500
Challapalca Pass — 14,500
" Umachuca " Pass — 15,600
Langui-Yanaoca — 14,200
Quenco-Pisac — 13,600
Yucay-Chincheros — 13,200
" Sanluis"-Abancay — 11-12,000
Aaci"Carahuacahua" to Huancarama - 11-12000
(Pisco Cura Valley — 2500-3000 meters)
Aca. Pisco - Andahaylas - 10,800
" Soroce ocha " Pass — 12,600
Chumbes - Matara — 13,500
(Ayacucho 9 — 9600)
Ayacucho - Cachi River - 12,200
Mantaro River - Pampas - 12,000
Pampas - Huancayo - 12,000
Acolla - Tarma — 12,200
Tarma - "Chichacaygri — 12,400
Huanuco (Valley - 6000 ft.)
Huanco - Jesus - Huanuco Valley - 11,000
Conalamba - (Puna) - San Marcos - 15,000
San Marcos - San Luis - 13,000
Llumya — 12-13,000 (Pomalamba)
Pomalamba - Mitcbamba - 12,000
Sihuas - Pampahuanchonga - 15,000
Cinchucu - Mollepata — 13,000
Mollepata - Huamachuco - 12,000
Yenasara - Cajabamba - 11,000
Cajabamba - Cajamarca - 10,000
Cajamarca - Hualgayoc - 12,000
Hualgayoc - Chota — 11,000
Chota - Cutervo - 9,000
(Chotan River - Neces Coast river drainage)
Tembracura - Olerinos - 3000 meters

TOUGH GOING

The trail plunges once more into a reptilian bellyfold and then cuts a zigzag tepee to a higher gap. Three rungs up, two rungs back down and you can't see what's beyond the next one. Looking back over the mountain jam you've already wended through, you see yourself as a myopic ant lost on a washboard of frozen tidal waves.

Flutes pipe in the breeze as two bundle-packed Indians approach in metronomic downswing; their spindly legs stretch under enormous bales of coca leaves. We find a wide spot and stop to let them by.

"Hòla, buenas tardes."

My words are snuffed out by the twitter of their wooden flutes. Where do they get the oxygen to play without pause? Their marble eyes register nothing. Don't see us, don't hear us. Beasts of burden with green lips and a wad of coca in the cheek on an unending high of highs - feeling no hunger, no cold, no fatigue, no pain - all the way from the Cordillera Oriental with the raw material for underground refineries

219

to make soma for our fatherland.

In the north we learned that, in Peru, you don't conquer mountains.

Every day, you get to climb the mountain all over again and arrive in the village, searching for feed and food. The Myth of Sisyphus is no myth in the sierra of Peru. That is how life is. Every day you push a great burden towards a summit and every night it rolls back down again. You learn to think not too far ahead. Not to look back. You learn to put one foot in front of the other and not ask too many questions. You can't stop, because your burden will bury you then.

We crossed thirty-one passes on our way north through the sierra.

If I could imagine looking down from above, like a condor, I would see a straight line across the gargantuan tangles of granite, a stone laid *camino*, twelve feet wide, made for walking the length of an empire, connecting all the tropical valleys like beads on a string.

But I am no condor. I am riding a horse deep down in the maze, caught up on trails that take you around the compass, just to put you in the next hamlet for another meal of barley soup that gives you back half the strength you have lost by the end of a day. You advance maybe five miles, travelling twenty, over tortuous switchbacks that twist your sense of direction and erode your will until you ask: closer, to where?

What had been the center of the Inca world: Cuzco, Pisac, Machu Picchu, Sacsayhuaman are now centers to the tourist world. You don't need our version. Everyone goes from Lake Titicaca to Cuzco and then on down to Lima. Tschiffely rode this way. Almost half a century later, people remember. An old man in Calea tells us Tschiffely fed each of his horses a kilo of sugar every morning. In Cuzco we learn that he used to bathe Gato and Mancha daily in the Apurimac River. Near Urcos we meet an elderly man who shows us a poster of Gato and Mancha still up on the wall of his house.

Tschiffely's ride was part of the tradition of The Grand Adventure that sent people (men, mostly) sailing, skiing, climbing, riding to the far corners of the earth. And reporting back to an audience of enthusiastic armchair travellers.

The world of our ride is a different one. The journey is personal. The world of this book is a different one yet. Extreme adventure travel is a mass movement now and a multi-billion dollar business. The earth is so much smaller now that there are so many people travelling to and fro. There is no one back home somewhere eagerly awaiting a report, because everything has already been studied in such minute detail.

Yet, now and back through history, the day-to-day life with the horses remains the same. Horses are what they are. They do what they do. Maybe that is why we need horses so much.

In Huancayo, Tschiffely set out for the coastal desert in his bid to join Buenos Aires with New York with two horses within a given timeframe. We continue north. We don't know where this journey is taking us. North is off the beaten path. That is where we want to be.

We have a new member of our troupe along with us now. His name is Andin. He is a purebred German shepherd that we acquired on a side trip down to Lima. He is just two months old and he travels in a burlap bag that Nathan has slung over his shoulder. Having him is a bit like having a baby along and it shows you how little we knew of what awaited us in the northern sierra.

There is a fork in the narrow trail from Conchabamba to Pampas. Pampas is a village tucked in he folds of the sierra, of no particular interest. We have no reason to go there rather than to some other village just like it. Pampas is just a somewhere, that's all. We ask a couple of *indios*: which trail do we take?

"That one!" Both of them say and point. "That one!"

After months in the sierra, we should have known to take the *other* one! Because by then we have been sent down the wrong way so many times. It is the *indio's* way of telling you that you're an intruder and not welcome here.

We climb for hours. We stop briefly on the summit, which is all of fifty feet wide, and then the trail takes us right back down again on the other side of the granite fold. We follow a narrow trail along the side of a mountain above a very deep gorge. We come to a place where a rockslide has taken out a twenty-foot section of trail, probably in the recent earthquake. We should have found some way of turning around and, like it or not, climbed back up and back down the way we had come and gone through some other village instead.

That's what I would do today.

We don't consider going back. Along the top of the avalanche area, we can see a faint trail where others have walked across on foot. Nathan follows the trail to the other side. It seems okay, so he comes back and takes India and leads her across. Caicique follows me without hesitation and close behind him Maracas. Nathan is on his way back to get Pampero, when Pampero decides not to wait for an escort. Instead of going up above the way we did, he plunges straight across the avalanche area. Shortcuts are his trademark. He'll hang way back on the trail when he has the pack, or it's his day off, and then catch up to us by taking out a hairpin curve and cut straight down a mountainside. He gets himself into some tough spots that way and after he does, he will stay close behind for a while. This time, there is no way out of the situation.

Time stops, breathing stops as we stand mute with horror and watch the mountain begin to move underneath Pampero. Small rocks roll across the slow moving sand, bounce down over the steeper slope and whip on down and down and down. Pampero is galloping in place, knees and hocks deep in sand. He is running for his life against the growing mass that is sending more and more pebbles and rocks toward the deep gorge hundreds of feet below us.

I don't know how Pampero makes it across.

We stop to take a picture on the other side of the rockslide. The picture shows me up close on Caicique, Maracas immediately behind, on a narrow trail above a deep canyon. The picture appeared with a story in Argosy Magazine. What amazes me, looking at it now, is how tough, nay how *nonchalant* I appear! You can't tell from looking at me that we almost lost Pampero just moments before. No hint that we had all been in danger of plunging down the gorge to our deaths. It wasn't until we talked to a mule driver in Pampas and saw the look in his eyes that we realized how very close we had been to disaster.

"Six good mules went down that gorge just days ago!" He says. "No one should go that trail. Didn't they tell you?"

They told us.

It is hard to get used to this hatred the *indio* has for you. You know it isn't personal. For centuries the *indio* of the sierra has lived in fear and resentment of white horsemen. Inca Garcilaso de la Vega wrote this about Pizarro and his handful of men who conquered the Inca Empire back in 1532:

"Here the Indians began to observe with great curiosity the horses, which they took for heavenly creatures and equals of their masters. Having remarked that they were continually chewing their bits, they concluded that this was their usual food and hastened to bring them bars of gold and silver ore, with which they filled their feed troughs. Then, addressing themselves directly to the horses, they said very kindly:

'Do leave your iron aside and eat this fodder, which is much better.'

And the Spaniards, laughing up their sleeves at their ignorance, encouraged the Indians to bring the horses all the gold and silver they could find, if they wanted to make friends with them."

At hacienda Mitobamba Don Julio Noriega tells us how it was in the good old days. Once upon a time, says he, once upon a time there was a beautiful and rich country called Peru. The elite of the sierra lived the best of lives. Everybody had lovely horses then. Everybody gave lavish parties, was fashionable and ate steak for breakfast. All the *indios* obeyed the patron as if by the touch of magic. The ladies of the sierra rode sidesaddle then and Don Julio Noriega has an exquisite stirrup from one such saddle, ornate and made of pure silver. An *indio* would run along the trail behind the lady's mount, indefatigably for hours he would run, ever ready to hold the reins of the steed for her dismount.

We sit in the dirty kitchen of Don Julio's hacienda, chewing toasted corn to clean our teeth after dinner and try to imagine this land he remembers. Don Julio has a half-breed woman here now. The woman stands barefoot on the dirt floor and holds the beautiful silver sandal up for display in her wide earthen palm. The ugly stepmother and the ugly stepsisters come to mind. You simply cannot imagine how there ever was a Cinderella of the sierra to step daintily into this silver sandal.

Don Julio wants to sell us the stirrup. He wants sixty-five dollars, which is almost half our monthly income from the sale of the house on Machichaco. We offer him sixty. He doesn't budge. We don't budge. I think about that sandal sometimes and wonder how, for five dollars, we could have left something so beautiful and worth ten times the price, maybe twenty. I would not have wanted it for a keepsake, but we could have sold it. Made a bundle. We don't seem to do that sort of thing.

We bought a sheep from Don Julio, at so much a pound. You weigh it live and he gets to keep the hide, that is the deal he makes us. He did not expect us to be there watching when the *peon* opens up the stomach of the sheep. Water comes gushing out, water the *peon* forced down the gullet of the unfortunate creature moments before it was hog-tied and put on the scale to be weighed in front of us.

Don Julio shows no shame that we should discover how he gained a pound or two in the equation. He looks at Nathan with a smirk. He knows how far we have ridden to get to Mitobamba and how far we have to ride to be out of here. He knows how tired our horses are. He knows we have no choice but to pay him for the water in the sheep and pay him three times the going rate for oats. You meet people like Don Julio, quite a few in this land that is Peru and that is not a fairy tale country.

The *patròn* of hacienda Ocobamba is away, he usually is. Most *patròns* usually are. Only a girl is there, living out on the back porch like a watchdog. We call out to her from across the yard and she comes, without haste, without hesitation, looking us over. Her left eye is enlarged, unseeing behind a cloud. It is one of those things you notice involuntarily.

We expect her to tell us that the *patròn*, all Saints and God himself are due back any moment now and that we'd better be gone. And you would not blame her. It is the job of the watchdog to chase away strangers.

There is something about this young girl - thirteen, she says - that sleeping on a mat like a dog has not rubbed out. You spot a Cinderella here, a beautiful soul. She understands our plight: we have come a long way and it is getting dark now in the narrow valley. She says we can share the back porch with her. There is grass for the horses in the grove of poplars, she says. We may cook out back, where she does.

She was brought to the nuns to learn how to read and write and keep records, she tells us. She loved it, the reading most of all. But then her eye began to go bad. The *madre* Superior made a point to inform the *patròn*. He himself came to the school. And he told her the *madre* and the doctor were planning for her to have an operation.

"He said the doctor would have to take out my eye! Both my eyes! And he would give me instead the eyes of a dog."

With that she returned thankfully to the hacienda with the *patròn*, terrified now of the *madre* Superior and the doctor.

"Who wants to live with the eyes of a dog?"

The sonofabich *patròn* you think, feeling the hard and the cold from the stones under your bedroll, like she does. The subservience in her voice makes you want to scream: let the Agrarian Reform take his hacienda, let the *peones* lynch him! There is no use telling the girl now that a cataract operation would have just taken the cloud from her eye. And your realize that getting rid of the *patròn* won't bring her Prince Charming. Fairy tales do not have happy endings in the sierra of Peru. She would merely be without a master until, maybe, some *pobre diablo* takes her in to share his mud floor. It is the fizzled potential, all these aborted lives that get to you.

In the narrow valleys, everywhere you stop belongs to someone and we are glad to head back up to the *puna*. It is a long, hard, slow climb and we're heavily loaded with meat and oats. But it is okay, because this time the trail won't tip right back down into another tropical valley. This time we get to stay a while and camp in a hollow and imagine ourselves back to the Patagonia as we watch the horses graze on tufts of hard yellow grass. We see a shepherdess move a flock of llamas and alpacas across in the distance, minding her business as we mind ours in this high country that belongs to no one. Only life in its simplest form is possible here. Hardy potatoes and barley have to be wrestled from the earth between frosts. A house is made not of brick, not of mud, but of grass and rests directly on the earth.

We are riding through the gray drizzle of a morning fog up on the *puna*, with no mountain vistas to fill us with awe, prisoners of a gray mist, when quite suddenly we come upon a grass hut set in the lee of a crag. A ray of sunshine breaks through the clouds just then and shines upon a large wool blanket spread out over the damp grass. A young man is working a needle and thread slowly, with large hands. The patch of sun plays on the yellow, orange and red tapestry and on the jet black of his hair. He looks up at us and he smiles. He tells us he has woven this bedspread for his young wife. It is for her birthday and he shows us where he is now embroidering her name and the year: 1970.

Never have we seen a weave such as this; it is a reflection of the sun itself, brought down in the name of love to protect a marriage bed of earth and domed grass. You ride on into the mist with a ray of their sun in your soul.

There is no beginning, that anyone can remember, to the rolls of white woolen cloth, used for sheets, that come off the loom of the family of weavers who live in a cave by the old Inca Road, on the southern edge of the plateau above Huanuco Viejo. Grandma and grandpa, bachelor brothers and unmarried sisters and who knows how many young ones are part of the cycle of shearing, washing, carding, spinning and weaving rolls of cloth that they bring to the fairs to exchange for raw wool and food staples. In this way, they keep it all going, never ending. We buy four meters, enough for a top and a bottom sheet.

"Now the *señores* will sleep warm," says the weaver. She smiles and resumes her work and we ride on across hard yellow grasses under a steel grey sky. All around the mesa the faraway mountains are electric blue.

We are glad for the wool sheets when evening catches us high up in the tundra world. Following the Inca Road along a very high ridge, with a 180-degree view toward the Cordillera Blanca to the west and the Cordillera Azul to the east, we come upon the ruin of a large stone house. We decide to put up our tent in the lee of two walls that are still standing and that offer a sense of protection in this barren place. We try to imagine what this house might have been for, so far away, so high up on this ridge. It is unlike any Inca structure we have seen before. It is very roughly made. But who but an Inca would build anything up here, at almost five thousand meters?

By sundown, the landscape turns white with frost and then the moon comes up and we are surrounded by an empty immensity, devoid of the familiar land-marks that make the earth feel like home. This ruin is nothing like the ruins in Switzerland or in Greece that we used to seek out, climb on foot for hours sometimes to get to and sleep in, if we could. We would listen there for the footfalls of our own history. Here we listen for sounds coming on the wind. We half expect the arrival of some otherworldly creature, invaders from an-other planet.

We are glad for the horses and the dogs. None of them seem to perceive anything strange and unusual up here. Chaco is curled up in his pre-sleep stance: a tight ball at the foot end of the tent with Andin right next to him. The horses are chewing on the frozen grass around the crumbling stone walls. They know there is more grain in the pack. They'll hang in close and be around in the morning.

The night is very cold, even with the wool sheets wrapped tightly around us. I wake up several times and finally check Nathan's wristwatch. It is just after five o'clock. I grab my jeans and my jacket and find my boots and step outside under a big full moon in a clear sky. The ground is white with heavy frost. Pampero and Maracas are still grazing on the frozen grass. India and Caicique just stand with their heads hanging. They look so tired, so thin. I decide to give the horses their ration of grain right now. Then I crawl back into the tent to wait for the sun to rise and thaw the landscape.

The pulsating pain is right behind my eyeballs and I can't tell if I am struggling to wake up from a bad dream or trying to go back to sleep to escape this bed of volcanic rocks that threatens to rise up and shake us off. Her voice is somewhere saying the horses can't go on and that my fever is getting higher and begging me to please stop. We're clambering up this endless staircase of polished stones, the horses slipping and sliding, three steps up and two back down and the pass just ahead is the same one we climbed yesterday and the day before and the one before. All blur together as I struggle through a black night with no moon or stars. I take the last step to the crest with my knees buckling. Then the mountain tilts forward and we're all falling in slow motion into a bottomless maze of shadows as I desperately reach for Pampero's reins to save him and myself. Cold hands cup my burning face and Elly is shaking me gently and I hear her saying, "Wake up, Nate!" And I crawl behind her out of the tent into the white tundra world and see the horses standing nearby the Inca ruin like ice statues and dawn smiles with pink pastel lips to lure us into another day of climbing. But the effete beauty of this rooftop world no longer seduces you as you strap the heavy pack on your silent horse with numb fingers and brain.

The top of the pass is not far from our campsite and then we begin the long descent towards the village of Conchucos. We stop for lunch, as we usually do and take the saddles off, as we always do, so the horses can roll if they want to and have a complete break and a chance to graze. They don't bother. They just stand together in a huddle, too tired to rest. They could use some grain, but we don't have any left to give to them. We manage to heat some water out of an unhealthy looking puddle of water for a cup of Milo. We use *ichu* grass as fuel, the same material the shepherds use to make their huts. What you do is light a clump on fire, hold the *pava* over it, balanced on the spare tent pole. It takes four or five good-sized grass clumps to boil your water, if you are lucky not to spill it moving from one clump to the next.

Then we just sit there and watch the horses. They look awful! Gaunt and bedraggled. Unrecognizable now from the horses we rode through the desert and that were always fit, shiny, and interested in their surroundings. We have lost a lot of weight too. Skinny looks good on both of us and our faces have a healthy tan from living outdoors. But looks are deceiving. Nathan coughs a lot. We feel weak and dull most of the time.

We have a fight. It is not the first one we have in the northern sierra. We feel so sick of it all. Sick of always being dirty, of being gypped by people like Don Julio, being sent the wrong trail and secretly being laughed at. We are sick of finding no kindred souls, of lacking comfort and most of all sick of seeing our horses get skinnier and skinnier. We look at each other and we don't like the face in the mirror.

We set out from Spain to live on horseback on the pampas of Argentina where everything is vast and plentiful. How did we end up boxed into this country that was not made for horses?

I write in my diary: there are only two ways of dealing with the sierra.

You resign yourself to it.

Or you get the hell out of it.

We did neither.

Looking for answers, why we did what we did, I read our diaries, covered with leather from what was a jacket I brought from Spain. The grease off your hands has turned the leather dark. It feels rich to the touch and caused a man in a donut shop in Calgary to come up to me and ask:

"Are you writing a book?"

And when I said yes, as a matter of fact I was, he asked if he might hold one of the diaries, just for a moment. With such reverence he held it lightly and turned it in his hands.

"It is so real," he said.

Yes.

It is a tough write as we sit here on our mountain in northern British Columbia and struggle to survive as horse loggers in a forest industry that has become a sawtooth range of politics and bureaucracy.

You realize you've never got it made.

You never get to stay on the summit.

In my diary, I wrote:

The sierra and its people pulled us close and held us and we almost suffocated. We learned what we had to learn. We can't just walk away from our

four horses in the high sierra. We had taken them out of the worst kind of place
that was the Patagonia and we brought them into an even worse place. You
can walk away from a bicycle or a car or a boat or any other thing and go do
something else, but your horse is not a thing. Your horse is your friend, your
whole world. The sierra is not a place for horses. Colonel Flores proved right
after all. Mules would not have been the answer. Our horses did not fail us.
We almost failed them.

We feel we have let ourselves fall apart. We have gotten into the habit of
complaining about circumstances rather than adapting to them. Talking about
it clears the air. We can be so bloody heroic sometimes, pushing ourselves
harder because neither Nathan nor I want to be the first to say: I'm tired, I'm
sick. I've had it. I quit! We push each other right to the edge. Now after the
storm, comes the calm and with calm a change in the wind.

We have been told that feed would be especially hard to come by in the
village of Conchucos. But the first man we ask, a *señor* Lara, offers us the use
of his alfalfa field, just north of the village. We set up our tent and then sit for
a long time and watch our horses graze on the luscious green. We make a fire
and roast some potatoes and go to sleep early. I wake up sometime during the
night to a loud snoring and look out through the tent flap. Pampero's head is
inches away from the tent. He is sleeping flat on his side and it is his snoring
that woke me up. The other horses are lying in the grass close by. I smile, for
the first time, it seems, in such a long time. This is more like it! I go back to
sleep again, feeling secure again, at home in the world.

We learn the story behind the strange stone house up on the *puna*. It is
known as the *Payahuachanga*, 'the-house-where-the-son-of the-Inca-was-
born'. The Inca was travelling along this road, so the legend goes, when one
of his concubines came into labor. The Inca ordered the soldiers travelling
with him to erect a house for his child to be born in. In one hour, they gathered
the rocks and put them together. Quite a fantastic feat! I suppose four thousand men could put up a three-room house in the same time it took us to make
our camp in its ruin.

The following day, we leave the horses in the field and walk down to the
village to look around, pick up a few things we need. We get a lot more than
we bargained for. Conchucos is twelve days into the annual celebration of
fiesta de las animas and the core of the party is at the house of this year's
mayordomo. A group of young schoolteachers we happen to meet in the plaza

take us there and make sure we have some beef and empanadas and *chicha morada*. Each year, the *maestras* tell us, one man is chosen to sponsor the animas. He has to provide the fireworks, the music and the food and the fiesta will go on until he runs out of money. He chooses the sponsor for the following year and, in this way, the village of Conchucos brings a rich man back down to the level of everyone else.

It is easier to join the party than it is to leave. We eat, we drink and we're boxed in by people high on *coca*, sleeplessness and *chicha*, shuffling to the monotonous flute music on a battery operated record player. Now and then the needle skips, repeats. No one takes notice. I am starting to feel claustrophobic in the stale air that reeks of home brew and urine. We see a hole in the crowd and head for it, but the crowd closes in to block our exit. This happens several times. Then a well-dressed young man comes to the rescue.

"You want to leave?"

"Yes!"

When he motions, the crowd loosens its inebriated embrace and parts to let us go. He is a man to reckon with in Conchucos, that is clear. He is also very drunk. Out in the street, he wants to set the record straight with us right away.

"For me," he says, "there is Che and Fidel. Nothing else."

He takes us to what he calls the General Headquarters of the Guerrilla. It is his father's house; a big two-story building painted pale yellow. We follow him to an upstairs drawingroom. He is talking about organizing thousands of *campesinos* along the Maranon River. We don't even know his name, or he ours. But he wants us to know there is no God and that the campesinos must govern the world.

He calls out to a *peon* down in the courtyard below and the *peon* appears in the doorway, passive, barefoot, poncho over his shoulder, a wad of *coca* lodged in his left cheek.

"Come in!" Bids our guide. Motions toward a chair.

"You're in your house, *hermano*." He says. "Make yourself at home, my brother." The *indio* obliges him by placing his poncho carefully on one edge of the chair. Remains on stand-by, passive, sucking on his wad of *coca*. Our guide puts an end to the awkwardness of the moment by giving the *peon* an order to go fetch some coffee. Taking his poncho with him, the *peon* promptly leaves the room and does not return. A maid brings coffee and sweet rolls. Tomás does not call her 'sister'. He does not acknowledge her in any way, but he tells us more about all the peasants he helped organize to take control over land on the Marañon River. We find out he is a schoolteacher. That his name is Tomas Parra. And, once more, that for him there is only Fidel Castro and Che Guevara. That God is dead.

"Long live the People's Revolution!" Says Tomás Parra.

We finish our coffee and try to take leave. We have to find oats and something to cook for Chaco and Andin and get back to camp before dark. Tomás tags along. In the street, right at the corner to the Parra house, we encounter two men, dressed in black suits. One carries a black briefcase, the other a stack of books. They stop and stare straight at Nathan.

"Remember, I waved to you from the mountain?" Says one of them.

"You are Nathaniel!" Says the other man. "Are you not?"

"I am," says Nathan.

"We are on our way to the City of God!" Says the first man.

"We have a lot to talk about, you and I," says the second man. "But we are in a hurry now to sit with a man who cannot be alone."

And they are on their way.

Tomás Parra has become very agitated by this strange encounter. He is tugging at Nathan's arm and insists we must accompany him back into The General Headquarters of the Guerrilla at once. There is a door directly off the street that leads into a small room on the ground floor. Clearly this is Tomás Parra's private domain. Portraits of Fidel Castro and Che Guevara share wall space with pinup girl calendars. He pulls a Winchester 30-30 out from underneath his mattress and begins to walk around in the small room, waving the gun.

"All I say," he keeps repeating. "God does not exist."

He talks only to Nathan. One moment he seems convinced that Nathan is sent by the church or by the CIA to spy on him. The next moment, he goes into another harangue about the death of God and the birth of the Revolution. He makes a fist with his left hand.

"Let's cut our wrists and become blood brothers!" He says.

The gun is making me uneasy. I make sure I stand between Tomás and Nathan at all times. Tomás is not interested in me. I don't feel in any danger. Nathan might be.

Tomás finally fires his gun: two shots out the door and up into the air. The sound reverberates loudly in the cubicle of his room and echoes up the street.

The noise seems to calm him. He shoves the gun back underneath the mattress. He agrees with Nathan that a double handshake will do as a seal of brotherhood, in lieu of blood letting.

"If I have a son, I will name him Nathaniel," he says solemnly.

Dusk is upon us. We really have to get back to our animals. Tomás won't let go. He takes us back into the inner courtyard and gives us a sack of oats from his father's granary. Then he walks with us back to camp, stumbling over the rocks in the trail. Behind him, the *peon* floats along in a *coca* trance, packing the fifty kilos of grain.

Chaco emerges from his bed inside the red tent with Andin in tow and growls a warning to Tomás and his *peon* before he bounds around us in greeting and in anticipation of what we may have brought him. The horses amble over from the far end of the field and we pour out a ration of the grain for them. Caicique gets to eat off the canvas cover we use to wrap up the tent and extra blankets. The twins eat together off a piece of tarp and we feed India in the big pot, away by herself so the geldings won't chase her. And while they eat, we make a fire with sticks we have gathered earlier in the day. We sit late into the night, the three of us, while the *peon* remains in the shadows.

Tomás is beginning to sober up. Now he believes that we are on a journey of our own, sent by no one, accountable to no one. He wants to know how it is we can live like this, outside of country, of profession, of family.

Nathan tells him about the *barrio*, about Benito.

About how we went down to Venezuela to save the world, but not on behalf of the CIA. When we understood what was behind Acción, we stopped trying to organize community projects; we did what we could to help individual dreamers instead.

Benito's dream was to have a street, a real street so you could drive a car right up in front of the block house where he would someday live. The house had a foundation already, built around the tin shack where he now lived. Reinforcing rods stuck up at the corners, ready for the wooden forms he would someday put around them and fill with concrete. Four rows of blocks were built up in front, where someday he would build a porch towards the street and sit in the cool of the evening.

Benito wanted his dream enough to go out in the heat of a Saturday or Sunday, with a pick and shovel and move dirt. Nathan went over to help and, one shovelfull at a time, the two of them advanced on the red clay of the hillside. One Sunday Antonio and Jose and Rafael came and joined them. The boys who had a *bolas* court over the hill came too and together they built a retaining wall out of bricks and cement and sweat. And then one day a *por puesto* taxi pulled up in front of Benito's shack and Benito and his woman got out on Calle Milagro.

"And you," Tomás addressed me for the first time. "What did you do?"

I told him then about making the rounds on behalf of the CARE program. The People of the United States donated oil and flour and dried eggs. The program was called Food for Peace and was distributed by the Catholic Church. The gifts came with strings attached. Recipients were to improve themselves in small and specific ways. I was sent out to see that they did.

In a shack made of scrapwood off packing boxes and hammered out tin cans, a man threw the flour out the door past me. It landed out in the street.

"I may be poor," he said to me, "but in my house I am the master."

I agreed with him. I never made another visit on behalf of CARE. I used my Pentax camera to record the lives of Dorka and Alexandra and Flores the way that they were, not the way that Acción or the CIA or anyone else thought that they should be. *The San Juan Review* published *Barrio World* and Luis liked my pictures enough to hire me to do the photos for his art exhibit.

It is quite late when Tomás stands up to take leave. He is sober now and does not stumble on the trail. Behind him, at his distance, the *peon* follows.

I don't know if the General Headquarters of the Guerrilla became the center for the Shining Path. The geographical place fits as the stronghold of the Maoist Revolutionary group of Peru. I don't know if Tomás Parra was one of the organizers. The profile fits that of a disciple of Guzman, the university professor from the north.

And I don't know if there is a young man in the village of Conchucos named Nathaniel, who tells of his father meeting a gringo on horseback during one *fiesta de las animas* and that is how Nathaniel got his name.

I like to think such a young man exists.

We named our second daughter Conchita Maria.

We had given no previous thought to what me might name a baby, boy or girl. We had no lists, no choices narrowed down. When the small new person entered our world in 1979, at the hospital in the village of Burns Lake in British Columbia, a name came to us from deep in a valley in the sierra of Peru.

It is dark and quite late when we rode into *hacienda* Yanasara. Large oak doors open at our approach and we rode into a cobblestone courtyard. We seem to be expected here. But that that is impossible!

A *peon* takes our horses and we are shown to a guestroom. An evening snack is brought to our room, along with a note from the *patron* and two books for us to read. One of the books is titled *Recuerdos*, Recollections. The author is Conchita Maria Cintrón. I start to read, but soon fall into that deep comfortable sleep you experience in your own bed after coming home from a long absence.

In the morning, we can see our horses right from the guestroom window. They are grazing in a field of alfalfa. They would not want to see us for a while! I pick up the book again and read about a little girl who grew up in Lima in the nineteen twenties. At age ten she was struck with an incurable passion for horses. For her birthday, she asked for and was given a packet of ten riding lessons offered by a colonel. When the series was over, the colonel continued teaching the child free of charge, so impressed was he with the natural ability of Conchita Maria.

That is how far I got by noon, when there is a knock of the guestroom door and a message delivered. Our host, Don Pachito, is downstairs to meet us. He is an unusually tall, very skinny, absolutely toothless and intriguingly eccentric man.

He raises bulls, black fighting bulls from stock imported from Spain. They run on the hard ground above the valley and are in high demand, he tells us, for the rings in Cajamarca, Ayacucho and Lima.

"Are you reading the books I sent down?" He wants to know.

I nod. "Yes."

"Good. Let me know when you finish. There are some others I want you to read while you are at Yanasara."

He asks no questions, no questions at all. The next day, we start to fill him in as to how we came here, riding a narrow trail for three hours in the dark because we could not find any feed or a place to stay in the village. Then someone told us Yanasara was a place of plenty. Don Pachito interrupts.

"Don't explain what no one is asking," he says. We will remember and, over the years, try and live by this simple advice.

We spend the evening at the hot spring, just the two of us in a big pool of tepid waters that bubble right out of the ground of Yanasara, which is a Quechua word that means soil-of-hard-maize. Back in our room, I continue reading about Conchita Maria. She was the horse girl that I was. Instead of Belgian draft horses and half-wild remounts, she rode the colonel's jumpers and the Andalusian horses used for *rejoneo* that belonged to a friend of the colonel's. Conchita Maria showed great aptitude for classical riding: she would collect the horse for the Spanish walk, move the shoulder, move the haunches, do the *passage*, do canter pirouettes.

The *rejoneo* is bullfighting on horseback. It is a dance and a fight to the death, the beauty and agility of the horse pitted against the brute force of the bull. It is the ultimate test of equestrian artistry. The rider must guide the horse with thought, with eyes, and the slightest shift in body position to within a hair's breath of the sharp horns of the enraged bull to plunge the *rejon* inbetween his shoulder blades. There is no room for error. Hesitation can spell death for the horse or his rider.

Nathan, meanwhile, reads a book of a different genre *El Retorno de los Brujos*, Return of the Magicians and his imagination goes wild, when at night we hear Don Pachito pacing in his rooms above ours and catch a glimpse of his shadow from the outside and smell incense from the candlelit room.

On our third day at Yanasara, an invitation comes to have lunch at a neighboring hacienda. We are to use horses belonging to Don Pachito, who is not going. I pick a lively looking chestnut stallion. Nathan gets left with a flea bitten Paso Fino well past his prime. The directions are simple: follow the trail up the valley bottom until you get there. We set out together, my chestnut stallion fretting and shying, dancing and prancing and huffing and puffing and sweating profusely. The old grey floats past us. By the time my frothing steed gets me to our destination, the grey is standing in the shade of a big tree. Nathan is relaxing on the veranda, nursing his second drink.

A large herd of purebred Lippizan horses graze in the alfalfa fields below: heavy white mares, each with a coal black foal running at side. So this is what Don Pachito sent us here to see! Obviously Don Pachito heard me when I mentioned my interest in the history of the Spanish horses in America! A few mares rescued out of the war-torn Central Europe were brought to this isolated valley in the sierra. We are looking now at the largest herd of purebred Lippizans in the world outside of Piber, Austria. These sturdy and gentle horses are close in origin to our Criollos, to the Paso Fino Nathan just rode, to the Chileno and to the tough little Morochuco ponies of the Puno region. All evolved from the

Andalusian horse of the fifteen hundreds. In America, the Spanish horses adapted to survive their new environments and the new tasks demanded of them. The Lippizan has remained astonishingly unchanged through the centuries as his stabling and feed and his training in the ancient art of classical warfare have remained much the same.

On the fourth day at Yanasara, Don Pachito accompanies us on a ride through the alfalfa fields, the creeks, the corrals and orchards of Yanasara. He speaks sparingly, in a high-pitched voice. Don Pachito had his balls crushed in a horse riding accident when he was just a boy. The cook told us this. His voice never changed. I can understand why Don Pachito would revere Conchita Maria, but I wonder: does he hate horses? Blame them for his condition, for having no family, only the hacienda and the bulls.

The slaughterhouse steers would look at her with large doleful eyes, Conchita Maria wrote. She felt bad for them and for what she was about to do to them. But then she thought of the horses and the bulls and the rush and what the colonel expected of her and she forced herself to go through with what she had gone there in the night to do. She plunged a *rejón* sword into the steer, deep enough to pierce the lungs. She told herself the butcher was on his way and the fate of the steer had been sealed beforehand. It is hard to imagine a beautiful young lady doing this as her homework so she could take her skill into the bullring and become the first woman invited to display her art in Cordoba, deep in the heart of Andalucia, Spain.

I cannot explain why I would name my baby girl for a woman who rode dancing horses and stuck swords into fighting bulls. As Don Pachito would have put it: no one is asking. Conchita Maria is a beautiful name for a beautiful girl who grew into a young lady who would drive Belgian draft horses in the forests of BC and then follow a dream to go dance with the purebred horses in Andalucia, Spain. The book Nathan read at Yanasara spoke of events that occur independently of each other, yet reveal unusual bonds between man, time and space. It spoke of a fiesta of coincidences, of synchronicity. Maybe that explains it, then.

On the fifth day, we leave Yanasara. I don't know why we don't stay longer, read more books. What drives us ever on? You can always find reasons. In the Patagonia, we had to get north before winter. In the desert there was so little feed, so many kilometers. In the sierra, habit maybe? We have become addicted, like the gypsies, to movement. Maybe we know that the longer we stay, the harder it will be to return to life on the trail because the sierra is not about dancing horses and black bulls, but about chickens and pig shit and the beginning of the rainy season.

The afternoon sky turns black and it begins to rain. We find shelter in an abandoned farm to wait out the worst, then continue up to Conabamba Valley in a light drizzle. We stop at several small fundos to ask for feed and lodging, but are turned away.

Things take a turn for the better just as it is getting dark and we are bracing ourselves for a miserable night in damp sleeping bags. We enter a dilapidated farm and find a friendly obese woman, Dona Claudette, who receives us with great interest. Her five children are about the filthiest creatures I have laid my eyes on. But even though there is pig dung all over the floor of her kitchen, we are delighted to have a roof and a plate of hot potatoes. By now we must have every intestinal parasite in the book, thanks to the total lack of hygiene of our hosts: fly eggs in the meat, flies in the milk and bugs in the soup. My tolerance for dirt and carelessness has been surpassed. I am becoming a fastidious person. I dream of clean bathrooms, polished floors, neat gardens, the smell of disinfectants, starched sheets, steaming dishwashers and shampooed children with electric blonde hair.

There is never enough space for all you want to include. You have to make a choice and say: here it is! Done! But wait, there is so much more, says another part of me and says Nathan. Our diaries are brimming with material! Yes, true. But time is up for the sierra of Peru. We move on now through the lowlands north of Cajamarca, where the jungle spills over from the Amazon headwaters.

The total and unexpected change of scenery makes us feel good. The jungle brings back memories of Venezuela and of southern Chile and makes the present seem like a continuum again. The sierra is like nothing else. Each part is disconnected from a whole and yet so monotonously the same. The sierra had a very isolating, fragmenting effect on us. We are looking now to The Promise Land of the Central Valley of Ecuador, forgetting what Horacio Español said as we set out across the Fry Pan basin:

"The worst is never behind you, only the best."

HORSE THIEF

As we wait for the *pava* to come to a boil for our morning coffee, we look out across the growing Chinchipe River. Small trees along the far bank quiver and bend as the rising current tugs at the lower branches.

Then the river roars.

In a flash it has become a giant juggernaut of brown waters, tossing tree trunks in and out of foaming troughs. Without warning it boils over with a torrent of mud heading our way. We grab saddles, panniers, the tent hung to dry on some bushes, and pile everything on high ground.

We did not reach our *pava* in time. The dirty waters swirl around the rocks that hold our campfire and for one brief moment the *pava* teeters sideways. Then it bobs out into the gurgling avalanche and disappears forever.

My sense of loss is acute. And quite out of proportion. I didn't lose my house, just a teapot. We will be able to get another one in the next general store, probably even in Zumba on the other side of the river, in Ecuador. In the meantime, any tin can with a wire will do the job.

The trouble is, this was not just a teapot.

This was the *pava* we watched blacken over our very first campfire on the Gallegos River, one year, ten months and five thousand kilometers ago. This pava held the clear waters of the southern Andes and remained empty when no water could be found in the desert. It boiled the liquids out of so many sloughs and ponds and creeks and rainwater puddles in Peru until we would dare make coffee out of it. This *pava* evolved from just another teapot into the hobo's icon Nathan wrote so poetically about at the very beginning.

When you have so few things, each thing has a distinct value. It becomes polished, or in this case, blackened with use. Its familiar shape is comforting as you travel through an ever-changing world. It is irreplaceable. The voice of a man named Moses, whom we met in Cajabamba, speaks to me over the roaring waters. I try to ignore it.

"They will make it to the United States border." He looked at our four horses grazing around the church in Cajabamba. The cemetery was the only place with any grass at all in that miserable village where we had come tired and trail-weary, hoping to find good feed and a place to rest for a couple of days.

"All except the big one with the crooked spike. He won't make it out of Ecuador," said this man named Moses.

Angry with myself, I push the thought away. What did a self-proclaimed *brujo* deep in the *sierra* know about horses! And I don't tell Nathan, because he would take the prophecy of Moses and bounce it around all over the place and then I would not be able to get rid of it at all. Caicique always looked the worst of the four when feed was scarce and poor. We didn't need this Moses to point that out to us.

"So much for our morning coffee!" I pretend that was all I cared about.

"Watch for the signs!" Nathan says.

Of course! Nathan would be on the same wavelength. 'Watch the signs' Moses told us. Losing our *pava* to the river could not be a good sign.

"Yeah. Such as don't camp on a jungle river in the rainy season," I say and shove this Moses out of my mind and busy myself with saddling and getting the gear together so we can escape from the cyclones of gnats and flies that surround us whenever we stop for a moment. I can't wait to get out of these fetid lowlands! The Central Valley of Ecuador where it is always springtime, that's where I want be! Caicique reads my mood and stomps off down the rutted trail toward La Balsa at a good clip.

There is not much to La Balsa: a few coffee plantations up on the bluff, banana trees growing in no particular pattern down the slope toward the river and a cluster of adobe huts under black thatch. Not a soul is astir when we arrive in the early afternoon. We unsaddle by a big tree at the river's edge and bathe the horses in a backwater eddy. We are submerged to our necks in the brown river when a chubby *mestizo* appears on the bank up above. He makes a quick retreat. Returns moments later wearing a *guardia republicana* cap and a gun holster strung over his hips and a pair of red boxer shorts. He is not wearing a shirt or shoes.

"You are having a bath?" He says at length.

"We are staying out of the bugs," Nathan says.

There is a long pause. A second *guardia* appears, also in his underwear and cap. No guns.

One of my favorite mementos of our journey is the stamp we receive when we present our documents in the adobe hut that is the seat of law and order on the Chinchipe River. It is a triangular stamp with *Puerto International La Balsa* written around the periphery. Coffee Merchant No: it says in the center. The *guardia* in the red underwear takes his time with the number. Finally he puts in a '0' and scribbles a couple of letters. His initials maybe? We don't ask. As long as this lawman is satisfied that we are legally able to exit Peru, it probably won't matter much to anyone else.

"Where do we cross into Ecuador?" Nathan asks.

We assume there is a bridge upstream and that La Balsa - The Raft - is merely a geographical name, the way you assume that whatever horse died to give Dead Horse Mesa its name is long gone by the time you get there.

There is no bridge. There is not even a raft. Just a little pile of balsam poles down on the riverbank, about twelve feet long and six inches in diameter.

That is it. That is how you get over to Ecuador.

The ferryman who supplies the rope and the paddle and the river expertise to take you and your stuff across is away in the village of San Ignacio. Might be back tomorrow. Might not be. We are too impatient to hang around La Balsa for an indefinite time with nothing to do but scratch the latest constellation of welts left by the last swarm of bugs that attacks you. The Guardias offer to help us cross. Too late I wish for more patience and less audacity when the raft tips over with all our saddles on their first trip across. A good thing

Nathan insisted on tying the saddles down with our lead ropes. The two *guardias* end up in the water, but manage to hang onto the raft and get back aboard and deliver our soaked gear onto Ecuadorian soil.

I have a choice of swimming with Nathan and the horses, or have the *guardias* take me across. I am not too keen on either option. I am a very poor swimmer. I have trouble just floating in water. Nathan finds this quite unbelievable; he is a great swimmer. He likes having water, even salt water, in his eyes and nose and ears. I don't. I opt for the raft. Nathan takes pictures from the Peruvian shore. We don't tip over and it is actually kind of fun. The *guardias* make a special trip to bring me the cameras and I find a good spot to take pictures of Nathan swimming across with the horses, in the narrow channel where the *guardias* tell him that people swim their mules all the time.

*Caicique goes belly deep into the churning spillway, then he stops and refuses to budge. I attempt to force him. We have to get across the river, **damnit**! He rears then and spins back to shore and refuses to go back into the water. One look into his wary eyes should have made me stop and reconsider.*

Instead, I jump on India. Trusting my better judgment, she plunges right into the river. Her hooves are off the rocky bottom suddenly and she has to swim hard. But in the narrows, the current is stronger than she is. An uprooted tree slams into us broadside and India lunges in panic, a scorching pain shooting up my right hip. I dig my fingers deeper into her mane and kick hard alongside her, talking to her. Together we have to break out of this vise grip that is pulling us toward the white water rooster tailing over submerged boulders.

Then the current spins us around and we're thrown up over the boulders and sucked down into the whirling maelstrom. We hit the bottom, still spinning. The river won't let us go. I know I can't hold my breath forever. And I can't let go of India. My lungs are exploding and everything turns from darkness to light and I'm swimming in the Ionian Sea with Doc in an underwater race to the rock and back to the pier. Just one breath. We swim like dolphins possessed, side by side, and the water is warm and very clear. Schools of tiny fish with zebra stripes and large eyes part before our reaching hands, turning to join the race. We touch the rock together and somersault into a fast turn, pushing with both feet and my lungs are aching and my heart is pounding so hard that the drumming in the temples is too loud to bear and I see the veins in his neck and face as he reaches and pulls, reaches and pulls. I match him stroke for stroke, pulling harder and harder and everything is pounding and becoming dim and I keep saying to myself: one more, just one more! He is no longer there as my hands touch the granite pier.

We hit bottom. India gets her legs under her. Lunging and bucking and twisting, she frees herself and me from the whirling death grip of the river. The spinning stops and we rise quickly, smashing through the blue mirror above.

*I burst out into the sky with a howl. I won! I won! To see Doc sitting there above, grinning like a Cheshire cat. But it isn't the young Greek doctor at all; it is the Peruvian **guardia** who sent me and my horse to swim the river in this spot. His moon face is full of worry now. The same guy who told me for sure, yes, that is where everyone crosses the river now hems and haws and can't look me in the eye.*

I pick up a stick and toss it into the middle of the river. The current pulls it through the funnel between rocks and into the maelstrom and I don't see it again. I wonder why I didn't do this before plunging headlong into the river. How many times did we have to learn to trust our own best judgment more than the advice of others? I try the same experiment downstream where the river widens. Here the stick floats calmly toward the opposite shore and into a quiet backwater behind a logjam.

Downstream, Caicique walks into the river without hesitation and the others all follow. Chaco stays right up alongside as Caicique swims with the current toward the logjam. Behind us the heavy-boned twins snort with the effort. They look like baby hippos, only their black noses and bulging eyes showing above water. India comes last, but she comes and I think that is a very brave thing for her to do.

"Get some dramatic shots?" I quip to Elly, who meets us on the bank, a camera slung from each shoulder.

"I didn't want pictures of you drowning on our way to Ecuador," she says. I don't find anything to say to that.

We are very well received by the major in command of the Ecuadorian army outpost in Zumba, when we appear the day after crossing the Chinchipe River. He even dispatched a scout to meet us and escort us to headquarters, up the hill from the quaint frontier town with its stores and bars facing a rutted main street. You could shoot a Western movie here - as long as you were okay with the jungle motif - with the town just the way it is. Wood frame houses are set up on piles, mules and scrub horses are parked at the hitching rails. Men emerge through the swinging doors of bars and young girls wave to you from upstairs balconies.

A rusty lion statue crouches at the gates to the old mansion on the hill above Zumba. A couple of ancient cannons on the lawn let you know this is now a military compound. Dressed in a blindingly white uniform, starched and impeccably pressed, the major makes you think of one of those Somerset Maugham characters who lived in a high society of one in some godforsaken outpost of the British Empire, keeping up all the little rituals and appearances.

Our horses are grained and put on good pasture. The major sends his captain to help us get settled in the married officers' barracks. The building leans slightly to the downhill on mossy posts, the stairs are sprinkled with rotting sawdust left by termites. Upstairs, on a wide balcony closed in by walls of moist foliage, a large woman sits fanning herself, sweating profusely. The captain introduces his wife. We exchange a few pleasantries before her conversation turns onto well-worn tracks.

"I suffered five days on a mule," says she, "to get in here to join my husband. Now my health is gone. And there is no way for me to leave." She mops her upper lip with a damp handkerchief.

"The airstrip will be completed soon!" Says the captain and you sense this is a mantra he repeats often and that might, someday, conjure up the real thing.

"I may not live that long, Leonardo," she says and you can see he has heard it before.

"For some reason the doctor doesn't understand, my system retains more and more liquid. Already I have gained over thirty kilos," she says to no one in particular.

"Why don't you go and lie down for awhile," says her husband.

She smiles weakly and leans forward to watch an insect that has landed on a Venus flytrap plant that grows in a tin can on the railing in front of her. The cupping petals close slowly around the prey and snap shut. She sighs, puts a hand to her forehead.

"Yes, I think I shall take a rest. This heat is unbearable."

A few days later, as we struggle through the worst trail of our entire ride, I will think of this poor woman imprisoned on her upstairs balcony. I will marvel that she made it in at all. I will understand why she cannot make it back out the same way she came in.

In spite of the heat and the bugs, we enjoy our stay in Zumba. The major is a superb host. We have not eaten such well-prepared food, served with such decor, for a very long time. The major plays chess and he is well read: *The Phenomenon of Man* by Theilhard de Chardin, Nathan's kind of stuff.

On the eve of our departure towards Loja, the captain comes to our room on official business. With apologies for the intrusion, he comes with orders from the major to search our things. He requests our documents and our exposed film. Turns out we have been prisoners in Zumba for the past three days. A General Rhon of the Ecuadorian Air Force was kidnapped by extremists and the whole country is on high alert. All individuals, in any way suspicious, are to be detained and interrogated. No one has yet claimed responsibility for the kidnapping. No one knows where the general is being held, or by whom. It was the major's choice to treat us as his guests rather than prisoners of his army. But now that we are leaving his jurisdiction he has to inform us. Our documents and our film will be forwarded to headquarters in Loja, where we are to present ourselves upon arrival.

"And what about us?" Nathan is visibly miffed at his intellectual sparring partner turned warden. "Do we go under armed guard?"

The major smiles. "That won't be necessary," he says. "There is only the one trail."

Inspired by the major's impeccable appearance, we spent a considerable amount of our time in Zumba giving ourselves and our things a thorough cleaning. We washed all of our clothes, scrubbed and oiled the saddles, even the pack saddle, polished our boots to a high shine, gave each other a haircut. We felt we were contributing our own little bit of order and the pride of good grooming to this outpost. We need not have bothered.

We leave Zumba at dawn. There is a gradual ascent through a tunnel of green. The air is cool and quite agreeable. All that is written and said about the seductive beauty of the jungle must refer to this one

hour of reprieve between dawn and the full onslaught of the day. In-
sects decorate the undersides of giant leaves with pointillistic configu-
rations, snakes doze in early pools of light. And not a ripple on the
surface of mulatto gold as we descend steeply and cross a river at the
bottom of a veiled gorge. Even the birds observe a moment of silence,
of ritual blessing before the daily Armageddon begins.

As we begin to climb once again, six mules heavily loaded with
rolls of barbed wire, barrels of cooking oil, kegs of nails and bottles of
Coca Cola come skidding down the rain-gouged trench of a trail, forc-
ing us up against mud walls. They are caked with red clay that cracks
and peels at the joints as they move. The shifting cargoes, the cinches
and cruppers, have chafed open sores into their flesh. Behind them
walk their drivers: barefoot, sinewy, stripped to their underwear, shirts
tied around their heads. I search for expression in faces creased with
sweat but find only masks of the living dead, green saliva dripping
from the wads of coca leaves lodged in their cheeks.

We move on through the undulating tube of green foliage. Minutes
stretch into hours as the horses stumble and trip over jagged stones,
plunge belly deep through red soup, clatter over ledges and slide down
yet another mist-lidded gorge. We can hear yet another loose shoe
rattle against submerged boulders. Someone is going to kick a shoe if
you don't stop and reclinch the nails, but you want to put if off until the
next dry ledge, until the next stream where you can wash the muck off
the hoof first. The choice is not yours. The shoe twists off between two
rocks and I have to get off and dig for it because this is shoe number
four already, Caicique's left hind. We only have two spares left now.

I wipe the slime off my hands and onto my jeans. Then I put
Caicique's muddy hind leg on my left thigh so I can rasp his hoof down.
I have to brace myself on my right knee, which gets soaked. Water runs
into my boot. Then Caicique yanks his leg free to kick at the mosqui-
toes under his belly and my face and chest get splattered with muck. I
drop the hammer. It sinks out of sight. As I am groping around in the
sludge to my armpit trying to find it, Caicique spooks at something and
backs up, knocking me over on my ass. The rancid goo gurgles up all
around me. By the time I finish and slide back on Pampero, there is
nothing to remind you of the spic-and-span fellow who left Zumba this

morning.

We wade on through fetid trench saunas, keeping our eyes to the ground, no longer bothering to swat at the bugs. You can't beat them anyway. The only relief from the mosquitoes comes with the brief **aguaceros**. *You find yourself listening for the distant drumming of rain on the canopies. Sometimes it roars right on past you like an elevated express train, leaving you in the hot backdraft without a cooling drop. Other times you'd get drenched in a deluge that makes your skin shrink and your teeth chatter.*

Each time another mule train splatters on by, you look at the **arrieros** *knee-deep in mud and you see less difference between you and them: matted hair, grit in the mouth, sweat and grime all over. Your horses too are getting galled from the cinches and developing sores on their backs and would start going lame because now you are all out of shoes.*

So many little choices led up to this. Thinking we were following a whim, exercising our free will, we arrived in Zumba. This trench through the jungle took us prisoners. We had no choice then but to endure. We thought if we could do that, we'll pick up our freedom along with our passports at the other end. We had no idea the terrible toll we would later have to pay.

If we had, we would have turned right around and crawled and clawed our way back over the sierra of Peru and taken whatever other route we would have, could have, should have taken to avoid these disease infested lowlands.

Free choice is a white elephant sale: you grab the bag you think you have a good feeling about.

But you never know.

In the morning, I wrote in my diary, we went for six hours straight. Much too long, but there was no place to stop until we got to the Palema River, where we rested for a few hours before making another horrible climb. Night was falling when we finally found a clearing and set up the tent, just as an aguacero whipped through. Everything that was clean and dry this morning was now dirty and wet.

And from the following day:

Mud. Mud. Mud.

Rain.

Steep stony trail down to a river. Had to stop midway down to put a shoe back on Maracas. Shoe number 5 in a day and a half!! At the river, we cooked up some corncobs for lunch but they were full of bugs. Got corn stalks for the horses and gave them two *panelas* of raw sugar to share.

Lots of mule trains passed us as we sat by the river, carrying a *quintal*, 100 kilos of coffee. The *arrieros* are rough looking types, walking in their muddy underwear, bullwhips in hand.

The trail improved a bit in the afternoon. We doddled along picking bananas, talking to people. Stopped in a field and planned to camp overnight. But when the owner of the field and the mosquitoes appeared we continued on. Finally found a pretty good place to stop, had a cup of tea, some dry Quaker oats and called it goodnight.

The following day:

Awoke before 5 am by someone passing on the trail. We could not hear the horses and got scared that someone had taken them, but they had merely left the good pasture to wander off down the trail. The bugs were driving them nuts.

Arrived in Valladolid at nine. Pampero had lost another shoe. By the time we found an old guy with a forge to shape muleshoes into horseshoes and tacked one on Pampero, it was too late to continue. Discovered that India would be out of commission for a while. She had several sores developing on her back.

The shopkeeper was pleased to have someone to talk to and as a gesture of appreciation he gave our horses lots of sugar cane. That was a language we understood!!

And the next day:

How they ever got the captain's obese wife and the major's record player across this damned trail will always remain a mystery to me.

The last part was not as bad as they had told us. We have seen much more dangerous trails but it was long and painful. We left at six thirty, just ahead of a mule train and arrived in Yangana at five, two hours ahead of the *arrieros* in spite of having stopped to shoe. Caicique and India this time.

"Good going!" Remarked the rough owner of the saloon where we had dinner. "You came in good time, well ahead of the *arrieros*".

Met a guy from the army who expressed his admiration for us, our horses particularly. He had seen a young American with Paso Fino horses at the border on the Pan-American three years before. Said they were not having an easy time. The guy was walking and the horses carrying alfalfa and oats.

"Your horses," said the army guy, "they are really amazing. They have been through hell and come out on the other side."

Yes.

But they don't have to turn around and go back for another journey of unspeakable torture and return, over and over again. In the almost two years on the trail, we had never before had a cinch or saddle sore and none of our horses had worked lame; we prided ourselves on our good care.

On the trail from Zumba to Yangana, India developed both cinch and saddle sores, as did Caicique. Maracas and Pampero had cinch sores. We lost eleven shoes on the way and when we arrived in Loja, India was lame.

Had we turned around and gone back over the same trail and then turned back and done it again and again after that, our horses would all have had open sores, they would all have been lame.

This is no mere purgatory: this is hell itself.

If I believed, with the Hindu, that how you are reborn into the next life depends on how you lived the one before, then I would know that the beasts of burden of the Zumba to Yangana trail had been the Jack the Rippers and the Hitlers in a former life. Only the very worst, the most hideous deviates, the scum of humanity could earn the karma of making this journey, laden with canned goods, barbed wire and Coca Cola bottles, going ten, twelve, fourteen hours at a stretch, knee-deep through black ooze or red, up hills and down, packs chafing, open sores full of worms, before the sharp prods of the bamboo sticks, pushed through the heat of the days and into the nights to reach a destination only to turn around and carry coffee and brown sugar loaves back out again, with no Sunday in-between, driven on by *arrieros*, driven by cocaine.

But I don't believe the poor beasts were horrendous criminals in another life. I believe they are exactly what I see before me: animals treated horribly by the men they serve. In my notes on horses in the Americas, I have this quote:

'The white man rides the horse until exhausted

'The *mestizo* rides him another day after that

'The *indio* rides him to where he is going.'

On the trail from Zumba, I found a fourth line to add:

'The *arriero* drives him through the gates of hell.'

Friedrich Nietzsche went mad when he witnessed a downed carthorse being flogged in the streets of Turin one winter day towards the end of his life. The great philosopher was committed to a mental institution as a direct result of this incident. Knowing this about him made him special to me and my philosopher of choice to study at Albert Schweitzer College. Maybe, in that one instant, Nietzsche understood there never would be such a creature as the Übermench, the Superman. The basis for his whole philosophy, his belief in the dawn of a new era for mankind evaporated. Nietzsche did not have to live to see the twist that the Nazis gave to his philosophy: millions of Jews tortured and killed, in the name of forwarding the interests of a Superior Human. Nietzsche saw the treatment suffered by that one horse and that was enough to annihilate his spirit. The one horse was his Holocaust.

'Don't flog a dead horse.' Men in suits use the expression all the time. Everyone knows what it means. Something is done. Over. Leave it alone.

But what does it really mean? That you should beat a live horse?

People do.

Abuses worse than in the sierra of Peru, worse than on the Zumba trail happen today in the United States, in Canada and in Europe. In the cover of darkness, the night before a Futurity run, three year old reiners are tuned up with barbwire bits and punished, punished, punished until they dare not take a breath on their own. In the jumper fields rails have spikes for teeth and the legs of jumpers are shaved and blistered to better feel the bite and know that the name of the game is to clear the fences at all costs. Behind the barn draft horses are taught to pull before the electric shock from a cattle prod. Horses are worked with their front legs nerved, their hocks injected, worked on pain-killers and performance enhancing drugs. Worked in fear. All for the sake of a ribbon. To be the best, the master of the game.

The best? That is the best we can be?

I think they have it all backwards. I think that sort of thing puts them at the back of the line, behind the *arrieros* of Zumba and those who would supply them with the cocaine. Not even ahead of the long forgotten thug who beat his exhausted horse on a street in Turin. How could any man treat in such a way a creature that gives its heart, its limbs and lungs and its very soul in our service, in peace and in war, pulling our plows and our logs, aggrandizing our vanities by stepping higher, faster, more brilliantly.

I won't go mad. I do get angry.

We report to cavalry headquarters in Loja well after dark on the sixth day after leaving Zumba. We are unsure what sort of reception is awaiting us. The university we just rode past is under military rule because of student protests. Are they going to arrest and interrogate us? As we rode through the rain this day, we have practiced imaginary speeches we will deliver before an imaginary panel of judges, in defense of our personal freedom and philosophy of life. We are reasonably ready for what may come.

The young lieutenant on duty immediately knows who we are. Our arrival is expected. But our reception is an anti-climax; the national crisis caused by General Rhon's kidnapping has passed and we are no longer suspected of guerilla activities. We are free to go. We can come by for our documents the following day.

Standing at the guard post, bedraggled and soaked to the bone, we realize we have counted on being detained at the cavalry in Loja. We don't have anywhere else to go. We are down to twenty dollars, until we get to Cuenca, which is ten days journey away. We desperately need to rest the horses for a few days.

"Would you be able to put us up for a couple of days, lieutenant?" Nathan asks. You learn to be right to the point.

So instead of being imprisoned as guerilla suspects, we end up staying at the officers' Casino and acting as Spanish interpreters for Major Musslewhite, US Army. He arrives the following afternoon to check and repair military vehicles and equipment supplied by the US. Charlie Musslewhite stays in the room next to ours. Charlie is a friendly guy and wastes no time in introducing himself, inviting us for a drink and sitting down with us to dinner in the Casino. Could it be his visit is timed so he can have a look at us also? He doesn't say that he is or isn't when Nathan asks him point blank: "Are you investigating us?"

Charlie Musslewhite speaks very little Spanish, having been transferred a few months earlier from duty in Vietnam. He shows signs of battle fatigue and unsteady nerves. His face is drawn and he has nerve twitches, jumping every time a door slams or a car backfires. What is particularly interesting is to hear a professional military man express doubts and even regrets about US presence in Southeast Asia. Apparently the disenchantment with the war has penetrated into the upper ranks of battle-hardened professionals - this fellow is a veteran of Korea. We talk with him late into the evening about his experiences in Vietnam, his close calls as a paratrooper, his family. We find him to be a very warm and human guy, struggling through a reality crisis, wondering what the hell he had been doing all his life fighting to "contain communism and promote freedom and democracy" throughout the world.

The horses are reshod by the cavalry farriers and checked over by a young veterinarian. We clean and repair equipment, treat our horses for sores and fungus infections, undergo medical exams, see movies and are buzzed around with the officers in their jeeps. The group of young cavalrymen at the Casino remind us of the officers we met in Viña del Mar and Arica: cocky, vain, horse-crazy playboys. They are enthusiastic about our adventure, yet seem incredulous that two softies like us could be enduring such an extended trial.

*Things are on the up and up. We push toward the Central Valley at twenty, thirty, forty kilometers a day, lured on by images of greener pastures, the mountain air pumping energy back into our tired blood. We have been through the worst and we are heading for the Promised Land. Clover, alfalfa, corn by the square mile. Luxurious **haciendas**, fine horses and black bulls from Andalucia. The reward we have dreamed of for months, now it is within our reach. With a little hustle, we'll be in Cuenca in less than a week and then. And then, ah sweet illusion! You get hooked and rush on, a soul possessed. And then and then.*

We ride through villages of proud Saragurus, subdued by neither Incas nor Conquistadores. Then we are back on the desolate paramo with no fences or dwellings in sight. No man's land, our land, steppenwolves we. We slow our pace, forget the race into tomorrow, and look for a place to camp. What is the hurry anyhow?

Sometime after midnight, Chaco's low warning growl brings us awake. We can hear the jingle of spurs and voices but can see nothing through the heavy ground fog. I crawl out of the tent and make my way toward the sounds. Three horsemen are standing near Caicique.

*"**Compañeros, Buenas Noches**. Looking for something?"*

They turn their mounts toward the sound of my voice. One of the men gives a hoarse chuckle.

*"**Señor!** We're looking for a black heifer. Maybe you've seen her?"*

"A black heifer?"

*"**Si, señor**. Black," he says.*

"Didn't see her. Come around in the morning if you like and we'll help you search."

*"**Gracias**, maybe we'll do that," he says and they move off into the mist. Their hoofbeats head east.*

I put wood on the coals and go over to tie Caicique further up the slope so he'll have more grass, before I escape the chill back into the bedroll.

"Looking for a black cow in the dark? Sure!" Elly says and rolls over and goes back to sleep. Chaco snuggles up at our feet and is soon snoring loudly. I drift into a light slumber, comforted by the peaceful sound of the horses' slow steady munching.

The horsemen are back within the hour. This time they ride up close to the tent. I can see unsheathed machetes resting across the front of their saddles.

*"**Gringo!** We'd like a word with you!"*

I start to move, but Elly puts a restraining hand on my arm - better stay where we are. This time they don't sound any too friendly.

"Still looking for your cow at this hour?"

*"Still looking, **Gringo**."*

Chaco starts to growl, baring his teeth as one of the men rides up towards Caicique. Elly has to hold him back by his collar. Our spare aluminum tent pole is lying by the opening next to the flashlight, one end blackened from being used to prod the coals in the fire. I get an idea. I slide the blackened end of the pole through the tent flap a few inches and switch on the flashlight for a second, then I turn the light so I can see the face of the horseman outside but he can't see mine.

"A man could get himself into trouble snooping around the camp of strangers," I say, with more assurance than I feel. "I think you fellows had better be moving on."

He hesitates a moment, then turns his horse and joins up with his companions. My heart is racing as I strain to make out words from their muffled voices. Would they believe I had a gun on them? What if one of them has a gun? I become aware of the faint sound of my watch marking the passage of seconds, waiting for what would be their next move. Then the earth reverberates from the impact of horses taking off at a gallop. The hoofbeats fade away, towards the west this time. We lie back and sigh.

"Good bluff!" Elly says.

"If they wake me up again, I'm going to blow kidney beans at them so fast they won't know what hit them."

*She pushes the blanket over my head and we laugh: relieved, happy, reckless, way up on the **paramo** in our portable dream capsule, far away where nothing can touch us.*

In the morning, two young men come galloping bareback horses out of the west. They stop to ask if we have seen some men driving a bunch of horses. A herd was stolen from their corral in the early morning.

"Three men stopped in looking for a black heifer just after midnight." I say.

"Black heifer! They took my best horse!" Says the young man astride the chestnut.

"Three men you said?"

"Yes, three. They were riding dark colored horses with no markings," I say.

*"Thank you, **compañero**," says the youth and they gallop off again.*

I look at Caicique and feel very, very lucky.

A week later, an invisible thief hits us from behind.

It all happens so fast.

On Friday afternoon the vet in Cuenca diagnoses Caicique with a blood disease, either piroplasmosis or tripasomiasis from the symptoms: stiff hindquarters, high fever, yellow around the eyes, chalky blood.

Monday afternoon his lungs hemorrhage.

Dr. Paez gives him two hours to live.

At dawn, twelve hours later, it takes a large overdose of Combelin injected into the jugular and every last ounce of courage I have to put an end to his angry and futile struggle for life.

When the sun comes up over the lush fields of alfalfa, flooding brightly over the paradise we had promised him, our indomitable Caicique lies dead at our feet.

I set in the wet grass, hearing Elly cry, the needle still in my hand, feeling nothing, unable to cry, staring out across the valley at the mountains.

And I see myself throwing more wood on the dying embers, see him getting up from the cold stones in the corral at Challapalca and go down to the river for a drink.

He will whinny and wait and we will all follow him. Caicique, always out front Caicique, the crazy horse she loves. There is nothing that can defeat you, nothing you have not already conquered.

Then the words of the man named Moses explode through my brain: "The one with the crooked spike won't make it out of Ecuador."

My forehead against his cold chest, the sobs tumble out uncontrollably.

We are all out of miracles.

Our keystone is gone.

We are orphans in an alien land.

I do not mourn.

Can not.

I rode Maracas far back at the very end as Nathan was leading the way through the Central Valley of Ecuador, and anger was burrowing tunnels through my soul and my heart was empty.

I was angry at Fate.

I raged, I cried.

I did not mourn.

We had done our part and Fate had no right to do this to us!

I had taken all the love of my childhood dream and I had placed it in a horse that was nothing at all like my dream and who did not always love me back. I settled for a cranky, coarse, cantankerous horse and desired no other. When I was so sick and so tired and wanted to quit in the sierra of Peru, I remained loyal and would not leave him. Even after he kicked me and sent me to the hospital in the most agonizing pain I have ever known, I put no blame on him. We had this little game, Caicique and I. A game of tag. He'd walk away and I would follow and grab his tail and he would stop then and turn his head so I could catch him. Only this time, in the village of Chincheros where Peter Fonda and crew had just finished *The Last Movie*, Caicique kicked out with both hind legs and sent me into a backwards somersault and knocked my wind out. Nathan gave me morphine and found a car to take me to the hospital in Cuzco while he stayed to arrange for the horses. The doctor found two distinct hoofprints, one on my shoulder, the other on my chest. But nothing was broken.

"You approach a bull by its tail," someone had told me, "and a horse by its head. Do it the other way around and you are in trouble." I had broken the rule and I took the blame and moved on and did not hold a grudge.

We did our part.

We gave up everything. We came through all the tough parts. This is one of the most beautiful places in the world. We have earned this, we really have. Most of all, Caicique earned this. He never faltered. Even when he was so sick, going across Cangrejos and Meseta de la Muerte and Pampa del Asador, when we had nothing to feed him at the end of a long day but the chewed down *vega* grasses of some *potrero*. We promised him a place just like this Central Valley of Ecuador. Deeper and deeper my thoughts burrow. I rage at Fate and at the infected tick that bit him somewhere on the jungle trails between Zumba and Loja.

After all he had conquered, all the close calls, to succumb to a tick!

Then, one night, we come to a rain-swollen creek.

It is getting dark. We stop and ask the family in the shack back up on the near bank if we can spend the night and join them by their fire, built right on the dirt floor of what is their kitchen, with no chimney to carry the smoke. They are celebrating the departure of Manuelito, not a year old yet.

I stare in disbelief at the mother smiling in her faith that her Manuelito is an *angelito* with God now. She is proud that God has chosen to take her sweet little baby boy to reside at His side in heaven.

And I look into the hollowness of my own inside.

I look at her smile.

She has lost a child.

I have lost a horse.

I feel ashamed then of my anger.

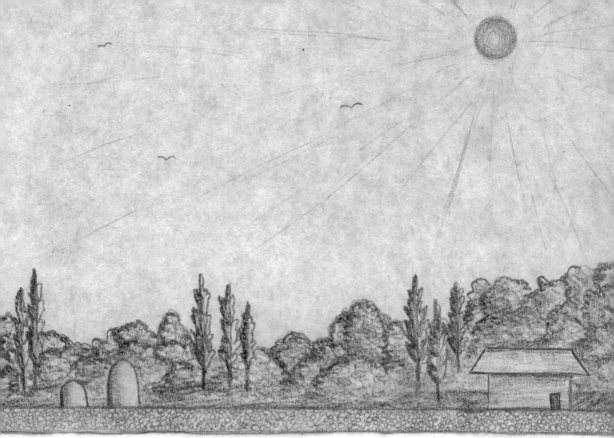

PIRATA

I try to relate more to Maracas. He's the other *twin*, smaller and darker by a shade than Pampero and with the shadow personality to his brother's; Maracas didn't have one of his own. He was Caicique's disciple, my second horse. He often carried the pack because he would follow behind without stopping along the way like Pampero or India did. Maracas never did anything on his own. He never got sick, or lame, or lost. If you had a *tropilla* of horses, you'd want them all like him. If you ran a pack string or a dude trail riding outfit, a whole bunch of Maracases is what you'd want: herdbound horses who just go along with what everyone else does, make no waves and endure whatever the trail brings them.

Guillermo named him Unquillo, for a Patagonian pampa grass. We called him Maracas because of how he would shake you like the Caribbean rattles, the *maracas*. He would go from single-foot pacing to trotting in front, loping behind. Then loping, but misfiring, with a different lead front and back. Then he'd fall back into single-footing, then trotting and keep switching like that.

He wasn't the horse you'd pick out of a herd for an afternoon's pleasure ride.

But here he is, twelve thousand kilometers past a day's ride and now my number one horse. I never ride Pirata, the bright-eyed sorrel gelding Nathan bought from a rancher in Cuenca. We needed a fourth horse right away because, in the middle of all this, Pepper, age ten, had come down to Ecuador to ride with her uncle and me.

Pepper dreamed it up on her own in a Chicago suburb from the pictures she saw and the stories she heard tell of our ride. She started taking riding lessons and used Christmas and birthday money to help buy a used saddle. Everyone thought it was neat that an ordinary kid from an ordinary American suburb would want to do an extraordinary thing like that and encouraged her dream. Her grandparents wanted an excuse for a firsthand look at The Adventure and so the trip to Ecuador was born.

It was really great that Nathan's parents would embrace the present lifestyle of this son they put through prep school and Harvard and who then chose to live like a gypsy.

How could we say to them: don't come?

Keep reading our diaries, look at our pictures, but stay where you are.

That is what we should have told Teddy de Mora, who tried to ride our dream and found it didn't work. I haven't told you about Teddy de Mora earlier because I didn't know how to fit her in. We met her one particularly rainy afternoon in Valdivia, Chile, where she lived with four sons, a whole lot of chickens and husband Octavio, who was a professor at the university and whom she met and married while he was a student at Davis, California. We were in Valdivia without the horses, taking a break from staying in Maria Angelica's house.

"I am riding with you!" Teddy said.

She was a rough and tumble rodeo girl, now suffocating in her role as wife-and-mother. She did not fit into the mold of Valdivia society; the university faculty wives made sure of that. She told us how she was invited to someone's house for an informal gathering.

"Come just as you are," they told her.

She came in her jeans and a shirt. Everyone else was dressed in their party best. They left her standing all alone while everyone was talking to everyone else. She found her way to the bathroom and looked in the mirror at her long straight brown hair quickly brushed and now she noticed the stains on her jeans and that her hands were not very clean with black still under short nails. She wanted to cry, but she waited until after she got out of there. She sat by the mouth of the river for a long time and wished herself far away from this life.

"I'll buy a horse and come on the trail with you!" She said to us. "I won't be any trouble, I promise. Please. Please. Please!"

We said okay. We told her she could not put her stuff on our packhorse and that we would not wait for her. We didn't expect she would actually come.

She took the egg money, which she kept in a glass jar out in the hen house, and bought a sorrel mare which she named Apolla and trucked her up to a little town called Quepa, where she joined us at the end of July, which is the middle of the rainy season in southern Chile.

Teddy was good company. She did a lot of the talking with the people where we stayed along the way. She played cards with the Carabineros in *retens*, she rode colts on ranches, she got wet and went hungry and she never complained.

I have a picture of Teddy rolling out her sleeping bag in a cave where we camped one night in early spring. Her bridle is hung from a bush, she's got her saddle for a pillow and she looks much younger than when we met her. I would have liked for her to have this picture. But we lost track of her after we parted ways in Santiago. Her trip ended quite suddenly on a big *fundo* right on the ocean, where we roamed the beaches and watched the sea lions and talked long into the night with Mario, the administrator. When he offered to buy Apolla, the ride was over for Teddy. Quilpolemo was the perfect place. She would be leaving her mare in good hands. We came with her to Santiago, by bus.

It was hard to leave Teddy all alone with her saddle and her tanned face in the elegant vestibule of her in-laws' house to face all the indignation of a clan who knew for certain that a-wife-and-mother does not abandon house and home and go live on the road with a pair of gypsies. They did not close the door in her face; the time with us on the trail did that.

We wished then that, for her sake, we had said no rather than yes.

And that's the thing. This isn't just a trail ride; it's a whole other dimension to life and the experience will shake the very foundations of what you thought life is about and who you are. This is not a time-out for us; we have nothing to go back to. Here and now is all there is. Every morning when we break camp, we leave everything familiar behind. Every night, we build a world anew. That world, that moment, is all there is. The unknown is our constant companion.

You can't have a guest along on a ride like that. With guests you are supposed to have a plan; they expect you to lead the way.

Last time we saw the parents was in Spain, four years earlier. We were hosts in our house on Machichaco and it was easy then to combine a holiday trip for them with a business trip for us along the northern coast of Spain. We travelled in our VW camper bus. Sometimes they camped with us and sometimes they treated us to a night's lodging in a hotel.

The business part of the trip was in the role of Advertising Executive for The New York Times, according to my business card. It was a fancy title for what I did, which was knock on the doors of shipping agencies and canneries to pitch advertising space in a special edition of The New York Times, featuring Spain. The most interesting part of the job was who got me the job. He was a Basque, from Guernica and one of many who found their way to our house on Machichaco. We referred to him as The-Man-Who-Knew-Hemingway. His conversation was seldom far away from an anecdote or a memory clip involving the great writer. Ernesto, he called him.

We were writers and The-Man-Who-Knew-Hemingway liked to help any writer, famous or not, in any way that he could. Broke as usual, one of us needed to find some kind of a job and he got me the interview with The New York Times. I took the train to Madrid, dressed up in a blue suit I had made my senior year in Nyköping and I wore gloves to hide the calluses and the cement under my broken fingernails. The head of advertising was Italian. I was blonde and Swedish. Maybe that was why I got the job, or simply because no one else wanted to drive around northern Spain looking for commission sales.

I didn't make any money. But we did have that trip with Nathan's parents and I still have a card saying Advertising Executive for Spain. It makes me smile when I look at it and remember extending my gloved hand to be kissed by some general manager in Bilbao or La Coruña.

And I could keep on taking you around on little loops like that, to avoid getting on with my story of how it was in Ecuador with the parents and Pepper visiting. It is complicated and difficult and it is tempting to leave all this out and move on to the next thing. There is so much to write about. Much has to be left out. Why not this?

This book is about doing what is hard. If I don't write about it because it is hard I would be dishonest. And in that case, why write at all?

Caicique died in Cuenca on November 23, two days after Pepper and the parents arrived.

I look at the sentence for a long time and I don't know what I should put down next. Getting to Cuenca had been on our minds for weeks. We pushed towards Cuenca because we had this rendezvous with the parents, even when we realized Caicique was more than exhausted and we should stop. Your attention to each and every member of your troupe is always more important than any obligation you can have to outsiders or to a goal, or deadline. It has to be. That is how you survive as a troupe.

But Nathan and I now had a second troupe, with very different needs. That is how come we left Caicique in the care of the *capataz* for a few hours and went in to Cuenca for dinner at El Rincon, an Argentine restaurant that served excellent *asado*. While we were good hosts to our second troupe, someone out at the farm, maybe the *capataz* himself, let our horses out to drink from the river.

Caicique was under strict orders from the veterinarian not to have any water. The autopsy showed he drank a large quantity of water and some got into his lungs. Fulminating pneumonia is what killed him. We lost him because we were not paying undivided attention to him. It does not matter how many people tell you in how many ways that it was not your fault.

It was.

We should have been with him and we were not. There is no way around that. It doesn't matter that he might have died anyway of Piroplasmosis, or about Moses' prophesy that he would not make it out of Ecuador. We should have never left his side. He survived the death sentence in Challapalca because our attention never wavered then.

It is very hard for anyone to grasp the amount of concentration required to live in a continuous dialogue between will and chance. People understand about karate; you wear white clothes and a special belt and you learn the moves, ever ready for the unknown. People understand that you learn karate as a philosophy of life: a system to move you beyond all systems. I don't do karate, but I do horse logging and it is like that. You always expect the unexpected. The task is simple: move logs from a here to a there, using one or two horses.

But each log behaves differently than any other log because of its shape or weight or how it was felled, or the ground conditions or if it's dry or wet, pine or spruce. You might know the trail, but it will be different each time. Your horses might hear something, or see something, or feel something that causes them to behave differently. You have to be alert to anything coming at you from anywhere and react by instinct based on accumulated experience. If you have students, or the occasional visitors, you have to slow the process down to a crawl because now your peripheral vision and senses have to take in them as well. You have to anticipate where they will be in relation to you and the log and anything going on around them and alert them to any danger.

Horse logging, like karate, is dramatic. Riding up the Americas on horseback entails hours of sitting in the saddle on a horse walking slowly through the landscape, as the rain falls on you or the sun beats on you or the wind whips you. You spend much time looking for feed for your horses and it is not anything like in the Western movies where riders gallop off at sunrise and go all day and their horses never tire and never eat or drink.

Pepper got bored on the trail. She wanted to gallop and jump, not just sit there for so many hours. In the villages, wherever we stopped, crowds would gather and people would speak to her in Spanish. She could not understand what they said and it bothered her. Reality was disorienting and exhausting and not at all what she could have imagined.

You cannot ask a ten-year-old to feel at home in a world that is so unpredictable and always changing. Pepper rode with us for most of two weeks. She decided that was enough. And it was. In this she had more sense than the rest of us. She went to Quito to stay at the hotel with her grandparents until their scheduled flight out of Ecuador.

It felt sad to put Pep's saddle, bedroll and bags in the trunk of the rented car. She was dropping out, just like I did at the same age, after I lobbied so hard to go to horse camp in Colorado and learn to be a real cowboy. I was fine until the family left St. Paul to go to Maine. I could not imagine them going there without me. The camp director would not let me use the phone to call home so I walked down a long and lonely and very hot road to find a pay phone.

I often wonder if the folks did the right thing in allowing me to quit, as with Pepper now. I arrived in Maine with my boots and my hat and

*everyone called me Cowboy Nate, but my self-confidence was shat-
tered. The sense of failure has driven me on ever since and none of my
subsequent achievements were good enough to make up for it.*

*Years later, I heard a taped version of the presentation Pepper made
in front of her whole school about her adventure. It made me smile and
think things turned out all right even if Pepper lost her interest in riding horses after her trip to Ecuador. She remembered the good times
with her grandparents, with pictures of all of us together riding up the
Chimborazo Volcano on borrowed horses and cooking hot dogs and
hamburgers on the open hearth at the hacienda when we got back. The
hamburgers, she said, were not like McDonalds but she ate a whole
one anyway.*

She did not talk about the night we had to keep candles burning in a room
upstairs in a barn because there were rats in there the size of cats. They were
the only rats I can remember on our entire ride and so many of them! Our hosts
sent up a bowl of potatoes, large ones, cooked with the skin and the dirt on
them. They brought up warm milk too. Chaco got the milk. We took the salt
out of the pack and Nathan and I ate potatoes while the rats stared from the
dark corners of the room. Pepper could not make herself eat, not even the
crackers we had in the pack. And who could blame her? Pepper could not in
her worst nightmares have imagined this to be part of The Adventure.

In the morning, we asked our hosts why they did not have cats around the
barn.

"We did!" They told us, "but the rats ate the cats."

We were glad Pepper did not understand. We did not translate for her.

When Pepper's younger sister Bonnie was sixteen and came to spend the
summer with us at the ranch in BC, we were hosts in a world of our own. We
were doing wilderness trail rides and summer camps for girls and we served
potatoes too, roasted in tin foil over the coals of a campfire. Nathan would tell
the girls to make sure to brush their teeth and clean their fingernails afterwards. Bears have a very developed sense of smell, he told them. You could
never know where bears might be lurking. The girls would laugh at him. But
a little part of them would wonder if he might be serious and they brushed their
teeth extra long that night and made double sure every scrap of food was either

put away or thrown into the fire and burnt so that there would be no bear eyes looking at them from some dark part of the forest. Theirs was a measured adventure in a wilderness setting with us as their guides; not a journey into a strange unknown. Bonnie took a part of this world back with her, the way you take a piece of sourdough home to start your own batch and she grew it into a cattle ranch in Wyoming. She was a girl from a Chicago suburb too.

December twenty-first was my mother's birthday. Elly and I went into Quito the night before. Elly got up early to round up a cake while I wrote up an Honorary Membership Certificate in the Hobos on Horseback Society to present to mom. Then we marched into their bedroom with a breakfast tray, singing and hollering the ancient tune of felicitation in Spanish.

After the party, Pep and I went across town to the bus depot, found one going south and after a bouncy one and a half-hour ride we were back with the horses. They were grazing peacefully in the paddock where we left them and when I whistled they all looked up, even Pirata. I thought: how amazing! With our horses, anywhere at all becomes home. As we walked in the gate, a peon came running toward us, his face pale and agitated.

"Your dog was hit by a truck! He is badly hurt!"

My boots were full of lead, my heart beat like a drum as I hurried towards the garage where they had put Andin. Once again we had placed the life of one of our companions in jeopardy by trying to spread ourselves too thin.

Andin cried out when he heard my steps approaching and tried to crawl out of the corner of the garage to meet me but his body was too traumatized to move very far. I sat down on the dirt floor with him and he put his head in my lap and tried to lick my face and his eyes were saying: "Where have you been so long? Why did you leave me?" His nose was bleeding, there were cuts on his paws and around his face and several toes seemed to be broken. His back was partially paralyzed, but it was impossible to determine the extent of the damage by look and by feel.

We wrapped Andin in blankets and Pepper stayed with him while I hitched in to Latacunga to try and get a veterinarian. He was out of the office so I left a message with the secretary, hitched back to check on Andin and Pepper and then continued over to La Avelina Restaurant where mom, dad and Elly were to meet us at one o'clock for mom's birthday party. I met their bus and I am sure that my face concealed nothing for they all looked frightened when they saw me standing there alone. I sent them to see Andin and Pepper and caught a bus back into Latacunga. This time I found Dr. Molina in his office and he agreed to come out immediately. He too thought that Andin had multiple fractures and suggested we take him into Quito where a friend of his had a clinic.

Then we went over to look at Pampero, who had come up suddenly lame when we were loping along on a soft, sandy trail. There was nothing stuck in his hoof. It wasn't hot. We managed to move Pampero to a nearby hacienda. The owners were very helpful and called in two veterinarians to look at him. Each had a slightly different approach to the problem. One prescribed penicillin. The other prescribed sulfur drugs. Neither of the veterinarians stooped down to examine the hoof and leg. Penicillin might be the cure for a lot of things, but an undiagnosed sudden lameness would not be one of them. Pampero's leg was now quite swollen. Dr. Molina suggested we move him by truck over to a neighboring ranch so he could be attended to by an old Chilean there who knew a lot about horses.

We had to split up again: Elly went into Quito with Andin and the folks and I stayed on duty with Pampero. I felt desolate after everyone had departed. How could things turn out so bad when we all tried so hard? The following day I sat with the horses in the sunny paddock most of the day, writing in my diary. The administrator and his family were civil enough to invite me for lunch, but I found them insincere and callous.

"It will cost too much to cure your dog," said the wife. "Why don't you just shoot him?"

In order to cure Pampero's leg, the administrator suggested tying his tail to his good leg - the wisdom of a man who had been around horses most of his life!

Elly arrived back late and first thing in the morning, I went to get a truck to take the horses over to the Chilean at La Avelina. The three

Criollos were predictably nonchalant about the whole thing. Pampero was standing firmly on three legs, his mouth stuffed full of the green barley we had brought them, even as the truck swerved and bounced. Pirata went wild. It took all my strength to hold him as he slid around and banged himself, tried to rear up and vault over the tailgate.

It seems to us that Providence might have concocted this whole thing so that we would meet up with Arturo Dragon. He is eighty-two years old, with the vigor of a man very much involved in living life to the fullest.

The first thing Arturo does is get down on his hands and knees in the grass. He puts his face right next to Pampero's left hind and smells deeply and noisily.

"*Hormiguera*," he snorts. "There is a pocket of pus deep inside the hoof."

He shakes his head when we tell him the battery of antibiotics prescribed by the two young veterinarians. He brings out a brown glass bottle with one of his own remedies. The brew makes your eyes sting from ten feet away! He goes back down on all fours and smears the concoction all around the coronary band.

"That will get the infection moving!" He says.

The following morning Pampero's whole leg is hot and quite swollen. Arturo nods and says this is a good thing. The medicine is pulling the infection out of the hoof and up where we can get rid of it. By evening, pus is erupting along the coronary band. The following morning Arturo says it is time to cool things down with another remedy of his. He tells us to leave Pampero in his hands and go be with the family in Quito.

This is Pepper's first Christmas away from her parents and her sisters, and without snow; nothing at all to remind her of Christmas' past.

For Nathan and his parents it is their first Christmas together since the Christmas of 1962 when Nathan and brother Caleb and I drove fifteen hundred miles through winter storms from Cambridge, Massachusetts to be with them in St. Paul, Minnesota. Fran and Carl and Pepper were there too. It would be our last Christmas together, ever.

We left Chaco on Arturo's balcony and hitched into Quito to celebrate Christmas Eve with Pep and the parents. They had decorated

*their hotel room with red and green yarn on the door and around the
lamps. Chicken dinner in the restaurant stood in for the traditional
turkey and then we retired upstairs to open the few gifts we had to
exchange. Most were practical jokes: a plastic gun for me, a check
for 365 happy days for Elly and me, two bottle caps of Nivea skin
cream for mom, a Chicklet box of Aspirin for Dad. We had a gay time
in spite of the Santa Lucia, the gingerbread houses, the spruce tree
laden with stars and candy that were in the back of our minds.*

*December 27 was our final day together. We brought Andin back
out to La Avelina, to be reunited with Chaco and the horses after nearly
a week of staying at the hotel with the parents and Pep. Both dogs
went wild upon seeing each other. Andin yapped for joy and for pain
both, his battered body unable to respond to equal his exuberance.
Chaco was a charge of TNT as always, his legs trembling with desire
to play, run and rough-house again, but trying to be gentle, sniffing
Andin all over.*

*Dad and I went out to the polo field with Pep to see her ride India
one last time. Mom and Elly stayed on the sundeck of Arturo Dragon's 'penthouse' to keep an eye on the dogs and watch Pep at the
same time. After a spill she took a few days earlier, Pep's confidence
was at a low and she asked me to ride the mare around the court first,
in case she bucked.*

*"Impossible!" I said. But away went the mare, her head between
her front legs and her heels high in the air. Pepper laughed and cheered
me on from the sidelines and after India was bucked out, Pep did a
few tight circles at the trot, then figure eights and a short canter, all
bareback. We rode double back to the paddock and walked over to La
Avelina restaurant for the parting feast.*

*Just as we stepped outside the restaurant, a bus bound for Quito
came to a stop. The conductor yelled that they had four empty seats
up front. We had no time for tears and clutches. Suddenly Elly and I
were alone once again in our mobile, topsy-turvy, marvelously myriad
world, standing on a highway in the backdraft wind of the bus taking
our loved ones back to their lives.*

Arturo belongs with Armando and with Guillermo and it is entirely befitting and not a coincidence that we would spend New Year's Eve with him, our second anniversary on the trail. Arturo did most of the talking. Maybe he sensed that our search for Freedom was a continuation of his own, that his story was part of our own unfolding story.

For Arturo going to school interfered with living and learning things and one day, without telling anyone, he sold his bundle of schoolbooks for a few *centavos*. That is all the money he had when he went to see the *arrieros* who ran the mule train with mail from Santiago de Chile across the Andes into Argentina.

"Take me with you!" He begged of them.

"It is cold on the pass, you will need a coat. And you will have to work hard." Arturo was thirteen years old. That was old enough, back then, to be taken seriously and to do with your life as was your destiny.

Arturo did not say much about the trail across the Cordillera, maybe he figured we had plenty of material to fill in the geography for ourselves. He told us about three Italians they found sitting in a snowdrift up on the pass. They were smiling, beyond pain already, beyond caring. The *arrieros* took their whips and began beating the defenseless men on their hands and across their faces. Arturo thought he had never seen such cruelty. The frozen Italians began defending themselves against the abuse. The *arrieros* got them angry enough to want to come back to life. They got them up and walking and holding onto the tail of the last mule in each train, the Italians made it down the other side of the mountain. Arturo understood then that things are not always what they seem; what he had perceived as cruelty was instead a great kindness.

Arturo stayed with the families of the mule drivers on the Argentine side of the Andes. He helped cut and bring in the firewood and in exchange he received his meals and he had a place to stay. But his shoes and his clothes wore out and he found himself in rags.

"Ah, how I learned to suffer!" He shakes his head. Then he laughs. "But I understood it was the price I must pay for my freedom."

He stayed with the mule drivers until one day at the market some people threw him into the ring with the burly son of his host.

"Let's see the Chilean use his fists!" The people yelled.

Arturo proved tougher than he looked. He beat his opponent. But his was a bitter victory; now he could not return to live under the same roof as his vanquished adoptive brother. Alone, he set out for Buenos Aires in search of an uncle who had a business there. He managed to locate the uncle and the man did the right and honorable thing: he clothed and housed his nephew and put him back in school. After a few months, Arturo cut loose once more. He stowed away on a ship bound for Valparaiso, Chile, via Cape Horn. Once in port, he contacted his family in Santiago. They did not open their arms to welcome him back. Instead he was remanded onto a ship whose crew was made up of delinquents and troublemakers.

Not long after the ship put out to sea, Arturo witnessed two mates fall from the yardarm and into the water. The ship stayed steady on her course, leaving the two boys for dead before they were. Arturo refused to go back up in the rigging after this. They flogged him, they made him peel potatoes for months on end. "But no one was going to make me toss my one life away! Besides, I had food down in the galley!"

Seven mates had perished at sea by the time they reached Rio de Janeiro. Arturo knew he had to get off this ship. His opportunity came when local officials were invited aboard for a fiesta. The crew were given dress uniforms and allowed to take part. When everyone was drunk, Arturo stole away and slid down one of the anchor lines into a small launch. He hid under the seat in the bow. Luck was with him and he made it to shore undetected.

Arturo gets up to enact his feelings as he sees the ship pull anchor and set back out to sea, leaving him behind on solid ground. He dances and waves and smiles, the eighty-two year old man as one with the boy who left everything familiar and safe because he had to know what lay on the other side of the mountains.

Arturo found his way to the racetrack in Rio and moved quickly from stableboy to rider to jockey. Horses ran well for him and he rode on tracks all over South America. He even made some trips to ride in the US.

"I moved with the high society people, especially when I was rolling in money, which was often in those days. After my money was gone, they all suddenly disappeared and did not know Arturo Dragon!"

"Friends of my pocketbook, the bastards!"

He says it without a trace of bitterness; an old man looking back and shaking his head at the credulity of himself as a young man, but judging the youth not for his naiveté. Regretting nothing.

A diploma with lots of swirls to the scripted letters hangs on the wall at the entrance to Arturo's apartment. It reads Honorary Doctor of Veterinary Medicine and it has a simple black frame. It is signed by the general in charge of the Ecuadorian cavalry. He shrugs when I ask him about this extraordinary document.

"The regular veterinarians complained to the authorities about me. 'Why are you allowing a *brujo* to do the work of a scientist?' They said. They demanded that only doctors of veterinary medicine be allowed to practice at the track and in the cavalry stables. The General knew I was the one who could get lame horses running again, that I saved many horses with colic, I cured moon blindness. They did not want to do without me. So they made this up."

"Do we call you *Doctor* Dragon?" I ask.

He laughs and laughs. "*Doctor Dragon*" he repeats and shakes his head. "They still call me *brujo*!" He says. "But they can't stop me from treating the horses."

It is impossible to tell if he prefers to be known as a witch doctor or as the *Doctor*. Or if he even cares. Imagine how good you would have to be to earn a doctorate with only an elementary school education! And this in a country where it isn't about what you know but who you know!

Arturo gave us the bottle containing the rest of the medicine he used to cure Pampero. He also gave us his recipe so that we should be able to make up our own batch as needed up the trail. I remember that a dozen eggs and kerosene went into the making, but we lost the piece of paper and with it a miraculous treatment for deep-seated abscesses. We joke sometimes that Arturo's formula would have made us rich. It wasn't meant to be.

It is difficult to drag ourselves away, yet once back in the saddle, riding through the silent morning along a narrow winding road with animals grazing amongst the cypress groves, I feel there is no other way to be living.

The mist lifts slowly off the valley. We begin to meet school children, bookbags slung over their shoulders, skipping and running down the path toward the neighborhood schoolhouse. The sun spreads his warm fingers over the earth and the day's pulse quickens. Leaves unfold. Birds take wing.

Andin and Pampero are able to move short distances only. Pampero's hoof is too tender for us to nail on a shoe, so we improvise with oval shaped sardine cans. The way it works is you remove the lid, with a key provided, and then you cut one end off the can with a knife and make two holes about an inch and a half from each end and two holes about four inches apart in the toe. Laced on with leather thongs, this tin slipper lasts half a day's ride across dry and rocky ground. It doesn't stay on through mud. Even the most humble and remote store in Ecuador will have canned sardines to sell. Neither Nathan nor I care much for them. Fortunately Chaco and Andin do because they get to eat a lot of sardines in the three weeks after we leave Arturo's.

We advance like that, slowly but steadily until one day when we tap his hoof with the hammer lightly, Pampero does not flinch. Nathan is able to put a shoe on him this day, the twenty-second of January. We are camping up in the high country on the Paramo del Angel, in view of the twin border towns of Tulcan and Ipiales in the valley far below.

Tomorrow, we leave for Columbia. We have spent less than three months in Ecuador. In that time, our world crashed. It is easy to get caught up in all the bad things. And in some ways, conflict is easier to write about than it is to write about the happy moments.

Strange, isn't it? We strive for happiness and peace and when we have it, we really don't know what to do with it. The moment goes so quickly by. You pass it over with a picture postcard: *wish you were here*! And you really don't mean that.

I look at the two dogs curled up on the other side of the fire. Andin is almost back to normal now. Three of his toes were broken, but no major bones were. I have a new saddle now. It has a horn and fancy tooling. It looks like an oldtime western saddle, maybe something that Butch Cassidy and the Sundance Kid left behind long ago and the saddle makers of Ecuador adopted as their own design. Fernando Diaz bought it for me because he has Caicique's saddle now. And how that came about was we were staying at the hacienda belonging to a friend of his. Fernando came over because he loves horses. He looked at our gear, interested as horsemen usually are. He mentioned he wants to start playing polo, as soon as he finds a saddle.

"Will mine do?" I ask.

"Well, yes, *señora*."

"It doesn't fit my other horse. If it fits yours, you take it."

It did fit the good bay horse he planned to use to play polo. We spent the day with Fernando Diaz, who was the best *rejoneador* in Ecuador. He put his purebred Spanish horse through its paces in the ring and let Nathan ride the beautiful grey, so responsive to the slightest shift in the rider's weight, so light in the hand, so attentive. Then Nathan acted the bull, charging at the horse as Fernando rode by, so that he could demonstrate how he stuck lances into the bull's neck as the horse spun and dashed out of the sweep of the horns, Nathan's arms in this case. Pepper and the parents laughed out of control as Nathan goofed around, snorting and pawing the dirt and lunging at Fernando's horse. We all had dinner together afterwards and the following day we borrowed horses for the parents and rode up the backside of the Chimborazo Volcano. What I want to take with me as we leave Ecuador is the memory of all of us together under a clear blue sky, sharing a simple picnic in the heart of the most beautiful country in the world.

I needed to try and remember what I had gained, not what I had lost.

Banco Mundial de la Prosperidad

INSTITUCION DE NOBLES DESEOS

N° 01971

Páguese por este cheque a   Quito, 2 5 de Diciembre de 19 7 0

Nathan y Elly Foote

365 TRESCIENTOS SESENTA Y CINCO DIAS DE FELICIDAD

Feliz Navidad
Próspero Año Nuevo

Sus Padres

BUENAVENTURA

Unceasing rain drums on the foliage, hisses on puddled clay. Bushes, trees, boulders, moss-tiled huts materialize out of the vapor banks, each enclosed within its own veil of tears and running away into a thousand trickling brooks; instant creeks merging into tumbling streams that cut wounds in the red soil. An overhanging barranco crumbles away and a grove of banana trees comes skating down a mud avalanche, exposed roots clinging to pedestals of clay, fanned leaves hanging limp. The switchbacks tighten into coils as the path steepens and the pounding of angry water on rapids rises up out of the narrow gorge to drown the piss-sizzle of the deluge.

Up to his knees in the swirling water, Pirata balks. I slack the reins and let the horse spin and return to the shore where the others are waiting, Elly huddles in her poncho to the rear where she always rides now, using only Maracas, refusing even to come near the blaze-faced sorrel who has usurped the lead from Caicique and from her.

"Nate, how could you buy him - with that name!" She said when I brought Pirata into the corral in Cuenca to meet the others. She is staring blankly at the muddy river now, turns her horse wearily and leads the retreat back up the slippery trail to a toadstool hovel that seems to grow right out of a shelf dug into the naked slope. The hard packed mud yard is speckled with chicken droppings and the hiero-glyphic etchings of claw, hoof and bare feet.

A small girl with a burlap sack draped over her head and shoul-ders leads us over to a shed where we pull off the gear and string a rope between two posts to hang the blankets so they will shed some of the wetness overnight, better to absorb the deluge of the next day. A man's voice comes though the driving rain:

"Give their horses some cornstalks, Veronica!"

They find fruit crates for us to sit on in their semi-circle around the tray of red coals on the clay floor and fill gourds with **sancocho** *from the big iron kettle and hand them to us. Our boots steam and curl at the toes, the garlic gruel driving out some of the numbness. We drink hot cinnamon water and smoke black cigarettes, talk little. Gusts of wind throw buckshot rain against the plastic window coverings, whip the burlap flap hung over the doorway. I steal a glance at the pale face of the mother who is rocking back and forth, eyes closed, nursing her youngest of ten. The elder daughter squats next to a wash basin rins-ing the dishes, humming to herself, in her faded dress and with no shoes for her callused feet.*

I am overcome by a sense of despair. Despair for the nursling in this big family with so little to share; for all the dreary, wet, sad, for-gotten villages we have ridden through in the province of Nariño, Co-lumbia. And I despair at feeling this way. Eight years ago, the Consci-entious Objector went to the barrio believing that, in some small way, he would change the world and that all the droplets of goodwill would flow into creeks and swell into a growing river and move the tides on the ocean of humanity.

The only change I am concerned with now is in the weather and in the scenery; I wish us far away from all this and to some sunlit Rocky Mountain Wilderness.

We share their food, their hearth, their mud floor for a night. The same rain beats on them as on us. But we are nomads; we move on, leaving behind the people of these lost villages. For them there will, with each generation, be more water in the soup, more toadstool huts.

What will happen to all the new people with no new places to go, no new soil to work? As I write this, statistics tell me there are now twice as many people on the South American continent as there were back then and I wonder how we can be so good at making charts and projections and be so utterly incapable of controlling development.

"I wish I had been born sooner, so I would have a longer life," said Conchita, age ten after visiting an Earth Day exhibit in Vancouver, BC. I asked her what she meant.

"Because all the water and the air and the land will be used up," she said.

I told this to an Argentine I met at Expo '86 in Vancouver.

"How very sad, such a negative worldview," said he.

Her despair should rightfully belong to him, I thought and I wondered how well did he know the hinterlands of his own continent?

I think about the hills of Nariño the night when the headline news on CBC radio is the birth of the six billionth human in Sarajevo, in the former Yugoslavia. I wonder: how did they pick who this sixth billionth would be?

The year is 2000 and I am driving through the night in our one-ton diesel pickup, pulling a gooseneck trailer with a couple of horses in it. Conchita is asleep in the back seat.

It is just after three a.m. when, coming up a gradual hill, the motor dies. We are out of fuel. I let the rig coast to a stop with the right wheels off on the gravel shoulder and step out of the truck. The night is clear and quite warm for September, with so many stars.

I have a cell phone, but it has no signal here. I have BCAA, but without a cell phone signal, I can't call anyone. I have a two-way radio but there is no traffic on this stretch of road at this hour. It strikes me as funny to have all these gadgets disabled by distance. A soft quietude wraps itself around me and I feel a great sense of security, stranded in the middle of this vast space. I watch Northern Lights sweep across the sky and try to make some sense of the news.

Six billionth!

And here am I on my way back to my mountain so far away on this road where no one will come for an hour, maybe two, and that is a rare privilege in a world teeming with six billion humans. We have just returned from Europe, Conchita and I, where we were surrounded by a constant hum, even camping by the ocean in Sweden you could hear the hum of cars. Like a swarm of relentless bugs. Day and night the sound pressed against you from all sides and what you notice, coming back home, is the absence of the hum. You can hear the small sounds clear and distinct. A brook trickling close by. A rustle in the bushes across the road. Eventually, the approaching sound of a diesel truck.

It is a big semi with two young men in their twenties. They find a gallon jug and siphon diesel from their tank, several canfulls, and put them into the blue oneton and they help me bleed the air out of the injectors and then I continue on into the morning while Conchita sleeps. She drives the last few hours to our mountain, where we look out across a valley of spruce and pine and snowcapped peaks in the far distance. Our backyard is inhabited by moose and deer and bears and birds and there is plenty of air and water here for my children and their children's children.

Flushed out of the hills of Nariño, we invade the urban labyrinth of Cali, reeking of mildew and mold, our boots cracked with the mud of a thousand places. Teenagers gather on sidewalks, saunter along, edging in closer, ready to groove with whatever is happening. Indoor moon faces slide across bay windows, children waving shyly, pin-curled mamas puzzling. A photographer wiggles across the white line, his necktie flapping on the hot pavement, angling for a snake-eyed view while a jack-in-the-box microphone emerges from the window of a station wagon. India lays her ears back, sidestepping away. The commentator brings us right into a million homes:

"Hear the clack of their horseshoes over the traffic. It is a fantastic sight. At five kilometers an hour! We're clocking them on our speedometer as they enter Cali, our city of the future."

"Tell our listeners. Don't you get bored riding all the time?"

*"The **gauchos** say whoever gets bored riding must have an empty head."*

"Well that is... terrific."

Wetting his lips, switching the channels:

"Here they are, citizens of Cali, entering our modern city, proud

home of the 1972 Pan American Games. Truly a symbol for us all. Athletic. Rugged. And very, very charming."

Honking from behind us: two hundred and fifty horsepower have given up the ghost right in the middle of the Avenida. The Argentine consul steps out the door of his black limo and stares helplessly as the gap between our horses and his horseless carriage widens. The driver opens the hood and a cloud of steam envelops him. The commentator snaps up the action.

"The Honorable Consul of the sister Republic of Argentina is just taking farewell of the adventurous couple and the rugged equines, natives of the republic of Argentina".

He pauses, readjusting the mike to catch something more from Elly.

"By the time you reach Alaska, señora, you will have the long distance record for riding, correct?"

"Our not being in a hurry tends to get us there. The tortoise and the hare, you know."

"Yes indeed. Right on, señora." He leans over to check the fuel and the temperature gauges on the dashboard of his vehicle. Glancing at his watch, he says.

"Our time is almost up, folks. But tell us, señora, after conquering the Andes and the deserts, how do you feel about facing the greatest challenge of them all, crossing the Darien jungles to Panama?"

"We don't plan to attempt anything that would jeopardize the lives of our horses," she says.

Silence accentuates disbelief. "Surely your honor as sportsmen is worth the risk?"

"Our horses mean far more to us than breaking some record. If no one has crossed the Darien before, it is probably for very good reason."

"A British expedition is underway, using canoes and amphibious jeeps. But our bets are still with you. We, the citizens of Cali, stand firmly behind you in this great undertaking. It is our belief that you will not let yourselves be outdone."

He cranks in the mike before she can make a comment.

"This is Pedro Velasquez, signing off for RRLD, your station of tomorrow. We have been talking to a fearless couple embarked on a

historic ride as they set out to do what no one else has ever attempted,
the conquest of the Darien jungles.
 "Adios and hasta manana."

Because we met someone, who knew someone, who knew the Swedish Consul in Cali, we came to stay the night at the villa belonging to the Swedish Consul, whose name was Vern Lindblad. His wife's name was Anita and she had on a nice hostess smile as she served us dinner on her terrace. But when her husband left the room to put their children to bed, her smile froze to a smirk and she began to give us a lecture. She told us we should not think anyone cared about this thing we were doing, that it had all been done before, many times before. Even should someone come herding rattlesnakes up the road, they would cause but a small ripple of notoriety, said Anita. We should not think ourselves anything so special.

She apologized for having no mattress, no spare bed or even blankets to offer. We didn't mind the bare floor; we did mind her invasion into what was our private realm, her presumption of understanding our reasons and interpreting them to us. I want to get up in the night and ride out of the confines of Anita's kingdom, which only reached the fence of a forty meters by sixty suburban house plot. We lay awake on our horse blankets on the floor in the library of the Swedish Consul and dreamed of a ranch in the Rockies, a world to call our own, where no one had the right to invite you for supper and then make you pay for it with insults.

I remember the woman Anita so many years later because you meet people like her, quite a few people like her, who are fascinated by your nomadic life and repelled by it, threatened to the very core because they think are stuck where they are and have the mind to perceive their own stuckness.

She thinks she wants your freedom. But she wants it for free.

You hold up some sort of mirror to her and she does not like what she sees, so she turns on you. There is no point in arguing with her and telling her she's got it all wrong, that you are not doing this for anyone else, certainly not for her. You want to leave her housefull of opinions, right then, in the middle of the night, because you don't want her acrimony to ooze out and drip on you. But it does, her bitterness is writ with indelible ink and spills onto this page, so many years later.

Now you can tell her what you didn't back then:

You want something?
This is how it works:
You go get it!
What's stopping you?

"Columbia, the door to South America!" Woo the tourist brochures.
For us, the exit.
From Cali, Columbia, we have three choices:
We might have attempted to take our horses across the swamps of the Darien Peninsula and into Panama. But not after riding the Zumba to Yangana trail and losing Caicique. The jungle is not an option for us. The level of risk to the horses is unacceptable. We could go north to Barranquilla or Santa Marta and try to ship out from there.
We went to Santa Marta when we worked in the *barrio* and spent magical days in the company of a man named Constantino. He was a rich guy, maybe he was a drug lord; we didn't ask. We went snorkeling with him in the clear waters of the Caribbean and he swam with sharks in the shallows over the corral reefs. He said there is nothing to fear about this but fear itself. Fear has a smell, he said and I would remember this. Sharks can smell fear from miles away. If you are not afraid, as they are not afraid, being the masters of the ocean, they will accept you as an equal and not attack you. We believed him. But we watched from the boat as he slipped over the gunnel to retrieve the knife he has dropped into the water. He swims in amongst a school of sharks, nudging them aside as he moves to pick up the knife. He returns to the surface with the knife between his teeth. We spent evenings with him by the pool in his mansion and we stayed only a couple of days. It was perfect. We want to keep these memories clear like the waters of the Caribbean and not return.
Our third option is Buenaventura.
Buenaventura has a nice sound to it, doesn't it? A tropical paradise kind of sound.
Don't be fooled.
It is a sticky, muggy, clammy, bug infested *cul de sac* that reeks of death and decay. There exists every kind of flying, creeping, wiggling, crawling insect vying for equine blood, each taking a turn, from pre-dawn mosquitoes to the giant horseflies of high noon, vampire bats who attack during the night and fungi in the grass that cause the hooves to slough.

There were no horses in Buenaventura. No donkeys even.

In this hellhole of a place sprawling at the edge of the tropical swamps, we found one of the most wonderful persons we have ever met. Her name was María de Botin and she lived at Finca Bombay, which is a large white wooden house perched on a hillside, ten kilometers out of the port. It was all lit up with the power from a diesel generator when we rode in after dark, worried about what we should do with the horses and with Chaco and Andin in the days ahead.

"Stay here," said María de Botin, "for as long as you need to. It will be my pleasure to have you."

You knew Maria wasn't going to frost over. She was the widow of a captain and lived here with her black adoptive son. His name was Martin. He was her brother in the faith, which was Jehovah's Witness. They lived their faith in practical ways and never tried to impart their version of The Truth onto us. They had a big ramada where the horses stood in the shade all day, out of the bugs. We swabbed their hooves with kerosene and disinfectants and bathed them with insect repellants made of garlic, red pepper and vinegar. There were places with grass not far away where we kept them tethered at night.

Each day we went into the port to try and arrange for passage. There were always ships in harbor, numerous shipping agencies handling cargo. It isn't far by sea from Columbia to Panama. But no one was much interested in transporting two ton of horseflesh on a short haul. I can see now why they would not be, but we could not then because we were in the situation, growing increasingly desperate to get out.

We climbed walls, getting nowhere but back down. We screamed and yelled and sulked and felt very sorry for ourselves and especially for the horses and we took it out on any and everyone in our path; we were a little grey twister coming at you. People slammed doors in self-protection, sent messages with secretaries that they were out or busy or otherwise unavailable.

Our wedged toes blistered, shirts glued to our backs, we haul ourselves across Plaza Bolivar as office workers emerge from their frost-gilded worlds. Another day gone! Three weeks in this hellhole and we are no closer to shipping out than we were after our first day of making the rounds in Buenaventura. Faces are becoming familiar in the crowd at the sidewalk cafes.

Julio, agent for Mexican Lines, beckons us over to his table.

"Pull up a chair. Relax." He orders a round of gin and tonic. "I thought Marquez got you a ship?"

"If we had the kind of money Grace Prudential wants to charge for taking our horses to Balboa, the two of us could take a cruise around the world!" Elly says hotly.

We run through the whole litany of rejections we have gleaned in Buenaventura on this day:

Italian Lines feared we would sue them if a horse broke a leg.

Norwegian Lines that a spark from a horseshoe might blow a tanker sky high.

The captain of the Naxos that he would lose his job if he took our circus aboard.

Swedish American told us to try shipping out of Barranquilla.

Polish Lines told us to go across the Darien swamps.

We tried seeing the mayor, but he was too busy.

The harbor pilot told us we should sell the horses.

The captain of the naval base was very friendly. But he had no ships to commandeer.

Julio nods. "Did I tell you about the German who drove his VW off the pier? Right into the sea he drove it! Had been here about two months then. Flew out of Cali the next day."

"Thanks, Julio," I say, "that helps a lot."

He attempts a laugh. "I have been stuck here for eight years!" He says and there isn't much we can say to that.

The tropical night smothers us like a soft sponge as we listen to Julio recite his litany of a wife walking out with two kids, leaving him with bottles of loneliness at this table in this plaza at the edge of this swamp, talking into the ear of strangers. Julio orders another round and then another and we let the camaraderie of miseries lull us into inertia and almost miss our ride back to Finca Bombay.

Just barely, out of breath, we catch Tonio's attention as he lurches the old gravel truck out of the landfill quay and rattles across the railroad tracks onto Calle Central. He offers us space in the cab, as he always does. We decline. We know better now than to ride up front on the broken old plastic seat that sticks to your clothes and your skin and where the smell of diesel and sweat and oil makes your head pound. We slouch down in the bottom of the damp metal box under the raunchy palm of the tropical night, not wanting to see, not hear, not care. But the rings of fetor and squalor creep in around us on the backdraft humidity: sour sawdust off the floor of the Tropicana, sunbaked sulfur in open rail cars waiting on the siding mixed with the acrid smog from the lumber mill burners. Then you pass the vacant lot with the bloated carcass of a dog and hold your breath for as long as you can. The smell of yesterday's refuse coming back in on the tide around the bamboo slum of Barrio Isleta makes you gag, wishing yourself far, far away out on a windswept pampa with no human around for miles.

Shocks recoil as the truck bounces onto the warped planking of the bridge to the mainland. The breeze off the lagoon brings up a motley collection of odors: kelp-snarled nets, barrels of chum on slimy decks, tarred ropes, creosoted piers, diesel rainbows adrift at each stern. Then, for just a second, you catch the cold exhalation from the blowers of the shrimp packing plant.

*We stand up and lift our faces into the heat swell humidity as the truck picks up speed. Tandem tires suck up a hot licorice aroma off the blistered asphalt, then the yellow line bends into a black-lipped grin on a steeply banked curve and we enter the neon jungle of the twenty-four hour upbeat and howl. The Cocacabana, the 007 Club, the NutHatch flash by. We even catch a glimpse of the officers from the **Bergaa** piling out of Avemar's company car at Casa del las Rosas, under the protective wing of **señor** Francia.*

The truck bounces on up the valley on the gravel road that is soft and slick in places from so much rain and the canopy of trees close in around houses and shacks more scattered.

The string of lights along the upper balcony of Finca Bombay blink through the trees. Tonio applies the brakes, almost as an afterthought and the truck groans to a stop below the old mansion that appears like a stern-wheeled ark stranded on this hillock, its diesel generator pecking at the hush. The blue running lights at the end of the porch cast a soft glow over the citrus grove. From the shaded arbor below the house, a horse gives a whinny, three more joining in. They know the sound of Tonio's gravel truck. We grab our bags of vegetables and fish packed

*in ice, gone soft now, and there is some meat for Chaco and Andin too.
The dogs time it perfectly: dashing down the path as Tonio roars off up
the road. Chaco spins and jumps and leaps and turns and leads the
way up the hill to the big ramada where the horses are munching elephant grass.*

*"I took the liberty of feeding them," Martin says, almost apologeti-
cally. "I thought you would not want to take them over to the medano
in the dark. The flies were especially tormenting today. Much moisture in the air."*

*Martin follows us up the stairs onto the large veranda and into the
kitchen out back where Maria stands by the kerosene burners making a
meal of grated carrots and cabbage and potatoes.*

Maria reminds me of my mother. Like my mother, Maria has a God to
give her structure and to explain to her all the big things about life and death so
she can concentrate on all the little things, living one moment into the next,
accepting them all as they come to her.

For the first time, in such a long while, we have a family with this
wonderful woman and her adoptive son who took in a pair of strangers riding
down the valley, on a dark night like this. Almost a month ago now. But we're
so busy trying to get out of town, we're missing the experience.

I watch a moth flutter around the glass lamp. Wings flap and flitter until
the moth falls down in exhaustion and crawls wingless to its death on the wood
floor. Another moth rises above the glass and flies straight into the source of
light and the source of heat. It leaves a momentary scent of burned tissue in the
night air.

And I think of the magician who had himself put in chains that were pad-
locked and the key thrown to the bottom of a large pool of water. People paid
to sit on the other side of a glass wall and watch him locate the key at the
bottom of the tank, unlock his chains and remove them one by one and rise to
the surface. He did this for years, always challenging more difficult knots,
more chains, deeper water.

Why?

Maybe for some of the same reasons we do what we do?

So why are we taking all this so seriously, I am thinking, why are we getting ourselves boxed into a corner?

Isn't this too a game?

"We're going about this all wrong!" I say into the silence of the open veranda, where the soft breeze of the night brings the song of crickets. Nathan is used to the one-liners I throw out of a stream of consciousness that is rushing through rapids, much too fast to pause to elaborate. He knows there will be another brief phrase from further downstream.

"We've been trying to change Buenaventura," I say. "But we're the ones that need to change. Buenaventura is what it is."

This was pretty cryptic, even for me. I needed to work out my thoughts on something concrete. I sat down with a glass of fresh guayabano juice Maria made and wrote a letter addressed to the general manager of Mexican Lines in Mexico City. You can say things in Spanish that would not translate well into English: I evoked Cervantes and his Don Quixote de la Mancha, who esteemed Mexicans as the most chivalrous of knights. After two years of chasing windmills in South America and finding ourselves at an impasse, I wrote, it is natural for me to turn to a Mexican for relief from my distress. I feel inspired writing. I spread it on pretty thick. If nothing else, it might give the manger a chuckle.

We talk and laugh and drink guayabano juice until late that night, Maria and Martin and Nathan and I, hatching plans.

"The manager of Grace Prudential is flying in to Buenaventura in a couple of days. How about we meet him on horseback? The airport is not far from Finca Bombay."

"Make him an honorary member of the Hobos on Horseback Guild."

"Bring him a horseshoe for good luck," Nathan says. "Maybe it will boomerang back to us."

"My husband so liked to entertain," says Maria. "How about we invite some of the agents out on Saturday. It would be like old times."

And as we reflect back on that night at Finca Bombay, we know we learned the most important lesson of our entire journey that night, maybe of our entire lives.

Buenaventura isn't just a place anymore. It is a state of mind. Simply this: control your reaction to circumstance, and you begin to control circumstance.

The response to the letter I wrote to Mexico city was swift. Julio, the agent, received a telegram and it said:

"Put them aboard the Monica. No charge."

"What did you write to them?" Said Julio and he actually smiled. It was a bit rusty, his smile, but nice.

"I don't remember word for word," I said. "I spoke of a damsel in distress. Of knights in shining armor riding to the rescue."

"Honestly?" He said. "*De veras*, you said that!"

"Something like that, yes," I said.

I wish I had kept a copy of this letter. I didn't.

The Monica was in port and slated to sail for Costa Rica in twenty-four hours. This was amazing! So sudden! One more day and night and we'd be out of here, forever. There was just one hitch to the company offer of free passage. Embarking the horses was subject to the captain's approval.

The captain of the Monica was an Englishman. The chivalrous tradition of Don Quixote was not part of his cultural heritage. He was not amused in the least when we came on board to see him.

"I cannot allow horses loose on my deck," he said. "Sorry we can't be of help to you." With that, the captain turned to take leave.

"They will be secured in boxes, sir." Nathan said.

"We have no boxes for horse transport," said he.

"We will supply the boxes, captain," Nathan said.

We had looked into building boxes. We had talked to the owner of the Sabanita mill about lumber. That was weeks ago. Now, in twenty-four hours, somehow, we would have boxes designed, built and delivered to the pier. We could not allow ourselves to doubt for a moment that this was possible.

"No passengers allowed on board, I'm afraid," said the captain. He remained in profile, poised to leave. For him, this conversation was clearly over.

"The horses will require grooms for the voyage," Nathan said.

"You are determined, it would seem, to board my ship."

"Yes, sir," Nathan said and that was all. I bit my lips over phrases such as 'you are our one and only hope' and 'we will be eternally grateful and mention you in our book', that sort of thing.

'Yes sir', was perfect. If I could just say nothing at all, we might make it. Nathan is a master of the art of subtle persuasion. He is a sailor too; he understands this kind of people.

"And how do you plan on getting off the ship in Puntarenas?"

Just another hurdle, we thought, smelling success already. The captain was bending just a little, under the relentless onslaught of our positive energies. That's what we thought. If we had known what awaited us in Puntarenas, we might not have tried so desperately to get aboard the Monica.

"Using the same boxes, sir," Nathan said.

The Captain turned around to face us. "You will sign on and off the crew list. You will quarter on deck. I will not be seeing you again."

Boxes got built, by Nathan and three *peons* at the mill in Barrio Las Llaves. Elephant grass and sugarcane was cut by Martin. Exit stamps, bill of lading, port authority documents were procured. Horses were bathed in antiseptic solution, Foote paraphernalia packed up and put in the Grace Prudential van along with the dogs and Martin and Maria, who came to see us off. Five weeks after arriving at Finca Bombay, we rode our horses into Buenaventura for the first time. Everyone we encountered seemed to be smiling and waving. On this day that we left, we felt embraced by a welcome that had not been there before. We felt like conquerors on this day. I would have liked to ride up Calle Central, straight across the Plaza Bolivar and wave good bye to all the shipping agents. But we came in the back way, past multicolored driftwood shacks with naked children and radios blaring, with no time for detours and little time for reflections on this day.

Longshoremen gather to watch us coax Pampero into one of the shipping crates with an armful of grass. He advances cautiously, grabs a huge mouthful, stretching his short neck to add every possible inch before he cautiously takes another small step ahead to get his teeth into the grass and another big mouthful. And so it goes. Halfway in, he reverses and backs out of the box at full speed.

We take some more cut grass and coax him back in again. This time, we tie a rope around the rear frame of the box and Nathan keeps it tight around Pampero's hind end. He advances as before: a big mouthful of grass for each few inches into the box. Almost all the way in now, Pampero throws himself into reverse. But this time he lunges to the left, through the side of the box. Repairs are out of the question. We have no tools and there isn't enough material left to work with anyway. Pampero reduced a sturdy looking hardwood crate into a pile of scraps. Just then a voice comes over the megaphone:

"Mr. Foote. You have exactly fifteen minutes to put order into that chaos down there."

"Yes, sir!" Nathan says.

"Now what?" I whisper to him.

"Let's load the empty boxes," he says. "Then the horses."

I can feel the captain's eyes on us as Martin and Jerry, a couple of longshoremen, and even Julio, help run grass up the gang way, stacking the bundles neatly on top of the hold. We put the cargo net around the empty boxes, one right after the other. Up on deck, Martin and Julio secure the boxes to the railing with a hemp rope. Next, we rig a car sling around Pampero's belly and tie an old shirt over his eyes.

"This is it! Your last chance to get out of Buenaventura!" Nathan says to him sternly. "Please don't screw it up, will you!"

He signals the derrick operator to take the horse up, real easy. As Pampero lifts off the dock, he lets out a loud snort. He paws briefly, then just hangs limp as he is hoisted alongside the ship. I am thinking how good we are at improvising, handling hurdles as they come, when the shirt slips off Pampero's eyes. He is thirty feet up in the air then and swinging up over the hatch. He begins to kick wildly, sending the net into gyrations. The operator turns to us with palms up: now what?

Pampero is not a complicated horse. He is unafraid. This is the guy who scrambled across the avalanche area, rather than take the detour above, and who would cut off switchbacks in the trail to go straight down a cliff because he had spotted a tuft of grass, or simply did not feel like going the long way around.

Nathan signals for the operator to keep on lowering the crane as Pampero marches in place, tipping fore and aft as they bring him down into the makeshift corral. Before his hooves touch the deck, our gourmand manages to snatch a big mouthful of elephant grass. The crowd along the quay burst into a laughing cheer.

But we are running out of time. We are also getting the hang of it. We make sure the shirt is tied tightly around Maracas' eyes, secure the cargo net around him and have Maracas off the quay and onto the Monica in less than five minutes. India is a cinch to load. She never moves at all in the net and lands nice and easy on deck. The inspector of sanitation for the port of Buenaventura arrives just as Pirata begins his journey up the side of the Monica. He watches the equine pendulum swining high up above.

"You need a permit to embark livestock," he remarks.

This balding little man with thin white arms coming out of a shortsleeved shirt has the power to reverse this whole process. He can make us unload the horses on some technicality.

"You did disinfect their hooves, didn't you?" He asks.

"Every day for six weeks!" Nathan assures him. "Trying to keep tics, flies, gnats, black widows, fungi and bats off our horses."

"*Bueno, está bien.* Glad you found a ship," he says and he hands me the pink slip we need to disembark in Costa Rica.

And that was all there was to that.

> *Together we stand on the bow hatch as the gap widens between the ship and the port. A black girl in a faded orange dress runs barefoot along the edge of the quay, weaving in and out of stacks of cargo and equipment, darting around groups of workers, running and waving all the way to the end of the docks where a red beacon blinks. Her warbling cry comes across the water:*
>
> *"Gringa, take me with you! Please take me away. Anywhere."*
> *"Gringo, gringa!"*

NO! Wait!

Warm tears run down both of my cheeks and I can't take my eyes off the black girl running to land's end.

This is all wrong.

We should be staying, not leaving. We should be riding our Criollos back into the mountains and the arid plains where we are at home. What are we doing, sailing away like this?

You belong in Latin America, said Luis. On this volcanic earth, home of the hybrid man. This is the future. And he gave us the crayon etching he made for Nathan's book *Barrio Mundo*, multicolored strings of cars enlacing the urban labyrinth against a background of black.

"Why are you going back to Europe, that decrepit old man!"

We wrote Luis from Machichaco.

Luis wrote back: "You will be back and you know it!"

And so it was: we returned. But we never saw Luis again.

My eyes overflow and there is a taste of salt in my mouth: now we are leaving Luis all over again. I feel cast out from my chosen homeland, orphaned.

Apprehensive.

Then the Monica turns to face the expanse of water and the horses raise their heads into the wind, their nostrils large, gulping sea air. They don't worry. Why should I? They are descendants of horses that survived the voyage from the old world to the new, that multiplied and spread all over the humid *pampas* in great numbers. They are phylogenetically programmed to know there is a better world at the end of a voyage, even of a little one like this.

Nathan and I stand side by side watching our horses drink the wind and I know it is right for the girl in the orange dress to stay, as it is right for us to take our world ever onward.

That's what Luis would have wanted, in the end.

After we left the barrio and visited New York and stayed the summer in Maine, Nathan wrote about Luis in my mother's apartment in Sweden. We were living between worlds then, aliens both in our native lands. We huddled together, working jobs to make money to free ourselves once again. And we wrote.

Nathan wrote about Luis:

> *When Luis walks the busy streets of Caracas, the human current parts before this boulder of a man, so unselfconsciously distinct. He walks with a slight limp, from a bullet he took in the hinterlands of his native Bolivia. He is a tall man, Luis and his head is extraordinarily large, framed by a bristly white beard. Along with his extraordinary size, Luis occupies an enormous chunk of psychic space.*
>
> *His words cascade and explode as he assaults the bloody dictatorships of Latin America in poems without beginning or end; brief moments in his hurricane of wrath and indignation. The news over the radio of a child purposefully crippled by its father to better serve him as a beggar to support his drinking sent Luis smashing bottles and destroying several of his own canvasses. All through the night he scratched, stabbed, tore at page after page: **La Matanza de los Inocentes**. I found him in the morning, utterly exhausted and asleep on the floor of his studio, scraps of paper spread out over his bed and all over the floor. Pages had blown out the open window onto the street below.*
>
> *Luis' paintings emerge from a different persona. He once told me*

that he paints out of disenchantment with what is. He is clutching at the last vestiges of love and faith by reinventing the entire creation on his own terms. The threshing floor of his imagination is grounded in the pristine soil of the tidal universe, part of the original cradle of being. His brush calls forth the renaissance of innocence: black, blood-red and wheat-colored women pregnant with immortal faith. His children are realities yet undiscovered; they are Luis' unborn dreams. They frolic in the air, plant clover with ringing laughter, smother the earth with virgin loveliness.

His imagination is in everything. He invents it all anew each day, sometimes every hour. He can talk for hours about the contribution to art by the astronauts pushing the horizons further into space and time. Art replaces borders with a new vision of things in their fluid interdependence, says Luis. Immortality exists for him only in an instant of total arrest when the universe wraps a man in blinding light.

Luis paints to burn limitless energy, to expend overflowing emotion and not in order to leave his mark on the world. He speaks of his art as moments, fleeting as puddles after a rain. Without the slightest shading of vanity and possessiveness then, the world offers herself to him. Luis trembles, sometimes weeps in sheer thankfulness.

I would like to be like Luis. But I know that I never will be.

So writes the young man that winter in Sweden of the sixty-two year old manchild Luis.

How never catches up with you! You have become Luis, Nathan! Synchronicity of events has brought me to this part of the journey and the book and back into your writings on Luis. You are now the sixty-two year old child. You are become the man about whom you wrote:

Luis is the counterpoint, the antitoxin. He explodes with love. He shatters the common definition of 'adult' and shows it up for the sham that it is. For him maturity has nothing to do with acceptance, compromise, settling down, adjusting to assembly line lives, saving money and things, filling out social security forms, insurance forms, old age pension forms.

Luis says that maturity is death. Life is incessant growth, tendrilling, spreading ever wider spiritual roots.

LINEA MEXICANA DEL PACIFICO

SERVICIOS MARITIMOS MEXICANOS, S.A.   MARITIMA MEXICANA, S.A.

AV. INSURGENTES SUR 432 - 4o. PISO   MEXICO 7, D. F.

(SPACES IMMEDIATELY BELOW ARE FOR SHIPPER'S MEMORANDA-NOT PART OF BILL OF LANDING)

FORWARDING AGENT-REFERENCES	EXPORT DEC. No:
DELIVERING CARRIER TO, STEAMER:	CAR NUMBER-REFERENCE

BILL OF LADING
(SHORT FORM INCORPORATING TERMS OF LONG FORM)
(TERMS CONTINUED FROM REVERSE SIDE)

SHIP **MONICA** FLAG **INGLESA** PIER PORT OF LOADING **BUENAVENTURA**

PORT OF DISCHARGE FROM SHIP **PUNTARENAS** (Where goods are to be delivered to consignee or on-carrier) DESTINATION OF GOODS (If goods are to be transshipped or forwarded at port of discharge)

SHIPPER NATHAN CLARK FOOTE Y ELLY JULIANA FOOTE

CONSIGNED TO ORDER OF NATHAN CLARK FOOTE Y ELLY JULIANA FOOTE AT PUNTARENAS

ADDRESS ARRIVAL NOTICE TO NATHAN CLARK FOOTE Y ELLY JULIANA FOOTE

MARKS AND NUMBERS	No. OF PKGS	SHIPPER'S DESCRIPTION OF CLASS AND CONTENTS OF PACKAGES	GROSS WEIGHT IN KILOS	GROSS WEIGHT IN POUNDS
S/M		RECIBIDO A BORDO		
	4	ANIMALES - CABALLOS CRIOLLOS ARGENTINOS EN DOS JAULAS DE MADERA.	1.600	
	2	ANIMALES - PERROS PASTOR ALEMAN	60	
	6	ANIMALES.	1.660	

ESTOS ANIMALES VIAJAN ACOMPAÑADOS DE SUS PROPIETARIOS Y SEGUIRAN EN TRANSITO A NICARAGUA Y OTROS PAISES AL NORTE POR SUS PROPIOS MEDIOS LOCOMOTIVOS.

FREIGHT PREPAID - FREE IN/OUT

NOTA:- EL EMBARQUE SE HACE POR CUENTA Y RIESGO DE LOS INTERESADOS SIN RESPONSABILIDAD PARA EL BUQUE, SUS ARMADORES, FLETADORES O AGENTES POR ACCIDENTES O MUERTE QUE OCURRAN DURANTE EL VIAJE.

IN WITNESS WHEREOF, 3 Bills of Lading have been signed of this tenor and date, one of which being accomplished, the others shall be void.

DATED AT BUENAVENTURA-COL.

B/L No: 5

FOR THE MASTER
LINEA MEXICANA DEL PACIFICO
BY

MEX TAX
SURCHARGE
TOTAL U.S. CURRENCY

F-D-P-44

BETWEEN HERE AND THERE

Elly seasick and with a cold, says my diary entry for Good Friday, April 9th. Chaco sick from overeating of the good food from the mess kitchen. Horses fine in spite of the rough sea. Maracas seemed to get a thrill from looking out at the white capped sea and showed no fear whatsoever, just curiosity at what was making the world roll and shake.

April 10.
Less sea than yesterday. Elly better (curious to refer to myself in the third person - I must really have been out of it!) Chaco worse, from eating even more since he cannot stand to let Andin have it all. Horses fine, of course and chewing away on the cut grass and sugarcane, but showing little interest in the corn. I began to feel boxed in. There is nowhere to go on a ship! After the *Utlande* experience, all the charm of cruising is gone for me.

Saw the lights of Puntarenas by 10 p.m. Went to sleep thinking: tomorrow we will be riding on the beach!

Tomorrow came and we realized that we were a long way from the beach. Puntarenas is a narrow finger of sand in waters so shallow that ships have to anchor far out in the bay. It is a port city without a harbor. Cargo has to be off-loaded onto flat-bottomed barges that are towed into the pier by tugboats. Thousands of sacks of soybeans were lifted out of the hull of the Monica while our horses remained in the deck corrals. On the morning of the second day, we were summoned to the bridge.

"You wanted to see us, Captain?"

"Not particularly," he said. He laid down his pen next to the logbook and stared straight at us, the way you remember a schoolmaster looking down at you, making you feel bad even if you hadn't been. "We have been here two days. You still haven't succeeded in getting your horses ashore."

"We had no idea the ship wasn't even going to dock," Nathan said. "The port authority won't allow us on their barges with the rest of your cargo. The Company promised to send a barge especially for the horses, but they have to wait for the sanitation inspector. He hasn't shown up yet."

"For a couple who seemed to have all the answers, you're not doing so well."

"The inspector is supposed to show up at any moment now," Nathan said.

"The ship departs for Mexico this afternoon."

"We don't want to go all the way to Mexico!"

"The horses of the Spanish explorers swam ashore. I imagine yours will too."

"You wouldn't!"

"May I remind you, Mrs. Foote, that you are on board this ship against my better judgment." He picked up his pen. "That will be all. Good luck. I won't be seeing you again."

The sanitation inspector from Puntarenas finally showed up. He was a rotund little man, not amused, not charmed, not impressed by us and our horses. He declared that he was unable to authorize entry for our horses onto Costa Rican soil. The barges were considered part of Costa Rican territory. We could therefore not put our horses on board a barge either, without obtaining proper documentation. There was no time to do this before the Monica pulled anchor in just a few hours. The inspector did sign and stamp the authorization for us to disembark from the Monica. That was all.

"I guess that means the captain can throw us into the sea legally," I said to no one in particular.

"Excuse me, *señor!*" Nathan turned to the sanitation inspector. "And who has jurisdiction over the tugboat?"

The inspector did a double take. *"Diga?"*

"The tugboat, who's in charge?"

"The captain of the tug, *señor.* "The tug belongs to Mexican Lines."

"And is not part of Costa Rican territory?"

"No, *señor*, independent."

The voluminous skipper took another drag on his cigar and stared at Elly who was bracing herself against the doorframe as the tugboat pitched and bounced against the side of the MS Monica. He broke into an uproarious laughter.

"He'd give you all a bath, eh?"

"He was not kidding," Elly said.

*"**El ingles** has been at sea too long. **Ahora** you want us to take the horses aboard the tug?" The captain and his equally statuesque mate laughed some more.*

"Mexicans seem to be the only people who care about horses."

Still chuckling, his rolls of fat jiggling, he looked out over the stubby bow padded with tires

"Where will you put them?"

"There is just enough space on your poop deck."

He cocked his head up towards the swaying gunnels of the big freighter, more than forty feet above.

"And who is going to put them down here? In this sea?"

"We will," I said with much more conviction than I felt.

"Go ahead, amigo. Give it a try."

He grinned and pulled a gold crucifix from under his damp T-shirt.

"Juan and I, we will pray!"

*The boatswain came over to help me adjust the cargo net around Maracas. I attached a **cabresto** to his halter and tied a ring into his tail for another rope, the way I had learned so long ago from Segundo when we put the first set of shoes on Maracas. With this, Elly should be able to guide him onto the poop deck with the help of the weighty first mate. I did not put on a blindfold this time; Maracas needed to see* *what we were doing so he could work with us.*

Up went our trial balloon, just as the Monica rolled on a big swell and sent Maracas on a flying trapeze over the port gunnel. Down below on the tug, Elly and the mate hauled in the guy rope tied to the bottom of the sling and I ran forward along the Monica's rail with another guy rope tied to his halter. The spinning lessened as we tightened the ropes and we began trying to center the horse over the bobbing, tilting target area, fourteen feet across by twelve, and forty feet down. I signaled to the derrick operator: GO.

He dropped the horse like a yo-yo, then held. Maracas was now dangling way out over the waves. The boatswain grabbed onto my guy rope and we both pulled hard until we had the gyrating horse positioned above the poop deck of the little tug that rolled and bobbed on the waves like a toy boat.

Down he went, another ten feet. More pulling and adjusting. Another ten feet and now the tug rose up to meet him on a giant swell. Maracas skidded and fell to his knees on the pitching oil-slick deck. The prayers of Captain Miguel must have been heard loud and clear just then for Maracas managed to lunge back on his feet. He stood with legs spread wide apart and looked towards the tugboat bridge where a perspiring Captain Miguel clasped his hands and raised them above his head.

"Blessed be Saint John and the Virgin!"

Four horses crammed together in an area no bigger than a large box stall intended for one, on a slick deck enclosed by a gunnel two feet high. How crazy was that? You do what you have to and you have no time to worry about all the ifs and the buts; it is only afterwards that you perceive the dangers.

Afterwards hadn't caught up with us yet as we were marooned at the Puntarenas pier, still very much in emergency mode. We had no feed left for the horses. There was none to be had in Puntarenas. The port authority would not authorize us to put the horses onto Costa Rican soil because the pier was under the jurisdiction of National Railroads and they in turn were answerable to Customs and the word from Customs was that no cargo could be transferred without proper documentation and this documentation needed approval from Sanitation. And so it went. They could keep playing this bureaucratic game of pass the buck for a long time if no one stopped them.

The only way to do that was go around them, right to the top. So at three in the morning, I boarded a train for San Jose. Four hours later I was at the doors to the Ministry of Agriculture, which opened at seven am in the capital of Costa Rica.

Powerful propellers churned up a rooster-tail of foam behind us as the tug steamed across the harbor. The Monica was gone. But we were, quite literally, not yet out of the water.

The deck tilted steeply starboard as Captain Miguel made a sharp turn, then he threw the tug into reverse and backed underneath the towering bow of the big Greek freighter anchored out in the bay. I waved up at a row of grinning faces and helped Juan haul in the two cables they tossed down to us. Someday I too wanted to be laughing at the picture of four horses corralled on a busy little tugboat, chewing on a salad of lettuce and cabbage leaves, bananas, pineapple and carrots, scavanged from the open market. But not just yet.

We made fast to the cleats on either side of the horses. Taut cables hummed under the strain, just two feet away from India on the one side and Maracas on the other as Captain Miguel threw the tug into its Herculean task at full throttle. With dual engines roaring and the deck vibrating and shaking underneath them, the horses continued to stare placidly at the grey hulk heaving and plunging through the waves behind us. Nothing seems to phase them!

Giving up my worrying watch for a while, I went into the galley for a plate of chili con carne and talked about the fighting bulls in Guadalajara with Captain Miguel. Afterwards there were several more barges to pull and it was late in the afternoon when we returned to berth. By then school children lined the wharf, laughing and shouting:

"Look! Like I told you. Four horses do live on the tugboat!"

Not a sign of Elly. Not a word from San Jose.

It was a sucking sponge of an evening on the harbor. Not a ripple on the oily surface, not a sound in the heavy air. The tug swung slowly, ever so slowly, in a circle around its anchor line just off the end of the wharf. Captain Miguel had given up trying to cheer me with beer and stories and gone down below to turn on the radio. I lit up another

Mexican cigarette, listened to the belly rumble of the hungry horses. I must have dozed off for a minute, an hour maybe, just before she appeared on the dock with a bouquet of flowers, looking beautifully angry. Her voice came across the water so clearly I thought she was right next to me:

"What are you doing on the tug?"

"Waiting for you," I said. "You got the permit?"

"No."

"No?"

"The minister phoned down here this morning at nine. I heard him. I was in the office. You were supposed to be off the barge first thing."

"No one told me. What took you so long?"

"Lunch. Ice cream. Tour of San Jose."

"Great! We toured the harbor pulling freighters. No food."

Elly made an about-face and disappeared towards the harborside buildings. She returned some time later with the antipathetic sanitation inspector in tow. He looked like she had routed him out of some bar, or blasted him out of bed. Silence reined between the three of us. Elly was mad. I was hungry and tired and sleepy. The inspector stuffed our saddles and all our gear into plastic bags and sealed them. Maybe he was mad too. I didn't know and I didn't care. He walked abruptly up to Pampero who must have been dozing and startled at the sight of a strange little man armed with a pail and a brush attacking his feet. Pampero snorted loudly and flew backwards into Maracas, who bumped Pirata, who bumped India and who swayed out over the gunnel precariously.

"Let me!" I said and grabbed the bucket and the mop.

The inspector seemed all too glad to have me perform the onerous task of disinfecting sixteen hooves. When I had finished, he glanced at his watch.

"A quarter past ten. Double overtime. That will be fifty dollars, señor."

Not **colones**, *dollars!*

"I'll need a receipt. For the minister," I said.

"We will call it twenty-five."

"I still need a receipt."

"Ten."

"You don't want to give me a written bill? I plan to write one up for you."

"Señor?"

"We're charging you personally for time lost and for the cost of my wife's trip to San Jose. Captain Miguel also has a bill he wants to present you."

The inspector took a step toward the ladder. *"Let's forget the whole thing,"* he said. *"A favor to my great American friends."*

"I'm not an American," growled Elly.

And I'm not your friend, I thought, but I let it go. We were getting closer, but we were not out of the water just yet and it was better to have a friend than an enemy ashore. At dead low tide, with the tug a good twenty feet below the wharf, the winch operator finally showed, with a full shift of longshoremen in tow. I was in no mood to pay fourteen men double overtime to be in our way.

"We don't need you," I said. *"We've been loading and unloading these horses for days and we're getting pretty good at it."*

*"Union rules, **señor**,"* said the foreman. *"You cannot unload unless we are here."*

Miguel helped me strap on the cargo nets and up and off they went, one right after the other. At last we sent up the plastic bags with our gear. I scrambled up the ladder with Chaco to find Elly all alone, holding on to her saddle, coughing and with tears running down her cheeks.

"What happened? Where is all the help?"

"When Maracas came down, snorting and kicking out in all directions, most of the union boys disappeared. Pampero took care of the rest of them."

She coughed again. *"What did he douse our tack with anyway?"*

"Formaldehyde."

"Lovely."

It would have been a beautiful ride along the beach, in the moonlight, under the stars, except for the damn formaldehyde that was giving us a headache and nausea, to the point of having to hold onto the *front of the saddles for fear of falling off. We rode until we found some vegetation and then we stopped and just plopped down on the dunes and fell asleep to the sound of the horses chewing on the hard grasses.*

Nothing could have made us move today, says my diary. We were supposed to take our passports into Puntarenas to have them stamped, but that could wait. Everything but a day of rest on the beach could wait. We found enough grass around the dunes to keep the horses happy. The Criollos looked as fat as ever. They are like rubber, they plop right back into shape. But Pirata looked battle-worn.

The next day we move on. In three days we are up in the mountains, where the climate is cool and life is an easy trail ride. In our diaries, I read of colorful and neatly kept houses, of a reserved yet courteous and well educated people. Pages are filled with the small things and chance encounters that form the body of a journey.

Nathan's diary is detailed and elaborative. His hand flows easily across the pages and he loses himself in the art of writing. His sentences become pregnant with images and ideas. He projects and expands and it makes wonderful reading. It is hard to leave so much of it out.

Saddle, unsaddle, saddle up again for the thousandth time, twice a day most days. We can do it blindfolded and I think about other things or other nothings, for the mind is trivial when it isn't either empty or compulsive. The point in writing about it is to entertain myself and others, so we can all laugh a little, cry a little and not twiddle our thumbs and tongues too uselessly and maliciously and I wondered if humor was more rare than the tragic sense and concluded that it was.

The trail went down and around and the footing was difficult. Saddles slid forward and we had to adjust them so that the cinches would not rub. Then we came to a river where we swam and shampooed our hair and the horses stood in a pool with cool water up to their bellies and gurgled water, for they enjoy drinking and slurping and washing out the corn from between their teeth and rolling in the sand and scratching each others' backs.

With no one around to object, or to charge us too much because we were gringos, we set up camp beyond a wooden fence where the grass was tall and where six pines stood close together on a flat place that was perfect for pitching the tent and making a fire pit right nearby. And we sat by the fire and looked at Andin's sore feet and put some ointment on them and planned how to make him shoes out of rags since the gravel on the road was wearing through his still tender paws, monstrous puppy that he is at nearly forty kilos.

Spent a day by the river, doing nothing except nothing. The horses would roll in the sand where the stream had flooded out a sandbar along the bank and with my back against a knotty pine, I thought about what the Criollos have taught us by grazing tranquilly wherever they find a bit of succulent grass, slurping water playfully from some brook.

We haven't always been very good pupils. We often get restless, impulsive, irritable and try to push them - and ourselves - beyond wise limits. When you roam, you enjoy being where you are, passing through. Itching to go means you are more interested in being someplace else, or never being where you are.

So let's keep trying to be good roamers, never too much in a hurry to get there (somewhere, anywhere). You might just miss a bird's song or a squirrel's hop from tree to tree or maybe even that thought trying to be born.

My diary is sparse. My handwriting is impatient, it has no time to form each and every letter nicely and becomes an irreverent shorthand that is cryptic even to me. I seldom write more than a page for each day. When I elaborate, it is on a typewriter, from notes (cryptic) that I keep separate from the diary.

At the top of the page, I record what the horses were fed. G stands for grain. I note down how many pounds and what kind: oats, barley, corn or concentrates. I note if they had hay, how much and what kind and if it was good, mediocre or bad. If on pasture, if it was good, bad, dry or green. In the left top corner, I note down the number of kilometers and what kind of accommodations we had: in a field, a mud floor, a ranch, camping. I compile the numbers in a month end report. I also keep track of the money. Sometimes when I scribble my numbers, I envision my grandmother sitting at her small red mahogany desk by the window in the living room. My grandmother used to write down absolutely everything. She wrote with a pencil, in a small notebook with black covers.

I keep track of the money by general category:

Food - Dogs - Horses - Things - Equipment – Various

Food and feed are always the largest expense. Equipment has sporadic entries, usually for clothes. When something is worn out, or we change climate, we replace it. 'Things' seldom has an entry and I am not sure why it remained a category. 'Various' would pick up movie tickets, cigarettes, that sort of thing. It was not a big category.

We were living within our means, relative to our income from the house on Machichaco. One thousand six hundred and eighty dollars was more than most families of eight would have, in most of the regions we travelled.

We seldom paid money to have a roof over our heads. In San Jose we did. We left the horses west of the city and took the dogs with us. It was hard to find a ride and even harder to find someone who would rent us a room with two big dogs along. But after *La Nación* ran a front-page story on our journey that sort of thing became much easier. Everyone recognized us as we walked by and people stopped us to get an autograph and to ask the questions people always ask. It was nice, for a little while. The reporter who interviewed us for the English speaking paper invited us to her house, but when we were told a group of people was coming, we went to the movies instead. We didn't want to be the appetizers at a cocktail party. We sat for a while in front of the National Theater and watched delegates to the meeting of The Organization of American States stroll by, on their way to some social function. Elegantly dressed women accompanied some of the men and there was gaiety in the warm evening air. Everything was relaxed and friendly and it seemed entirely possible that the problems of the Americas would be resolved.

Clodomiro Almeyda was there, the foreign minister now of Salvador Allende's Chile. We looked for *señora* Irma, but we didn't see her in the crowd. Maybe she had stayed behind in Chile. It would have been nice to say hello.

La Nación is read all over Costa Rica and instant recognition followed us across the republic. People came looking for us to offer pasture and lodging. School children lined up to applaud as we rode past. We were completely unprepared for our reception at the border to Nicaragua. A major who smells strongly of after shave and cologne steps out of the air-conditioned border post at Peañs Blancas and says:

"No way!"

"We obtained the ambassador's personal invitation to the Republic of Nica-ragua," Nathan says. This is entirely truthful. We made a point of meeting with the ambassador. "Just last week. In San Jose."

The major shows us a telegram which states that, effective immediately, no hoofed animals coming from Panama can enter the Republic of Nicaragua.

"We did not come from Panama," Nathan says.

The major pulls ultimate rank. "Orders from General Somoza himself," he says. Somoza is the dictator of Nicaragua, as was his father before him and his grandfather before him. The only one to outrank Somoza would be God him-self.

"We have not been to Panama," I say. "We came from Columbia directly to Costa Rica."

"I have clear orders. Our border is closed to all horses, mules or donkeys coming from Panama."

"But we didn't *come* from Panama!"

I was getting mad.

I get a nudge from Nathan. "Remember Germany!" He says in a loud whisper.

I do remember Germany, so I turn around and walk away and don't say another word.

We were en route from Greece to Sweden in a dark blue VW Bug Nathan bought in Germany, drove for over a year in Europe on Z plates, which are export plates you get when you intend to take the German vehicle back home with you.

"You have no license plate on the front of your vehicle!" Said the German guard.

"It is lost, sir. Probably on some dirt road in Greece or Turkey," Nathan said.

"You cannot cross the Republic of Germany without a license plate on the front of your vehicle," the guard said.

"I am due to embark in Oslo in two weeks," Nathan said. "Returning to study at Harvard."

The mention of his illustrious alma mater falls on deaf ears.

"You cannot drive this vehicle across The Federal Republic of Germany without a front plate," the guard said.

"Where can I acquire such a license plate?" Nathan said, no hint of exasperation in his voice.

"This is not possible," said the guard.

"How then will I get across Germany?" Nathan said.

"By rail perhaps?" Said the German guard.

Insurance was in order. Registration was in order. Driver's license and personal documents were all in order.

Nathan was being so diplomatic and so patient.

I got angry.

Too many words in fluent German, too loudly spoken, brought the border guard out of his complacency. Two guards practically lifted me into the commander's office where I received a lecture on my duty to show respect for German authorities. As punishment for swearing at a German officer they confiscated our cash. This wasn't a whole lot, but it was all the money we had from singing in the streets in Salzburg, Austria, with Claes and Eric. The border officials made me count the money to the last *pfennig* and then sign a form stating I was donating this sum to the Red Cross.

This donation still didn't get us into Germany. Broke, we drove back to Austria. Someone told us of a dirt road further west with a combined Austrian-German border station. The guards there found our documentation to be in order and waved us through, with no mention of the missing front plate.

"Now what?" I asked when Nathan caught up with me sitting in the grass on the Costa Rican side of the border, watching the horses graze.

"Nothing," Nathan said.

"How do you mean *nothing*?"

"We'll have to wait them out," Nathan said.

We unsaddled and pitched our tent in plain view of the Nicaraguan border control. The horses would be fine; there was plenty of grass. Chaco made friends on both the Costa Rican and the Nicaraguan side and he had plenty to eat. Nathan and I went to see a woman who lived in a shack close by and she agreed to cook for us. Her kitchen had a dirt floor, hard-packed from her moving barefoot between the kerosene stove and the small wooden table where she kept her dishpan and her white enamel plates. She had two pots, aluminum ones. She would polish them each day with steel wool until all traces from the smoke off the kerosene burner were gone and they shone in the rays of light that seeped in through the cracks in the wall when the sun was still low. She cooked rice in one pot and black beans in the other. She did this in the morning and then three times a day, every day, she put the beans and the rice on tin plates for us. You would think you would get bored but we did not. It was what mutton was in the Patagonia: good eating and you felt completely nourished from this food and you did not mind the sameness, did not even notice it. She would add spices and some very small piece of meat or maybe chicken just for the taste at dinnertime and her meals were so good that it is one of the things that I cannot leave out. We stayed there for most of a week.

On the fifth day of our siege, we receive a dinner invitation from the major in charge of the Nicaraguan border post. Chaco, by now a well loved friend of the Garcia family, escorts us over. The major has come up with a solution. We are to draw blood from each of our horses. He will seal the samples and we will personally deliver them to the government laboratory in Managua for analysis. In this the major went out on a limb for us. General Somoza's orders were absolute. An edict. Everyone always talks about the bribes, the hassles at the borders in Latin America. There is another side to this and that is that Latins understand a rule to have a certain elasticity; a law as something made by humans and inherently bendable.

We took the four vials of blood with us on the bus to Managua and waited for the results. They were negative and we took the bus back to the border at Peñas Blancas. We were free to proceed.

Directives from Major Garcia were to cross the country as quickly as possible and avoid publicity. That was fine by us. The Nicaraguan landscape, at the end of the drought season, was drab and parched. Days were exceedingly hot. We decided we would travel by night, when it was cool and quiet. We travelled through the desert like this and it was nice.

So here we were, clippety-clopping right up the middle of the Pan-American around two in the morning. We stopped at a spring earlier, where grass grew tall and cut enough for the horses and stuffed it in the canvas cover we used for the bedroll. We strapped it across India's back and tied it with one of the stakeout ropes. With our own supply of grass along, we could stop anywhere, anytime we got tired.

"We must be a sight to behold, body bag and all!" Nathan jokes. "Right out of a Western movie!"

That is fine, as long as there is no one out there watching us. Most of the time there is no one. When two sets of lights approach, slowly and noisily from the opposite direction, we move off to the side of the highway to give plenty of room for the trucks to pass us. But instead of passing, they gear down and jerk to a halt in the middle of the road. Orders are barked and soldiers pour out the back of the lorry.

"Drop your weapons!"

Nathan lets go of the flashlight he has been carrying. You can hear the plastic crack as it hits the asphalt. Damn! It is a brand new Eveready and quite expensive, I am thinking as it clatters over the pavement toward the right side of the road. We never seem to be able to keep a flashlight for very long. Something always happens to it.

"Dismount!"

Three soldiers surround Nathan. They practically pull him off Pirata. Drag him across the road and slam him up against the side of the green truck. Frisk for weapons. I smell liquor in the night air.

Suddenly I feel a hand on my thigh. I turn my head and look down into a male face that is much too close. There is no time to think. Instinct makes me pull back on the reins with much more force than I ever did before. Pampero responds with equal forcefulness. In this moment, he has become my warhorse: he rears up, paws the air above the head of the startled officer.

"Lieutenant!" I say with a voice inspired from I don't know where. "I am the daughter of the Norwegian Ambassador to Nicaragua. You get your men under control immediately, or my father will have General Somoza courtmartial you!"

I don't know why the *Norwegian* ambassador. I have no idea if Norway even had an ambassador to Nicaragua. Or why I, a Swede, would think to call upon the Norwegians rather than on my own countrymen. No matter. It wasn't what I said. It was the authority with which I spoke that made the man back off.

Show no fear and the sharks won't bite.

My unconscious made the connection to Santa Marta, Columbia, watching Constantino swim with the sharks in the blue Caribbean. The uniform takes a few steps backwards. I keep looking straight at him and he continues to back up.

"There are bandits around these parts, *señorita*," he says. His voice is subordinate to mine. "You must take precautions, *entiende*!"

The soldiers are ordered back up in the lorry and the convoy continues up the highway. Nathan bends down to pick up the flashlight. Miraculously, it still seems to work. We are both disproporionately pleased about this. Nathan wastes no time getting back up on Pirata and we continue right up the middle of the highway as before until, on the right side of the highway, off a curve, we spot a steep embankment. We stop. Look down into the thick brush below.

"What if they ask themselves what the heck the daughter of the Norwegian ambassador is doing riding a horse out here in the middle of the night?" I say.

"They'll be back!" Nathan says.

We head down the embarkment. Nathan leads, I walk last and take care to run a branch over our tracks so they will not be readily visible, at least not to a bunch of drunk soldiers in the dark.

The convoys do return.

Now they have searchlights turned on. A loudspeaker barks orders into the night:

"*Gringos*, come out! We know you are there. *Gringos* give yourselves up!"

We remain very quiet, far down in the thicket. Each of us has hold of a dog. Chaco growls in his low, menacing, puma-like way. The sound is more of a faint purr and won't be heard from ten feet away. We are worried that Andin might give us away with a loud bark. Nathan has a grip around his nose with both hands. We allow ourselves no thoughts other than: stay quiet, don't move. We are not afraid. That comes much later, years afterwards, when we read about four nuns being raped and murdered one night on a highway in El Salvador and realize how easily our journey might have come to a tragic end on that dark piece of Pan-American.

The trucks travel back and forth a couple of times, then they continue on down the Pan-American. All is silent again. We stay in the thicket until the sun comes up. Then we ride on up the highway and find shelter in a finca called El Limon where we sleep. We continue in broad daylight after that.

It wasn't bravery that saved us that night. Years of travelling, always wary, taught us that all you control is your own reaction. And that is how you can control a situation.

And it was luck.

Luck stayed with us for a time.

BEFORE THE WIND

Mariachi music and the pounding of hooves, hats off and stamped-ing applause: the young charras of Rancho Grande de la Villa come charging in, flowing crepe and silk behind them. The girl out front, the most lovely of them all, leans into the turn as her dappled grey breaks into the arena at full gallop, the red-yellow-green banner of Mexico flowing just above her raven curls, the staff braced against her single lady's stirrup of pure silver. Now, matched to a hair, two blood bays throw up a wave of red sand as they cut in sharply behind the leader. The twin daughters of the charro Jimenez raise their left hands as they pass the VIP box, pink lace kerchiefs waving. And on come the rest: six, eight, twelve double links form a spinning star that closes around the flag girl, her grey going into piaffe, held by just one delicate finger on the reins.

The crowd rises with the rapid staccato of trumpets:
TA-TA-TA-TA

Here come the charros, gold-laced sombreros tilted forward over embroidered jackets. The sun snatches a glitter of silver bits and spurs the size of saucers, of wax buffed muscles under quivering velvet: roan, palomino, black. The finest horses in the whole republic!

The drums of the mariachis roll louder, announcing the guests of honor. This is our cue. We kick up to a choppy dog trot as we enter the arena, fire blackened pots swinging from the patched canvas pack, and move up between a half moon of charras and of charros, jolting to a halt just before the grandstand. We are reasonably clean for the occasion, but definitely plain.

Not a sound. The mariachis seem to have forgotten their cue.

Then comes a wild howl from behind the gates and a yapping bundle of yellow vaults over the barricade and careens into the arena. Bouncing to a stop, Chaco turns in his tracks with an exuberant yap-yap-yahOOOOOO and makes a dash for the horses. Around and around them he cavorts, jumping up to kiss one after the other on the muzzle.

Someone way up in **sombra** *yells:* **OLÉ!**

The mariachis churn up a rendition of 'She Wore a Yellow Ribbon' for the supercharged yellow mongrel drag-tailing serpentines and figure eights, dodging in and out of the skitterish charro horses. He feigns back and forth, spins out and plays tag with his tail. Elly slaps her hand against her thigh. Without breaking pace, Chaco bounds right up in front of her saddle and off the other side.

Olé! Olé!!! *Responds the crowd.*

Tongue hanging out rakishly, he skids to a stop and raises his left paw.

The arena reverberates with stamping feet. **"Mucho!!"**

The **presidente** *of the charros steps to the mike and lifts a hand for silence, smile stretching the chin straps of his sombrero.*

"This guest of honor has clearly earned every coin on his collar. Each one, I have been told, from a country that he has walked through. It gives me the greatest pride to introduce to you this valiant dog who, over the past three years, has lead this singular equestrian expedition all the way from the Straits of Magellan to our Aztec capital."

His arm takes a graceful slice of the sky, the resonant voice quivers with emotion and his grandiloquence recalls the horse of Cortez, en-

shrined as a deity in the wilds of Guatemala. The radiance of clapping swells to a deluge. Chaco turns and turns, drinking it all in. True to form, the Criollos hold their heavy heads at half-mast and doze off, even as the charro swears to forever revere them and bestow upon them eternal glory.

But aren't we forgetting someone?

What about Andin?

He wasn't there.

Life on the road had been killing Andin, a little bit each day.

He was a year and five months old when we reached Mexico City. He had grown exceedingly tall, but with so little flesh now over his bones. Both of his eyes were runny and clouded over. His paws were sore almost all the time. He always seemed to be stepping on something, or getting stepped on by somebody, or run over by somebody. The long march through the south of Mexico on a diet of tortillas and beans had been hard on all of us; only Andin showed it physically. He was an emaciated shadow of the dog he was born to become.

Tears came to the eyes of the husky Swiss American in charge of the SPCA in Mexico City when he laid eyes on Andin. The dog looked up at the man and wagged his tail slowly. Then he lay down by his feet with a sigh deep from the bottom of his soul and closed his sore and tired eyes. Tears of pity and of guilt brimmed in my own eyes as I signed Andin into the shelter, forever out of our lives. I did not look at Nathan. We had never been right for this dog, nor he for us. His whole life with us had been a pilgrimage in search of his true home, his rightful master. Utterly exhausted now, Andin found him.

About a year later, we received a picture of a big handsome German Shepherd, an outstanding representative of his breed. It was almost impossible to recognize in him the mournful creature we left behind. The picture was taken in a park, which the attached note explained to be the garden around the house that was now Andin's home.

It would never have occurred to us to pick up a Thoroughbred horse along the way. A highly bred horse would not survive, we knew that. So whatever possessed us to yank a six-week-old purebred and papered pup out of his sheltered home in Miraflores, Lima? I search in my diary and in Nathan's for clues.

There were a series of significant coincidences leading up to Andin becoming a part of our lives. When Caicique kicked me up at Chincheros, Peru, a German family named Fritsch offered Nathan a ride to the hospital in Cuzco. A month later, at a first class hotel in the Montero Valley, outside Huancayo, we had another chance encounter with the Fritsches. They were up for a week-end getaway; we were camped for the night in a field of grass next to the hotel. We spent an enjoyable evening together at the hotel and then they walked back to camp with us. Chaco was sitting in the door of the tent and the four horses were lying down in the grass all around it.

"What a marvelous, marvelous life!" Said Herr Fritsch who was a CEO at Bayer.

We took them up on their invitation to come down and stay with them in Lima. We needed a rest. Both of us were battling a recurring cold, a nasty chest and stomach virus and general fatigue from five months in the sierra. Frau Fritsch put us both to bed on arrival. We awoke the following day feeling brand new and, for one unforgettable week, we became members of this very traditional European family. Punctuality, hot showers, daily routine, it all felt pleasantly exotic - for a time.

The Fritsches had one puppy left of a litter of purebred German Shepherds. It was clear to all of us that this pup was meant to link our family with theirs. Andin would make the journey on behalf of the Fritsch family. It was a wonderful idea, it just wasn't a reasonable one for Andin, who was born to stay put.

We stayed two weeks in the Mexican capital. I spent much of that time in the library belonging to one Colonel Jorge Luis Lepe, retired. He lived with his wife and his books in a small apartment in an old house with nine-foot ceilings. The library walls had shelves all the way up and all the way around the room, over the doorway even, and the shelves were filled with books. All the books were about horses, horsemanship, equine history and riding. I was introduced to the colonel after a search for books on horses and horsemanship at the national library turned up a scant two volumes, both of which I had read before.

My eyes paused on a two-volume edition: *Handbok För Hästvänner* by Carl Gustaf Wrangell.

"May I?" I asked.

"Of course, *señora*."

"One of the best books ever written on horsemanship!" Remarked the colonel.

"You read Swedish?"

"I don't have to read Swedish to know that," said the colonel.

The handbook was first published in 1897, the two volumes totaling 1332 pages, with almost nine hundred illustrations. Wrangell was a cavalryman and a nobleman. He travelled Europe buying horses on behalf on the Swedish government. His handbook intends to supply you with all you should need to know about horses, beginning with the origin of equus. He tells you about the breeds of the world and how to raise, break, train, shoe, jump, drive, ship, diagnose and treat a horse for common and not so common ailments. His illustrations are lavishly detailed. Need a design for a ladies sidesaddle skirt or instructions on how to throw a contrary horse? Wrangell has them for you! My mother found a 1910 edition of his book for me and, someday, I will finish an abbreviated version of Wrangell's handbook in English so you too can meet this most amazing horseman.

Colonel Lepe was a horseman, a teacher and also a writer. His own works were simply printed on unbleached stock in a paperback edition. The colonel is as brief as Wrangell is elaborate, both shared a sense of exasperation with the vast majority of men who abuse and misuse the most noble creature on earth. Let me give you a sample from the colonel's Equestrian Concepts:

"Much advice give those *charros* who have never been able to follow any.

"If *charros* would dedicate half the time, interest and care that they spend on their dress and saddles to their riding, they would be much better riders.

"There are horsemen who judge themselves on what they believe themselves capable, while the rest only appreciate them for what they really do.

"Mediocre riders may talk, but only good riders can observe."

I wanted to read everything in the colonel's library: Xenophon's book on horsemanship, cavalry manuals from many lands, scientific studies, books of fiction, travel books, children's books and every book ever written on the subject of the horses of the Americas. But there was so little time.

I wish I could just stand in the center of the room, close my eyes and concentrate very hard to open up every single pore in my body so that the words from the books might flow in through them and when I left the room, as I would have to do, the content of this singular library would be with me, right beneath my own skin.

I told this to the colonel. He smiled. "You do not have to read all of them," he said. "Just read the right ones. You have the time."

I decided I would read *Tractado de la Caballeria*, Treatise on Horsemanship, written by one Juan Suarez de Peralta, who was a citizen and native of Mexico in the Indies.

"Becoming a good horseman requires three basic things," wrote Juan Suarez.

"First of all a great interest in and love of horses, a willingness to care well for them under any and all circumstances.

"Secondly, the would-be horseman should never tire of riding, all day long if necessary, in order to acquire a good seat so that whatever he does on horseback comes easily and naturally. The third thing is for him to keep in mind always that he knows nothing. He therefore should make every effort to learn from anybody who knows something and stay clear of any false pretense."

De Peralta's book was first published in 1580, in Seville, Spain. The colonel's copy was from a limited edition printed in Mexico in 1950. Four hundred and twenty years later, Peralta's three rules of horsemanship still apply. I copied out the whole section on 'how to break a colt and make a horse of him' and I would like to share it with you here.

"Get hold of the colt and immediately put a halter on him and then (if feasible) have a groom wash him down with water all over, including the head, which is where the most water should be used, though not thrown so harshly as to frighten the colt. Thereafter he should be put in an open stall and there given a good feed, twice a day. His front and back legs should be washed and he should be sacked out as many times as possible during the course of the day.

In this way, he tames down very quickly and two days after he was started, he may be saddled (while blindfolded). The cinches should not be tightened too much so as not to irritate him and cause him to throw himself, a bad habit that could stay with him, but saddled gently and walked around without either tiring nor hurting him in any way.

Proceed little by little in this manner and tighten the cinches until they are the way they are supposed to be. Then a groom may get up on the colt's back, after he has been snubbed up to the tail of a well broke horse. He should be tied to the tail first, later on to the neck of the *madrina*, which is the horse to which he is snubbed, so that he is better secured and the *madrina* doesn't get its tail pulled out.

Once on his back, the rider should hold onto the front of the saddle with one hand, onto the cantle with the other, so that he feels himself well balanced, grip tightly with his thighs and hold himself upright in the stirrups, making sure to keep his feet away from the colt's sides until he calms down, then ease down on him and take the reins in his left hand and with the right continue holding onto the saddle as before. The bit must not be pulled at, neither intentionally nor by accident. The reins in hand serve the sole purpose of keeping the colt from twisting the bit in his mouth and in this manner the rider may start to show him how to hold his head and carry himself well. It is recommended to put some salt on the bit.

In this same manner, the colt should be taken out for two or three days until he is tame and care should be taken not to take him too far at one time so that the colt does in each lesson what is expected of him, not submits out of sheer fatigue. After having led him around in this way for a few days, he may be untied and let to follow behind the *madrina* for another two. And he must be worked every day, without letting one day pass in between.

And after he has followed the *madrina* loose for three days, he may be ridden anywhere by himself, but without running him, and guiding him with a *cabezon de la brida*, with a twisted rope attached to the bottom to serve as reins and this rope should be so fastened that pulling on one side of it, it should force the colt to close his mouth and turn in the desired direction. This should be carried on the colt at all times until he knows how to run and stop and is a finished horse, because the longer he carries it, the better he will hold his head and the more he will tend to work with his mouth closed and without having his mouth ruined. It should be clear that the hand should always be light and the rope loose at all times."

There, in 618 words, you have it!

For the further training of the colt, Suarez recommends much work in circles and figure of eights. "And this," he cautions, "should be done in complete solitude. The rider must never let himself be persuaded to show off his mount in public before he is ready. For as the rider attempts to show things the colt does not yet know well and becomes irritated when the colt does not respond, he will end up discrediting both himself and his horse in the eyes of those looking on and perhaps ruin his horse as well. Once his horse is finished, he may show him proudly before anybody and receive much satisfaction."

How did the horses of Spain accomplish the conquest of the Americas? I looked for answers in the many books on the shelves in Colonel Lepe's library.

I did not find them there. I did not find the answer in history, but in watching a little grey carthorse in Ronda, Andalucia, years later. He didn't weigh more than nine hundred pounds and looked to be a late teenager. With four tourists in the carriage, it was a heavy load for such a small horse. I looked him over carefully. There was not a bump on him, not a mark from the harness. He was brighteyed and responsive even towards the end of a day of pulling the carriage up and down the streets. I understood then how it was the Spaniards conquered the Americas. It would not have been mounted on the heavy-necked prancing horses of the parades and the fiestas, but riding unassuming hacks such as this, who survived the voyage, survived the daily marches into the unknown. And I thought, as so many times before, how undeserving we are of the horse, yesterday and today.

From Mexico City north, the continent fans out before you. You can set course anywhere you want. It was, a little bit, like the Patagonia. Yet very different. Our journey had changed since the day we headed out from El Zorro and into the vastness of the plains.

We still did not have a geographical goal, that is true. Nathan's boyhood summer haven, his mother's birthplace and now his parents' retirement home on Mount Desert Island, Maine, was not a destination we considered.

Nathan's birthplace, Stockton, California, might have had some sentimental appeal, you'd think. The Californians we encountered along the way assured us people would really dig this whole trip of ours out there. A longhair from Frisco was particularly euphoric about us riding into a California sunset. We met him as we were trapped on a traffic cloverleaf during rush hour in Guatemala City. He drove his red car right up on the grass to groove with us, oblivious of the cars honking and spewing fumes all around us. He went on and on about our being one with nature. He pretty much scared us off from any notion we might ever have entertained of riding west and making a road show of ourselves.

Nathan's boyhood camp was in Colorado. My Colorado connection came from what my godmother had told me of riding horses in the Rocky Mountains when she was young. I don't remember details. I do remember how she looked when she told me her stories. I could imagine her with windblown hair, tanned and laughing, and I knew Colorado would be a good place for me too. The University of Colorado in Boulder had offered Nathan a full scholarship to attend their post graduate school after Harvard. Instead, we went to work in the *barrio*. We didn't go to Colorado this time either. We went to Texas.

Texas had never been part of any dream for either one of us. We have no family, friends or connections in Texas. We never considered Texas, until we began to hear of the trials and tribulations of a young man named John Popham The Third who set out from San Antonio, Texas to ride to Buenos Aires on two American Quarter Horses, along with his pistol and elevated sense of drama. His ride ended in the south of Mexico.

Somewhere along the way, the idea of heading for San Antonio, Texas was born. There was a growing wave of interest in our ride. National Geographic was considering a story. We were corresponding with the managing editor of Reader's Digest. I n those days, you could do that. We were beginning to realize that the journey on horseback could become the springboard to the ranch we dreamed of in the Rockies, if we played our cards right. And that is what we thought we were doing, when we decided to head for San Antonio.

Guillermo Halliday might fly up to San Antonio, maybe even Dr. Emilio Solanet, who owned Gato and Mancha, the two horses Tschiffely rode from Buenos Aires to Washington in 1924 and who was following our ride with great interest. The rodeo at San Antonio in February would be a grand occasion to tell the world about our ride. Then we would ride towards the Rockies. It was just a matter of time to get to Alaska after that and a world record in long distance riding. It would be a piece of cake. We were veterans now. Our horses had never been in better shape. All the tough geographical challenges were behind us.

And we rode along with an old fellow on a skinny nag and he told us about this rich patron who was riding toward a village and he stopped to ask an Indian how long it would take him to arrive there. The old native looked him up and down and then said: "At a walk, you'll be there pretty soon. But if you gallop, you won't get there until tomorrow afternoon." The rich man spurred his fine horse angrily and galloped away, for he had misunderstood the Indian's meaning. The next afternoon the tired patron entered the village with his saddle over his shoulder, for his horse had given in long before.

The old cowhand nodded us farewell and we passed through a gap in the stone wall and followed the trail up and around a hill and spot-

*ted a dam and a lake surrounded by wildflowers and by wild bulls, black as coal, property of the Labastida clan. We soon arrived at their Hacienda Santo Domingo, which was marked, on the yellowed maps in the history books in the **hacienda** library that smelled of stale pipe tobacco. The Labastida family wrote history, about themselves and others of their class, and without them the world would stop turning because there would be no ice cream palaces, bullfights, stock markets or for that matter revolutions. A king on the hill is a prerequisite and only the rich live on in time because they have tombstones, while the rest have wooden crosses, so history belongs to those who can pay for it.*

Javier Labastida invited us for dinner. The priest who was also invited did not arrive, but the place set for him at the long table remained reverently empty while we all drank beer in silence and thought about important things that might have been said if we, or he, had felt more communicative.

*The mother cows were braying under the moon up on the hill and the following day we found ourselves riding loaned mounts on the roundup to brand the bull calves. We rode up past the lake to the stone corrals with Pilar and Jesus, two cocky young people who were only too conscious of their superior status amongst the hands on their daddy's **hacienda**. But when a lasso burned through Jesus' palm, he became conscious of his inferior stature and his swagger wilted. His sister was rubbing salt in his wound and the foreman chuckled as he threw a bull calf and planted the red iron on its flank, the air filling with the acrid smell of burning hair and live flesh. The calf was let free again, but now with an inescapable number on his hide. In exchange for the number he would have a noble death; he would have fifteen minutes at the height of his power and beauty to impale death on his proud horns before sinking to his knees, not so much in defeat as in mortal confusion at the treachery of man.*

*It was silent in the glade where the old bull ring stood even though there were many people sitting on the wall watching Churro Rivera work a heifer in the selection ritual for the future mothers. A sharp **olé** rang out as Churro led the heifer in a series of complete circles without moving his feet from the spot. This heifer was good because she kept* *her head down and followed through and she was beautiful and brave and was fighting for her life. Churro positioned her near the **picador** and she charged and sank her young horns into the padded flank of the horse as the blunted lance stung her just between the shoulder blades. Dr. Manuel Labastida was making notes on his pad and Churro nodded in satisfaction and said that she was like her father whom he had fought the year before. Now a novice **torero** was given a chance with the cape and he was nervous and awkward next to Churro, who was one of the best **toreros** in Latin America and there was tension in the silent glade. Finally the heifer was let out because she had passed the test and her sons would someday charge into the rings of Mexico.*

*The next one was let in and I sat in the shade and thought about having a **rejoneador** for a son who would fight bulls on horseback like the Piralta brothers in Spain. This heifer was not so good because she held back and raised her head and Manuel gave the signal to Manolo and Churro and the spectators on the wall leaned forward. There was death in the air and the sword was driven in three times before she fell to her knees, yet the crowd was pleased at this unexpected sacrifice early in the morning and the sky turned red and the earth black.*

We always seem to be in some desert when Christ's birthday comes around. Our third Christmas on the trail came to us in Matehuala, on our way towards the US border at Laredo, Texas. Matehuala is a grey adobe village that has not changed for hundreds of years, probably not unlike Bethlehem. It's only real claim to distinction is that it is halfway between San Luis Potosi and Monterey and many tourists stop overnight in the luxurious sleeping bins attached to the main artery that cuts around the village. We arrived at a stable and it appeared that we would have to camp out in the hayloft. But along came Victor Mahud, of Arab descent, and he invited us to rest in Las Palmas Motel (run by Holiday Inn). He was a friend of the Labastida clan and a jet-setter, telepathic liar, playboy, name-dropper. We meet the strangest people in the strangest places! He told us about his link with the CIA and the Arab underground and his trips to New York and Havana (Fidel was his 'intimate friend'), to Lebanon and Columbia on undefined government assignments, his plans to live in Turin, Italy after marrying an American girl and I wondered if he was a complete mystery even to himself.

Later we met a Russian leather tanner and a butcher. Both invited us for Christmas dinner and so we made the rounds. We learned how they cure hides and make sheepskin rugs at the Russian's tannery, then we ate lunch and had dinner with the butcher, his wife and pile of children and I was as always enthralled by the sheer expanse of happenings in one day in this life of ours! We have become quite good at talking with people on all different planes: Kensyian economics, the war in the Middle East, curing hides, slaughtering lambs for Christmas tables (all have something in common). We wound up the day reading **Rayeuela** by Julio Cortazar and visiting the horses in the corral at midnight to fill the water trough.

Colonel Armando Arroyo of Queretaro, Mexico gave us a white wool blanket with his initials AA in the center and a simple geometrical border out of black wool. This blanket always goes right over the top sheet on our bed and it has been there ever since. It would have pleased him, I think, to know this.

"It is heavy!" Says Raya who bought us a quilt made of synthetic material and that does not weigh much at all.

"I like the weight!" I tell her.

"Isn't it getting kind of worn?" She says.

"I like it!" I say.

"Okay," she says with the tone that means I am being stubbornly and peculiarly me. She accepts my right to be so, even when she does not approve.

The colonel owned a motel by the highway between Monterey and Laredo. The colonel is long gone. Maybe Motel El Retiro is still there. It was a very nice motel. We took a picture of the horses parked in the carport while we unloaded the pack. Then we took them across the highway to a field and settled in on the queen-size beds and enjoyed room service, courtesy of the colonel. The waiter brought a tray with three plates of T- bone steak, each with its baked potato and buttered vegetables. The third plate was just like the other two, but came without utensils. It was meant for Chaco. And Chaco stayed right there with us in the room, on his very own queen-size bed.

I don't really know why the colonel would treat us so royally or why he would give us one of the blankets he had commissioned as gifts to his friends. Why such a grandiose gesture bestowed upon a pair of strangers? Maybe he did not have so many friends to give blankets to?

Northern Mexico was like that. Maybe because the plains are arid and windswept and, like in the Patagonia, people react to natural adversity by taking good care of one another. True. But when I re-read Nathan's diary, I wonder if maybe Raya is right. Why are we keeping this blanket so close to us? He had a pearl inlaid revolver, Nathan writes, which you can see under his open jacket. The colonel makes sure that you do. He never turns his back to us and his bodyguard is always with him. He shows us pictures of himself with Pancho Villa. That would explain how a man such as Colonel Arroyo would own so much land and apartments in Mexico City and we did not doubt that he did; he was on the right side of the revolution and these were the spoils. His wife was the age his daughter might be, but the colonel had no daughters. The people in the village told us about an accident involving failed brakes in a brand new car and the colonel's first wife and their two children. The man Nathan describes was not the kind of man you would want to keep close. He reminds me now of Anthony Quinn's character in the movie Revenge.

But this isn't about the colonel. Someone, not the colonel, wove this blanket so tight and with such skill and care that after more than ten thousand nights, this blanket shows very little wear. Remember those cold winter mornings when you, Raya, Conchita and Naomi would snuggle and giggle together on a bed made of two by eight planks, in a house made of logs that we cut and peeled and fashioned into a home? This blanket is about continuity through all the changes that life brings and through all the geography before that. Every morning that I make the bed I connect to the trail and the open sky and you cannot buy something like that. And why would you ever want to replace it?

HARMLESS LITTE SCHMOOS

A flashflood of orange sweeps across the land as the sun lays its head in the lap of hills. We watch through a narrow cleft in the stone wall, nestled together in the hay. Like children, I was about to say, listening for the clatter of phantom horses and carriages racing through the dusk, for these stones to give back words and laughter from long ago. Tonight this abandoned wayfarer's inn is our castle. No matter the roofs are gone, that pigeons nestle in the broken walls. Sliding my left hand along the sill, I cover hers, our fingers interlocking, our silver rings clinking together. She smiles.

"Your ring is just about worn out," she says. "You can't see the NE design anymore."

"We'll have another one made," I say.

"Another? Can't be done."

"Sure it can. We'll go back to Greece, someday. Find that old silversmith in Athens and have him make another pair."

She shakes her head. And as I look across the old Camino Real to another part of the ruin where four horses stand motionless under the whisper of a new moon and on across the chalklands to where a moving chain of headlights on Route 80 saws the night in half, I know she is right.

*Sixteen horseshoes on cobblestone, our **castanets** of ringing steel, play along the chalk shoulder of the Camino Real as we rise in graceful bolero and crest another low rolling hill, the last rolling hill, we now see. On the empty flatlands of Matehuala stretching out below us, the old Camino Real makes one last wistful swirl, then surrenders herself to the monotony of Route 80.*

*I feel ambushed. Inside me a voice like a slighted lover wails: betrayal! After leading us on, taking us along from ridgetops to **arroyo** shadows, all the way from Chiapas de Corso, how can you abandon us now to this black slash of a highway!*

The hot silence of the plains throws the accusation back in my face:
*"Shame on you, **gringo**: you're going home!"*
The words catch on a hook at the end of the spinning lure:
HOME.
Three times I left. And for the third time now, I become a salmon jumping sandbars to get back to the native pool. My eyes hopscotch across the desert landscape, darting from one clump of mesquite to another as I argue with the blacktop road, with myself.
There is no place back there; we cut all umbilicals.
Right out here, behind a bush, is home!
*Why always north, **gringo**?*
Yes, why north?
*Swimming the heat waves, perched on blue crackling flames behind a bush at the bottom of the world, I see a shiny teapot chuckle to a boil, a cupping hand of smoke blackening its base and I hear a heavy maul pounding at the rim of the **meseta**, watch Segundo, loose **bombachas** swinging, red shirt soaked with sweat, his grin turning to a frown. We leave him driving a **tropilla** toward the Cordillera; meet him again on the other side of the mountain driving posts for a fence.*
Bouncing along now on my sturdy Pampero while Segundo talks

inside of me, joking and stirring up fistfuls of conflicts, I try to figure out if we have learned anything over these years.

Years! Three, almost.

*Just a few hundred miles shy of the border and urging my horse on north, while at soul-root I want to spin right around and race back south, back to the **pampas**, back to where it all began.*

Segundo is grinning and shaking his head.

*"And here I am, **amigos**, driving posts to fence myself in." He shrugs. "We all wind up yanking our own tails."*

So I am a flip-switch renegade who travels every-which-way at once in my head. I drive a tent stake with the words: here we'll stay, and by morning I'm burning to move again. I court every side trail, take any excuse for a detour, then want to push a hundred miles to make up for lost time.

The roads join and we have to ride the ditch beside the slick blacktop. The horses bolt sideways at the sudden diesel kickback and roar of a Greyhound bus bound for Chihuahua and then settle down into a sleep-walker's shuffle through the noonday heat. Adaptable creatures. In another few days even a supersonic blast won't phase them.

Up the line, Elly leans out with her hooked stick and snags another empty pop bottle, flips it up into her lap and slips it into the gunny sack hanging from her saddle horn. It's her way of dealing with the endless monotony. Ever the here and now realist, she turns her disgust of high-way litter into a treasure hunt. Hey, she'd say, I picked enough bottles to buy a horse when I was a girl and I could have bought a horse with the money. So what's wrong with turning a bag of bottles into a bag of feed for my horse at the end of a day? Nothing wrong with it. Maybe I too can find something to distract me from my growing apprehension about where we are headed: Texas. It will be fun, I tell myself. But a nagging voice keeps telling me this is all wrong; we didn't set out to prove anything to anyone. We should be going up Eagle Pass into New Mexico, as we had planned, instead of to a rodeo in San Antonio.

Elly has stopped, waiting for me to catch up.

"Maracas picked up something," she says. "He's dead lame."

I get off Pampero, eager to cover the fact that I was daydreaming and didn't notice a thing. I pick up Maracas' right front. What have we this time, a piece of glass, a tuna can lid? I probe around the frog and dig out a shiny blue bottle cap, bloodied around the milk tooth edge. In the center a yellow crescent grins at me:

SMILE

I will not, you little bastard! Just look at what you did to Maracas! The face shines: Oh come on, I didn't mean to!

The hell you didn't. Ten years ago you wouldn't have dared talk back.

"Nate?"

"It's a bottle cap," I say, "and it's telling me to smile."

Something else is different about it too: there is no can opener dent on its chin. Again it speaks as I study its side:

TWIST OFF

Another startling innovation: increased accessibility. No wrenching or prying necessary. Just like the tear-off tabs speckled all over the highway shoulders. An army of aluminum shmoos. Harmless little schmoos, recyclable too.

Keep America beautiful.

Just drop me in Mexico.

Out of the north comes a line of Airstream trailers and it is a sight to behold. I mean, really! Forty, fifty torpedo shaped capsules whizzing across the chalklands with bumper-to-bumper zeal and still they keep on coming, more than sixty, who knows how many; a silver thread of tinsel spun from the shores of Lake Michigan and melting behind you, maybe five or ten miles behind you, back into the rolling heat swells and each and every one completely supplied and equipped to cross and re-cross an entire continent. Just imagine for a moment: sixty propane stoves, sixty mini refrigerators, sixty trail bikes tracking behind. It strikes you as unreal, a fantasy of sorts, yet familiar and ultra American. Hear the echo of the old 'westward ho' in the wrenching of trailer hitches and the roar of muffled horsepower putting mile upon mile behind them, racing toward the promise of sprouting wings under the Mexican sun.

From a distance these cocoons look identical. Look again! Each one has a name of its own, listen to the nostalgic ring of Rover 11, Gypsy Cruiser, Wanderer, Pathfinder, Wrangler. The faces of the men behind the wheels are bracketed with silver hair and they look neither right nor left, their eyes sucking at the dotted line: they're still dream- ing, still and forever yearning to get there. After forty years behind a desk or counter these pioneers are eager to explore, to discover some distant hideaway: Mazatlan this season. With hook-ups.

We ride up the dusty street of a shantytown on the southern edge of Nuevo Laredo, Mexico. It is January 20, 1972.

An old woman looks straight at me from her doorway. "Beautiful mare you have," she says and smiles a toothless smile and I am reminded of another old woman, who knelt down to rub my numb feet, who draped me in her own dry clothes, with whom I shared a gourd of *máte* and who opened her bedroom and Samhuesa's to Nathan and to me, way back in the south of Chile.

"Thank you!" I say and smile back at her. We have no idea then that this old woman is the godmother of the Pruñeda Family, with many grown sons and grandsons to defend the family position as number one in the cross-border drug trade of Nuevo Laredo. We do not know then that we will be returning to ask this old woman to help retrieve something stolen from us, much later than we ever thought we would still be in Nuevo Laredo.

We ride right down to the US Department of Agriculture quarantine corrals on the south shore of the Rio Grande, where cattle are kept in pens, dipped and ready to be shipped to feedlots north of the border.

"Nice *caballos*!" The Mexican cowboys look with admiration at the horses that have crossed deserts and high mountain ranges and jungles to get this far. "All fat and shiny!" Knowledgeable and appreciative hands run over the backs of Pampero and India, who like the attention. Maracas keeps a distance behind his brother. Pirata stays clear of strangers.

"And where are you two staying while the *americanos* test the blood of your horses?" The Mexican veterinarian asks.

"Haven't thought about it," Nathan says. "Right close by, I suppose. Un- less, of course, you mind our camping here."

"Camping! No way!" Says the Mexican veterinarian whose name is Alfonso von Ziegler. "We have lots of room in our house. You'll come stay with us!"

His is a very comfortable villa. You can stand in the shower for as long as you want and our room is upstairs next to their daughter Amelia's. We appreciate the hospitality but we have a hard time falling asleep to the hum of the airconditioner. We tell ourselves we must be patient. There are rules for bringing in horses to the United States of America. We have to follow protocol.

What we don't know then is a whole lot.

Circumstance put us at the Texas border at the worst possible moment, just a year after an outbreak of Venezuelan Encephalomyelitis that claimed the lives of thousands of horses in Texas. Each year, the virus had progressed a little further from its country of origin in a seasonal, predictable migration northwards with the flies that transmit it. Mexico moved to protect its valuable equine population with live vaccines. The United States did not, because the United States was bound by a rule of their own making that says a live vaccine cannot be imported or used unless there is a confirmed case of the corresponding disease within the US borders.

By the time there was one case, there was an epidemic.

The American Quarter Horse Association blamed the policies of the United States Department of Agriculture for the loss of valuable stock and lobbied for much tougher laws governing the movement of equines from south of the border.

The USDA acquiesced. A month before we arrived, new rules were put into place. We knew nothing of this coming in, too much going out.

In charge of implementing the new rules at the Laredo, Texas crossing was a career bureaucrat, a man a year away from retirement. His name was Dr. Spruell. We never learned his first name; he wasn't that kind of a man. His assistant was a war veteran, recently returned from Vietnam. His name was Earl.

The two of them arrived each morning in a grey sedan with a US Flag on the driver's side. They changed into grey coveralls, wasting no time with chitchat and went on to the tick inspection station to check and disinfect cattle. They drew blood from our horses for the laboratory at Bethesda, Maryland to test for Venezuelan Equine Enchephalomelitis, Equine Infectious Anemia and Piroplasmosis Equina. Every morning, they stopped by to take the temperatures of our horses. On the tenth day, when we come to see our horses, Alfonso hands us a folded piece of paper. I can tell from how Alfonso does not look at us this morning that he knows what the note says.

I still have that piece of paper. It is yellow with blue lines and a red margin line, legal size, torn off a pad. I don't need to look at it to remember. Every word is burned in my memory.

I'm very sorry but your horses all 4 have Equine Piroplasmosis. They can't ever enter the US. It will be up to Dr. Van Ziegler as to the disposal of them.
Dr. Spruell

Disposal of them!
DISPOSAL!
Like they were some garbage!
My blood is boiling.
I am sick of being greeted ignominiously by these United States.
In 1962, arriving in New York, nineteen years old, coming to America to marry Nathan, a customs official asks what is in the blue box that is sitting on top of my clothes in the suitcase he has asked me to open.
"It is personal!" I reply.
I don't make any move to comply with his directive. The box contains a brand new Ortho diaphragm, fitted for me by my Swedish gynecologist. I don't see how this uniformed New York official has the right to ask me to show it to him.
"Open it!" He repeats.
"It is personal! It is a birth control device, if you have to know!"
I can see Nathan on the other side of the rope barrier, right in the front line of the people waiting for the passengers from the Swedish America Line 'Gripsholm'. All I want to do is run into his arms. It has been six weeks since I saw him off in Oslo, Norway. I was planning to attend journalism school in Stockholm that year; Nathan was going to finish Harvard. Once we were both done with prior commitments, we'd get together and figure out what would come next. I decided I could not wait that long. I wasn't planning a career writing in Swedish anyway. I could get some kind of job in Cambridge, or in Boston, or study something. It did not really matter. All that mattered was that we be together.
"Did you say birth control device?"
"Yes."
The uniform calls out to a colleague across the aisle. He comes over and then several more gather until there are six of them surrounding me and my

suitcase with the little blue box on top of my clothes. The uniform asks me again to open the box. I do as they ask. The cluster of middle aged men stand for what seems a very long time and stare down at the rubber ring. They step out of earshot and confer. Then two of them return to me.

"Please pick up your box and come with us!" Says one of them.

Flanked by the two uniforms, carrying the blue box, I am walked through the customs building and out onto the pier where my ship, the Gripsholm, is docked. They walk me all the way to the water's edge.

"Throw it in!" Says one of the uniforms.

"You want me to throw the box into the river?" I am incredulous.

"Into the river!" Orders the uniform to my right.

I do as they say and watch my little blue box bob away from shore and sail out on the murky waters of New York harbor.

At a Manhattan drugstore, a couple of hours later, the pharmacist asks no questions when I present the prescription I had kept from my Swedish gynecologist. I get the same item, made by the same company. At twice the price.

"They made you do what?" Exclaimed the doctor I saw in Berkeley a few months later. Her husband was an activist in the American Civil Liberties Union.

Five years after that, our friend Pat sent me a clipping from the New York Herald Tribune, European edition, published in Paris. It relates the successful conclusion of a court challenge by the American Civil Liberties Union to have an antiquated law repealed in the State of New York. A law dating back to the last century, prohibiting the importation of birth control devices into the State of New York. The ACLU action was sparked, states the Tribune story, by the experience of a Swedish girl who arrived in New York in October 1962, engaged to be married and was made to dispose of her prescription birth control device into the Hudson River.

The United States was in the wrong back then.

The United States is in the wrong now.

They think they're going to **dispose** of our horses?

I don't think so.

Like bulldogs on a tight leash, we walk up the alley toward the tick inspection station where Dr. Spruell and Earl are processing a corral full of steers. I feel certain that they have seen us coming but neither man acknowledges our presence. They go on working, with synchronized precision. Spruell makes a sweep with his gloved arm underneath the belly of a steer caught in the cattle squeeze, nods. Instantly, Earl pulls the lever to open the front of the squeeze, jabs with the electric prod through the steel bars. The steer belches and splashes into the poisonous bath ahead of the chute. Earl pulls the lever to close the front as Spruell pulls the lever to open for the next animal in line. Instantly Earl is back there with his prod. The animal lurches forward from the shock, but falls. Earl is right there with an electric jab into the ribs of the animal struggling to regain his feet. The steer falls back against the rails. Gets another jab. Another. The animal lunges up, wrenching a foreleg out from between the rails. Spruell plunges a gloved arm under the steer, slides from collarbone to penis with one swift swoop. He gives a brief nod to the Mexican assistant with the tabulator.

"Clean."

One hundred and eighty nine. A chill ices my brain looking at the young Vietnam veteran's face, so strangely blank, as he jerks the electric stick back and forth like a bayonet and watching Spruell, sweat running down his rutted pale face as he plunges a gloved arm underneath a steer. These men are operators within a system. That's it. All of it. Neither man assumes any responsibility for any consequences of any policy forwarded by this system.

The Hereford fights his way to the surface of the brown liquid and plunges forward into the cattle car parked on the siding.

"Dr. Spruell, could we have a word with you!"

He doesn't look up. "When I am finished," he says.

"Now!" My voice is louder than I had intended.

"Go ahead. Say what you have to say."

He does not look up. I am talking to the back of his head.

"What do you mean, our horses have Piroplasmosis!"

"Their blood shows the presence of antibodies."

"Antibodies? That means they have immunity to the disease".

"Law says they can't be admitted to the United States if the blood comes back positive."

"Our horses are healthy and in excellent condition. And you know

335

it."

*"We found an irregularity in the temperature on your **tobiano**, indicating disease."*

"What kind of irregularity?"

"Elevated temperature. Over several days."

*"The **tobiano** is a mare! She was in heat."*

"I wouldn't know about that. But the blood work alone is conclusive."

"Conclusive of what?"

Dr. Spruell turns around finally. "Look," he says, "I am sorry."

"You are sorry!" Elly counters hotly. "I lost a horse to Piroplasmosis. In Ecuador. Fifteen months ago. We know what this disease looks like. It comes on very suddenly. Your horse has trouble moving. He runs a high fever. If he does not get treatment in time, he dies. It all happens very fast."

"I am sorry about your loss."

"Really! So sorry that now you want to dispose of four perfectly healthy horses!"

"That, as I said, is up to the Mexicans."

Elly turns abruptly and walks away. She knows she is too angry. She has learned to walk away until she can refocus. My anger works differently. I suppress mine deep down inside where it turns to ice and helps me think more clearly.

"The particular tick that can transmit the disease does not exist in either Mexico or in Texas."

"Any bloodsucking insect could transmit the disease," he says, still not looking, running his gloved hand under the belly of another steer.

"Veterinary books deny that."

"I don't make the laws," says Spruell. "It is not my job to form an opinion. I am just here to enforce the rules."

Hot or cold, it is all the same to this man. I turn and walk back down the narrow alley between creosoted bars. Earl catches up to me, the electric cattle prod balanced in the cleft of his elbow.

"Just wanted to warn you," he says, marching into step. "In case you were thinking of trying to ride across the river some night."

I keep putting one foot in front of the other, afraid of slowing down,

afraid I might stop then and turn and smash a fist into his clean shaven
mask of a face.
"I had a little talk with the Rangers," he says. "They'll be waiting
for you."

There are no entries in Nathan's diary, or in mine, for the month of February or for the month of March. Events are seared deep in our souls. We need no diary notes to evoke them.

Alfonso von Ziegler, the Mexican veterinarian, offers us the use of his farm just south of town, until we can figure out what to do. Humberto and Hilda and Alfonso and his wife give us their friendship, they treat us like family. Don Jorge, head of Mexican customs, even loans us a golden Mustang to drive.

A few days after we move out to the farm, Dr. Spruell sends a message via Alfonso. It concerns a drug that is being developed to sterilize the blood of antibodies to Piroplasmosis. He suggests we contact a Dr. Hamstead in Bethesda, Maryland for particulars. This is what we learn:

A research group of a hundred mustangs were injected with Piroplasmosis, then treated with the drug called Amidocarb. A series of eight shots were administered to this sample group over the period of a month. Clinical signs were of a moderate to very severe colic following each shot. Two weeks after the termination of the treatment, tests came back clear of Piroplasmosis. The blood was completely sterilized of all antibodies.

There were no fatalities in the sample.

We don't like this. Removing all their natural immunities would make our horses vulnerable to any disease. We don't like it at all. But we see no alternative. Obviously, we won't leave the horses in Mexico. If we try and ride them across the river, the Rangers will confiscate and dispose of them.

On February 7th, we administer the first Amidocarb shots to our horses. We stay with them for hours, expecting them to colic. None of the Criollos react in any way whatsoever to the first or the second shot. Pirata shows mild discomfort after the second injection.

From February 7 and every single day until March 23, we take the temperature of each of our horses when they come in from the field for their grain in the morning. The charts are textbook for a healthy horse. Pampero, Maracas and Pirata keep steady between 98 and 99 degrees Fahrenheit during the entire period. India's temperature goes up two degrees for the duration of her heat cycle.

Our life at the ranch settles into a sort of normalcy. We take turns at the Hermes portable. We write articles, work on the outline for the book we plan to write about the ride. Nathan writes a wonderful story called 'Pampero and I'. On February 14th, we receive a telegram from New York. A telegram, no less! Argosy magazine wants to publish a three-part series about our ride. A cover is a real possibility. The editor wants to see slides. Things seem to be going our way.

At times, early when the sun rises over the mesquite and we watch the four horses come in, we can forget about everything but the beauty of the morning and celebrate the day for what it is.

One evening we return late from grocery shopping in Laredo, Texas. The headlights of the Mustang sweep across the porch where our saddles hang over the railing. But between the packsaddle and my Ecuadorian saddle there is now a gap. The Mexican saddle, presented to Nathan by the *charros* of La Villa is missing.

We rest uneasy this night.

In the morning, we follow tracks in the light dust across the field to a shack made of cardboard and tin. No one is home. Neighbors provide the information that the occupant is one Antonio Sanchez. He is known as a petty thief with connections to the Pruñeda clan.

"What a shame about your saddle," say the people, "*qué lastima*."

"The police won't be able to help you. No one messes with the Pruñedas!"

The toothless old woman who complimented us on India when we first rode into Nuevo Laredo is a Pruñeda. She is, they tell us, the godmother of the clan. We decide to go straight to her with our problem.

"You are out of your minds!" Says Hilda, Humberto's wife. "Those people are all beasts and killers. Just last week there was a story in the paper of the Pruñedas blowing up a house. With the people in it!"

She shows us the article. Pictures of the burnt out shell of a building, charred bodies on stretchers. The story speaks of a drug war between rivaling factions and a bomb blast killing five.

"It is not our war," Nathan tells Hilda and we drive the yellow Mustang back to the house where the old woman took notice of India as we rode by a month earlier.

A young man stands in the doorway. He is taller than the average Mexican. He looks us over carefully. I expect him to frisk Nathan, he has that kind of look about him, but he doesn't.

"We have come to see the *madrina*," Nathan says.

The young man motions for us to follow him inside. Old mattresses and liquor bottles are strewn on mud floors in what seems to be several one room shacks arbitrarily shoved together under one tin roof. We pass through a series of burlap curtains into a smoke filled kitchen where the old woman and an old man sit warming themselves by a tray of smoldering coals, in a scene familiar from so many huts and shacks on our way. Momentarily I think we must be terribly mistaken, that this woman cannot be the one with power to cause splintered beams and roofing tiles to spin end over end into a black sky. We squat down to get beneath the layer of acrid haze that smarts our eyes.

"The couple who rode past a month ago, *madrina*," says the youth.

"I remember. The *señora* was riding a paint mare."

She nods. Motions toward the young man and he steps outside the room.

"What has brought you here?"

"You are the only one who can help us," Nathan says.

"Oh?"

"A petty thief stole the saddle given to me by the *charros* in Mexico City."

Her dull eyes become momentary sharp. "Why didn't you go to the police?"

"We knew better."

There is a long silence. The youth remains close behind the burlap curtain. A longhaired mongrel dog is slowly licking the infected toes of the old man's bare and swollen foot. Next to him, the old woman sits motionless, a bony hand resting on her thigh. I feel misplaced. The scene is so incongruous, so at odds with what we had imagined the inner sanctum of the Mafia to be. Finally the old woman speaks.

"You know who might have taken your saddle?"

"Yes."

"How do you know?"

"I tracked him."

"So why didn't you get it back?"

"Why would he give it to me?"

Her lips pursed, she seems to be suppressing a smile. She nods slowly. Then she stands up with a grace that surprises me. She turns her back to us. "Pablo, show the **señores** out," she says.

The young man brushes the curtain aside and holds it there. We rise.

"Thank you, *señora*," Nathan says.

"*Gringo*, I promise you nothing."

The three Criollos have no visible reaction to any of the shots. No colic. No variation in temperature. Pirata colics after the third shot, colics worse after the fourth. With four more shots left to go after that, we decide to discontinue treatment for him. If he is not cleared when the USDA tests the horses again, we will give him away to a friend of Alfonso's. We are to wait two weeks after giving the last two shots before having Dr. Spruell take another blood sample for analysis.

Ten days after the last shot, Maracas fails to come in for his morning grain. When one of your horses goes missing out of a bunch, you know you must rush off to find him. Maybe he is hung up on a wire or got caught somewhere. Maybe someone stole him.

Maracas isn't caught or hung up or stolen. He is lying in a pool of his own blood, not far away. He has no external wounds or injuries of any kind.

Nathan runs to the Mustang and drives away to get to a phone, to get help. I stay with my little horse who stands up and pisses blood into the dry dust and then follows me to the shaded porch and collapses. I sit there with him for such a very long time while his life ebbs away, one drop at a time.

I grab a line and repeat it to myself: I will cry tomorrow. Scarlet O'Hara repeated it over and over in Gone With The Wind. The phrase gave her strength to face the sorrow of today.

I will cry tomorrow.

But my tears don't listen; my tears keep on flowing down my cheeks onto his and together they disappear into the dust. There is no room for tomorrow as I sit cradling my horse's head in my lap.

His tears are dark red and there are spots of blood in his nostrils too. Maracas is crying soundlessly. His pain and mine won't wait for an uncertain tomorrow.

I dab his face with a cloth dipped in cold water. I don't know if it helps him, but doing something helps me as I wait for Nathan to return with the miracle drug that will make my little horse all better again.

Static clogs the connection. Word fragments rasp through the receiver, as though coming from the other side of a subway tunnel. The operator cuts in again:

"Please deposit another three dollars, sir."

I feed coins into the slots and listen to them jangle down into the box, mechanical sensors weighing their value. Then the voice from the government lab in Bethesda, Maryland breaks through again:

"I didn't quite catch what you were saying, Mr. Foote. Blood in the urine?"

"I said two of our horses are hemorrhaging, doctor."

A long silence. "That is highly unlikely."

"Our horses are pissing blood, doctor!"

"Give me the details." The tone is clear and cold now. "When did they receive the final injections?"

"Ten days ago. They seemed to be doing fine. Until last night."

"In my sample of a hundred mustangs, not one displayed abnormal symptoms at such a late interval. Of course, other variables may have influenced the normal rate of detoxification."

The black box is ticking off precious seconds.

"Doctor Hamstead. Just tell me what to do to stop it."

"We are still in the experimental stages, Mr. Foote. This does not follow the syndrome at all."

"What is the antitoxin? Give me the name of the product you use to control the poisoning."

"When the liver becomes overly saturated with any chemical substance and given the molecular structure of this particular drug... "

"HOW DO YOU STOP THE BLEEDING, DOCTOR?"

"You might try coagulants. Vitamin K, for instance. There is still much that needs further research."

"You mean I have to sit here and watch my horses bleed to death one drop at a time?"

My words ricochet around the booth like trapped moths, making me feel dizzy, nauseous.

"Believe me, Mr. Foote, I am sorry. But you assumed responsibil-

ity when you decided to use this drug. It has not been placed on the market yet, as you know."

The static sweeps back like a wave. I grip the receiver, wanting to wring it as hard as I can to force just the slightest spark of hope out of the black cable snaking three thousand miles across the homeland. I try to speak, but I can't. A woman's nose pinched plea breaks in:

"Sir. You were momentarily cut off. Will you please deposit another three dollars."

"The hell with your goddamn research! The hell with a government that kills by proxy. Our horses are dying!"

I cry helpless rage inside the glass walls of the isolation booth as the rush hour traffic drifts past outside. I drop the receiver and drive a fist into the folding glass doors and stumble out into the street. Behind me, the dangling voice is still pleading:

"Sir. The three dollars, sir."

THE ALAMO

I see a green Chevy pickup coming down the narrow drive towards the ranch. I hear gears grind as the driver shifts down. One of Alfonso's friends? Someone looking for us? Either way, they won't be able to see me; I am making sure of that. I draw up my knees closer to my chest, making myself as small as possible behind the *mesquite*.

The gears grind again, as the pickup jerks to a stop by the gate. A boy gets out of the passenger side to open the wire gate. Closes it again after they drive through. He need not have bothered. There is nothing here anymore to keep in. Maracas is gone. So is India. Manuel took Pirata to his new home. Nathan and Chaco are taking Pampero back down to the quarantine corrals for another test. I bite my lip hard, so hard I can taste blood.

The strangers stop by the brick house. They leave the motor running. The driver gets out and now I see that I know who it is. The boy jumps up in the back of the pickup box and struggles to lift a saddle up on the side so the old woman can reach it. She grabs it the way someone does who has handled saddles before and carries it up on the porch and puts it back with the other saddles on the railing.

Twenty-four hours ago, I would have stood up and waved and shouted and ran down to the house and I am pretty sure I would have embraced the godmother of the Pruñeda Family and said thankyou-thankyou-thankyou for doing this for us! I would have found her a photograph of India and written something on the back for her: Affectionately to Doña Pruñeda, something for her to remember us by. And I would have rushed off to tell Humberto and Alfonso and all their friends that the head of the Nuevo Laredo drug Mafia got our saddle back for us. See, miracles happen! You all thought we were nuts to go to the drug Mafia and ask this favor, but it worked!

I don't do any of those things. I remain immobile behind the *mesquite* and watch them drive the green Chevy slowly back out again.

On a night without stars, I set on the naked gravel at the USDA quarantine corrals on the outskirts of Nuevo Laredo, Mexico, numb from the cold and grateful to be so numb that I can't feel the sharp stones under me, cradling the head of my horse, talking to him. I stroke the soft nose resting on my knee, run my hand back along the cropped mane, over the sweat-polished shoulder to his trembling abdomen. It contracts again with pain. He lifts his head, ground his teeth together.

"Easy, Pampero. I won't let you suffer any longer. Not like the others. I know you want to go. To catch up with them." My voice sounds hoarse, unreal. "They will be waiting. Don't worry, I can see them all... Maracas, India; they're with Caicique now. Running together, in and out of clumps of sage and mata verde. I'll send you home, Pampero, home to the **pampas** *that gave you a name. So many miles ago." His chin touchs my knee, his body relaxing again.*

I stare out through the five-strand barbed wire fence at the headlights of cars darting in and out of the red light compound only a hundred yards away; taxis bringing **gringos** *from the other side of the river. Doors slam. Raucous laughter grates like fingernails on glass. High above, an enormous martini glass tilts drunkenly, spilling pink neon across the dark sky.*

My grip tightenes on the .38 police special, the handle cold and wet. I lift it slowly and take careful aim at an oncoming car, at the silhouette of the anonymous passenger in the backseat, following it until it ducks in through the walls and disappears. Then I focus on another blank face. And another, one thought pounding through my brain: they deserve to die, not you Pampero, not you!

But the rage is so far down inside of me that it cannot reach my finger on the trigger. I let the gun sink back to the ground and turn away.

The lights of Laredo, Texas make a purplish bruise on the under-belly of a cloud to the north. To have travelled so long - more than three years - and so far and to have come to this! We could have crossed the Rio Grande on a night like this and we would have been in the Rockies now, sipping tea by the glowing embers of a campfire, the horses standing vigil nearby.

I don't even know what I have done wrong. What we have done wrong. We crossed fourteen borders, this one led home. How could our dream have become this nightmare?

The music of a honky-tonk piano oozes over the walls of the red light compound, a boogie-woogie palpitating. Pampero lunges to his feet, staggers forward a few steps, loses his balance and falls over. His short legs kick out, again and again, then he freezes, chest heaving, blood dripping from his nostrils. God, no! Not his lungs too! I crawl next to him, press my face against his neck, feeling the soft warm fuzz just behind his ear and whisper, "Don't fight, Pampero. Lay still. I won't leave you. The last hurdle is coming. You'll fly right over. And they'll be there, waiting, hear them whinny. Smell them on the wind."

Somewhere across the washboard boundary, a bottle smashes, a woman screams, the shrill rising voice breaking into giggles, then with a drunken male voice splicing in, ruptures into a warbling howl of laugh-ter. Headlights rake across us huddled together, little Pampero and I, tosses our shadows against the pens, across the low buildings and cat-tle cars, tangled in black threads of barbed wire as a car spun out of the gap and sped off into the night.

I bring the pistol up, my throat tightening. I am choking. The gun shakes as I bring the muzzle into the dent just behind his left eye. An-ger pounds at my temples: he's innocent. We're innocent.

Or is living a dream a crime? Tell me, what is the crime?

A sharp convulsion rushs through Pampero's whole body. He lifts his head and whinnies once, then lets it fall back heavily onto my knees. Very slowly, using all the strength I cane find, I press my finger against the trigger now, closing my eyes to see his companions: Caicique, India, and Maracas, whom I had sent on before him, galloping across the Patagonian desert, their tails and manes torched crimson in the dying light of the Andes.

A wailing siren shatters the stillness, a factory whistle calling in the day I never wanted to see, and muffled the mercy shot which no one in this sleeping land could hear.

My groping left hand finds nothing. Nathan isn't on the left side of the bed, where he always is. It doesn't matter what bed it is, or where the bed is, he is always within reach on the left side. I feel panic, but it is so deep down, so very far away and I am so, so tired. I want to get up and search but I know I cannot even get started doing that because I would have to first summon enough strength to find the center of the nervous system that commands my body and sends a message to prepare for action, to each of four extremities and corresponding limbs and torso and hips and head and coordinate movement between all these body parts and it is a task much too immense to attempt, to even consider the possibility of.

It might be day, it might be night or something in between, I can't tell. The room is dark. The air is cold. It is too cold. I am cold here alone on this bed. I am shivering. Then again I am hot too. First one, then the other and I can't seem to hold onto either.

I think it is later and that I am waking up from somewhere because I hear the mention of my name. It is a woman's voice. I think it is familiar.

"Asleep?"

This time it is a man's voice asking.

"She doesn't know where she is anymore."

I can't come up with a name to go with the voice. Definitely familiar. The man's voice too. Friendly voices. They are talking about me. They are concerned about me. Why am I so cold? So afraid?

"Where is Nathan?" It is the man's voice.

They are looking for him too! I have to hold on here. Stay awake. I need to find the answer, for later, for when I can take command of this body.

"Outside, with the kids."

"Humberto, where is the gun?"

"Still in the glove compartment I suppose."

"Go out and get it, Humberto, please!"

I am trying to hold on, but I can't. I have taken too many sleeping pills and I drift away again and much later I find out that Nathan isn't on the bed with me because he is riding a red bicycle around the block with Hilda and Humberto's kids. He dubbed it the Laredo 500 and maybe that is how many times they biked around the block altogether. Nathan makes a great ten-year-old, especially this morning, after he turned the gun on Pampero.

Shoot, euthanize, slay, abolish, annihilate, bump off, butcher, decimate, dispatch, destroy, execute, exterminate, hit, knock off, liquidate, massacre, put away, rub out; there are so many words for killing and none at all to convey what it is for a peaceful and kind man to pick up a gun and in full command of his faculties, pull the trigger and kill his best friend.

Friendly fire. Deliberately aimed.

Murder by another name.

Nathan runs five hundred bicycle laps around the block.

I sleep.

We drink a lot of contraband liquor.

Chaco finds his own solace amongst the canine street population of Nuevo Laredo. When we notice that Chaco too has blood in his urine, we put him in the yellow Mustang and drive across the border. No one asks any questions.

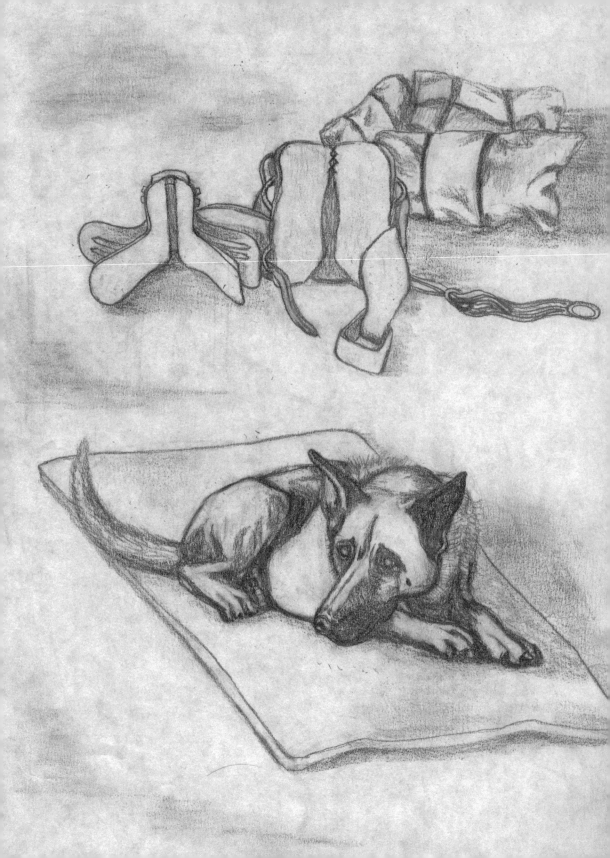

THE PROMISE LAND

"Your dog has canine syphilis." Dr. Kahn looks at us each in turn and his face is grave. "It works like a cancer in dogs. This is a bad case. He has lesions way up inside. I have to suggest euthanasia as your most reasonable course of action."

My scream implodes so deep inside of me it swallows its own sound and tears my entrails into little pieces. I double over in a pain so intense I believe it might obliterate me and, in that moment, I would let it. Just like that, I would let go for someplace beyond all this pain. Then I look into Chaco's deep amber eyes. Chaco is looking at me from the edge of the examining table and I see beyond the table to a yellow pup collapsing behind a *calafate* bush. Limp with exhaustion, he would get up, he would go on beyond his limits and he would find a hidden source of strength to thump his tail, to jump up and dash around. I see him running in and out of the horses' legs to keep out of the way of packs of dogs that would rush out of every farm and hamlet. I see him lying on a bed of hay with the horses eating around him and I see him jumping up to kiss

Pampero on the muzzle, picking up India's lead and bringing her over, see him standing so proud in the arena in Mexico City, knowing he is being honored and I see the immeasurable pain in his eyes when his friends left him, one after the other. I have to turn my eyes away because there are so many tears in them and I don't want him to see me thus because, in his eyes, there are still tomorrows. Even without his buddies, there are new horizons.

Nathan finds words to speak. His words carry the absolute calm of the hollow center of a black storm; they are matter-of-fact words.

"How do we cauterize the lesions." He says and it is not a question.

"The problem is getting them all," Dr. Kahn says. "If you don't get them all they will spread further. To the kidneys, the liver, the brain."

"What about laser surgery? Have you tried that?"

Dr. Kahn looks at Nathan and in the moment Nathan seems transformed from the owner of a patient, to a different category. Not a colleague, exactly, but no longer simply a client.

"That way you wouldn't have to touch anything," Nathan says.

"It might work," Dr Kahn says.

"And you could do this?"

"We can attempt the laser surgery," the vet says. "There are no guarantees, you understand. These lesions go very deep."

"When can you operate?"

Dr. Kahn looks at the dog, he looks at me and he looks at Nathan. He understands that this big yellow dog sprawled on his examining table is all that is left of a whole world.

"His convalescence is going to be difficult," he says. "I have a little house next to the clinic. No one is living there at the moment. I can move my schedule around and we will do surgery first thing in the morning."

"Why do you have to go on with the ride?" Asked brother Caleb who called and talked to us each in turn. We were staying in Dr. Kahn's little house and could be reached by telephone for the first time in years. Talking helped and it didn't.

Because we don't know what else to do.

Because we cannot leave our dream end with the ashes from three funeral pyres spread by the wind over the landscape of Nuevo Laredo, Mexico.

We will never survive anywhere else if we do not go on deep inside ourselves and look for a new beginning.

We can never run away from this pain.

"I understand," brother Caleb says and he tries to.

"I wish there was something I could do or say that would help." He is very sincere, brother Caleb, but he understands not. How could he? How could anyone possibly?

We had the dream before we had the horses. Our horses carried us and gave substance to the dream, our daily life a structure and a rhythm all its own. With the horses, we pushed freedom to the edge. Without them, the edge crumbled and we crashed into the abyss.

Without them we are lost. If we walk away now, we would walk away from each other because the pain of each would be magnified in the eyes of the other. I don't know if I knew all this in words back then, or if Nathan did. We did know we had to go forward. Like Arturo, we learned the terrible price of Freedom.

It wasn't about the trip; having followed us this far, can you understand that?

It was about living our lives as we set out to do and if we faltered now, our lives would dissolve.

It wasn't about going from a here to a there, you understand.

It was about being here, being now.

If we walked away, we would be shipwrecked, we would be swallowed up. Arturo Dragon risked everything for freedom. He would endure cold and hunger and loneliness, as long as he kept that one thing which was his freedom. To him life was freedom and it was worth everything and could not be relinquished and I knew Arturo would know there was only one way possible out of this. There was no way back, because there was no back there to go to: freedom is forward.

Dr. Kahn was guarded about the prognosis. "I think we got all the lesions," he said. "If they do not recur within six months, he should be okay."

There was a letter waiting for us at the post office. It was addressed to Nathan and Elly Foote, Horseback Riders, General Delivery, Laredo, Texas.

The letter was postmarked Finley, Oklahoma on April 5, 1972 and it was from a man named Gilbert Jones. He writes in big block letters that fill up the

353

envelope and both sides of an unlined piece of paper with Medicine Spring Ranch in bold letterhead.

We know this man only from a 3X6-inch ad I had cut out of a Western Horseman magazine. Spanish Mustangs, said the ad, raised wild on a million acres of forest land in the Kiamichi Mountains. I went through my wallet the night Maracas died by the porch of Alfonso's house and found the ad tucked away in a pocket and the tiny piece of paper torn out of a magazine was the only lifeline I had when blood was seeping from all his body orifices, even his eyes, and there was nothing we could do to stop the bleeding and I lost my second horse.

My little horse that had moved from being a mere shadow figure to being his very own number one. Very slowly, one day at a time, I had come to see he was more than just a follower. He was a little bit slow, but always ready to please, no matter what I asked of him and I had come to understand that of the four, he trusted us completely, unconditionally. He wasn't interesting, he was utterly, totally loyal to each and every one of the other horses and to both of us and he never questioned a decision; his was to do, not ask why.

He wasn't the kind you fell passionately in love with. He was the kind that you tended to take for granted until one day, when it was too late, you realized that you loved him.

There is an old Swedish pop song I used to sing as a girl, at the top of my lungs walking some lonely gravel road or in a field where no one was around to remind me I can't hold a tune:
"Old Blackie,
comrade on the long journey,
and when your journey is over,
awaits a field of clover,
for you, my faithful old friend."

Even out on the loneliest of roads now, in a vast field in the middle of nowhere, I can't sing this song to myself because it makes me think of Caicique and Maracas, my two horses, and my voice breaks after the first stanza.

I wrote this in my diary on April 7, 1972:
When I received Gilbert Jones' letter with its crooked letters and language that spoke of a simple earnest man, offering us the pinto and the grey, I knew

we had found a new direction. When I wrote him our last night at Alfonso's place, I felt like a traitor to the horses that had died there on the spot where we had all been so happy. Yet I knew I had to write that letter. It wasn't an act of will. Something made me sit up all night, crying as I typed, yet feeling it had to be done. It was a kind of spiritual self-surgery, to remove a tumor so that the wound could close up and I could go on living.

Where did that absolute certainty that this was the right, the only way, come from?

I don't know. It was just there.

This is part of what Gilbert wrote in his letter to us:

I HAVE THIS 6 YEAR OLD PINTO HERE. HE BUCKS IS ABOUT ALL WRONG WITH HIM. HE IS GENTLE, HOBBLE BROKE, ALSO STAKE BROKE. REINS OK. JUST HE NEEDS RIDING. I SOLD HIM AND TRADED FOR HIM BACK IN-TENDING TO KEEP HIM AS USING HORSE. I LET MY NEIGHBOR HAVE GREY ABOUT LIKE HIM. HE WILL BUCK SOME ALSO BUT BOTH HAS BEEN RODE CONSIDERABLE & I THINK WILL BE OK IF RODE. THEY WAS COMING 5 YEARS OLD WHEN BROKE. RANGE RAISED, NEVER FED UNTIL WE WENT TO RIDING THEM. ABOUT 14 HANDS 900 TO 950 POUNDS. NO TOUGHER HORSES EVER LIVED & IF YOU ALL CAN RIDE THEM THEY ARE ALL YOU ALL WILL NEED TO ALASKA. I AM SURE I CAN GET GREY FROM NEIGHBOR. I WILL DONATE THEM TO YOU. NO CHARGE AS THE OTHER RANCHER DID THE FOUR.

We cross Texas at night, by car, with Martinez' cousin Jose who is returning to work in Chicago in his old station wagon. He offered to take us to Medicine Springs, near Finley, Oklahoma, which is on his way only because he is a good man and makes a big detour to take us there.

Towns with immaculate streets float by, ghostlike, sending tentacles of flashing neon after us as we race across the empty tablelands. I stare into the blinding glare of oncoming headlights and try to empty my mind to the monotonous hum of tires on asphalt. Then a pebble wedged between the threads begins clicking on the pavement and I am transposed to another long drive through a night. We are heading south, toward the boot of the Patagonia with Miguel in his Mack semi, at seventy miles an hour on the gravel road. Just the three of us: Elly, Chaco and I with our saddles and gear and a dream of roaming the Americas on horseback.

I gasp with the pain.

I'd do it all over again, if I could change just the one thing, make just one choice a different one and ride across the border somewhere quietly. Martinez said he could show us where to cross the Rio Grande, which is not very grand at all and where hundreds of wetbacks go across every night. No one need have known. We'd be riding up in Colorado somewhere by now. I'd be home. I am an American. Who would care what kind of horse I was riding?

I would gladly start out again, knowing how hard it was at times, if I could change that one fatal choice of heading for San Antonio, Texas. I would go back; but I am not at all certain I have the strength to weave another dream forward.

The wail of a siren is closing in and a purplish blue light floods over us. Jose swears under his breath, shoves the gears into neutral and brings the station wagon to a stop. A broad rimmed hat with the emblem of the Lone Star State pinned in the center fills the view out the driver's side.

"Let's see your driver's license!"

Jose pulls out his wallet, flips through several cards.

"Here it is, sir," Jose says.

"You're in a mighty big hurry!" Says the ranger.

"I am sorry, sir."

"Insurance, please."

Hard eyes move from my soiled sombrero to the backseat where Elly is sleeping against a mound of saddles and tack. A glint of recognition comes over his stern features and he pushes the insurance document back into Jose's hand.

"Take in any money at San Anton?"

"Not this time around," I say, surprised at how steady the words came.

"Watch your speed, okay," he says. "You want to make your next rodeo in one piece.

Jose nods.

"Good luck to you all then," he says.

The patrolman makes a screeching U-turn on the thruway behind us and accelerates rapidly in the opposite direction. We drive on north through the night and when morning comes we are in Oklahoma.

Northwest of the small town of Finley, we turn onto a gravel road and following directions towards Medicine Springs Ranch we find a narrow dirt road that takes us deep into the forest of the Kiamichi Mountains.

A soft light sifts through the pale spring leaves that quiver faintly on the first breath of dawn. Then a horse breaks out of a thicket and begins loping just ahead of us. It seems to float through the dappled veil of foliage, hooves barely touching the ground. As translucent shadows roll over the buckskin and white tobiano, I think that I have been sleepless too long in the night; that I am dreaming awake now the image of India, so sleek, so graceful as she cuts in and out of the slender trees and drops from sight into a hollow. Then with a sudden burst of speed, she rises back into the clearing just ahead of the station wagon as Jose slows to a stop at a barbed wire fence.

The image of India remains before me when I step out of the car to open the gate for Jose. As she pivots on her hind legs and stares straight at me my heart stops between beats; I remember her anger, how she came at me, knowing what I was about to do; gentle little India coming at my gun with all the furor of a life that did not want to be extinguished so soon. Then the horse turns its head and I see that his left eye is clear blue like a glass ball and that I do not know this dun and white horse. I can see now that he is smaller and leaner than India.

A screen door slams and Gilbert Jones comes down the path from a small house hidden amongst broad-canopied oaks. He shoves his hat back off his broad forehead, then tugs it down again to shade his grin. I grip his callused hand firmly and Gilbert leads the way over to the station wagon, so eager to see, to ask, to welcome us to Medicine Springs, the place where the Choctaw warriors of old would come to heal their wounds.

357

"What rig you using, the Sawbuck or the Decker?" He asks.

"A kind of Decker. The old packsaddle Guillermo Halliday gave us."

I drop the tailgate and open up the rear window. Chaco lifts his black nose toward us, but makes no effort to rise from the old saddle pad coated with buckskin hair. I cluck my tongue and try to coax him out. His yellow eyes are fixed on mine, wide and questioning, but he does not move.

"He doesn't want to leave that pad." Tears brim in Elly's eyes. "It belonged to Pampero."

Gilbert looks down on his hands. "Bertha has a spot all picked out for him by the stove," he says and his voice has become husky. "He'll be mended by the time you gentle down the mustangs enough to hit the trail again."

"That tobiano, buckskin and white, is he one of them?" I ask.

"Yes," Gilbert says.

SPICE RACK

I use Spanish words the way you do spices: you don't have to use them, but they add flavor.
Some have an English equivalent, some need an explanation:

A

abrazo	hug, embrace, common way to greet friends
agua	water
aguacero	heavy rain, a real deluge
aguardiente	liquor - lit. water with teeth
ahora	just now
algarrobo	carob tree
allí ésta	there it is; that's it!
alojamiento	lodging
altiplano	high plateau of the cordillera, around 4000 meters
amargo	bitter Arg. máte without sugar
amigo	friend
angelito	little angel
anima	soul
apacheta	cairn (Peru)
arriero	driver of herd or flock of animals
arroyo	ravine
asado	roast
asador	spit
atalaya	watchtower
azoturia	blood disease in horses, protein shock
azúcar	sugar

B

bagual	Arg. wild or feral horse
bajo	low
baqueano	native expert
barranco	precipice, gorge
bien	good, well

bocado	mouthful of food, Arg. bit
boledoras	three round rocks encased in rawhide, used to down prey in Argentina
boliche	Arg. general store and pub
bombachas	Arg. baloon pants made of wool, used by gauchos
bombilla	Arg. gourd used to drink mate
botas de potro	boots made from hind legs of horse with hide left on
brida	bridle, also to mean horsemanship
brujo	sorcerer, wizard

C

caballo	horse
cabezón	halter, lit. big head
cabresto	lead Arg. usually of twisted rawhide
calafate	bush found in the Patagonia
camanchaca	Chile. thick fog along coastal desert
campesinos	rural laborer
campo	open country
capatáz	foreman
caracol	snail
casa	house
ceniza	Peru. ash mixed with coca leaves to produce high
centavos	cent
charro	Mexican cowboy
coca	Plant used to make cocaine Peru
coirón	Arg. Chile. hard yellow grass
colon	Costa Rican currency
comandancia	military or police headquarters
compadre	close friend
companero	friend, buddy
Criollos	Arg. native horse breed

D

de nada	don't mention it; it's nothing
destacamento	detachment, station

diablo	devil
domador	horse-breaker

E

empanada	Chile. meat pie
enterrar	to bury
entender	to understand, grasp
estancia	Arg. Chile. hacienda, farm

F

facon	Arg. knife often silver-handled carried by gaucho
faja	sash, worn by gaucho
feria	fair, holiday
fundo	rural property

G

galpón	barn, large shed
Garbanzo	Peru. weed in altiplano
gateado	tiger-striped
gaucho	Arg. cowboy
guayabano	guava

H

hasta	until
hermano	brother
hierba	grass
hijo	son, child
hormiguera	lit. anthill, deep seated infection, itch

I

inocente	pure

K

kronor	Swedish currency

L

lástima	pity
latigo	cinch strap
lienzo	riding ring
limosna	alms
luminoso	shining

M

madrina	Arg. leadhorse, often a mare
maestra	teacher
mañana	tomorrow
mariachis	Mex. group of musicians
mata	bush, shrub
mata negra	black bush
máte	hierba máte, Argentine tea
mayordomo	boss
medano	sandbank
meseta	plateau
mestizo	hybrid, mongrel

N

nada	nothing
niños	kids
ñire	Arg. iron oak

O

olé	bravo!

P

paja	straw
palenque	Arg. heavy pole set in center of corral
pampa	Arg. plain
paramo	Col. high mountain wilderness
pasajero	Arg. transient, traveller on horseback
patrón	boss-man

363

patrona	boss-lady
pava	Arg. container to boil water, tea pot
picador	in bullfights: rider with lance used to injure and anger the bull. Horse padded for protection
penca	big leaf plant
pingo	Arg. horse
pobre	poor
posada	Chile. resting place
potrero	pasture
potro	colt
puestero	Arg. postman, shepherd
puesto	Arg. shepherd's post
puna	arid tableland

Q

quebrada	ravine
Quechua	Peruvian native indian
quepu	colored threads and knots used by the Inca
querencia	homing instinct
quintal	hundred-weight, 100 kgs

R

ramada	arbor, roof of branches
rebenque	Arg. gauchos riding crop
recado	Arg. gaucho saddle
recuerdos	memories
retén	Chile. police post
riata	rope

S

salitrera	Chile. salt mine or field
sancocho	stew
señor	Mr.
señora	Mrs.

señorita	Miss.
sombra	shade
soroche	mountain sickness

T
taba	bone, Arg. game of throwing a bone
tierra maldita	damned land
torero	bullfighter
tortas fritas	Arg. deep fried bread used for long journeys
tobiano	two colored horse
tropilla	Arg. herd of horses

U
| usted | you, formal address |

V
| vega | meadow |
| de veras | really, for real |

Y
| yegua | mare |

POSTSCRIPT

We wanted our book to have our fingerprints all over it.

Technology caught up to us, so we could produce this book right here on our mountain in northern British Columbia. Our children grew up so they could help with the process.

The man who asked to hold my diary in a donut shop in Calgary gave us the idea for the cover. "It feels so real!" He said. I hope this book finds him. He wanted to read it.

Reg Leith, a volunteer fireman, an auto body man and a designer of houses, is the man behind the cover. Reg also took on the task of mastering the PageMaker program for the final look of the book between the covers. This is his first book design. Surely not his last.

Conchita Maria created the theme drawings from our sparse directions and her own imagination. She is a painter and a singer/songwriter. This is her debut as an illustrator.

CuChullaine O'Reilly, a rider and a writer, read the manuscript in its infancy. He heaped on superlative praise, at a time when it is so critical to have someone encourage you.

Thanks to the persons who read and copy read the book along the way and to the good people at Bookmasters who helped make this happening a thoroughly enjoyable experience.

Thanks everyone!

Captain Reg Leith, Book designer

Conchita Maria invites you to visit her website. Several of her paintings are now available in limited edition prints: gicleé on canvas.

www.conchitamaria.ca

You will find us at
www.ridingintothewind.com

Our toll free order line:
1-800-247-6553

Open 24/7
All major creit cards accepted

Canadian customers may also order on line:
www.ridingintothewind.com

RIDING INTO THE WIND, THE SEQUEL

Yes, it all ended so suddenly.

Slowly, we pick up the pieces to weave a new dream.

We ride on.

It is another journey. Another story. The challenges are different than they were in South America. The trail and the book are full of surprises. One day, Chaco cuts his foot on a piece of roadside glass. A forced stay turns into the discovery of an old homestead. We decide to stop and let one dream evolve into another. Saddle tramps endeavor to become homesteaders on a mountainside. We build a log house, go to work in the forest with draft horses, have three daughters. And, as always, we forge our life, our way.

The sequel is due to appear in 2005. The same team that put this book together will be back. If you have enjoyed our company and want to be notified when the sequel becomes available, write or e-mail us and we will put your name on the advance publication list.

What they say:

Riding Into the Wind shakes the lethargy out of you. It assaults you in the use of language and snaps your head back from the surprise of its graphic descriptions.
Riding Into the Wind rips up the rules and dares all of us who write and ride to keep up or get out of the way!
And you can quote me on that!

CuChullaine O'Reilly, Publisher
Glasgow, Kentucky

WOW!!! The story haunted me when I wasn't reading and mesmerized me when I was. Finished the 20th chapter today. Tremendous! Elly, I cried with you. I sat out on the patio watching the two puppies and read the last two chapters. Such heartbreak. You two had such adventures, adversity and tragedy. Remarkable. I feel like I went with you. The book is so descriptive.

Kathy Borgers
Santa Barbara, California

A rare find! Its wonderfully rich descriptions resonate in a way non-fiction seldom does. A thoroughly enjoyable read that I highly recommend to fiction and non-fiction readers alike.

Cherylynne Greenard-Smith
Burns Lake, British Columbia

relaxed and at home with
people who had no chips on
their shoulders so that dialogue
was possible and we sat
outside under the moon and
looked at the volcano and philoso-
phized with tongue-in-cheek and
then went back to the fire in
the low-ceilinged livingroom simply
decorated and spoke about man's
inability to be satisfied with
what he's got and at that
very moment none of us would
have asked for ~~——~~ anything else
because it was one of those rare
full moments when

you finish the sentence if
you want or just leave it
hanging as you wish

love

my morning

get so